Emerging Issues in
Mental Health and Aging

Margaret Gatz, Editor

American Psychological Association
Washington, DC

Published by
American Psychological Association
750 First Street, NE
Washington, DC 20002

Copies may be ordered from
APA Order Department
P.O. Box 2710
Hyattsville, MD 20784

Composition and Printing: National Academy Press, Washington, DC
Cover Design: imaginagency, Washington, DC

Library of Congress Cataloging-in-Publication Data

Emerging issues in mental health and aging / Margaret Gatz, editor.
    p.   cm.
   Includes bibliographical references.
   ISBN 1-55798-317-8 (alk. paper)
    1. Aged—Mental health—United States.   2. Aged—Mental health services—United States.   3. Mental illness—Treatment—United States.   4. Mental illness—United States—Prevention.   I. Gatz, Margaret.   II. American Psychological Association.
RC451.4.A5E44   1995   95-23748
362.2'084'6—dc20   CIP

British Library Cataloguing-in-Publication Data
A CIP record is available from the British Library

Printed in the United States of America
First Edition

Contents

Contributors

Carroll L. Estes, PhD, Director, Institute for Health and Aging, University of California, San Francisco

Sanford I. Finkel, MD, Director of Geropsychiatric Services, Department of Psychiatry and Behavioral Sciences, Northwestern University

Margaret Gatz, PhD, Professor, Department of Psychology, University of Southern California

Roberta R. Greene, PhD, Dean, Indiana University School of Social Work

Maureen C. Halpain, MS, Program Manager, Department of Psychiatry, University of California, San Diego

Dilip V. Jeste, MD, Professor of Psychiatry and Neurosciences, University of California, San Diego, and San Diego Veterans Affairs Medical Center

Brian Kaskie, MA, Predoctoral Trainee, Leonard Davis School of Gerontology, University of Southern California

Ira R. Katz, MD, PhD, Director, Section of Geriatric Psychiatry, University of Pennsylvania, and Philadelphia Veterans Affairs Medical Center

Bob G. Knight, PhD, Merle H. Bensinger Associate Professor, Leonard Davis School of Gerontology, University of Southern California

Laurie A. Lindamer, PhD, Postdoctoral Research Fellow, Department of Psychiatry, University of California, San Diego

Jana M. Mossey, PhD, Associate Professor, Department of Medicine, Medical College of Pennsylvania and Hahnemann University

David Naimark, MD, Geriatric Psychiatry Fellow, Department of Psychiatry, University of California, San Diego, and San Diego Veterans Affairs Medical Center

Jane Ann Pancake, BA, Graduate Trainee, University of Kentucky ElderCare Program

Leonard I. Pearlin, PhD, Professor of Medical Sociology, Department of Psychiatry, University of California, San Francisco

Larry Rickards, PhD, Director, Intergovernmental Initiatives, Homeless Programs Branch, Center for Mental Health Services

Anita L. Rosen, PhD, Senior Staff Associate for Aging, National Association of Social Workers

Lon S. Schneider, MD, Associate Professor of Psychiatry, Neurology, and Gerontology, Department of Psychiatry, University of Southern California School of Medicine

Marilyn McKean Skaff, PhD, Assistant Research Psychologist, Program on Human Development and Aging, University of California, San Francisco

Michael A. Smyer, PhD, Dean, Graduate School of Arts and Sciences, Boston College

Elinor Waters, EdD, Associate Professor, Human Resources Development Department, School of Education and Human Services, Oakland University

Foreword

On May 2 through May 5, 1995, more than 2,200 representatives of one of the most powerful constituencies in the United States convened for the White House Conference on Aging. This conference was the culmination of more than 650 preconference activities held throughout the nation.

In a very real sense, this conference and those that preceded it placed major emphasis on the aging process. This meant that pressing issues in the field of mental health received major consideration. One of the significant events prior to the White House Conference on Aging was the February 24–26, 1995, White House Mini-Conference on Emerging Issues in Mental Health and Aging, for which I had the privilege of serving as Honorary Chairman.

This interdisciplinary book, published by the American Psychological Association and edited by Dr. Margaret Gatz, a researcher and clinician at the University of Southern California, grew out of papers presented at that White House Mini-Conference. The contributors cover such topics as promoting mental health policy, encouraging optimal health as people age, expanding and consolidating the scientific research in late-life psychiatric disorders, and increasing access to mental health services. Each chapter contains material of interest to psychologists, psychiatrists, social workers, nurses, counselors, and others involved in mental health services for older adults. The book makes an important contribution to the health care debate and should be required reading for policy makers in this area.

To all interested in what constitutes quality of life for older individuals, this is a very timely publication. It emphasizes the contributions older persons can make to society. The field of mental health is enhancing these contributions in a very real way by underlining the essential fact that mental health is bound up with the physical health of all aging persons and by emphasizing what older persons can bring to society because of their expertise and creativity. It stresses that their increased opportunities to focus on central relationships with family, friends, and community can lead to emotional fulfillment for both the giver and the recipients of these relationships.

Rabbi Abraham Heschel delivered a memorable address at the opening session of the White House Conference on Aging in 1961, when I was Secretary of Health, Education and Welfare. In his closing remarks, Rabbi Heschel said, "Older persons need a dream, not only a memory."

Delegates to the May 1995 White House Conference on Aging demonstrated that they are prepared to draw on their memories in order to fuel the action needed to deal with the issues of our day. It remains for all of us to ensure that the American dream for older Americans includes optimal psychological health. The field of mental health has made, and will continue to make, significant contributions to this end.

Arthur S. Flemming, PhD

Preface

This book addresses the major mental health issues that will confront the growing population of older Americans: (a) promoting recognition of mental health as an integral component of general health and personal well-being, (b) promoting optimal mental health as people age, (c) expanding and consolidating the scientific knowledge base of late-life mental disorders, and (d) increasing access to mental health services.

The contents of this book were originally developed as background papers for the White House Mini-Conference on Emerging Issues in Mental Health and Aging, held February 24–26, 1995, in Washington, DC. This Mini-Conference, sponsored by the Coalition on Mental Health and Aging, was a preconference in support of the 1995 White House Conference on Aging, billed as the convention to set policy for the next millennium.

A Mini-Conference on the Mental Health of Older Americans was held 15 years ago as a preliminary to the last White House Conference on Aging, attended by delegates representing the four traditional mental health professions (American Nurses Association, American Psychiatric Association, American Psychological Association, and National Association of Social Workers). At the 1995 conference, the same mental health professions were featured, although the roles of other service providers were emphasized: primary care physicians, case managers, occupational therapists, and other community service providers, such as clergy.

The White House Conference in May 1995 was viewed as only one part of a national process that began with local, state, and national preconferences such as the Mini-Conference on Emerging Issues in Mental Health and Aging. This process will continue with postconference events, for which this volume—especially the resolutions passed by delegates at the Mini-Conference—provides a significant resource.

Beyond this specific purpose, the book provides selective reviews of literature about psychological and sociological characteristics of normal aging, describes clinical features of psychiatric disorders in older adults, introduces empirically supported treatments for late-life psychopathology, presents theoretically anchored preventive intervention strategies, and recommends mental health care policies necessary to promote mental health and to ensure access to treatment for those suffering from mental disorders.

This book would not have been possible without the help of a great number of people at every stage of its development. I would first like to thank all who contributed their efforts to the Mini-Conference, where this book had its genesis. The members of the Conference Planning Committee, listed in Appendix B, are really the ones who put the agenda together, including the topics for the background papers that became the chapters of this book. Special thanks go to Nancy Coleman, Rita Munley Gallagher, and Susan Cooley for their leadership and to Charlotte Mahoney and Ida Fairley at the American Association for Retired Persons for their assistance.

The material in the chapters was reviewed at several stages. Those who commented on earlier drafts of the background papers, before the conference took place, include Elizabeth Brown, Kathleen Buckwalter, Michael Duffy, Barry Fogel, Mary Jo Gibson, Linda Gonzales, Lisa Gwyther, Ann Hurley, Stanley Jacobson, Lissy Jarvik, Lucille Joel, Powell Lawton, Wendy Lustbader, Gabe Maletta, Barry Meyers, Jennifer Moye, Trudy Persky, Sara Honn Qualls, Peter Rabins, Ray Raschko, Eloise Rathbone-McCuan, Larry Rickards, Joan Rogers, Barry Rovner, Vicki Schmall, Paul Stiles, Larry Thompson, Richard Veith, and Antonette Zeiss. At the conference, the synthesizers, who prepared integrative summaries of the chapters, were Cornelia Beck, Gene Cohen, Patricia Parmelee, and Myrna Lewis. Finally, thanks to the Center for Mental Health Services, Substance Abuse and Mental Health Services Administration; the National Institute of Mental Health; and the Social Outreach and Support Section, Programs Division, AARP for their support of the conference.

Another round of appreciation goes to those who worked on the book manuscript: Donna Polisar in Los Angeles, Al Gabor in Chicago, and Mary Lynn Skutley, Peggy Schlegel, and Susan Bedford in Washington, DC. Last of all, heartfelt thanks to Mac Klein, who endured me during this rush to production.

Margaret Gatz, PhD

Introduction

Margaret Gatz

In the United States today, there is a larger percentage of adults over age 65—one of every eight Americans—than there has been at any other time in the history of the nation. Between 2010 and 2030, as the "baby boom" cohort reaches age 65, this proportion is estimated to reach one in five. Racial and ethnic diversity will become greater within the older population as it continues to grow. These enormous demographic changes present major challenges for the design and delivery of health care, including mental health services, and for the creation of supportive housing and new living arrangements.

A range of mental health issues will become increasingly relevant. Although most older adults do not have mental disorders, a significant portion do have serious mental health needs that have major effects on individuals, their families, and society. For everyone, growing older requires adaptation in the face of changing personal circumstances, which creates an obvious role for preventive mental health efforts.

The purpose of this book is to suggest how best to meet changing demands in the prevention and treatment of late-life mental disorders. It focuses on a continuum of mental health needs, including promotion of optimal mental health as people age, prevention and early intervention in mental disorders, and effective treatment of acute distress and severe mental illness. It provides suggestions for expanding and consolidating the scientific knowledge base of late-life mental disorders. It also stresses policy requirements for improving access and creating the most effective system of mental health services for this population.

Mental Disorders in Older Adults

Older adults with mental disorders include both those whose conditions occur for the first time in old age and those whose conditions had their initial onset earlier in life and continue as chronic or recurrent disorders into old age.

Mental disorders observed among older adults include depression, anxiety, schizophrenia and delusional disorders, personality disorders, Alzheimer's disease, vascular dementia, delirium, and substance-abuse disorders. These disorders are disparate, encompassing chronic mental illnesses, disorders with a clear neurological basis, symptoms that represent secondary consequences of physical ailments or their medical interventions, understandable reactions to normative stressors of old age, and subclinical conditions with important consequences for older adults' lives. Consequently, these diagnostic entities also reflect distinct stakeholders with respect to research, practice, and advocacy.

Estimates of the rate of mental disorder among older adults, cited in a number of chapters in this book, generally range from 18% to 28%. For most conditions other than the dementias, rates of disorder are lower in older adults than in younger adults. However, age, life expectancy, cohort, and chronicity also need to be taken into account when estimating rates of disorder 15 or more years from now.

Because onset of dementia escalates with age, as the number of Americans age 85 and older continues to increase, the number of individuals affected by dementia will likewise climb. Because the baby boom cohort has already shown relatively high rates of depression, anxiety, and substance abuse, we can anticipate that these trends will accompany them into old age, resulting in a dramatic rise in overall prevalence of mental disorder among older adults.

Promotion of Well-Being in Old Age

Another point of view to be incorporated under the rubric of mental health and aging is represented by the wellness movement, which emphasizes emotional well-being as an essential component of successful aging. Some conceptual convergence with respect to enhancing mental health and treating mental disorder is afforded by recent interest in redefining prevention and early intervention as part of an intervention spectrum.

Challenges in Meeting the Mental Health
Needs of Older Adults

As this book makes clear, practitioners from various professions, researchers from different disciplines, and assorted consumer groups unite in the view that the resources devoted to address mental disorders in older adults continue to fall far short of what is needed now and will be needed in the future.

Recommendations for addressing these shortcomings encompass expanding research into etiology of disorders in order to improve prevention and early identification, increasing involvement of consumers and families to ensure appropriate access to mental health services, and training health and mental health service providers to recognize and respond to mental health needs of the aging population. Finally, it must be emphasized that mental health policy is inevitably interlinked with trends and reforms in the health care system, including long-term care.

Overview of the Book

In chapter 1, Rosen, Pancake, and Rickards introduce the issues, beginning with a brief history of the evolution of the mental health policy in the United States, especially as it relates to older persons. They demonstrate several recurring policy themes and catalogue an array of policy disincentives that help explain barriers to improvement of access to mental health services for older adults.

In chapter 2, Schneider describes some of the major advances in the understanding and treatment of mental disorders. Treatments that

have proved effective are presented, with an emphasis on psychopharmacological findings. Schneider also takes a look at factors that complicate
treatment of older adults.

Next, in chapter 3, Jeste and his colleagues expand on severe and
chronic mental disorders in later life. They point out that psychoses in
later life, often overlooked in quick reviews of the mental disorders of old
age, may be among the most expensive mental illnesses. Together, chapters 2 and 3 offer a solid review of the strengths and limitations of the
research knowledge base related to late-life mental disorders.

In order to have a basis for understanding how to promote optimal
mental health as people age and how to create responsive service systems,
mental health specialists need a knowledge base that encompasses age-
related changes in physiological and cognitive functioning, the interpersonal and social context of aging, and the types of attributions that older
adults make about their life situations.

Pearlin and Skaff in chapter 4 and Mossey in chapter 5 elegantly
outline the knowledge base that is relevant to understanding these adaptive
processes. Pearlin and Skaff explain what makes stressors stressful and how
older adults maintain their well-being regardless of stress. Mossey provides
data documenting the important influence of self-perception on health
outcomes and on use of health services.

In chapter 6, Smyer suggests how research on developmental processes can become the basis for a continuum of approaches to intervention,
from prevention to treatment. Using the Institute of Medicine's recommendations for a prevention research agenda, he defines three types of
preventive efforts: *universal preventive interventions* targeted to all members of
a group, such as the elderly; *selective preventive interventions* targeted to
subgroups at risk for specific disorders, with these groups identified by
research into risk and protective factors; and *indicated preventive interventions*
targeted to individuals with detectable symptoms or biological predisposition, as yet not diagnosed with a disorder.

In chapter 7, Waters reviews a variety of preventive mental health
and educational programs designed to promote optimal aging. She emphasizes placing programs in settings that older adults frequent, such as senior
centers, neighborhood and community centers, and religious organizations, and even electronic support groups on Internet. In chapter 8, Greene

traces the evolution of the family from unheralded caregivers of the aging to advocates for social change.

Characteristics of successful systems of mental health care are presented by Knight and Kaskie in chapter 9. They first analyze the special problems that arise in providing services to older adults, then they derive a set of program principles from observing the common features of a set of exemplary community-based mental health service programs. These principles can be used to evaluate alternative systems of mental health care delivery that might arise depending on the direction taken by health care reform.

In chapter 10, Katz considers the infrastructure requirements in order for research to meet changing needs in the treatment of late-life mental disorders. In his view, clinical research and clinical care must take place in the same settings and must inform one another. He evaluates primary care settings, community-based services, nursing homes, and other long-term care sites.

Gatz and Finkel, in chapter 11, focus on the continued shortfall with respect to geriatric training among physicians, psychologists, nurses, and social workers. Reasons for the shortfall include curricula that lack material on aging, a scarcity of mentors, and an absence of financial incentives. The authors propose a philosophy and content of training and urge greater attention to interprofessional education.

In chapter 12, Estes examines barriers that inhibit efficient and low-cost interventions to prevent or treat mental disorders. She focuses on processes in the delivery of mental health services that are changing as a consequence of policy and funding shifts during the past 20 years and the subsequent implications for access to mental health services by older adults. These processes include rationalization of care and its corollaries, specialization and fragmentation; privatization and competition, including the emergence of managed care; deinstitutionalization and transinstitutionalization; medicalization; and informalization, or allowing certain groups of mentally ill to drop out of the formal delivery system altogether. The chapter offers a concise explanation of the dilemmas to be faced in meeting the needs of future older adults.

The book ends with four appendixes. Appendix A contains the final resolutions passed by the delegates to the White House Mini-Conference: Emerging Issues in Mental Health and Aging, held February 24–26, 1995, in Washington, DC. These recommendations pertain to (a) mental health and aging policy, especially a call for parity in the reimbursement of mental health services, coordination of services, and availability of in-home services; (b) access to mental health care, including outreach, improved screening and early identification of problems, and culturally acceptable services; (c) expanded education and training; (d) an expedited research agenda; and (e) consumer involvement. These resolutions are the collective resolutions of the participants. They do not necessarily reflect the positions of the individual participants or of the organizations or agencies that they represent. Appendix B lists the members of the Planning Committee for the Mini-Conference, Appendix C gives a record of the delegates to the Mini-Conference, and Appendix D lists the members of the Coalition on Mental Health and Aging.

CHAPTER 1

Mental Health Policy and Older Americans: Historical and Current Perspectives

Anita L. Rosen, Jane Ann Pancake, and Larry Rickards

Mental health policy in the United States has not kept abreast of the service requisites of older people, advances in understanding of aging, or the demographics of aging. Although the need for mental health services for older adults and the efficacy of appropriate interventions have been well established (Birren & Schaie, 1990; Birren, Sloane, & Cohen, 1992; Finkel et al., 1993; Jeste, Naimark, Halpain, & Lindamer, this volume; Knight & Kaskie, this volume; Schneider, this volume; Smyer, this volume), policies affecting access to services, service system coordination, the financing of care, and the training of professional and nonprofessional service providers have frequently lagged far behind need. As a consequence, millions of older people whose mental and emotional problems are serious enough to warrant professional care will not receive services (Colenda & van Dooren, 1993; Flemming, Rickards, Santos, & West, 1986; Knight, 1989; Smyer, Cohn, & Brannon, 1988).

Unfortunately, issues germane to mental health and aging policy have received little attention at the national level. However, the rapid growth in the population of older persons creates the potential for significant increase in the incidence of mental illness and cognitive disorders, with their associated cost to society and human toll (Advisory Panel on

1

Alzheimer's Disease, 1993). This demographic change demands increased attention to policies affecting access to and availability of mental health treatment and prevention programs for older people (Pope & Tarlov, 1991; Smyer, this volume).

Current debates on mental health financing, locus of administrative responsibility for care, community versus institutional care, and quality of care all have long-standing historical roots. A brief review of mental health policy in the United States reveals that current themes have a long history of both helping and hindering the policy debate on mental health and aging. Among the most prominent themes are contradictory public attitudes toward people with mental illness; stereotypical and ageist attitudes toward aging; a bias toward institutional care that has largely neglected community-based services, especially for older persons; lack of parity between mental health and physical health financing; lack of interest in geriatrics by mental health and physical health professionals; reliance on an acute-care medical model of health services; and lack of attention to prevention and early intervention in mental health.

The impact of this policy context on the elderly has been compounded by the indifference of policy makers and mental health providers to gerontological issues, and the lack of leadership in geriatric mental health and training (Binner, 1988; Evans, Buchwalter, & Fulmer, 1993; Gatz & Finkel, this volume; Hagebak & Hagebak, 1983; Jeste, Naimark, Halpain, & Lindamer, this volume; Katz, this volume).

A BRIEF HISTORY OF MENTAL HEALTH POLICY

To understand current issues of mental health policy for the elderly and to address the needs for designing policy for the next century, it is important to acknowledge historical precedent.

Early Attitudes, Treatment, and Financing

Historically, persons with mental illness in the United States were cared for by their families or in institutions (Grob, 1992) and generally were viewed in a negative manner. In institutions they were treated as criminals or undesirables and were cared for as cheaply as possible (Bell, 1989; Friedlander & Apte, 1982). By 1830, prisons and then almshouses were the most common public institutional settings for those with mental illness. Although the almshouse originally served the old and infirm, it became the public institution for housing poor families and people with mental illness. Thus, almshouses became overcrowded with a diffuse population and developed into cruel, unpleasant environments. This warehousing of diverse "undesirables" on the local level was the primary public policy in the United States until the 1830s.

Dorothea Dix led a movement to replace prisons and almshouses with more humane treatment settings in state-supported mental hospitals (Bell, 1989; Friedlander & Apte, 1982). However, by the 1880s, the hospitals that had offered such promise became overcrowded and filled with patients needing chronic care. As the hospitals experienced increases in long-term care cases, a growing population of elderly patients (5%-10%), and a lack of trained staff, their orientation shifted from curative to custodial, and the use of physical restraints resumed (Grob, 1992).

In the late 19th century, funding was split between the states and the local communities. Efforts by Dorothea Dix to garner federal support for mental health services had failed. States paid for sites and construction of facilities, and local communities paid hospitals for maintenance and care of the most dangerous and deranged (Friedlander & Apte, 1982).

Cost containment was the reason for dividing financial responsibility between local and state systems. This "turfism" (protection of individual agency interest) and cost shifting between localities and states resulted in fragmented, inadequate services. States relieved local communities of the burden of care, but the result was the transfer of patients, many of them elderly, from almshouses to state mental hospitals (Grob, 1992)— essentially a lateral shift from one kind of custodial care to another. The effect on elderly people with mental illness was significant: In 1880, 24% of them lived in almshouses but by 1923, only 5.6% did. At the same time, divided responsibility between state and local authorities regarding programming and funding resulted in about two thirds of mentally ill people remaining in the community either as paupers or with family or being relegated to almshouses (Grob, 1992).

Staffing, Services, Leadership, and Research

In conjunction with longer stays and the growing proportion of elderly people in mental hospitals and asylums in the late 1800s, other problems included overcrowding, fragmentary etiological knowledge, and inadequate numbers of trained staff (Bell, 1989; Grob, 1992). Although the mental health professions developed during that period (medicine, psychiatry, academic and clinical psychology, social work), the numbers of experienced personnel were limited (Group for the Advancement of Psychiatry, 1987).

In addition, mental health service and research interests diverged instead of combining to provide leadership. In 1880, the National Association for the Protection of the Insane and Prevention of Insanity was formed by social workers and neurologists. The association was successful in drawing attention to abuses and need for reform, but it later dissolved for lack of consensus on goals—social workers wanted more reform of institutions, and neurologists wanted more research.

During the early 20th century, mental health professionals and laypeople advocated new methods of dealing with mental health problems (Group for the Advancement of Psychiatry, 1987), including psychosocial etiology and treatment approaches. Though these efforts were a substantial improvement over past approaches, they were directed primarily toward children and younger adults. Mental health etiology, prevention, and treatment programs for elderly people were generally ignored (Park, Cavanaugh, Smith, & Smyers, 1993).

The Great Depression of the 1930s hurt mental health services, particularly facilities housing aged and chronically ill patients. Budgets dropped, programs were curtailed, and expansion was halted. With an increasing expectation that mental illness could be treated medically or surgically and the concurrent lack of funding for public programs, the use of electroconvulsive therapy and prefrontal lobotomies grew. The new methods were considered a medical breakthrough, but they were also relatively inexpensive methods of controlling severely ill, chronic care patients (Friedlander and Apte, 1982). Again there was retreat from concepts of treatment back to control and restraints.

An Emerging Federal Role in Mental Health

World War II was a turning point with respect to locus of mental health service delivery and funding. Because large numbers of men had been excluded from military service for psychiatric reasons, and because the war had produced many psychiatric casualties, national attention was drawn to mental health issues (Mechanic, 1989a).

> The national attention led Congress to establish a national health policy for increasing psychiatric services. Veterans Administration (VA) hospital facilities were greatly expanded, as was their recruitment and training of psychiatric personnel. The VA's psychiatric training program was the first major step on a national level to increase the number of trained mental health professionals (psychiatric social workers, psychologists, and psychiatrists). (Friedlander & Apte, 1977, p. 419)

A postwar shift in psychiatric thinking emphasized life experience and the role of socioenvironmental factors, the efficacy of community and outpatient treatment for people with mental illness, and a belief in prevention and early intervention at the community level. In addition, the introduction of psychotropic drugs held promise for a more normal existence outside institutions (Grob, 1992). Therefore, new interest was directed toward a community-oriented approach. However, this community approach was directed at child guidance services and at adults who could afford private outpatient psychiatric care. Psychiatrists began practicing in the community because treating outpatients and younger clients was seen as more desirable than providing services to elderly, chronically mentally ill patients in mental hospitals (Grob, 1992).

The turn toward community care affected debates on mental health policy (Mechanic, 1989a). The community mental health movement was strengthened by the passage of the National Mental Health Act of 1946, which created the National Institute of Mental Health (NIMH). The avowed intent was to apply the traditional public health approach to mental health (Mechanic, 1989a).

In 1955 the Mental Health Study Act was passed, authorizing an appropriation to the Joint Commission on Mental Illness and Health to study and make recommendations on mental health policy. The study report, *Action for Mental Health*, argued strongly for an increased program of services and more funds for basic long-term mental health research.

The Community Mental Health Centers Act of 1963 strove to achieve the goals of *Action for Mental Health* through *deinstitutionalization*— discharge of most long-term inpatient residents as well as prevention of unnecessary new admissions (Gatz & Smyer, 1992). Deinstitutionalization was predicated on the belief that community-based services would be readily available and that the need for institutional services would soon be minimal. The effect of deinstitutionalization on elderly, chronically men-tally ill people, however, was actually only a transinstitutional shift. By 1977, nursing homes had surpassed state mental health facilities in number of patients with chronic mental illness (Gatz & Smyer, 1992). As in the 1880s, one form of custodial care had been exchanged for another. More recently, many inpatient services have shifted from state mental hospitals to psychiatric units in general hospitals (Gatz & Smyer, 1992), which are more appropriate to short-term, less chronic intervention.

Although the community mental health centers (CMHCs) created under the 1963 act were initially organized as comprehensive care centers to provide services to individuals regardless of age, little attention was given there to older adults. After a trend toward providing services for special target populations emerged in the 1970s, Congress mandated in 1975 that newly funded CMHCs should provide specialized services to older adults, a requirement that was reemphasized in 1978 amendments to the act. Though CMHCs made some progress in expanding services to older people, neither the 1975 nor the 1978 amendment provided ad-equate incentives for full implementation. Thus, the proportion of older persons served by CMHCs has remained at 6% (Flemming et al., 1986).

In retrospect, negative views of mental hospitals and a shift in focus to community-based care did not fully anticipate the consequences for those with chronic mental illness. Issues such as prevention, whether a person had a home to go to, whether family members could give at-home care, and whether home care created family hardships were not well con-sidered in the Community Mental Health Centers Act (Rochefort, 1993).

Retreat of Federal Leadership

During the 1960s and 1970s, Congress and the executive branch redirected already limited mental health funds to a new interest: alcoholism and substance abuse (Mechanic, 1989a). An umbrella agency was formed—The Alcohol, Drug Abuse, and Mental Health Administration—which incorporated the National Institute of Mental Health, the National Institute on Alcohol Abuse and Alcoholism, and the National Institute on Drug Abuse. These agencies initially had responsibility for a variety of service programs, demonstrations, research efforts, and professional training programs and were also involved in planning and public education (Mechanic, 1989b). In general, mental health issues of elderly people were not the thrust of federal interest.

The Vietnam War and disillusionment with the programs of the Great Society resulted in curtailment of funds for mental health programs during the Nixon administration (Mechanic, 1989a). Federal leadership intitiatives in mental health training, research, health centers, and professional development were reduced or eroded by inflation.

When the Carter administration began in 1976, problems associated with inadequately funded programs and the deinstitutionalization process were clearly evident, especially the need to develop community services for the most chronically disabled patients (Mechanic, 1989b). In 1977 Carter established the Presidential Commission on Mental Health, which found a need for financially, geographically, and socially accessible community-based services that also served the needs of various social and racial groups (Mechanic, 1989b). The Mental Health Systems Act of 1980, a product of the Commission, provided for special staffing and coordination grants for CMHCs with identified aging programs.

The Reagan administration took office 1 month after the signing of the 1980 act and it was never implemented. This represented a retreat from earlier congressional commitment to provide community mental health services to older adults.

In 1981 the bulk of federal mental health services moneys as well as funds from many other health and social programs were returned to the states in block grants but with cuts in funding levels. Other federal programs that mentally ill people depended on were cut, including social services and housing subsidies. The block grant funding combined substance abuse and mental health money while decreasing funding for both. Less money was available to provide needed community-based care. Channeling the funds through states increased state influence on mental health programs once again (Gatz & Smyer, 1992). Federal, and thus national, leadership was diminished.

The diminution of the federal leadership role was felt particularly in such areas as services, clinical training, and the sponsorship of national meetings and work groups to promote national policy leadership in mental health (Surles, 1993).

CURRENT FEDERAL ROLE IN MENTAL HEALTH AND AGING POLICY

A broad assessment of programs of the past several decades demonstrates how policy decisions have led to generally inadequate mental health services for older Americans (Greene, this volume; Roybal, 1988). Counterproductive policy, coupled with financial and other disincentives for medical and mental health professionals, resulted in mental health problems of elderly people often going undiagnosed, untreated, or inadequately treated. For example, though efforts have been made to classify and understand mental and cognitive disorders of elderly people, treating very old patients is still considered an undesirable area of practice (U.S. House Select Committee on Aging, 1993). Illness often is attributed to age alone, and there is a dearth of geriatrically trained health care providers (Estes, this volume; Safford, 1992).

Medicare and Medicaid

In modern times, the Social Security Act of 1935 was one of the most important federally legislated measures concerning elderly people. Included in the act and its amendments were old-age and survivor benefits programs, which provided some basic security for older Americans. Thirty years later, Medicare and Medicaid were established under the Social Security Act to provide health insurance for people aged 65 or older and selected others (Medicare) and for the poor (Medicaid). These programs were based on an acute-care medical model of providing relief from major medical costs. Today Medicare covers 97% of older adults (Hellman & Hellman, 1991).

8

Medicare has uniform national criteria and is not linked to income level. It is composed of two parts. Part A, known as Hospital Insurance, provides up to 60 days of full coverage for hospitalization annually, certain extended care services, and home care. Payroll taxes deducted during the recipient's working years pay for Part A programs, and there is no additional monthly premium.

Part B, known as Supplemental Medical Insurance, has voluntary enrollment and carries a monthly premium that provides insurance for physicians' care and certain ambulatory care programs. Under Part B, Medicare covers 80% of approved charges, and the recipient is responsible for an annual deductible amount, 20% of Medicare-approved charges, any additional amount that providers charge, and fees for noncovered services.

Medicare does not meet all the care expenses of older adults. For example, coverage for care in skilled nursing facilities is limited to posthospital, subacute care (Rosen & Wilbur, 1992), and Medicare does not pay for prescription pharmaceuticals, dental care, or hearing aids. Medicare covers only 40%–50% of the actual health care costs of the average older adult (Hellman & Hellman, 1991). Like private health insurance, Medicare lacks parity of health and mental health coverage. For example, the lifetime coverage limit on inpatient care in mental hospitals is 190 days; no similar limit exists for inpatient care in general hospitals beyond the standard maximum for any benefit period. Although outpatient mental health coverage recently has been improved by the lifting of an annual cap, and psychologists and social workers are now considered eligible, independent providers, there are still significant limitations: Unlike outpatient health care services, which are covered at 80% in Part B, mental health services are reimbursed at only 50% of approved costs. The high costs of many medications for mental illness (e.g., Jeste et al., this volume) are not covered, and mental health services in the home are generally precluded.

In short, with Medicare the federal government has failed to take the lead in providing a model for mental health services to older people. Instead, the Medicare system creates financial barriers and disincentives for providers and patients alike and discourages mental illness prevention, early intervention, and rehabilitation (Binner, 1988; Gatz & Smyer, 1992).

Medicaid, a joint federal-state program for people with low income and limited assets, is the largest government payer for long-term care services (U.S. Government Accounting Office [GAO], 1995). Today Medicaid covers about 50% of nursing home services to elderly people, most of whom have some type of dementia or cognitive disorder (Greene, this volume). Means testing, which varies from state to state, is the basis for eligibility. Medicaid, combined with various demographic and other policy factors, has been a key factor in the shift from mental hospitals to nursing homes in the provision of services to mentally impaired elderly people (see GAO, 1994).

Mandatory features of all state Medicaid programs include general hospital inpatient care, physician services, outpatient general hospital care, and nursing home care, although restrictions and payment levels vary. Optional services include case management, psychosocial rehabilitation, clinical services entailing outpatient therapy, partial hospitalization, and home-based personal care by nonphysician providers. Availability of optional services is extremely limited.

For elderly people with chronic mental illness or dementia, Medicaid offers primarily custodial nursing home care (GAO, 1995). Although outreach, prevention, early intervention, and psychosocial services might prevent or eliminate the need for nursing home care among these people— and although nursing home care is a major financial burden for states (GAO, 1995)—those services are limited, unavailable, or even discouraged (Colenda & Van Dooren, 1993; Wykle & Musil, 1993). Some states have begun experimenting with Health Care Financing Adminstration waivers of program requirements in an attempt to use less costly home- and community-based services. However, much of this experimentation is being conducted for those who are most physically impaired (GAO, 1995).

Omnibus Budget Reconciliation Act of 1987

Because of the large increase in the numbers of elderly people with chronic mental illness in nursing homes, the Omnibus Budget Reconciliation Act (OBRA) of 1987 established guidelines for applicants to nursing homes. OBRA 1987 requires states to review the care of current nursing home residents with mental disorders. If screening establishes that treatment is needed for mental illness but not physical disability, the person is to be excluded from nursing home care. In part because appropriate alternative care is usually unavailable, this screening program has not met its intended goal, and many nursing home patients are residents solely on account of psychological diagnoses or cognitive disability.

In fact, many elderly people in nursing homes still need mental health services because of the strong comorbidity of physical and mental illness (Brandler, 1992; Brody, 1985; Bruce & McNamara, 1992; Prager & Jeste, 1993). Such mental disorders include dementia, schizophrenia and other psychoses, depressive disorders, and anxiety disorders (Jeste et al., this volume; Smyer, 1994). Emotional distress related to adverse environment or physical symptoms is another example of comorbidity. OBRA legislation specifies extensive requirements for addressing these comorbid mental health needs in nursing homes. However, research has demonstrated that mental health needs of older nursing home residents are significantly neglected (Burns et al., 1993; Lombardo, 1994; Smyer & Garfein, 1988) because of the disincentives that militate against providing such services. Many nursing homes lack psychosocial services and overuse physical restraints and psychotropic drugs in response to chronic mental illness, though the intent of OBRA legislation was to eliminate this ineffective, inhumane, custodial reaction.

The Older Americans Act

Other important legislation related to older people includes the Older Americans Act of 1965, which established a nationwide network of regional, state, and substate agencies such as area agencies on aging (AAAs). The agencies are responsible for the planning, coordination, and delivery of a variety of community-based social services, including multipurpose senior centers and nutrition, recreation, transportation, information, and referral services (Rosen & Wilbur, 1992). Mental health services have not been a significant aspect of most AAA programs in the past and thus have not advanced public understanding of prevention and early intervention (Lebowitz, Light, & Bailey, 1987). Little if any case identification occurs. The great leeway allowed these state and local agencies has not provided an environment for national mental health leadership.

Federal Oversight

Congress established the House Select Committee on Aging and the Senate Special Committee on Aging in the 1980s to address aging issues. Despite hearings held by both groups, and efforts of various other entities to address problems of mental health treatment of elderly people and assistance to their families, the results have been characterized as remaining fragmented, inappropriate, and inadequate (Committee on Government Operations, 1988; U.S. Bipartisan Commission on Comprehensive Health Care, 1990; U.S. Senate, 1993). Furthermore, the 104th Congress's elimination of the House Select Committee on Aging suggests a lack of interest in providing federal leadership for aging issues.

OTHER FORCES CURRENTLY AFFECTING AGING AND MENTAL HEALTH POLICY

Managed Care and Mental Health

Rapid growth in managed care (Health Insurance Association of America, 1994) has affected the mental health system, including mental health services for Medicare- and Medicaid-eligible people (Estes, this volume; Knight & Kaskie, this volume). Managed care programs are systems that integrate the financing and delivery of health services in order to control medical costs and utilization. Traditionally, managed care programs have sought to address cost and quality issues of primary, acute-care medicine. Managed care has been reflective of overall national health care policy in that it has not, until recently, attempted to integrate acute and long-term care. However, since more and more employees are now being covered by managed care plans, the next decade of retirees will be greatly interested in Medicare managed care plans. In addition, on account of the rising costs of Medicaid, many states have opted to seek Medicaid waivers of federal regulatory requirements (either Section 2175 of OBRA 1981, or Section 1115 of the Social Security Act Amendments) so that they can experiment with cost-effective services, including managed care models.

What this growth in managed care portends for mental health and aging is a matter of considerable debate. Some studies have shown that managed care organizations have made respectable attempts to provide cost-effective, quality services for chronic illness. However, current concern largely centers on two main areas: mental health "carve-out" plans, and geriatric education and training.

As a result of cost escalation for mental health and substance abuse services in HMOs, those insurers contract with third-party mental health management vendors outside the normal benefits plan. These carved-out, contracted arrangements have been shown to favor outpatient care; use less expensive, nonmedical therapists; limit numbers of visits; and prefer less expensive group and family interventions (Knight & Kaskie, this volume; Wetle & Mark, 1990). Not only are these methods of intervention not the most effective for providing mental health services to many older people (Knight & Kaskie, this volume), but they also lessen the opportunity for practicing some of managed care's greatest assets: interdisciplinary team practice and continuity of care. The second major concern regarding managed care is that limits on specialized services and managed and closed systems of medical providers are disincentives to promoting academic medicine, research, and geriatric and mental health training to professional staff (Katz, this volume).

Barriers to Service

The turf issues and cost shifting that occurred in mental health in the late 1800s between state and local governments are being repeated in the 1990s with slightly different players, and turfism still stands in the way of a coordinated, adequate service delivery system (Armour, 1989). None of the health professionals and agencies involved in mental health care for elderly people has adequately addressed issues of collaboration, outreach, case identification, or continuity of care: In CMHCs, only 6% of clients are elderly; among private mental health practitioners, fewer than 5% of clients are elderly (Colenda & van Dooren, 1993); and the professionals who provide most intervention for older people—acute-care-oriented physicians—lack training in both geriatrics and mental health (Reuben et al., 1993).

A further barrier is created by current congressional interest in returning to a block grant concept of service delivery, which lessens federal

13

leadership in mental health and aging. At the same time, most states have demonstrated no ability to develop national models (Mechanic, 1993), and their increasing reliance on managed care providers to deliver services tends to exacerbate the fragmentation problem and creates gaps in public leadership in such areas as research and training (Knight & Kaskie, this volume). Block grant funding also exacerbates the problem of fragmentation of service delivery. It is counterproductive to development of a continuum of care (Greene, this volume) and was shown during the Reagan administration to diminish research and training efforts.

Another barrier is the lack of parity in research moneys and training stipends for gerontological mental health compared with other parts of the health care system. One positive example is the recent psychogeriatric demonstration training program of the Department of Veteran Affairs (VA) to develop an integrated continuum of care with a variety of mental health professional providers (Stone, 1994). As with postwar efforts at enhancing mental health provider training, the VA is attempting to respond to the aging of its target population by demonstrating leadership.

Further, insufficient study has been given to two important issues: First, the aging minority population is growing rapidly, but little attention has been paid to the special mental health needs of that group (Markides, 1986). Second, although much of the care for mentally ill elderly people is being provided by informal caregivers, there is little public support or policy to address the financial and emotional stress and the mental health problems of those caregivers (GAO, 1995; Odell & Safford, 1992).

SUMMARY

A historical review suggests a number of recurring themes in mental health policy, especially in relation to older persons:

1. Lack of parity between traditional health care and mental health care in services, training, and research, due in part to continuing financial and social disincentives.

2. Imposition of an acute-care medical model on financing, programming, and research approaches to the chronic conditions of mental illness.

3. Government programs that contain policy disincentives against providing preventive and early interventional mental health services.

4. Fragmentation, turfism, and lack of leadership in policy making, financing, training, and service systems of mental health programs for older people.

5. Overreliance on inpatient (custodial) treatment rather than prevention, early intervention, and appropriate home- and community-based mental health care services for the elderly and their families.

In addition to these continuing themes, it should be noted that maintaining the mental health of the elderly has generally been neglected or misunderstood by the public, professionals, researchers, and policy makers. While there have been some gains in improving mental health services for elderly people since the last White House Conference on Aging in 1981, the mental health of older people has not been considered a priority among policy makers. With the significant growth of the elderly population in the next century, mental health policy must shift to a more organized, proactive, and age-sensitive orientation, or the costs to society will be overwhelming.

REFERENCES

Advisory Panel on Alzheimer's Disease. (1993). *Fourth report of the advisory panel on Alzheimer's disease 1992* (NIH Publication No. 93-3520). Washington, DC: U.S. Government Printing Office.

Armour, P. (1989). Mental health policymaking in the United States: Patterns, process, and structures. In D. Rochefort (Ed.), *Handbook on mental health policy in the United States* (pp. 173-192). Westport, CT: Greenwood.

Bell, L. (1989). From the asylum to the community in U.S. mental health care: A historical overview. In D. Rochefort (Ed.), *Handbook on mental health policy in the United States* (pp. 89-120). Westport, CT: Greenwood.

Binner, P. (1988). Opinion: Mental health funding policy; a critical look. *Administration and Policy in Mental Health, 16,* 40-43.

Birren, J., & Schaie, K. (1990). *Handbook of the psychology of aging* (3rd ed.). New York: Academic Press.

Birren, J., Sloane, R., & Cohen, G. (1992). *Handbook of mental health and aging* (2nd ed.). New York: Academic Press.

Brandler, S. (1992). Antisocial behavior in old age. In F. Turner, (Ed.), *Mental health and the elderly: A social work perspective* (pp. 304-327). New York: Free Press.

Brody, E. (1985). *Mental and physical health practices of older people: A guide for health professionals.* New York: Springer.

Bruce, M., & McNamara, R. (1992). Psychiatric status among the homebound elderly: An epidemiologic perspective. *Journal of the American Geriatrics Society, 40,* 561-566.

Burns, B. J., Wagner, H. R., Taube, J. E., Magaziner, J., Permutt, T., & Landerman, L. R. (1993). Mental health service use by the elderly in nursing homes. *American Journal of Public Health, 83,* 331-337.

Colenda, C., & van Dooren, H. (1993). Opportunities for improving community mental health services for elderly persons. *Hospital and Community Psychiatry, 44,* 531-533.

Committee on Government Operations. (1988). *From back wards to back streets: The failure of the federal government in providing services for the mentally ill.* Washington, DC: U.S. Government Printing Office.

Evans, L., Buchwalter, K., & Fulmer, T. (1993). The mosaic of needs for elderly with mental health concerns. *The Gerontologist, 33*(2), 280-281.

Finkel, S., Dye, C., Garcia, A., Gatz, M., Greene, R., Hay, D. P., Smyer, M., & Wykle, M. L. (1993). *Report of the interdisciplinary coordinating group on mental health and the elderly.*

Flemming, A., Rickards, L., Santos, J., & West, P. (1986). *Mental health services for the elderly: Report on a survey of community mental health centers, Vol. 1.* Washington, DC: Action Committee to Implement the Mental Health Recommendations of the 1981 White House Conference on Aging.

Friedlander, W., & Apte, R. (1977). *Introduction to social welfare* (4th ed.). Englewood Cliffs, NJ: Prentice-Hall.

Friedlander, W., & Apte, R. (1982). *Introduction to social welfare* (5th ed.). Englewood Cliffs, NJ: Prentice-Hall.

Gatz, M., & Smyer, M. (1992). The mental health system and older adults in the 1990s. *American Psychologist, 47,* 741-751.

Grob, G. (1992). Mental health policy in America: Myths and realities. *Health Affairs, 11*(3), 7-22.

Group for the Advancement of Psychiatry. (1987). *Psychiatry and the mental health professionals: New roles for changing times.* New York: Brunner/Mazel.

Hagebak, J., & Hagebak, B. (1983). Meeting the mental health needs of the elderly: Issues and action steps. *Aging, 1,* 26-31.

Health Insurance Association of America. (1994). *Source book of health insurance data.* Washington, DC: Author.

Hellman, S., & Hellman, L. H. (1991). *Medicare and medigaps: A guide to retirement health insurance.* Newbury Park, CO: Sage.

Knight, B. (1989). *Outreach with the elderly.* New York: New York University Press.

Lebowitz, B., Light, E., & Bailey, F. (1987). Mental health center services for the elderly: The impact of coordination with area agencies on aging. *The Gerontologist, 27,* 699-702.

Lombardo, N. E. (1994). *Barriers to mental health services for nursing home residents.* Washington, DC: American Association of Retired Persons Policy Institute.

Markides, K. (1986). Minority status, aging, and mental health. *International Journal of Aging and Human Development, 23,* 285-300.

Mechanic, D. (1989a). *Mental health and social policy in the United States* (3rd ed.). Englewood Cliffs, NJ: Prentice-Hall.

Mechanic, D. (1989b). Toward the year 2000 in U.S. mental health policymaking and administration. In D. Rochefort (Ed.), *Handbook on mental health policy in the United States* (pp. 477-503). Westport, CT: Greenwood.

Mechanic, D. (1993). Mental health services in the context of health insurance reform. *Millbank Quarterly, 71,* 349-364.

Odell, C., & Safford, F. (1992). Working with traditional and non-traditional families of the elderly. In F. Safford & G. Krell (Eds.), *Gerontology for health professionals.* Washington, DC: National Association of Social Workers Press.

Park, D., Cavanaugh, J., Smith, A., & Smyer, M. (1993). *Vitality for life: Psychological research for productive aging.* Washington, DC: American Psychological Association.

Pope, A., & Tarlov, A. (Eds.). (1991). *Disability in America: Toward a national agenda for prevention.* Washington, DC: National Academy Press.

Prager, S., & Jeste, D. (1993). Sensory impairment in late-life schizophrenia. *Schizophrenia Bulletin, 19,* 755-772.

Reuben, D., Zwanziger, J., Bradley, T., Fink, A., Hirsch, S., Williams, A., Solomon, D., & Beck, J. (1993). How many physicians will be needed to provide medical care for older persons? Physician manpower needs of the twenty-first century. *Journal of the American Geriatrics Association, 41,* 444-453.

Rochefort, D. (1993). *From poorhouses to homelessness: Policy analysis and mental health care.* Westport, CT: Auburn House.

Rosen, A., & Wilbur, V. (1992). *Long-term care: Needs, costs and financing.* Washington, DC: Health Insurance Association of America.

Roybal, E. (1988). Mental health and aging: The need for an expanded federal response. *American Psychologist, 43,* 189-194.

Safford, F. (1992). Differential assessment of dementia and depression in elderly people. In F. Safford & G. Krell (Eds.), *Gerontology for health professionals* (pp. 51-67). Washington, DC: National Association of Social Workers Press.

Smyer, M. (1994). Mental health services in nursing homes. *Dimensions, 1*(3), 5-6.

Smyer, M., Cohn, M., & Brannon, D. (1988). *Mental health consultation in nursing homes.* New York: New York University Press.

Smyer, M., & Garfein, R. (1988). The mental health problems of nursing home residents. In M. Smyer, M. Cohn, & D. Brannon (Eds.), *Mental health consultation in nursing homes* (pp. 66-81). New York: New York University Press.

Stone, W. (1994). *Psychogeriatric programs in the Department of Veterans Affairs: An integrated continuum of care.* Presentation at the American Association of Geriatric Psychiatrists Annual Meeting, Tampa, FL.

Surles, R. (1993). Significant changes in mental health: 1972–1992. *Administration and Policy in Mental Health, 21,* 123-128.

U.S. Bipartisan Commission on Comprehensive Health Care. (1990, September). *Call to action: Final report.* Washington, DC: U.S. Government Printing Office.

U.S. Government Accounting Office. (1994, December). *Aging issues: Related GAO reports and activities in fiscal year 1994* (GAO/HEHS-95-44). Washington, DC: Author.

U.S. Government Accounting Office. (1995, April). *Long-term care: Current issues and future directions* (GAO/HEHS-95-109). Washington, DC: Author.

U.S. House Select Committee on Aging. (1993). *Shortage of health care professions caring for the elderly: Recommendations for change*. Washington, DC: U.S. Government Printing Office.

U.S. Senate Special Committee on Aging. (1993, July 15). *Mental health and the aging*. (Forum before U.S. Senate Special Committee on Aging, No 103-10, pp. 84-90). Washington, DC: U.S. Government Printing Office.

Wykle, M., & Musil, C. (1993). Mental health of older persons: Social and cultural factors. *Generations, 17*, 7-12.

Wetle, T., & Mark, H. (1990). Managed care. In B. S. Fogel, A. Furino, & G. L. Gottlieb (Eds.), *Mental health policy for older Americans: Protecting minds at risk* (pp. 221-238). Washington, DC: American Psychiatric Press.

CHAPTER 2

Efficacy of Clinical Treatment for Mental Disorders Among Older Persons

Lon S. Schneider

ental disorders that are manifested in old age have a major impact on individuals, families, and society. This chapter reviews the most severe mental disorders experienced by older individuals and focuses on the efficacy of currently available empirically based treatment approaches. While the chapter focuses more on biological and psychopharmacologic treatments, psychotherapy and other psychosocial treatments are also discussed.

The emphasis is on medically stable individuals who may need acute inpatient and short- or long-term outpatient mental health care. The challenges posed by special populations such as the medically ill and residents of long-term care facilities are only briefly discussed. Though the impact of substance abuse is increasingly important, with its long-term

The author gratefully acknowledges the contributions of Lissy Jarvik, Charles F. Reynolds, Barry D. Lebowitz, Enid Light, Larry Thompson, and Margaret Gatz. Work was supported in part by NIH MH 19074 and AG 05142. Portions are adapted from a 1993 report submitted to the National Advisory Mental Health Council titled Health Care Reform for Americans With Severe Mental Illnesses: Treatment Efficacy for Geropsychiatric Patients with Severe Mental Illness. A condensed version of this report was published as "Efficacy of Treatment for Geropsychiatric Patients With Severe Mental Illness," by L. S. Schneider, in volume 29 of *Psychopharmacology Bulletin*, pp. 501-524, 1993.

medical and neuropsychiatric consequences for elderly people, it is not covered in this chapter because of space limitations.

The chapter emphasizes research published in the past decade, in which randomized, placebo-controlled, double-blind methodology has generally been used to establish the efficacy of particular treatments of severe mental disorders in elderly people. Whenever possible, conclusions have been drawn from the results of the most methodologically sound work. The weaknesses inherent in the literature, however, often necessitate rendering tentative conclusions concerning the efficacy or lack of efficacy of particular treatments. In areas where such methodological rigor has not been attained, open-trial studies have been cited to substantiate potential efficacy for clinical practice and future research. Efforts have been made throughout to identify the limitations of current knowledge and to point out the numerous areas in which much more needs to be learned.

Although the following points are not specifically discussed in the review of particular disorders and their treatment, they can be useful to keep in mind as the reader progresses through the chapter.

1. The most important step in treatment is accurate psychiatric diagnosis. Unfortunately, accurate diagnosis for elderly people is often given short shrift for a variety of reasons.

2. The special vulnerability of frail elderly people requires emphasis. Interindividual variability increases with aging. Yet in many studies, elderly people are lumped into a single group even though they may differ in age by more than 30 years and have strong differences in such factors as health status and social status.

3. The distinction between acute and maintenance treatment is important. Relieving a patient's acute symptoms is not enough; relapse must be prevented as well. For example, more than 50% of people who have had one depressive episode have subsequent episodes.

4. Substance abuse is overlooked among elderly people of today, yet it is likely to become increasingly common as younger generations grow older.

5. The extent of posttraumatic stress disorder among elderly people as a result of proximal trauma or of distant war or childhood trauma is only

beginning to be appreciated. For example, we might expect an increase in posttraumatic stress disorder and major depression among Vietnam War veterans as they age.

SEVERE MENTAL DISORDERS IN THE GERIATRIC POPULATION

The severe mental disorders in the elderly age groups and related treatment considerations are listed in Table 1. These disorders are classified into six groups: delirium, dementia, depression, mania, psychotic disorders, and anxiety disorders. Onset of these disorders may occur in early adult life and follow a clinical course into older age, or onset may occur during the older years.

At present, knowledge in clinical diagnosis and treatment of elderly people is accumulating rapidly; new textbooks are appearing with impressive regularity (e.g., Salzman, 1992; Shamoian, 1992). These developments have been supported by two separate initiatives: the search for cognition-enhancing agents as part of drug discovery in Alzheimer's disease (Khachaturian, Phelps, & Buckholtz, 1994; Lebowitz, 1992); and the extension of findings regarding the treatment of depression in midlife adults to elderly people (Schneider, Reynolds, Lebowitz, & Friedhoff, 1994). In addition, there has been a resurgence of interest in the treatment of anxiety disorders (Salzman & Lebowitz, 1991). This review will concentrate somewhat more on depression and dementia, since there is more systematic research in these areas than in other psychogeriatric areas. In particular, treatment recommendations from the 1991 National Institutes of Health (NIH) Consensus Development Conference on the Diagnosis and Treatment of Depression in Late Life are discussed.

In each of the disorders described in this chapter, psychopharmacologic treatment is emphasized. Minimizing side effects of psychotropic drugs is a matter of concern in geriatric psychopharmacology, as is reducing the unwanted effects of all treatments in medicine. It is clear that elderly people are at significantly greater risk than younger patients for movement disorders (e.g., Harris et al., 1992) and for anticholinergic (Tune, 1992), behavioral (Pomara, Deptula, Singh, & Monroy, 1991), and hypotensive and cardiovascular effects (Pascualy, Murburg, & Veith, 1992).

TABLE 1   Severe Mental Illnesses Among Older Persons

Illnesses	Treatment Considerations
Delirium	
An acute physiological brain dysfunction complicating medical illness, or the result of trauma. Manifests as confusion, alteration in level of arousal, attention, and behavioral disturbances. Increasing age, medical illnesses, medication use, and dementia are risk factors for its development.	Diagnose and treat the underlying cause; use environmental manipulation and medications such as haloperidol to treat behavioral symptoms. Common precipitators are medical illness, medications, intoxications, and postoperative states. Environmental manipulations and nursing support are used. Benzodiazepines are used for sedative or hypnotic withdrawal; physostigmine is sometimes used for anticholinergic states.
Dementia	
A syndrome characterized by memory and cognitive impairment in the presence of a clear sensorium. Primary dementias include Alzheimer's disease, vascular dementia, and dementia due to Parkinson's disease, Huntington's disease, Creutzfeldt-Jakob disease, Pick's disease, and human immunodeficiency virus. Secondary dementias are those due to alcohol abuse, medical illnesses, or other specific causes. Dementias are generally chronic and progressive.	For Alzheimer's disease: Memory and cognitive impairment and behavioral symptoms are the main areas for treatment. Medications are under development to treat the specific cognitive impairments (e.g., memory loss); one medication, tacrine, is available by prescription. Most patients have severe cognitive impairments beyond the range of medications under development. Behavioral symptoms such as agitation, hallucinations, delusions, aggression, and depression occur in most patients over the course of the illness. Treatment aimed toward ameliorating these symptoms improves quality of life. Various medications may be effective. It is important to try to determine possible causes of behavioral symptoms. For vascular dementia: Several drugs are under development, aimed at altering the vascular pathology. Behavioral symptoms are similar to those in Alzheimer's disease and are treated similarly. Psychosocial interventions: Day care, behavioral intervention, and interventions directed toward caregivers may improve quality of life and delay the need for institutionalization.

TABLE 1 *Continued*

Illnesses	Treatment Considerations
Depression	
Syndromes characterized by a pervasive depressed mood. Subtypes include major depression, major depression with delusions, major depression with melancholia, and dysthymic disorder. Minor depression or subsyndromal depression is becoming recognized as clinically important. Depression may be acute, remitting and relapsing, or chronic. Anxiety disorder may occur with depression. The syndrome may occur in the context of medical illnesses, dementia, and medication use. In elderly people, depression is often unrecognized.	Moderate to severe depression requires hospitalization for acute treatment, medication, and/or convulsive therapy. Depression with delusions or hallucinations requires neuroleptics in addition to antidepressants, and/or convulsive therapy. Concomitant medical illnesses are common among depressed elderly people. Response to antidepressant treatment may take 6 weeks or longer in elderly people. Psychotherapy and psychosocial support is useful in outpatient treatment. Structured psychotherapies may be as effective as medication in some depressed outpatients. Relapse after successful acute treatment is common. Maintenance therapy to prevent relapse or recurrence is important. Nursing home residents and recently bereaved groups have increased prevalence.
Mania	
Characterized by persistently elevated or expansive mood, accompanied by several other symptoms; a mood disorder. Often occurs in people who have recurrent depressive episodes.	Recurrence is common. Acute and maintenance pharmacologic treatments are important. Depressive episodes may occur also.
Psychosis in Late-life	
A constellation of syndromes including schizophrenia, late-onset schizophrenia, paraphrenia (late-onset delusional disorder), depression with delusions or hallucinations, psychotic symptoms in dementia, and symptomatic psychoses (due to specific diseases) characterized by impairment of reality testing, usually evidenced by delusions or hallucinations. Symptoms often markedly interfere with daily functioning.	Psychotic symptoms occur in a variety of illnesses. Treatment considerations depend on the specific illness. Schizophrenia is characterized by chronicity and progressive deterioration in about one third of patients. Depression accompanied by delusions requires antipsychotic medication in addition to antidepressants and is often marginally responsive or unresponsive to medication. Convulsive therapy is more effective for acute treatment of delusional depression. Psychotic symptoms occur frequently in dementia (above).

continued

TABLE 1 *Continued*

Illnesses	Treatment Considerations
Anxiety Disorders	
Fear or apprehension resulting from anticipation of danger, often accompanied by motor or autonomic signs or by hyper-vigilance. Includes generalized anxiety disorder (unfocused), agoraphobia with and without panic (physical symptoms), panic disorder, phobia (focused), obsessive-compulsive disorder, and secondary anxiety disorders.	The distinctions between anxiety disorders and depression accompanied by anxiety and between a primary anxiety disorder and anxiety secondary to medical illnesses are important. Many physical illnesses may present with anxiety-like symptoms.

NOTE: Adapted from L. S. Schneider, 1993, Efficacy of treatment for geropsychiatric patients with severe mental illness. *Psychopharmacology Bulletin, 29,* 501–524.

Excessive sedation, ataxia, and "cognitive toxicity" are troublesome side effects of many psychotropics (Pomara et al., 1991). The efficacy of a particular drug is attributable to its ability to modulate selective neuro-receptors in the central nervous system. By contrast, the nonselective modulation of other receptor systems may lead to unwanted side effects with a particular drug.

While these and other potential side effects occur with all medical treatments and are a clinical concern, space limitations do not permit extended discussions of these effects in this chapter. The decision to treat an individual patient with psychotropic drugs requires an assessment by the psychiatrist that the potential benefits outweigh the risks. Even when the benefits outweigh the risks, physicians still must take steps to help the patient minimize and manage side effects.

Delirium

Clinical Features

Core clinical features of delirium include reduced ability to maintain and shift attention to external stimuli, disorganized thinking, reduced level of consciousness, perceptual disturbances, disturbances of the sleep–

wake cycle, disorientation, and memory impairment. In particular, 38% of patients with delirium syndrome manifest agitation and 33% have hallucinations or delusions (Ross, Peyser, Shapiro, & Folstein, 1991). Prevalence estimates range from 10% to 30% of hospitalized patients.

Important causes and precipitating factors for delirium are intoxications from drugs and other chemicals and endogenously produced toxins due to hepatic, renal, endocrinological, metabolic, and infectious disorders. Important pharmacological precipitants include sedative-hypnotic medications, anxiolytics, antidepressant medications, anti-inflammatories, analgesics, antibiotics, anticonvulsants, antihypertensives, cardiovascular drugs, anti-gastrointestinal ulcer drugs, anticancer medications, and over-the-counter medications. Postoperative delirium is particularly common and is associated with increased mortality (Tune, 1991).

Treatment

Treatment involves identifying and treating an underlying cause of the syndrome when possible. Although controlled studies are very few, many authors (and clinical experience) suggest the following treatment approaches (Rabins, 1991): Provide a predictable, stable environment; use medications judiciously for specific symptoms; and restrain patients to prevent harm to themselves and others.

The choice of medication depends, in part, on the syndrome being treated. Withdrawal from sedative-hypnotics, including alcohol, generally requires the use of a benzodiazepine such as lorazepam, intramuscularly or orally, in repeated, frequent doses. Physostigmine salicylate (1 to 2 mg given intravenously) is useful for delirium due to drugs with anticholinergic effects. Haloperidol (and other neuroleptics) in individualized doses is effective for delirium accompanied by hallucinations, delusions, and severe agitation (Adams, 1988; Tesar, Murray, & Cassem, 1985). Haloperidol and benzodiazepines are combined on occasion (Menza, Murray, & Holmes, 1988). Although neuroleptics and benzodiazepines are effective for the symptoms mentioned above, they may also aggravate delirium and therefore should be used with appropriate, close monitoring.

Dementia

Clinical Features

Dementia is an organic mental syndrome characterized by cognitive impairments, particularly memory impairment, accompanied by impairments in abstract thinking, judgment or insight, language, or the ability to carry out familiar movements or properly use common objects, as well as possible changes in mood, personality, and behavior.

For purposes of treatment considerations, there are three overlapping clusters of symptoms: those related to memory and cognitive impairments, abnormal symptomatic behaviors, and impairments in activities of daily living. In practice, dementia patients have symptoms from all clusters that can serve as a focus for treatment. An overview of treatment considerations is provided in Table 2.

The most common dementia syndrome is Alzheimer's disease (AD), a neurodegenerative disorder characterized by decline in memory, cognition, behavioral, and neurological function, progressing to increasingly severe dementia and death. Other dementia syndromes occur with vascular disease (e.g., multi-infarct dementia), Pick's disease, Parkinson's disease, Creutzfeldt-Jakob disease, Huntington's disease, hydrocephalus, alcohol abuse, schizophrenia, and various medical illnesses.

Epidemiology

The prevalence of dementia is greater than 5% among people older than 65, increasing to more than 30% in those over 85. Most dementia represents AD; about 10%–15% is caused by vascular disease; another 10%–15% is a mixture of both. The lifetime risk of AD ranges between 14% and 26% (Terry, Katzman, & Beck, 1994). Less frequent causes of dementia include various medical illnesses and medications. The incidence of AD increases dramatically with advancing age and is approximately the same for men and women. The prevalence of AD, however, is twice as great in women as in men, and the difference in prevalence becomes larger with increasing age, suggesting differences in longevity. Nevertheless, dementia and AD are significantly underrecognized in the

TABLE 2   Overview of Treatments for Symptoms of Dementia

Symptoms	Treatment Considerations	Comments	References
Cognitive or memory impairments	Reversal or prevention of cognitive deterioration is the treatment goal. This is currently an area of active pharmacologic investigation. There is no evidence that social interventions, "retraining," or education is meaningfully effective in improving cognitive function per se.	One cholinesterase inhibitor, tacrine, is available by prescription. Other cholinergic drugs are under investigation. Such drugs are likely to confer modest improvements in memory in a minority of Alzheimer's patients. Long-term efficacy is not known. Use in other dementias is not tested.	Davis et al., 1992 Farlow et al., 1992 Knapp et al., 1994 Tariot et al., 1992 Wadworth & Chrisp, 1992
Impaired social function and activities of daily living	Environmental manipulations to allow patients with dementia to function better may be helpful. Experimental medications that seem effective for cognitive symptoms may affect daily activities and social function also. Psychosocial interventions directed toward caregivers may postpone nursing home placement.	There are no drugs currently available. Drugs that improve cognition would be expected to improve cognition-dependent social function. Drugs that limit further deterioration would be expected to preserve basic activities of daily living.	Mittleman et al., 1993
Behavioral symptoms (depression and mood-related symptoms)	Depressive symptoms may occur in 10% to 20% of dementia patients with Alzheimer's, usually earlier in the course than psychotic symptoms appear. Antidepressant medication may be helpful.	A randomized trial of imipramine showed no significant advantage over placebo. A trial of moclobemide (not available in the United States), however, suggested more efficacy than placebo.	Hebenstreit et al., 1991 Reifler et al., 1989 Reynolds et al., 1987

continued

TABLE 2 *Continued*

Symptoms	Treatment Considerations	Comments	References
Behavioral symptoms (hallucinations, delusions, agitation, aggression)	These symptoms, which most patients have during the illness course, influence quality of life and institutionalization. Environmental manipulations may be helpful in reducing symptoms. Various medications may be effective; neuroleptics are best studied.	Several placebo-controlled trials with neuroleptics, usually haloperidol or thioridazine, indicate efficacy for an acute treatment period of 8 weeks or less. There have been many case reports, but there have been very few controlled trials with other medications such as anti-depressants, anti-convulsants, ß-blockers, or serotonin uptake blockers.	Nyth & Gottfries, 1990 Salzman, 1987 Schneider, Pollock, & Lyness, 1990 Schneider & Sobin, 1992 Sunderland & Silver, 1988

NOTE: Adapted from L. S. Schneider, 1993, Efficacy of treatment for geropsychiatric patients with severe mental illness. *Psychopharmacology Bulletin, 29,* 501–524.

United States. Institutionalized patients and those with a rapidly progressive course are often not recognized. The prevalence of dementia in the United States is also markedly greater in African Americans than in Whites (Heyman, Fillenbaum, & Prosnmitz, 1991; Schoenberg et al., 1985).

Manifestations

In addition to the manifestations of cognitive impairment and impairments of activities of daily living, agitation and other symptomatic behaviors are principal problems in the clinical management of patients with AD and other dementia. Disruptive symptoms such as outbursts, violence, sleep disturbance, motor restlessness, delusions, hallucinations, and misidentifications each occur in approximately one third of various AD patient samples. Between 50% and 75% of AD patients show significant disruptive behavior at some time during their illness (Schneider & Sobin, 1992). There is considerable variability in the behavioral patterns of patients with dementia. Some behaviors, such as wandering and agitation, appear to be particularly characteristic of AD and increase in frequency with duration of illness.

The consequences of progressively impaired cognition and agitated behaviors for patients with dementia—regardless of the etiology—include the inability of families to care for patients at home and subsequent institutionalization, loss of autonomy, loss of function because of physical restraint, and withdrawal of caregivers' emotional support. A disruptive patient may not receive appropriate clinical care and is more likely to be treated with medication or restraints.

Treatment of Cognitive Symptoms

The goals of treatment for dementia are to reverse, prevent, or slow cognitive and intellectual deterioration. The development of effective medications for this purpose is an area of intense research. There are several empirically and theoretically based approaches. The most pronounced neurotransmitter abnormalities in AD—the loss of various aspects of acetylcholine function—provide a rationale for experimental drug therapies. Phase III efficacy trials of several cholinesterase inhibitors and cholinergic agonists are nearing completion. One drug, tacrine, is available by prescription, although it is covered by few pharmacy benefits management programs. The therapeutic effects of these medications are modest but still of clinically significant benefit to a minority of patients. Between 25% and 50% of patients may benefit from tacrine (Schneider, 1994). (High rates of side effects are a particular issue with these drugs. With tacrine and related medications, reversible liver toxicity is a major side effect. With cholinesterase inhibitors and cholinergic agonists in general, nausea and vomiting are not infrequent).

Several other medications marketed in the United States are not approved by the Food and Drug Administration (FDA) for AD or dementia but may nevertheless be prescribed by some clinicians for treating cognitive symptoms. They include selegiline ((−)-deprenyl), nimodipine, anti-inflammatory medications, physostigmine, and ergoloid mesylates (Hydergine). Several clinical trials suggest that selegiline ((–)-deprenyl) may be effective, at least acutely, in improving cognitive function (Tariot, Schneider, Patel, & Goldstein, 1992). Over-the-counter preparations including vitamin B_{12}, vitamin E, lecithin and other sources of choline, and *Gingko biloba* have not been demonstrated to be of benefit. Well-controlled trials have failed to demonstrate significant therapeutic effects for acetylcholine precursors such as lecithin and phosphatidylcholine (Becker & Giacobini, 1988). Only pilot studies suggest that anti-inflammatory medications such as indomethacin may have an effect (e.g., Rogers, Kirby, & Hempelman, 1993).

Drugs such as selegiline ((–)-deprenyl), other monoamine oxidase B inhibitors, vitamin E, and the anti-inflammatory corticosteroid prednisone are being studied in ongoing clinical trials, some funded by the NIH, to help decrease the rate of deterioration in AD, but results are not available.

One drug, ergoloid mesylsates (Hydergine), has been approved by the FDA for "idiopathic decline in mental capacity." The package insert states, in part:

> A proportion of individuals over 60 who manifest signs and symptoms of an idiopathic decline in mental capacity (i.e., cognitive and interpersonal skills, mood, self care, apparent motivation) can experience some symptomatic relief upon treatment with Hydergine®. . . . The identity of the specific trait(s) or condition(s), if any, which would usefully predict a response to Hydergine® . . . is not known. It appears however, that those individuals who do respond come from groups of patients who would be considered clinically to suffer from some ill-defined process related to aging or to have some underlying dementing condition (i.e., primary progressive dementia, Alzheimer's dementia, senile onset, multi-infarct dementia).

Despite numerous clinical trials in elderly populations, the role and efficacy of ergoloid mesylates (Hydergine) in dementia remain uncertain. For the most part, these trials did not use homogeneously diagnosed groups (or appropriately diagnosed dementia patients), and the criteria for improvement have focused on behavior and functional activities. On these outcomes, ergoloid mesylates (Hydergine) have been demonstrated to be consistently more effective than placebo, but overall the improvements are very small. There is no general agreement on the role of ergoloid mesylates

(Hydergine), if any, in the treatment of dementia (Schneider & Olin, 1994).

Potential areas of experimentation in pharmacologic treatment include the use of growth factors to stimulate cell maintenance and growth and the use of compounds to compensate for neurotransmitter deficits, alter brain metabolism, alter neuron membrane function, regulate calcium homeostasis, and prevent the accumulation of abnormal proteins (including beta amyloid and abnormal cytoskeletal proteins).

In summary, there is only one FDA-approved, modestly effective treatment for the cognitive symptoms of dementia at present, although the situation may change with continuing clinical research.

Treatment of Behavioral Symptoms

The ideal management of these behaviors involves the search for treatable physical, environmental, and psychiatric precipitants before the use of behavioral or pharmacologic treatments (Leibovici & Tariot, 1988). Behavioral interventions and environmental manipulations may be effective in many cases. Pharmacotherapy is far more commonly used than behavioral interventions for treatment of behavioral symptoms; research on the nonpharmacologic treatment of behavioral disorders in dementia is underdeveloped (Rabins, 1989). Randomized, controlled treatment trials of disruptive behavior in dementia are few and have mainly been limited to neuroleptics and benzodiazepines (Schneider, Pollock, & Lyness, 1990).

Neuroleptics. The use of neuroleptics for treating symptomatic behaviors in dementia has been extensively reviewed (e.g., Salzman, 1987; Schneider et al., 1990; Sunderland & Silver, 1988). A meta-analytic review to assess the clinical efficacy of neuroleptics in dementia identified 17 placebo-controlled studies of neuroleptics in dementia, only 7 of which used a double-blind, placebo-controlled, parallel-group design to assess patients with primary dementia (Schneider et al., 1990). The results showed that, overall, neuroleptics were more effective than placebo but with only a small magnitude of effect, suggesting that a minority of patients benefited from treatment beyond the benefit obtained with placebo. In these double-blind studies, the placebo response rate averaged 37.5%, and the neuroleptic nonresponse rate was 40.5%. There is no evidence that particular neuroleptics are differentially efficacious, although haloperidol and thioridazine appear to be most widely used. In summary, neuroleptics appear to be modestly effective in controlling agitation.

Benzodiazepines. Benzodiazepines are consistently more effective than placebo in controlled trials. Short-acting drugs such as oxazepam seem to have fewer side effects than chlordiazepoxide and diazepam, but direct comparisons are lacking. There are no dose–ranging studies, nor are there direct comparisons among benzodiazepines (Schneider & Sobin, 1992). Neuroleptics are consistently more effective than benzodiazepines in direct comparisons. Because most of the benzodiazepine trials used mixed-diagnosis samples, their generalizability to dementia populations is limited.

Nonneuroleptics. In the past decade there has been an increasing number of clinical reports advocating the effectiveness of certain non-neuroleptic and nonbenzodiazepine medications, such as anticonvulsants and antidepressants, in patients with dementia and symptomatic behaviors. These medications have not been as well studied. The medications include lithium, β-adrenergic blockers, trazodone, carbamazepine, buspirone, selegiline ((–)-deprenyl), and serotonin uptake blockers. Most of these medications were tried not specifically in patients with dementia, but in patients with various organic mental syndromes. That the literature consists almost entirely of clinical series and case reports makes interpreting the efficacy of individual medications difficult. The few placebo-controlled studies generally are of small sample sizes and show no or very modest efficacy for the study medication. One notable exception is the serotonin uptake blocker citalopram, not available in the United States, which was clearly more effective than placebo in improving behavioral symptoms in patients with AD but not in those with multi-infarct dementia (Nyth & Gottfries, 1990). Despite their widespread use, there is very little published empirical evidence for the effectiveness of nonneuroleptic medications for treating behavioral symptoms in elderly patients with dementia.

In summary, while the use of nonneuroleptics in patients with AD and agitation appears promising, controlled studies are needed, paying attention to diagnosis and specific behavioral syndromes and comparing various agents with neuroleptics and one another.

Treatment of Depression in Dementia

Depressive symptoms occur in 10% to 20% of patients with AD dementia, usually earlier in the course than psychotic symptoms appear. Cognitive impairment may be a secondary symptom of major depression, or major depression may be secondary to dementia. Response of elderly patients to antidepressant treatment for mixed depression and cognitive impairment has only recently received limited investigation. A randomized trial of the antidepressant imipramine showed no significant advantage over placebo (Reifler et al., 1989). A placebo-controlled trial of the monoamine oxidase inhibitor moclobemide (not available in the United States), however, suggested its efficacy (Hebenstreit et al., 1991). Reynolds et al. (1987) reported an open trial with the antidepressant nortriptyline in inpatients with mixed symptoms of depression and cognitive impairment, compared with elderly depressed people without cognitive impairment. Ten of 16 mixed-symptom patients showed significant improvement in both depression and dementia rating scores, suggesting that these patients responded to treatment used for elderly people with depression and intact cognition.

Interventions With Caregivers

In addition to effective treatments for dementia aimed solely at the patient, interventions with family or other caregivers may be effective at delaying institutionalization. Delaying nursing home placement might be expected to substantially improve the quality of life of both dementia patients and their caregivers. In one study, caregivers were randomly assigned to receive either routine support from an AD center or comprehensive psychosocial intervention involving individual and family counseling, support group participation, and frequent consultations. Consultations reduced nursing home placement by half at the end of a year, suggesting that comprehensive counseling reduces socioeconomic impact of the illness and improves quality of life in both patient and caregiver (Mittelman et al., 1993). However, another study was unable to demonstrate that the availability of day treatment postponed nursing home placement (Rosenheck et al., 1993).

33

Conclusions

Randomized, controlled trials of treatments for symptomatic behaviors in dementia have been largely limited to neuroleptics and benzodiazepines (Salzman, 1987; Schneider et al., 1990; Sunderland & Silver, 1988). In direct comparisons, neuroleptics are more effective than benzodiazepines. Most reports of nonneuroleptics used in agitated dementia have been cases or case series concerning patients with a variety of organic brain syndromes. A notable exception is a randomized trial of citalopram in which the drug was effective for behavioral symptoms in AD but not in vascular dementia (Nyth & Gottfries, 1990). Other medications used to treat agitation have not been formally assessed. Nevertheless, many clinicians have extensive, nonsystematically acquired clinical experience in the use of some of these medications. Trazodone and carbamazepine seem to be prescribed frequently in preference to neuroleptics, but results have not been conveyed through the literature. Interventions directed toward spouses or other caregivers may be effective at maintaining elderly people with dementia at home.

The importance of further determining essential efficacy for psychotropic medications in dementia populations is stressed by the Omnibus Budget Reconciliation Act of 1987 (Public Law 100-203), which, in part, was intended to protect nursing home patients from the inappropriate use of psychotropic drugs as "chemical restraints." The law and its proposed guidelines (*Federal Register*, February 2, 1992) affect primarily the use of neuroleptics. The increased scrutiny of neuroleptic prescribing may encourage the use of other medications described above for the treatment of symptomatic behaviors, although there is less evidence of their efficacy, but it may also redirect attention to behavior modification and environmental manipulations.

Depression

Background

Recent work on the treatment of depression in late life has been summarized in the panel report from the 1991 NIH Consensus Development Conference on the Diagnosis and Treatment of Depression in Late Life. The panel report (Freidhoff, 1994) provided the following overview:

> Depression in the aging and the aged is a major public health problem. It causes suffering to many who go undiagnosed, and it burdens families and institutions providing care for the elderly by disabling those who might otherwise be able-bodied. What makes depression in the elderly so insidious is that neither the victim nor the health care provider may recognize its symptoms in the context of the multiple physical problems of many elderly people. Depressed mood . . . may be less prominent than other depressive symptoms such as loss of appetite, sleeplessness, anergia, and loss of interest and enjoyment of the normal pursuits of life. There is a wide spectrum of depressive symptomatology as well as types of available therapies.

The report commented on why the illness is underdiagnosed and undertreated:

> Because of the many physical illnesses and social and economic problems of the elderly, individual health care providers often conclude that depression is a normal consequence of these problems, an attitude often shared by the patients themselves. All of these factors conspire to make the illness underdiagnosed and, more importantly, undertreated. (p. 494)

Clinical Features

The term depression is used broadly to describe a syndrome that includes a constellation of physiological, affective, and cognitive manifestations. Criteria for diagnosis include depressed or irritable mood (most important); loss of interest or pleasure in usual activities; changes in appetite and weight; disturbed sleep; motor agitation or retardation; fatigue and loss of energy; feelings of worthlessness, self-reproach, or excessive guilt; suicidal thinking or attempts; and difficulty with thinking or concentration. However, often the symptoms are unrecognized in elderly people who have multiple physical illnesses. Medical illness should not preclude a diagnosis of depression. Major depression can be further subdivided into depression with delusions, depression with melancholia, and bipolar disorder. (In bipolar disorder, manic and hypomanic episodes occur in addition to depression).

Dysthymic disorder is characterized by a chronic disturbance of mood occurring more days than not for at least 2 years with the associated symptoms listed above. The distinction between depression and dysthymia (or depression in partial remission) can be difficult; they may co–occur in the same patient.

The presentation of depression in elderly people may vary with regard to symptoms, age of onset, and course. Late-onset depression is associated with a lower frequency of family history of depression but a higher frequency of cognitive impairment, cerebral atrophy, deep white matter changes, recurrences, medical comorbidity, and mortality (Alexopoulos, 1994; Caine et al., 1994).

Epidemiology and Risk Factors

The Consensus Development Panel (Freidhoff, 1994) summarized the epidemiology of depression in the elderly:

> Depressive symptoms occur in approximately 15 percent of community residents over 65 years of age. The prevalence of major depression among the elderly living in the community is usually estimated at less than 3 percent. The rates of major or minor depression among elderly people range from 5 percent in primary care clinics to 15 to 25 percent in nursing homes. The rates of new cases of depression in nursing homes are striking: 13 percent of residents develop a new episode of major depression over a 1-year period, and another 18 percent develop new depressive symptoms.

> There is a sharp drop in the rates of treatment of depression among the elderly compared with younger adults. . . . Only about 10 percent of the elderly who are in need of psychiatric treatment ever receive this service. (p. 497)

The lifetime risk of depression approaches 20% to 25%. The risk factors for depression in elderly people, although similar to those of younger age groups, have some important differences: being female, unmarried, widowed, or recently bereaved; experiencing stressful life events; and lacking a supportive social network are associated with elevated rates of depression (Zisook, 1994). There is an excess co-occurrence of physical illnesses (e.g., stroke, cancer, dementia) with depression, confirmed in numerous studies (Reynolds et al., 1994). Although depression may be an effect of such coexistent disorders, it might also enhance vulnerability to certain illnesses.

Subgroups of elderly people who are at greater risk for major depression include the chronically physically ill (of whom up to 50% may have major depression), institutionalized elderly people, the recently bereaved, and, often unrecognized, family members caring for chronically ill relatives. Among family caregivers the prevalence of major depression may be as high as 40%.

Course of Depression and Suicide

As in younger people, the course of depression in elderly people is characterized by exacerbations, remissions, and chronicity. Sixty percent of patients who recover from an index episode have at least one subsequent episode. Recurrence is a serious problem: up to 40% of depressed patients continue to experience depression chronically. Delusional depression is associated with greater mortality (Murphy, 1994). Mortality rates by suicide and other causes are higher among elderly persons with depression than among their nondepressed counterparts. This increased mortality cannot be completely accounted for by sociodemographic factors and pre-existing physical illnesses.

The best source of information about elderly suicide is Conwell (1994), who provides this summary. The rate of completed suicides for older people is more than twice that of the general population (26.5 per 100,000 in 80- to 84-year-olds, versus 12.4 per 100,000 overall). Elderly White men are at highest risk. More than three fourths of elderly people who complete suicide had visited a primary care physician within the month before their suicide. Most were suffering from their first episode of major depression, which was only moderately severe, yet the depressive symptoms went unrecognized and untreated.

Treatment

The goals of treatment for depression are to: (a) decrease symptoms of depression, (b) reduce risk of relapse and recurrence, (c) enhance quality of life, (d) improve general and medical health status, (e) decrease mortality, and (f) decrease health care costs. The two major categories of treatment for depression are biological therapy (e.g., pharmacotherapy and

electroconvulsive therapy) and psychosocial therapies (e.g., psychotherapies such as cognitive-behavioral, interpersonal, and psychodynamic).

The largest body of treatment efficacy data is available for biological therapies, although some data support the efficacy of particular focused,
time-limited psychotherapy such as brief psychodynamic, cognitive-behavioral, and interpersonal psychotherapies in defined populations. Since
the type and severity of depressive syndromes influence the choice of
treatment approach, treatment of depression should be conceptualized as
either acute or maintenance. In general, the more severe depression—
with melancholia, delusions, active suicidal ideation or plans, or concomitant medical illnesses—require intensive treatment. Patients often require
hospitalization, either medication with an antidepressant and a neuroleptic,
or electroconvulsive therapy or both, and intensive psychosocial support.
Moderately severe depression and dysthymia, with fewer melancholic
symptoms, without delusions, and without intense suicidal ideation may
require outpatient treatment with medication or psychotherapy or both,
managed at weekly intervals or more often. The acute treatment response
is relatively well defined; chronic maintenance therapy to prevent relapse is
less well defined (Reynolds et al., 1992, 1994).

Exhibit I to this chapter presents the Consensus Development
Panel's review of treatment, and Table 3 presents an overview of treatments for major depression in elderly people.

Acute Treatments

Medications. Supporting the efficacy of acute treatment there have
been approximately 30 randomized, placebo-controlled, parallel-group
clinical trials in elderly patients with depression. Medications used have
included nortriptyline, imipramine, doxepin, buproprion, desipramine,
nomifensine (not currently marketed), monoamine oxidase inhibitors such
as phenelzine, and other medications.

Two trials are of particular note. A double-blind study (Georgotas
et al., 1986) compared nortriptyline and phenelzine over 7 weeks with
respect to efficacy and safety in older depressed outpatients, reporting a
response rate of approximately 60% for both nortriptyline and phenelzine,
versus 13% for placebo. Additional benefit was found from extending

TABLE 3 Summary of Acute Treatments for Major Depression in Older Persons

Treatment	Efficacy	Comments	References
Antidepressant medications	Numerous (more than 30) randomized, placebo-controlled trials of several tricyclics, bupro-prion, trazodone, and others. Trial results are for acute treatment responses.	Adequate doses, plasma levels, and treatment duration are essential in order to maximize response. Response may take 6 to 12 weeks, somewhat longer than in younger patients. Side effects may limit use.	Friedhoff, 1994 Georgotas et al., 1988 Gerson, Plotkin, & Jarvik, 1988 Katz et al., 1990 Klawansky, 1994 Nelson, Jatlow, & Mazure, 1985 Plotkin, Gerson, & Jarvik, 1987 Salzman, 1994 Schneider, 1993
Psychostimulants	Evidence for short-term efficacy; onset of action is rapid; randomized trials results are limited; responders are usually converted to a standard anti-depressant.	Particularly in medically ill, hospitalized patients; when there is an increased risk from other antidepressants; and when rapid response may be needed.	Pickett, Masand, & Murray, 1990 Satel & Nelson, 1989
Combined antidepressants and neuroleptic (antipsychotic) medications	More effective than either medication alone for depression with delusions or severe agitation.	Not well studied in eldery people. However, convulsive therapy is more effective than the combination.	Abrams, 1992 Nelson, Price, & Jatlow, 1986
Augmentation of antidepressants with lithium, thyroid medications, carbamazepine	Patients nonresponsive to several weeks of treatment with standard antidepressant medications may respond rapidly after these medications are added. Evidence is based on case series and reports.	May be useful in patients who are not responding or only partially responding to standard antidepressant medications. Constitutes acceptable clinical practice.	Finch & Katona, 1989 van Marwijk et al., 1990 Zimmer, Rosen, Thorton, Perel, & Reynolds, 1991

continued

TABLE 3 *Continued*

Treatment	Efficacy	Comments	References
Electroconvulsive therapy	Clearly effective in severe depression; depression with melancholia, and depression with delusions and when antidepressants are not fully effective. Sometimes combined with antidepressants.	In medication-resistant patients, acute response rate is approximately 50%. Relapse rate is high, requiring attention to maintenance antidepressant treatment. Effects are more favorable with increasing age.	Abrams, 1992 Sackeim et al., 1994
Psychotherapy	More effective treatment than waiting list, no treatment, or placebo; equivalent to antidepressant medications in geriatric outpatient populations generally, with both major or minor depression. About half of studies are group interventions. Therapy orientations were cognitive, interpersonal, reminiscence, psychodynamic, and eclectic.	Studies have been in elderly outpatients who were not significantly suicidal and for whom hospitalization was not indicated. There is no evidence of efficacy in severe depression. Distribution of responses may be different from the response to medication.	Gallagher & Thompson, 1982 Gallagher-Thompson & Thompson, 1994 Jarvik et al., 1982 Niederehe, 1994 Scogin and McElreath, 1994 Sloane et al., 1985 Thompson et al., 1988
Combined antidepressant medication and psychotherapy	Effective in outpatients using manual-based therapies; the relative contributions of each component are not well understood.	Combined therapy has not been adequately studied in elderly people.	Gallagher-Thompson & Steffen, 1994 Reynolds et al., 1992 Reynolds et al., 1993

NOTE: Adapted from L. S. Schneider, 1993, Efficacy of treatment for geropsychiatric patients with severe mental illness. *Psychopharmacology Bulletin, 29,* 501–524.

treatment to 9 weeks with either drug (Georgotas et al., 1989). Nortriptyline also has been demonstrated effective for major depression and dysthymia in a placebo-controlled trial among frail elderly patients living in an institutional setting; the sample was much older than is usual in such studies (Katz, Simpson, Curlik, Parmelee, & Muhly, 1990). However, 34% required early termination of treatment because of side effects.

There is a consensus that the therapeutic range of steady-state plasma nortriptyline levels is between 50 and 180 ng/ml (Georgotas et al., 1986; Katz et al., 1990). Plasma levels may be important in monitoring other antidepressants as well. Problems do occur sometimes, however, in the clinical interpretation and accuracy of levels. Low doses of antidepressants may be effective in elderly people even though they are not effective in middle-aged or younger adults. Although opinions differ on the overall efficacy of the low doses, there are double-blind studies suggesting that low doses have produced remissions in elderly patients. It is not clear whether low dosages are associated with a decreased frequency of side effects.

Studies support the efficacy and safety of fluoxetine, trazodone, or paroxetine when compared with standard antidepressant treatment (Altamura et al., 1988; Feighner & Cohn, 1985; Feighner, Boyer, Meredith, & Hendrickson, 1988; Dunner et al., 1992), and, in one study, when compared with placebo in elderly depressed outpatients. Although antidepressant medication is effective in depressed elderly people, it may not be as effective as portrayed in the popular press. For example, in one recent multicenter study of elderly depressed outpatients, the response rate for fluoxetine (Prozac), although statistically and significantly higher than that for placebo, was only 32%, versus a placebo response rate of 18% (Tollefson et al., 1995). Therefore, although selective serotonin uptake inhibitors such as fluoxetine, sertraline, and paroxetine are prescribed frequently for elderly people and appear to be largely safe when used alone, efficacy issues persist.

Elderly people respond to various antidepressant medications during acute treatment, including nortriptyline, desipramine, trazodone, doxepin, and others. Claims for the efficacy of nortriptyline can be based on well-controlled studies (Georgotas et al., 1986; Katz et al., 1990). Side effects, especially anticholinergic side effects, may limit use, however. Sev-

LON S. SCHNEIDER

eral comprehensive reviews (Gerson, Plotkin, & Jarvik, 1988; Jenike, 1989; Salzman, 1994) have concluded that amitriptyline and imipramine cause significant orthostatic hypotension and probably should be avoided by elderly people, and that anticholinergic effects limit the use of many antidepressants by elderly people. The following recommendations were made by the Agency for Health Care Policy Research in its guidelines for the treatment of major depression (Rush, 1993):

> Secondary amines are especially preferred in the elderly, in whom the anticholinergic side effects of the tertiary amines may reduce adherence or be particularly severe. . . . In a patient who is older . . . determining the blood level to gauge the minimal therapeutic dosage . . . may be particularly helpful. Thus an antidepressant with better established therapeutic and toxic levels, such as nortriptyline, may be preferred over another for which such levels are less well studied. (pp. 55-57)

Augmentation of Antidepressant Medication. The addition of another medication to augment antidepressant response is a common practice in younger depressed patients. Augmentation with lithium, carbamazepine, and thyroid medications is used in younger depressed patients but has not been systematically studied in older people, despite the reporting of three open trials of lithium generally showing equivocal results. The necessary lithium dose was less than half that for younger adults.

Psychotherapy and Combined Medication/Psychotherapy. Success rates in acute treatment success rates have ranged from 61% to 84% in studies using interpersonal psychotherapy (IPT) or IPT plus medication (Rothblum, Sholomskas, Berry, & Prusoff, 1982; Schneider, Sloane, Staples, & Bender, 1986; Sloane, Staples, & Schneider, 1985) and from 50% to 70% in studies using cognitive-behavioral therapy (CBT) or CBT plus medication (Gallagher & Thompson, 1982, 1983; Thompson, Gallagher, & Breckenridge, 1987), over treatment durations ranging from 6 to 16 weeks.

There is a dearth of data on treatment response to combined psychotherapy and pharmacotherapy among elderly depressed patients. Reynolds et al. (1992) reported a treatment success rate of 79% in 61 elderly outpatients treated openly with combined nortriptyline and IPT. In one randomized trial in depressed outpatients, the combination of CBT and antidepressant medication (desipramine) was more effective than the

42

psychotherapy alone, which was superior to the medication alone (Gallagher-Thompson & Thompson, 1994). Despite this trial, there is inadequate information on the comparative efficacy of psychotherapy and medication separately or in combination for the acute therapy of elderly people with depressions.

Recent reviews of CBT for depression in elderly people (Teri, Curtis, Gallagher-Thompson, & Thompson, 1994) and of psychosocial treatments in general (Niederehe, 1994; Scogin & MacElreath, 1994) show that, overall, psychosocial interventions are more effective than no treatment in elderly outpatient populations with depressed symptoms. In a quantitative overview of psychotherapy studies, 17 interventional studies were identified in which the magnitude of effect for psychotherapy, generally compared to no treatment, was similar to that of medication compared with placebo in other studies (Scogin & McElreath, 1994). Most of the trials used group therapy approaches. The therapy orientations were cognitive, psychodynamic, reminiscence, and eclectic. Psychosocial interventions for geriatric depression research tend to be done in diagnostic groups composed of both patients with major depression and patients with subclinical depression. Only 4 of 17 trials included outpatients with only major depression, and 3 of 17 trials included outpatients with only subclinical depression; the rest were mixed depression groups (Scogin & McElreath, 1994). By contrast, medication trials tend to be performed on patients with major depression.

In clinical practice, the combination of pharmacotherapy with psychotherapy is very common and might be considered a standard of care. Psychotherapy and medication improvement rates are superior to no treatment and to placebo treatment. Psychotherapy studies are done with outpatients, generally self-identified patients seeking specific psychiatric treatment for depression. The dearth of information on maintenance studies of psychotherapy for elderly depressed people is also noteworthy, as discussed below.

Electroconvulsive Therapy (ECT). Convulsive therapy is clearly a preferred treatment for depressions that are especially severe or are accompanied by melancholia. Stronger indications for ECT in patients with melancholic or severe depression include delusions or hallucinations, stupor, suicidal behavior, severe medical disease, poor medication response, intolerance of medication side effects, and patient preference (American Psychiatric Association, 1990; Sackheim, 1994). Old age itself is a relative indication for ECT, with a better response rate and fewer required treatments in older patients than in younger ones (Abrams, 1992).

Maintenance Treatment of Major Depression. Chronic, prolonged depression occurs in a substantial minority of patients. The long-term prognosis for depression in late life is generally thought to be poor, with less than one third having a good outcome after 1 to 3 years of follow-up (Murphy, 1983, 1994; Roth, 1955). Antidepressant medication seems effective in maintaining remission and preventing relapse. The limited available data suggest that more than 80% of elderly people who recover from depression can be kept relapse free with antidepressant maintenance therapy for 8 to 18 months (Georgotas, McCue, Cooper, Nagachangdran, & Chang, 1988; Reynolds et al., 1989). A significant minority, however, continue to have intermittent depressive symptoms. Patients who had more prior episodes had a greater risk of relapsing.

When a patient improves, terminating antidepressant treatment on the grounds that the patient doesn't need the medication anymore may be as erroneous as terminating antihypertensive medication because the patient is now normotensive. Emerging research evidence indicates that to prevent relapse, medications should be maintained for at least 9 to 12 months at the same dosage used to treat the acute episode (Reynolds et al., 1992). Practice guidelines for maintenance therapy are detailed elsewhere (Reynolds, Schneider, Lebowitz, & Kufper, 1994).

Patients who fail to respond to medication but who subsequently improve with ECT are at high risk for relapse. Such patients, who tend to be the most severely impaired, need more intensive maintenance treatments; alternative pharmacological treatments or maintenance ECT to decrease the likelihood of relapse should be considered. Patients with chronic depression often show only partial, but significant, benefits from maintenance medication treatments.

Ongoing trials combining medication with psychotherapy include one comparing CBT combined with desipramine (Thompson, Gallagher-Thompson, Hanser, Gantz, & Steffen, 1991) and another combining IPT with nortriptyline. A maintenance study of 91 patients for 2 years after psychotherapy demonstrated a general efficacy for the time-limited psychotherapy in the absence of maintenance psychotherapy (Gallagher-Thompson, Hanley-Peterson, & Thompson, 1990). In the preliminary report of that study (Reynolds et al., 1992), nortriptyline combined with IPT for 9 weeks of acute treatment and 16 weeks of continuation therapy was associated with full remission in 79% of the patients; the relapse rate was 25% when treatment was discontinued.

In one of the few comparisons of psychotherapy (CBT) with antidepressant medication (desipramine), the results were analyzed both before and after intervention and at a 1 year follow-up (Thompson et al., 1991). End-point analysis showed no significant difference in depressive symptoms between the psychotherapy-treated patients and patients treated with a combination of psychotherapy and desipramine. But both groups showed significant improvement in comparison with the desipramine-only group. In this study, patients who were more depressed at baseline did not show a greater effect in favor of medication than patients who were less depressed. A 1-year follow-up showed no significant difference among the three treatments; approximately one third showed improvement from their initial baseline.

Treatment of Major Depression in the Medically Ill

Patients with major depressions and concomitant medical illnesses often do not receive optimal care for their depression. When the depression is recognized, potentially effective medication is usually withheld because the depression is assumed to be "caused by" the medical illness or the illness is considered a contraindication to the use of medication. There is relatively little evidence concerning the efficacy of antidepressant medication in medically ill elderly people, but the existing information is positive. There are at least three randomized clinical trials with nortriptyline indicating efficacy in medically ill patients (Katz et al., 1988; Lipsey et al., 1984). The Lipsey et al. trial was on patients with poststroke depression.

Stimulant drugs have been used in the treatment of depression in medically and neurologically ill elderly patients. Many experienced psychopharmacologists favor psychostimulants for medically ill patients because of their favorable cardiovascular profile. A critical review of this practice (Satel & Nelson, 1989) concluded that although uncontrolled studies were generally positive, . . . ten placebo-controlled studies of stimulant drugs in primary depression, with one exception, indicated little advantage of drug over placebo. . . . Studies in medically ill patients with depression were promising but uncontrolled. Side effects have not been severe, and these drugs may pose less of a risk than tricyclics in the medically ill or elderly. Habituation is suggested, but there are no placebo-controlled studies to confirm this. (p. 237)

In brief, the stimulant drugs do not appear to be as effective as conventional antidepressants in primary depression, but they are clinically useful in refractory cases or in special circumstances, such as those involving elderly medically ill patients, and have a more favorable side-effect profile. Placebo-controlled trials are needed to explore these issues.

On the basis of these limited data, elderly patients with concomitant major depression and significant medical illnesses should be treated with antidepressants, supplemented by psychosocial interventions, and can be expected to respond. ECT may be required for severe or refractory major depression. Considerable clinical experience indicates that patients may respond to psychostimulants over the short term, although large-scale formal studies have not been undertaken.

Major depression in patients with dementia is potentially responsive to treatment. Medication and ECT should be used as necessary, and treatment response should be monitored carefully. Studies suggest that moderate depression in patients with moderate dementia may be successfully ameliorated but that a tricyclic antidepressant may not be the specific agent (Hebenstreit et al., 1991; Reynolds et al., 1987).

Treatment of Depression in Caregivers

Nearly half of spouse and family caregivers may suffer from major depression. Both CBT and brief psychodynamic psychotherapy have been demonstrated effective in treating family caregivers of medically ill elderly relatives. Although both types of psychotherapy were reported as equally effective, patients who had been caregivers for shorter times showed better improvement with psychodynamic therapy, and patients who had been caregivers for more than 3-1/2 years showed greater improvement with CBT (Gallagher-Thompson & Steffen, 1994). There is very little research in this important area, important also because elderly caregivers constitute a definable population at extraordinarily high risk for major depression.

Summary

There are several effective treatment approaches to major depression in late life. Treatment requires adequate prescribing, patient education, and regular patient monitoring for compliance and symptom changes, side effects, and the development of intercurrent medical disorders that may complicate antidepressant therapy. Side effects from medication can be minimized by careful monitoring of the patient's clinical state and plasma drug levels. Even though treatment for depression in late life is effective overall, it is not known why a substantial minority of patients respond neither to medication nor to psychotherapy. Are these patients different from those who do respond? Would responders have improved if other treatments had been combined with medication or psychotherapy? Is there a basis for differential response? A major limitation for both researchers and clinicians is the fact that depressive disorders are clinically heterogeneous and are defined syndromally (i.e., on the basis of descriptive characteristics without a specific mechanism or set of factors that are responsible for the disorder).

Controlled intervention research is needed with respect to chronic and subsyndromal depressions in late life and with respect to depressions secondary to medical illnesses. Studies should include controlled evaluation of stimulant medication in patients who cannot tolerate standard antidepressants.

Both antidepressant medications and brief structured psychotherapies have efficacy in the acute treatment of elderly depressed outpatients with major unipolar, nondelusional depression, but the relative efficacy of specific medications and psychotherapies is unclear. Research on the indications for continuation and maintenance therapy using medication or psychotherapy or both is needed, particularly for patients with chronic, recurring illness. Maintenance treatments are important, however, to prevent relapses or repeated episodes.

The consequences of unrecognized and untreated depression in the elderly include increased use of health care services, longer hospitalization stays, and increased morbidity and mortality from medical illness and from suicide.

Mania

Clinical Features

Mania is characterized by a distinct abnormal, persistently elevated or expansive mood accompanied by grandiosity, talkativeness, decreased need for sleep, racing thoughts, distractibility, and other symptoms. The presentation is similar in older patients except that there may be more confusion, irritability, distractibility, and paranoid ideation. Episodes also may be longer and cycles more frequent. A characteristic of mania is recurrence, requiring maintenance pharmacologic treatment. The patient's history and the severity of the episode are considered in determining the need for maintenance treatment.

Epidemiology

Acute mania is relatively uncommon in elderly people; prevalence is less than 1%. However, about 5% of acutely hospitalized geropsychiatric patients have acute mania (Stone, 1989). A first episode of mania may occur in late life, either after previous depressions or de novo. Secondary mania may result from a variety of medical illnesses and drugs and is an important differential diagnostic consideration. Both prescription medications and illicit drugs are important causes of secondary mania.

Treatment

Both acute and maintenance treatments must be considered. There have been few if any randomized treatment trials for mania in elderly people. Yet, there is no reason to believe that lithium is ineffective; and as with younger patients, it is considered a first-line treatment. Because of marked but predictable age-related changes in pharmacokinetics and pharmacodynamics, the dose of lithium for elderly people is much smaller, and the therapeutic plasma level is probably about half that for younger patients (Mirchandani & Young, 1993). Patients who have underlying dementia or intercurrent, serious medical illnesses are more sensitive to side effects. Confusion and cardiovascular, renal, gastrointestinal, thyroidal, and neurological side effects are common. Later age of onset of mania and cognitive impairment is associated with poorer response to lithium in elderly patients (Young et al., 1992).

Alternatives to lithium include neuroleptics, anticonvulsants (carbamazepine, valproic acid, clonazepam), calcium channel blockers, and convulsive therapy. Indications for ECT include severe medical illnesses, poor response to lithium or other medication, and imminent danger to the patient. (The concomitant administration of ECT and lithium is to be avoided). There have been no controlled trials with elderly people. These drugs may be used alone or in combination with lithium both for treatment of an acute episode and for maintenance.

Maintenance pharmacologic therapies are intended to prevent recurrences of manic episodes, decrease their frequency, and lessen their intensity. Medications include those listed above. Doses may be the same or smaller than for the treatment of an acute manic episode. The relative rarity and the severity of manic episodes in elderly people make clinical trials especially difficult to perform.

Psychotic Disorders

Clinical Features

Psychotic symptoms (e.g., hallucinations, delusions) occur in various disorders, including delirium, dementia, depression, mania, schizophrenia, late-onset schizophrenia, and late-life delusions. Because late-life psychoses and their treatment are described in detail in the next chapter (Jeste, Naimark, Halpain, & Lindamer, this volume), the discussion of them in this chapter will be brief.

Late-Onset Schizophrenia. The onset of schizophrenia is usually in late adolescence or young adulthood. Schizophrenia with onset prior to age 45 has a highly variable course; about half the patients showing improvement or attenuation of symptoms with aging. Schizophrenia first occurring after the age of 45 may be a different subtype of the illness. Compared with earlier-onset patients, well-systematized persecutory delusions may be most prominent along with auditory hallucinations. Illness course is chronic and relatively unremitting. Relapses are common when medications are discontinued.

Late Paraphrenia. Late paraphrenia (or late-onset delusional disorder) is characterized by a well-developed, nonbizarre paranoid delusional system, with or without hallucinations, in patients without significant cognitive impairment, depression, anxiety, or personality disorder. The illness course is variable, having remissions and relapses, or it may be chronic, leading to residual symptoms. There is little evidence of a course leading to dementia (Roth, 1955). (There is, however, evidence of subcortical brain lesions [e.g., Miller, Lipowski, & Lebowitz, 1991].) Complete loss of psychotic symptoms is unlikely. Most patients show symptomatic improvement, and 20% to 25% are symptom free (Post, 1966; Rabins, Pauker, & Thomas, 1984).

Symptomatic Psychoses. These are psychoses due to exogenous causes such as medications, toxins, or medical illnesses. Treatment is symptomatic involving identifying the possible causes and treating with neuroleptics for specific symptoms.

Treatment

The efficacy of treatment of psychosis occurring in delirium, dementia, depression, and mania was discussed earlier. Treatment of schizophrenia and late-life delusional disorder are also discussed by Jeste and his colleagues in this volume.

Neuroleptics are the most effective treatment for both early- and late-onset chronic schizophrenia, both improving acute symptoms and controlling relapses (Jeste, 1990). Neuroleptics also may be effective for delusional disorder although there is little if any formal information. It seems that neuroleptics decrease agitation and the intensity of the delusion but do not suppress it. Patients with psychosis have impaired insight into their illness. As a consequence, they often are brought to medical attention involuntarily and often do not comply with treatment.

One serious risk of long-term neuroleptic use is tardive dyskinesia, a movement disorder characterized by involuntary, irregular, repetitive abnormal movements. Risk factors for tardive dyskinesia include increasing age, being female, increased dosage and duration of treatment, and possibly organicity (Jeste, 1990). The role of the atypical neuroleptic clozapine has not been established in these disorders in elderly people.

Anxiety / Phobic Disorders

Clinical Features

Although situational anxiety is common in elderly people, pathological anxiety develops with no apparent reason, severely disabling an adult who had been functioning adequately. Accurately diagnosing symptoms of moderate to severe anxiety in their own right is important for two reasons: to improve daily functioning and because many of the symptoms can easily be confused with even more severe geropsychiatric disorders such as dementia and major depression. These symptoms include impaired concentration, attention, and memory; dizziness; disabling fear; severe insomnia; and constant hypervigilance. The several anxiety disorders include generalized anxiety, phobic disorders, panic disorder, obsessive-compulsive disorder, and posttraumatic stress disorder.

Depressive and anxiety symptoms are often intermixed in elderly people. Anxiety is an important component of depression and dysthymic disorder, and depressive symptoms occur with anxiety disorders. Depression and anxiety may mimic cardiovascular disease, endocrine and neurological illnesses, and dementia. Factors associated with anxiety include alcohol abuse and dependence, sedative or hypnotic abuse and dependence, chronic pain, primary sleep disorders, various medical illnesses, and use of various prescription medications.

Epidemiology

Anxiety disorders are fairly common in geriatric age groups; the combined prevalence of phobia, panic, and obsessive-compulsive disorders is 5.5% in people older than 65 (Regier et al., 1988). The prevalence of generalized anxiety disorder has not been reliably estimated but is probably greater.

Manifestation of Particular Types of Anxiety Disorders

Phobic Disorders. The key feature of these disorders is the persistent, excessive, or unrealistic fear of a particular object or situation, leading

---

to avoidance of the object or situation or to intense anxiety when exposed. This fear, or the process of avoiding the fear-provoking object, significantly impairs normal social activities and relationships (American Psychiatric Association, 1987). Some apparently phobic behavior may be driven by depressive mood or memory impairment.

Panic Disorder. Panic attacks are characterized by unexpected episodes of intense fear. Accompanying symptoms include such somatic symptoms as shortness of breath, dizziness, sweating, numbness, and chest pain. Frequent episodes constitute a disorder.

Obsessive-Compulsive Disorder. This disorder is characterized by recurrent, persistent ideas or impulses that are usually experienced as unwanted and that cannot be ignored or suppressed. Compulsions are excessive or unreasonable repetitive behaviors performed in response to an obsession. These behaviors cause marked distress and can be disabling, causing significant interference with functioning (American Psychiatric Association, 1987). The onset of the disorder is principally in young adulthood. New onset in late life is relatively rare. However, the illness persists into old age.

Treatment Considerations

Treatment for these disorders (Table 4) is necessary when symptoms adversely affect social and daily function. There are relatively few clinical trials of medication or psychosocial interventions for anxiety disorders specifically in elderly people. In one review (Salzman & Lebowitz, 1991), only 6 placebo-controlled trials for anxiety in elderly patients were identified: 5 using oxazepam and 1 using diazepam. Nevertheless, there is little reason to doubt the efficacy of these interventions. Benzodiazepines are the preferred acute or subacute treatment for many anxiety disorders (although not for panic disorder). Trials in younger patients have not suggested that any one benzodiazepine is therapeutically better than any other. Therefore, the choice of a particular benzodiazepine depends partly on the expected treatment duration, characteristics of the patient, and the pharmacologic properties of the drug. (For detailed prescribing guidelines, see Salzman, 1992). Clinical recommendations for the use of benzodiaz-

TABLE 4 Treatment of Severe Anxiety Disorders in Older Persons

Disorder	Treatment	Comments/References
Generalized anxiety disorder	Benzodiazepines (e.g. diazepam, chlordiazepoxide, oxazepam, clonazepam, lorazepam, alprazolam), buspirone, ß-adrenergic blockers, antidepressants, antihistamines, and neuroleptics.	These drugs tend to impair memory. Buspirone, which has been extensively reported in open trials, affects cognition less. Neuroleptics should be used only for severe agitation when it is related to psychosis or organicity. Refs: Pomara et al., 1991 Salzman, 1992 Salzman & Lebowitz, 1991
Panic disorder (periods of intense fear)	Tricyclic antidepressants, monoamine oxidase-inhibitors, alprazolam, clonazepam.	
Phobic disorder (unrealistic fear of an object or situation, leading to avoidance)	Psychosocial and behavioral therapies, and medication.	
Obsessive-compulsive disorder (recurrent ideas or impulses that cannot be ignored or suppressed)	Clomipramine; serotonin uptake blockers (fluoxetine, sertraline). Behavior therapy for rituals.	Peak onset in young adults. Rare as a primary disorder in elderly. Obsessive/compulsive symptoms may occur in other disorders. Refs: Jenike, 1991

NOTE: Adapted from L. S. Schneider, 1993, Efficacy of treatment for geropsychiatric patients with severe mental illness. *Psychopharmacology Bulletin, 29*, 501–524.

epines are derived from efficacy studies in younger adults and from studies of pharmacokinetics and toxicity in elderly people (Salzman & Lebowitz, 1991). For longer term pharmacologic treatment of anxiety disorders beyond 1 to 2 months, antidepressants such as nortriptyline, desipramine, or trazodone may be useful.

Other medications include buspirone, ß-adrenergic blockers, antidepressants, and neuroleptics. Extensive clinical experience and extensive uncontrolled, open clinical trials groups of elderly people suggest that buspirone has efficacy and considerable safety in the short term (Salzman & Lebowitz, 1991). This drug's efficacy for anxiety usually emerges after several weeks of treatment and is probably best for generalized anxiety disorder. Studies of ß-blockers for anxiety are in younger patients. There are case series on the use of ß-blockers for agitation in elderly organically impaired patients only (see above). The drugs may be useful for suppressing autonomic symptoms, but they are also associated with hypotension and cognitive impairments. As with ß-blockers, there are no clinical efficacy data and few published clinical experiences with tricyclic antidepressants and monoamine oxidase inhibitors. Yet the clinical impression is that they are useful for panic disorder, longer term treatment of anxiety, and mixed anxiety and depression states. Extremely severe incapacitating anxiety (usually with agitation) may occasionally respond better to low doses of neuroleptic medications than to ß-blockers.

Tolerance and habituation may develop with many of these medications, especially the benzodiazepines. Although long-term use may be beneficial for some, it may be a hazard for others. Medications may be best for patients with anxiety associated with chronic physical illness, pain, and secondary depression. There is substantial knowledge of age-related pharmacokinetic and pharmacodynamic effects of many benzodiazepines (Pomara et al., 1991; Salzman, 1992; Salzman & Lebowitz, 1991).

Results of studies in younger adults indicate that tricyclic antidepressants and monoamine oxidase inhibitors are probably most effective with panic disorder. Alprazolam and clonazepam may be useful as well.

For obsessive-compulsive disorder, there are various approaches. Patients with only obsessive thoughts may benefit from antidepressant therapy including clomipramine, but its strong anticholinergic effects may not be tolerated by elderly people. There are randomized controlled trials of clomipramine and fluoxetine in younger patients with obsessive-complusive disorder, but not in older patients. Benzodiazepines are not effective for the obsessive-compulsive symptoms per se, but they may be helpful for associated anxiety. Behavior therapy may be particularly effective for rituals, but not in patients with obsessive thoughts alone or in patients with depression.

CURRENT AND EMERGING ISSUES IN TREATMENT EFFICACY

Cohort Differences

The elderly people of a generation ago are different from the elderly people of today and the next generation. Different generations have different experiences. The gradually increasing health and longevity of the American population will lead to an increasing proportion of the population being elderly and therefore susceptible to illnesses related to aging. As the population better survives cardiovascular disease, cancer, and infectious disease, a larger proportion will become old. For example, the prevalence of Alzheimer's disease is projected to increase dramatically, by a factor of 5, in the oldest old (above age 85) while remaining relatively constant in the younger 65 to 75 year-old group (Pieri et al., 1989). It has also been observed that onset of major depression is occurring at younger ages in cohorts born after World War II than in cohorts born earlier (Klerman & Weissman, 1989); the implication is that the prevalence of depression among elderly people will increase as these cohorts become old. Moreover, substance abuse, with its long-term medical and neuro-psychiatric consequences, is overlooked among elderly people of today, yet it is likely to become increasingly common as younger generations grow old.

There may be cohort differences in risk and protective factors— for instance, the increasing use of estrogen replacement therapy to prevent cardiovascular disease, severe osteoporosis, and hip fracture. Estrogen is a potent trophic hormone for cholinergic neurons. Recent evidence sug-gests that chronic estrogen deficiency (i.e., living from menopause to old age without estrogen replacement) may have a role in both depression and dementia occurring in late life (National Institute of Mental Health work-shop, September oral presentation, 1994; Henderson & Paganini-Hill, 1994; Palinkas & Barrett-Conner, 1992).

Gender

In general, psychiatric disorder in elderly people is more prevalent in women than in men. There is evidence, however, of a narrowing of the gender gap, of a greater increase in risk of depression among young men (Klerman & Weissman, 1989). The effect of this trend will become evident in the next generations of elderly people.

The prevalence of Alzheimer's disease is twice as great in women as in men, and the difference in prevalence becomes larger with increasing age. Yet women are relatively underrepresented in Alzheimer's disease clinical trials, comprising only 50% of the subjects whereas 65% to 70% would be expected. The caregivers of patients with dementia are more often wives and daughters than husbands and sons. Hence, women are disproportionally affected by the illness in two ways.

As mentioned above, women may be more sensitive to medication side effects than men, and estrogen replacement status may have a bearing in treatment response.

Multicultural and Minority Concerns

The prevalence of dementia is markedly greater in Blacks than in Whites (Heyman et al., 1991; Schoenberg et al., 1985). The prevalences of depression and dysthymia are higher in Hispanic elderly people than in Whites (Kemp, Staples, & Lopez-Aqueres, 1987). Minority group members and women are often underrepresented in clinical research on disorders of the aging. They are also underusers of medical care, and they experience barriers to obtaining care. There are significant public health effects of not providing care for minority elderly people.

RESEARCH DIRECTIONS

This review of severe mental disorders in the elderly populations suggests a number of general and specific research needs.

General Recommendations

1. Further develop efficacy data for acute and maintenance antidepressant, anxiolytic, and antipsychotic therapy. With respect to depression, these questions must be answered: Under what circumstances should medication be used alone? In combination with psychotherapy? Or

should psychotherapy be used alone? In these studies, treatment interventions should be focused on the family as well as the patient.

2. Include more very old patients, age 75 and above, in clinical trials. In particular, mechanisms to add elderly patients to ongoing industry-supported trials of investigational compounds should be explored.

3. Increase the number of older patients with medical co-morbidities in treatment research. The close relationship between physical illness and depression in elderly people needs to be better researched and understood.

4. Expand research on the clinical utility of therapeutic drug monitoring.

5. Encourage research on patients who respond little or not at all to existing treatments.

6. Develop appropriate assessment and treatment methods for ethnic minorities, including methods to reduce the barriers to care.

7. Understand further the multiple, complex drug interactions that might affect or contribute to depression and cognitive impairment in elderly people, who tend to be prescribed large numbers of drugs.

8. Encourage long-term treatment research into continuation and maintenance treatments with closer monitoring of response and greater attention to long-term outcome.

Recommendations Regarding Depression

With respect to depression in elderly people in particular, additional specific research recommendations are abstracted in Exhibit II.

Recommendations Regarding Alzheimer's Disease and Other Dementias

1. Establish realistic expectations for response in dementia, for both patients and caregivers. Although one study using intensive caregiver interventions was able to demonstrate postponement of nursing home placement (Mittleman et al., 1993), another study was unable to demonstrate that the availability of day treatment postponed nursing home placement (Rosenheck et al., 1993).

2. Develop better care and management programs for dementia patients at long-term care institutions.

3. Develop safe and effective treatments for the cognitive and behavioral symptoms. Treatments to slow or stop the progression of the disease could have major policy ramifications. Delaying the onset of Alzheimer's disease by 5 years or delaying the time to institutionalization by 5 years would halve the incidence of the illness and halve its prevalence in nursing homes (Jorm, 1987).

CONCLUSIONS

Although knowledge is far from complete, research-based guidelines for treatment of mental disorders in older adults are substantially more clearly defined today than they were even a decade ago. There is a body of data based on clinical trials demonstrating the clear efficacy of treatments for elderly people with mental disorders. As significant as this information is for geriatric clinical practice, it is important to acknowledge that much of it has been developed from relatively atypical older patients and settings. More must be learned about treatment response of some of the people with greatest need—in particular, medically fragile or very old people, and those in nursing homes and residential care facilities. The treatment of elderly people with subsyndromal depressive syndromes or mixed symptoms of depression and anxiety—sources of considerable disability—has been largely ignored in treatment research. Also ignored is minor cognitive impairment that is not severe enough to be considered dementia but is severe enough to affect daily function and quality of life.

These gaps in knowledge, together with other areas of investigation identified throughout this review, constitute a significant agenda for future research in treatment of older adults. At the same time, however, dissemination to clinical practice of known effective treatments for mental disorders in elderly people is essential to ensure that appropriate and adequate treatment is available. As shown by the NIH Consensus Development Conference on the Diagnosis and Treatment of Depression in Late Life and the AHCPR depression guidelines, in primary care, providing adequate treatment within the currently available knowledge base is at least as challenging as pursuing the next levels of new knowledge.

REFERENCES

Abrams, R. (1992). Efficacy of electroconvulsive therapy. In R. Abrams (Ed.), *Electroconvulsive therapy* (2nd ed., pp. 10-38). New York: Oxford University Press.

Adams, F. (1988). Emergency intravenous sedation of the delirium, medically ill patients. *Journal of Clinical Psychiatry, 49*(Suppl. 12), 22-26.

Alexopoulos, G. (1994). Biological markers in geriatric depression. In L. S. Schneider, C. F. Reynolds, B. D. Lebowitz, & A. J. Friedhoff (Eds.), *Diagnosis and treatment of depression in late life: Results of the NIH Consensus Development Conference.* Washington, DC: American Psychiatric Press.

Altamura, A. C., Mauri, M. C., Colacurelo, F., et al. (1988). Trazodone in late life depressive states: A double-blind multicenter study versus amitriptyline and mianserin. *Psychopharmacology, 95*, S34-36.

American Psychiatric Association. (1987). *Diagnostic and statistical manual of mental disorders* (3rd ed., rev.). Washington, DC: Author.

American Psychiatric Association. (1990). *Task Force on Electroconvulsive Therapy.* Washington, DC: American Psychiatric Press.

Becker, R. E., & Giacobini, E. (1988). Mechanisms of cholinesterase inhibition in senile dementia of the Alzheimer type: Clinical, pharmacological, and therapeutic aspects. *Drug Development Research, 12*, 163-195.

Caine, E., et al. (1994). Clinical and diagnostic heterogeneity in depression in late life. In L. S. Schneider, C. F. Reynolds, B. D. Lebowitz, & A. J. Friedhoff (Eds.), *Diagnosis and treatment of depression in late life: Results of the NIH Consensus Development Conference.* Washington, DC: American Psychiatric Press.

Conwell, Y. (1994). Suicide in the elderly. In L. S. Schneider, C. F. Reynolds, B. D. Lebowitz, & A. J. Friedhoff (Eds.), *Diagnosis and treatment of depression in late life: Results of the NIH Consensus Development Conference.* Washington, DC: American Psychiatric Press.

Davis, K. L., Thal, L. J., Gamzu, E., Davis, C. S., Woolson, R. F., Gracon, S. I., Drachman, D. A., Schneider, L. S., Whitehouse, P. J., Hoover, T. M., Morris, J. C., Kawas, C. H., Knopman, D. S., Earl, N. L., Kumar, V., & Doody, R. S. (1992). Tacrine in patients with Alzheimer's disease: A double-blind, placebo-controlled multicenter study. *New England Journal of Medicine, 327*, 1253-1259.

Dunner, D. L., Cohn, J. B., Walshe, T., & Cohn, C. K. (1992). Two combined, multicenter double-blind studies of paroxetine and doxepin in geriatric patients with major depression. *Journal of Clinical Psychiatry, 53*(Suppl. 2), 57-60.

Farlow, M., Gracon, S. I., Hershey, L. A., Lewis, K. W., Sadowsky, C. H., & Dolan-Ureno, J. (1992). A 12-week, double-blind, placebo-controlled, parallel-group study of tacrine in patients with probable Alzheimer's disease. *Journal of the American Medical Association 268*, 2523–2529.

Feighner, J. P., Boyer, W. F., Meredith, C. H., & Hendrickson, G. (1988). An overview of fluoxetine in geriatric depression. *British Journal of Psychiatry, 153*(Suppl. 3), 105-108.

Feighner, J. P., & Cohn, J. B. (1985). Double-blind comparative trials of fluoxetine and doxepine in geriatric patients with major depressive disorder. *Journal of Clinical Psychiatry, 46*, 20-25.

Finch, E. J. L., & Katona, C. L. E. (1989). Lithium augmentation in the treatment of refractory depression in old age. *International Journal of Geriatric Psychiatry, 4*(1), 41-46.

Friedhoff, A. J. (1994). Consensus panel report. In L. S. Schneider, C. F. Reynolds, B. D. Lebowitz, & A. J. Friedhoff (Eds.), *Diagnosis and treatment of depression in late life: Results of the NIH Consensus Development Conference.* Washington, DC: American Psychiatric Press.

Gallagher, D. E., & Thompson, L. W. (1982). Treatment of major depressive disorder in older adult outpatients with brief psychotherapies. *Psychotherapy: Theory, Research, and Practice, 19*(4), 482-490.

Gallagher, D. E., & Thompson, L. W. (1983). Effectiveness of psychotherapy for both endogenous and nonendogenous depression in older adult outpatients. *Journal of Gerontology, 38*(6), 707-712.

Gallagher-Thompson, D., Hanley-Peterson, P., & Thompson, L. W. (1990). Maintenance of gains versus relapse following brief psychotherapy for depression. *Journal of Consulting and Clinical Psychology, 58*(3), 371-374.

Gallagher-Thompson, D., & Steffen, A. M. (1994). Comparative effects of cognitive-behavioral and brief psychodynamic psychotherapies for depressed family caregivers. *Journal of Consulting and Clinical Psychology, 62,* 543-549.

Gallagher-Thompson, D., & Thompson, L. W. (1994). Psychotherapy with older adults in theory and practice. In B. Bongar & L. Beutler (Eds.), *Foundations of psychotherapy: Theory, research, and practice.* New York: Oxford University Press.

Georgotas, A., McCue, R. E., Cooper, T. B., Nagachandran, N., & Chang, I. (1988). How effective and safe is continuation therapy in elderly depressed patients? Factors affecting relapse rate. *Archives of General Psychiatry, 45*(10), 929-932.

Georgotas, A., McCue, R. E., Cooper, T. B., Nagachandran, N., & Friedhoff, A. (1989). Factors affecting the delay of antidepressant effect in responders to nortriptyline and phenelzine. *Psychiatry Research, 28*(1), 1-9.

Georgotas, A., McCue, R. E., Hapworth, W., Friedman, E., Kim, O. H., Welkowitz, J., Chang, I., & Cooper, T. B. (1986). Comparative efficacy and safety of MAOI's vs TCA's in treating depression in the elderly. *Biological Psychiatry, 21*(12), 1155-1166.

Gerson, S. C., Plotkin, D. A., & Jarvik, L. F. (1988). Antidepressant drug studies, 1964–1988: Empirical evidence for aging patients. *Journal of Clinical Psychopharmacology, 8*(5), 311-322.

Harris, M. J., Panton, D., Caligiuri, M. P., Krull, A. J., Tran-Johnson, T. K., & Jeste, D. V. (1992). High incidence of tardive dyskinesia in older outpatients on low doses of neuroleptics. *Psychopharmacology Bulletin, 28,* 87-92.

Hebenstreit, G. F., Baumhackl, U., Chan-Palay, V., Groner, E., Kasas, A., Katching, H., Krebs, E., Kummer, J., Martucci, N., Radmayr, E., Rieder, L., Saletu, M., Schlegel, S., Lorscheid, T. (1991, August). *The treatment of depression in geriatric depressed and demented patients by moclobemide: Results from the international multicenter double blind placebo controlled trial.* Paper presented at the Fifth Congress of the International Psychogeriatric Association, Rome.

Henderson, V. W., Paganini-Hill, A., Emanuel, C. K., Dunn-Meleana, E., et al. (1994). Estrogen replacement therapy in older women: Comparisons between Alzheimer's disease cases and non-demented control subjects. *Archives of Neurology, 51,* 896-900.

Heyman, A., Fillenbaum, G., Prosnitz, B., et al. (1991). Estimated prevalence of dementia among elderly Black and White community residents. *Archives of Neurology, 48,* 594-598.

Jarvik, L. F., Mintz, J., Steuer, J. L., & Gerner, R. (1982). Treating geriatric depression: A 26-week interim analysis. *Journal of the American Geriatrics Society, 30,* 713-717.

Jenike, M. A. (1989). Treatment of affective illness in the elderly with drugs and electroconvulsive therapy. *Journal of Geriatric Psychiatry, 22*(1), 77-112.

Jenike, M. A. (1991). Geriatric obsessive-compulsive disorder. *Journal of Geriatric Psychiatry and Neurology, 4,* 34-39.

Jeste, D. V. (1990). Neuroleptic treatment of chronically mentally ill elderly: Suggestions for future research. In E. Light & B. D. Lebowitz (Eds.), *The elderly with chronic mental illness.* New York: Springer.

Jorm, A. F. (1987) Sex and age differences in depression: A quantatitive synthesis of published research. *Australian & New Zealand Journal of Psychiatry, 21,* 46-53.

Katz, I. R., Simpson, G. M., Curlik, S. M., Parmelee, P. A., & Muhly, C. (1990). Pharmacologic treatment of major depression for elderly patients in residential care settings. *Journal of Clinical Psychiatry, 51*(Suppl.), 41-47.

Katz, I. R., Staff, D., Mickly, C. & Bari, M. (1988). Indentifying persistent adverse effects of anticholinergic drugs in the elderly. *Journal of Geriatric Psychiatry & Neurology, 1,* 212-217.

Kemp, B. J., Staples, F., & Lopez-Aqueres, W. (1987). Epidemiology of depression and dysphoria in an elderly Hispanic population: Prevalence and correlates. *Journal of American Geriatrics Society, 35,* 920-926.

Khachaturian, Z. S., Phelps, C. H., & Buckholtz, N. S. (1994). The prospect of developing treatments for Alzheimer disease. In R. D. Terry, R. Katzman, & K. L. Bick (Eds.), *Alzheimer disease.* New York: Raven.

Klawansky, S. (1994). Meta-analysis on the pharmacotherapeutic treatment of depression in late life. In L. S. Schneider, C. F. Reynolds, B. D. Lebowitz, & A. J. Friedhoff (Eds.), *Diagnosis and treatment of depression in late life: Results of the NIH Consensus Development Conference.* Washington, DC: American Psychiatric Press.

Klerman, G. L., & Weissman, M. M. (1989). Increasing rates of depression. *Journal of the American Medical Association, 261,* 2229-2235.

Knapp, M. J., Knopman, D. S., Solomon, P. R., Pendlebury, W. W., Davis, C. S., & Gracon, S. I. (for the Tacrine Study Group). (1994). Controlled trials of high-dose tacrine in patients with Alzheimer's disease. *Journal of the American Medical Association, 271,* 985-991.

Lebowitz, B. D. (1992). Developments in treatment of Alzheimer's disease. *Psychopharmacology Bulletin, 28,* 59-60.

Leibovici, A., & Tariot, P. N. (1988). Agitation associated with dementia: A systematic approach to treatment. *Psychopharmacology Bulletin 24,* 49-53.

Lipsey, J. R., Robinson, R. G., Pearlson, G. D., & Price, T. R. (1984). Nortriptyline treatment of post-stroke depression: A double-blind study. *Lancet, 1,* 297-300.

Menza, M. A., Murray, G. B., Holmes, V. F., et al. (1988). Controlled study of extrapyramidal reactions in the management of delirious medically ill patients: Intravenous haloperidol versus intravenous haloperidol plus benzodiazepines. *Heart Lung, 17,* 238-241.

Miller, N. E., Lipowski, Z. J., & Lebowitz, B. D. (1991). Delirium advances in research and clinical practice. *International Psychogeriatrics, 3.*

Mirchandani, I. C., & Young, R. C. (1993). Management of mania in the elderly: An update. *Annals of Clinical Psychiatry, 5*, 67-77.

Mittelman, M. S., Ferris, S. H., Steinberg, G., Shulman, E., Mackell, J. A., Ambinder, A., & Cohen, J. (1993). An intervention that delays institutionalization of Alzheimer's disease patients: Treatment of spouse-caregivers. *Gerontological Society of America, 33,* 730-740.

Murphy, E. (1983). The prognosis of depression in old age. *British Journal of Psychiatry, 142*, 111-119.

Murphy, E. (1994). The course and outcome of depression in late life. In L. S. Schneider, C. F. Reynolds, B. D. Lebowitz, & A. J. Friedhoff (Eds.), *Diagnosis and treatment of depression in late life: Results of the NIH Consensus Development Conference.* Washington, DC: American Psychiatric Press.

Nelson, J. C., Price, L. H., & Jatlow, P. I. (1986). Neuroleptic dose and desipramine concentrations during combined treatment of unipolar delusional depression. *American Journal of Psychiatry, 143*(9), 1151-1154.

Niederehe, G. (1994). Psychosocial therapies with depressed older adults. In L. S. Schneider, C. F. Reynolds, B. D. Lebowitz, & A. J. Friedhoff (Eds.), *Diagnosis and treatment of depression in late life: Results of the NIH Consensus Development Conference.* Washington, DC: American Psychiatric Press.

Nyth, A. L., & Gottfries, C. G. (1990). The clinical efficacy of citalopram in treatment of emotional disturbances in dementia disorders: A Nordic Multicentre study. *British Journal of Psychiatry, 157,* 894.

Palinkas, L. A., & Barrett-Connor, E. (1992). Estrogen use and depressive symptoms in postmenopausal women. *Obstetrics and Gynecology, 80*(1), 30-36.

Pascualy, M., Murburg, M. M., & Veith, R. C. (1992). Cardiac risks of antidepressants in the elderly. In C. A. Shamoian (Ed.). *Psychopharmacological treatment complications in the elderly.* Washington, DC: American Psychiatric Press.

Pickett, P., Masand, P., & Murray, G. B. (1990). Psychostimulant treatment of geriatric depressive disorders secondary to medical illness. *Journal of Geriatric Psychiatry and Neurology, 3*(3), 146-151.

Pieri, L., Cumin, R., & Hinzen, D. H. (1989). Nosological and epidemiological aspects of Alzheimer's disease. *DN&P 2,* 248-253.

Plotkin, D. A., Gerson, S. G., & Jarvik, L. F. (1987). Antidepressant drug treatment in the elderly. In H. Y. Meltzer (Ed.), *Psychopharmacology: The third generation of progress* (pp. 1149-1158). New York: Raven Press.

Pomara, N., Deptula, D., Singh, R., & Monroy, C. A. (1991). Cognitive toxicity of benzodiazepines in the elderly. In C. Salzman & B. D. Lebowitz (Eds.), *Anxiety in the elderly.* New York: Springer.

Post, F. (1966). *Persistent persecutory states of the elderly.* Oxford: Pergamon.

Rabins, P. V. (1989). Behavior problems in the demented. In E. Light & B. D. Lebowitz (Eds.), *Alzheimer's disease treatment and family stress: Directions for research* (pp. 322-339). Rockville, MD: U.S. Department of Health and Human Services.

Rabins, P. V. (1991). The impact of care delivery settings and patient selection in shaping research questions and results: Psychosocial and management aspects of delirium. *International Psychogeriatrics, 3*(2), 319-324.

Rabins, P., Pauker, S., & Thomas, J. (1984). Can schizophrenia begin after age 44? *Comparative Psychiatry, 25,* 290-295.

Regier, D. A., Boyd, J. H., Burke, J. D., Rae, D. S., et al. (1988). One month prevalence of mental disorders in the United States. *Archives of General Psychiatry, 45,* 977-986.

Reifler, B. V., Teri, L., Raskind, M., Veith, R., et al. (1989). Double-blind trial of imipramine in Alzheimer's disease in patients with and without depression. *American Journal of Psychiatry, 146,* 45-49.

Reynolds, C. F., Frank, E., Perel, J. M., Imber, S. D., Cornes, C., Morycz, R. K., Mazumdar, S., Miller, M. D., Pollock, B. G., Rifai, A. H., Stack, J. A., George, C. F., Houck, P. R., & Kupfer, D. J. (1992). Combined pharmacotherapy and psychotherapy in the acute and continuation treatment of elderly patients with recurrent major depression: A preliminary report. *American Journal of Psychiatry, 149,* 1687-1692.

Reynolds, C. F., Lebowitz, B. D., & Schneider, L. S. (1993). The NIH Consensus Development Conference on the Diagnosis and Treatment of Depression in Late Life: An overview. 32nd Annual Meeting of the New Clinical Evaluation Unit: Symposium on diagnosis and treatment of depression in late life (1992, Boca Raton, FL). *Psychopharmacology Bulletin, 29,* 83-85.

Reynolds, C. F., Perel, J. M., Frank, E., Imber, S., Thornton, J., Morycz, R. K., Cornes, C., & Kupfer, D. J. (1989). Open-trial maintenance pharmacotherapy in late-life depression: Survival analysis. *Psychiatry Research, 27,* 225-231.

Reynolds, C. F., Perel, J. M., Kupfer, D. J., Zimmer, B., Stack, J. A., & Hoch, C. H. (1987). Open-trial response to antidepressant treatment in elderly patients with mixed depression and cognitive impairment. *Psychiatry Research, 21,* 111-122.

Reynolds, C. F., Schneider, L. S., Lebowitz, B. D., & Kupfer, D. J. (1994). Treatment of depression in the elderly: Guidelines for primary care. In L. S. Schneider, C. F. Reynolds, B. D. Lebowitz, & A. J. Friedhoff (Eds.), *Diagnosis and treatment of depression in late life: Results of the NIH Consensus Development Conference.* Washington, DC: American Psychiatric Press.

Rogers, J., Kirby, L. C., Hempelman, S. R., et al. (1993). Clinical trials of indomethacin in Alzheimer's disease. *Neurology, 43,* 1609-1611.

Rosenheck, R., Neale, H., & Galley, P. (1993, Apr). Community-oriented mental health care: Assessing diversity in clinical practice. *Psychosocial Rehabilitation Journal, 16,* 39-50.

Ross, C. A., Peyser, C. E., Shapiro, I., & Folstein, M. F. (1991). Delirium, phenomenologic and etiologic subtypes. *International Psychogeriatrics, 3*(2), 135-147.

Roth, M. (1955). The natural history of mental disorder in old age. *Journal of Mental Science, 109,* 281.

Rothblum, E. D., Sholomskas, A. J., Berry, C., & Prusoff, B. A. (1982). Issues in clinical trials with the depressed elderly. *Journal of American Geriatrics Society, 30*(11), 694-699.

Rush, A. J., & Depression Guidelines Panel. (1993, April). *Depression in primary care: Volume 2. Treatment of major depression: Number 5. Clinical practice guidelines* (AHCPR Publication No. 93-0551). Rockville, MD: U.S. Department of Health and Human Services, Public Health Service, Agency for Health Care Policy and Research.

Sackeim, H. A. (1994). The use of electroconvulsive therapy in late life depression. In L. S. Schneider, C. F. Reynolds, B. D. Lebowitz, & A. J. Friedhoff (Eds.), *Diagnosis and treatment of depression in late life: Results of the NIH Consensus Development Conference.* Washington, DC: American Psychiatric Press.

Salzman, C. (1987). Treatment of agitation in the elderly. In H. Y. Meltzer (Ed.), *Psychopharmacology: A generation of progress* (pp. 1167-1176). New York: Raven.

Salzman, C. (Ed.). (1992). *Clinical geriatric psychopharmacology* (2nd ed.). Baltimore: Williams & Wilkins.

Salzman, C. (1994). Pharmacological treatment of depression in the elderly. In L. S. Schneider, C. F. Reynolds, B. D. Lebowitz, & A. J. Friedhoff (Eds.), *Diagnosis and treatment of depression in late life: Results of the NIH Consensus Development Conference.* Washington, DC: American Psychiatric Press.

Salzman, C., & Lebowitz, B. D. (Eds.). (1991). *Anxiety in the Elderly.* New York: Springer.

Satel, S. L., & Nelson, J. C. (1989). Stimulants in the treatment of depression: A critical overview. *Journal of Clinical Psychiatry, 50*(7), 241-249.

Schneider, L. S. (1993). Efficacy of treatment for geropsychiatric patients with severe mental illness. *Psychopharmacology Bulletin, 29,* 501–524.

Schneider, L. S. (1994). Comments on metaanalysis from a clinician's perspective. In L. S. Schneider, C. F. Reynolds, B. D. Lebowitz, & A. J. Friedhoff (Eds.), *Diagnosis and treatment of depression in late life: Results of the NIH Consensus Development Conference.* Washington, DC: American Psychiatric Press.

Schneider, L., & Olin, J. T. (1994). Overview of clinical trials of Hydergine in dementia. *Archives of Neurology, 51,* 787-798.

Schneider, L. S., Pollock, V. E., & Lyness, S. A. (1990). A metaanalysis of controlled trials of neuroleptic treatment of dementia. *Journal of the American Geriatrics Society, 38,* 553-563.

Schneider, L. S., Reynolds, C. F., Lebowitz, B. D., & Friedhoff, A. J. (Eds.). (1994). *Diagnosis and treatment of depression in late life: Results of the NIH Consensus Development Conference.* Washington, DC: American Psychiatric Press.

Schneider, L. S., Sloane, R. B., Staples, F. R., & Bender, M. (1986). Pretreatment orthostatic hypotension as a predictor of response to nortriptyline in geriatric depression. *Journal of Clinical Psychopharmacology, 6*(3), 172-176.

Schneider, L. S., & Sobin, P. (1992). Non-neuroleptic treatment of behavioral symptoms and agitation in Alzheimer's disease and other dementia. *Psychopharmacology Bulletin, 28,* 71-79.

Schoenberg, B. S., Anderson, D. W., & Haerer, A. F. (1985). Severe dementia: Prevalence and clinical features in a biracial U.S. population. *Archives of Neurology, 42,* 740-743.

Scogin, F., & McElreath, L. (1994). Efficacy of psychosocial treatments for geriatric depression: A quantitative review. *Journal of Consulting and Clinical Psychology, 62,* 69-74.

Shamoian, C. A. (Ed.). (1992). *Psychopharmacological treatment complications in the elderly.* Washington, DC: American Psychiatric Press.

Sloane, R. B., Staples, F. R., & Schneider, L. S. (1985). Interpersonal therapy vs. nortriptyline for depression in the elderly. In G. D. Burrows, T. R. Norman, & L. Dennerstein (Eds.), *Clinical and pharmacological studies in psychiatric disorders: Biological psychiatry—New prospects: Vol. 5.* London: Libbey.

Stone, K. (1989). Mania in the elderly. *British Journal of Psychiatry, 155,* 220-224.

Sunderland, T., & Silver, M. A. (1988). Neuroleptics in the treatment of dementia. *International Journal of Geriatric Psychiatry, 3,* 79-88.

Tariot, P. N., Schneider, L. S., Patel, S. V., & Goldstein, B. (1992). Alzheimer's disease and (–)-deprenyl: Rationale and findings. In I. Szelenyi (Ed.), *Inhibitors of monoamine oxidase B pharmacology and clinical use in neurodegenerative disorders*. Basel, Switzerland: Birkhäuser.

Teri, L., Curtis, J., Gallagher-Thompson, D., & Thompson, L. W. (1994). Cognitive/ behavior therapy with depressed older adults. In L. S. Schneider, C. F. Reynolds, B. D. Lebowitz, & A. J. Friedhoff (Eds.), *Diagnosis and treatment of depression in late life: Results of the NIH Consensus Development Conference*. Washington, DC: American Psychiatric Press.

Terry, R. D., Katzman, R., & Beck, K. L. (Eds.) (1994). *Alzheimer Disease*. New York, Raven Press.

Tesar, G. E., Murray, G. B., Cassem, N. H. (1985). Use of high-dose intravenous haloperidol in the treatment of agitated cardiac patients. *Journal of Clinical Psychopharmacology, 5*, 344-347.

Thompson, L. W., Gallagher, D. E., & Breckenridge, J. S. (1987). Comparative effectiveness of psychotherapies for depressed elders. *Journal of Consulting and Clinical Psychology, 55*(3), 385-390.

Thompson, L. W., Gallagher, D. E., & Czirr, R. (1988). Personality disorder and outcome in the treatment of late-life depression. *Journal of Geriatric Psychology, 21*, 133-146.

Thompson, L. W., Gallagher-Thompson, D., Hanser, S., Gantz, F., & Steffen, A. *Treatment of late-life depression with cognitive/behavioral therapy or despramine*. Paper presented at the 99th Annual Convention of American Psychological Association, San Francisco, 1991.

Tollefson, G. D., Bosomworth, J. C., Heiligenstein, J. H., Potvin, J. H., Holman, S., and the Fluoxetine Collaborative Study Group. (1995). A double-blind, placebo-controlled clinical trial of fluoxetine in geriatric patients with major depression. *International Psychogeriatrics, 7*, 89-104.

Tune, L. E. (1991). Postoperative delirium. *International Psychogeriatrics, 3*(2), 325-332.

Tune, L. E. (1992). Neurological side effects of psychotropic medications in the elderly. In C. Shamoian (Ed.), *Psychopharmacological treatment complications in the elderly*. Washington, DC: American Psychiatric Press.

van Marwijk, H. W., Bekker, F. M., Nolen, W. A., Jansen, P. A., van Nieuwkerk, J. F., & Hop, W. C. (1990). Lithium augmentation in geriatric depression. *Journal of Affective Disorders, 20*(4); 217-223.

Wadworth, A. N., & Chrisp, P. (1992). Co-dergocrine mesylate. A review of its pharmacodynamic and pharmacokinetic properties and therapeutic use in age-related cognitive decline. *Drugs and Aging, 2*, 153-173.

Young, R., Kalayam, B., Tsuboyama, G., Stokes, P., Mattis, S., & Alexopoulos, G. S. (1992). *Mania: Response to lithium across the age spectrum*. Paper presented at annual meeting of the Society for Neuroscience.

Zimmer, B., Rosen, J., Thorton, J. E., Perel, J. M., & Reynolds, C. F. (1991). Adjunctive lithium carbonate in nortriptyline-resistant elderly depressed patients. *Journal of Clinical Psychopharmacology, 11*, 254-256.

Zisook, S., & Schucter, S. R. (1994). Diagnostic and treatment considerations in depression associated with late life bereavement. In L. S. Schneider, C. F. Reynolds, B. D. Lebowitz, & A. J. Friedhoff (Eds.). *Diagnosis and treatment of depression in late life: Results of the NIH Consensus Development Conference*. Washington, DC: American Psychiatric Press.

EXHIBIT I

Recommendations of the Consensus Development Panel on Safe and Effective Treatment of Depression in the Elderly

Pharmacotherapy: Treatment of Acute Depression

There is now evidence from approximately 25 randomized, double-blind trials that antidepressants are more effective than placebo in the treatment of acute depression. Approximately 60 percent of patients clinically improve, but many of them retain significant residual symptomatology.

Available information from randomized controlled clinical trials in elderly patients is meager compared with that for younger patient groups. The number of patients in research studies drops off sharply after the sixth decade of life. There are very few studies of treatment of depression in the very old (80+), one of the most rapidly growing segments of our population. Therefore, clinical recommendations are primarily extrapolated from experience with young or middle-aged adults or based on a small number of elderly patients. There also is little research with elderly medically ill depressed patients; therefore, available evidence may be difficult to generalize to typical elderly patients presenting for treatment in clinical settings.

Most of the antidepressants are thought to be equally effective in elderly adults. The most commonly used and studied antidepressants have been nortriptyline and desipramine because they have a more favorable side effect spectrum than traditional antidepressants such as amitriptyline and imipramine. Most clinicians avoid these latter two medications because they cause significant orthostatic hypotension, which can cause falls and fractures, and because elderly patients are especially sensitive to their anticholinergic, cardiovascular, and sedative side effects.

Based primarily on clinical experience, many clinicians favor the newer antidepressants trazodone, bupropion, and fluoxetine because they have fewer anticholinergic and cardiovascular side effects. Contrary to widespread clinical opinion, the use of monoamine oxidase inhibitors, especially phenelzine, has been generally found to be safe and effective, but they have not been widely used for the treatment of geriatric depression.

There also is little known about patient factors that predict response, including clinical symptoms, demographics, subtype, comorbidity, or radiologic findings. However, there is considerable evidence that response depends on adequate length of treatment, dose, and blood level of medication. Significant antidepressant response in elderly patients often occurs later than in younger patients and requires at least 6 to 12 weeks of therapy.

Full clinical response is primarily dependent on achieving therapeutic doses that produce adequate blood levels. The measurement of plasma levels in elderly patients is even more important than in younger patients because of the increased importance of attaining appropriate therapeutic levels but remaining below levels associated with toxicity. Medication compliance by elderly people is especially important and difficult. It has been estimated that 70 percent of patients fail to take 25 to 50 percent of their medication. Lack of compliance, producing wide fluctuations in plasma levels, has been shown to be predictive of poor outcome.

Maintenance Treatment

There is an increasing recognition that the majority of major depressions are recurrent; therefore, the central issue in treatment is the prevention of recurrence. Although there are relatively few clinical trials of maintenance treatment in elderly patients, continuation of antidepressants has been shown to confer significantly greater protection against recurrence than placebo. Although clinicians often reduce doses during the maintenance phase, preliminary evidence suggests that continuation of the dose and plasma level that was effective in the acute treatment phase offers increased protection against recurrence. Evidence suggests that treatment should be maintained for 6 months after remission from a first episode of major depression and 12 months or longer after a second or third episode. Approximately 80 percent of patients maintained on doses that lead to their recovery maintain their remission over extended followup.

Electroconvulsive Therapy (ECT)

ECT has an important role in the treatment of depression in elderly adults. The most recent study conducted by the National Institute of Mental Health indicated that patients over 61 constitute the largest age group who receive ECT. The evidence for short-term efficacy of ECT is strong. However, relapse after effective ECT is frequent, and alternative treatment strategies, including maintenance ECT, or maintenance antidepressants post-ECT, require further study. ECT is often stated to be safer than antidepressants, although this has not been documented in controlled trials. Limited data suggest that advancing age heightens the probability of transient post-ECT confusion, especially in the very old. Additional risk factors include receiving psychotropic medication during ECT, concurrent major medical illness, and preexisting cognitive deficits.

Psychosocial Treatments

A comprehensive system of care necessitates the inclusion of psychosocial treatments because of the broad range of functional and social consequences of depression in elderly people. Biological treatments will not be able to resolve all of the problems associated with depression in the elderly. For example, significant and continuing life events, altered life roles, lack of social support, and chronic medical illnesses might well require psychosocial support and new coping skills. Also, some patients will strongly prefer nonbiological interventions, and others will not be suitable for biological treatment because of side effects, interactions between drugs, and comorbid medical conditions.

There are only a handful of controlled studies on the efficacy of psychosocial interventions with elderly people dealing primarily with cognitive behavior therapy, behavior therapy, interpersonal therapy, and short-term psychodynamic therapy. These treatments are all moderately effective and have durable effects with outpatient volunteers in comparatively good physical health. There are no clear comparisons with placebo or pseudotreatment control groups, with the old-old, or with medically ill elderly.

Marital and family interventions have not been adequately studied. Marital therapy has been found to be effective in treating depression in younger adults, and social support is a particularly important factor for elderly people. There are some promising strategies for treatment of family caregivers of the frail elderly who themselves often experience high levels of burden and are highly vulnerable to depression.

A number of problems in the use of psychosocial treatments require study. Many elderly people do not see themselves as depressed and/or will not admit to it and reject referrals to mental health professionals. Special effort might be needed to engage these individuals in treatment. Patients with significant physical illness and disabilities (e.g., visual and hearing impairment) and cognitive impairment may require special approaches. Special consideration should also be given to the dissemination of any programs that prove effective so that therapists and caregivers to the elderly are sensitized to the ability of elderly people to respond to active psychosocial interventions. Senior centers, nutrition programs, volunteer services, and other community-based programs should be integral components of any comprehensive psychosocial intervention system.

Special Populations

The evidence is contradictory concerning whether concurrent medical illness has an adverse effect on response to pharmacotherapy. Although medical comorbidity probably results in increased vulnerability to side effects, vigorous but careful treatment is still indicated. However, there are very few controlled trials of treatment of secondary depressions after the medical condition is stabilized. Also, patients with known brain lesions should be treated with the same guidelines and doses as patients without known brain lesions, except as specifically contraindicated. Based on the limited data available, these patients can be expected to respond as well as patients with primary depressions.

The prevalence of major depression in nursing home populations is high and is generally unrecognized and untreated. These patients respond equally well to standard doses of antidepressants, although their medical fragility can lead to treatment-limiting side effects in as many as one-third of these patients.

About 800,000 persons are widowed each year; most of them are old and experience varying degrees of depressive symptomatology. Most do not need formal treatment, but those who are moderately or severely dysphoric appear to benefit from self-help groups or various psychosocial treatments. Remarkably, a third of widows/widowers meet criteria for a major depressive episode in the first month after the death, and half of these remain clinically depressed 1 year later. These depressions respond to standard antidepressants, although there is limited research as to when in the course of these depressions antidepressant medications should be instituted or how medications should be combined with psychosocial treatments.

SOURCE: From A. J. Friedhoff, 1994, Concensus Panel Report.

EXHIBIT II

Recommendations of the Consensus Development Panel on the Most Promising Questions for Future Research

Improve diagnosis and identification of those elderly persons most likely to benefit from specific treatments—biological, psychosocial, or combinations thereof.

Clarify the relationship between subcortical brain abnormalities, depressive and cognitive symptomatology, and early- versus late-onset depression in the elderly.

Clarify the pharmacokinetic changes in the very old and the prognostic value of metabolic subtyping.

Clarify the cause and effect relationship between depression and medical illness.

Initiate prospective cross-sequential studies to identify general risk factors (including life stress and specific illnesses and disabilities) and their relationship to the course of depression.

Study the basis for differential occurrence of depression and suicide rates in demographic subgroups.

Determine whether ECT is effective as a continuation and maintenance treatment in late life depression.

Study the treatment of pathological grief. Which psychological and pharmacological treatments are effective, and when in the course of grief should they be used?

Conduct clinical trials and observational studies of treatment in the very old, the elderly in minority and underserved communities and in institutional settings, and the elderly with medical illness.

Develop and evaluate psychosocial treatments that are specifically linked to the needs of the elderly. Determine how psychosocial and biological treatments may complement or provide alternatives to each other.

Develop demonstration projects focused on innovative models of care delivery, particularly those that emphasize coordinated services and outreach efforts to depressed elderly people.

Carry out long-term clinical trials with broad-based assessment of outcome (including economic and social impact) to determine the extent to which effective recognition and treatment benefit patients and society.

Conclusions and Recommendations

Depression in late life occurs in the context of numerous social and physical problems that often obscure or complicate diagnosis and impede management of the illness. There is no specific diagnostic test for depression, so an attentive and focused clinical assessment is essential for diagnosis. Because elderly depressed people often do not present themselves for evaluation or because their depressive symptoms are not typical, the illness is underdiagnosed and undertreated. This is particularly true when it is secondary to physical illness, even though these secondary depressive symptoms also respond to treatment.

Estimates of depression in elderly people vary widely as a function of setting, threshold of diagnosis, and definition of depression; however, there is a consensus that the size of the problem is underestimated. The highest rates are found in nursing homes and other residential care settings. Risk factors appear to operate similarly in young and old, although the hallmark of depression in older people is its comorbidity with medical illness. The course of recovery and frequent recurrence is similar in young and old; however, suicide is dramatically increased in elderly depressed, as is mortality from other causes.

Depressed elderly people should be treated vigorously with sufficient doses of antidepressants and for a sufficient length of time to maximize the likelihood of recovery. Maintenance treatment with antidepressants should be continued with the same doses that produced remission of the acute episode. ECT is often effective for depression in the elderly but is generally underused or unavailable. Psychosocial treatments can also play an essential role in the care of elderly patients who have significant life crises, lack social support, or lack coping skills to deal with their life situations. These approaches may also be indicated in patients who cannot or will not tolerate biologic treatments.

The system of care currently provided to elderly depressed persons is inadequate, fragmented, and passive. Ageist attitudes among some health care providers compromise their ability to recognize depression in their elderly patients and to intervene in an appropriate and timely fashion. The prevalence of depression is particularly high among patients in nursing homes, but staff in many of these facilities are not equipped to recognize or treat depressed patients.

Families and primary care physicians remain at the front line in recognizing depression and facilitating patient access to professional help; however, large numbers of elderly people live alone, have inadequate support systems, or do not have contact with a primary care physician. The isolation of these individuals compounds their depression, and specialized efforts are needed to locate and identify them and to provide in-home care relevant to their needs. Although lack of services is a major problem, a greater problem may be our inability to deliver services to those community-dwelling elderly people who need them the most.

SOURCE: From A. J. Friedhoff, 1994, Concensus Panel Report.

CHAPTER 3

Strengths and Limitations of Research on Late-Life Psychoses

Dilip V. Jeste, David Naimark,
Maureen C. Halpain, and Laurie A. Lindamer

Near or above the 50s the elasticity of the mental process, on which the treatment depends, is as a rule lacking—old people are no longer educable . . . the mass of material to be dealt with would prolong the treatment indefinitely.

—Sigmund Freud (1924)

Modern culture has tended to concern itself with youth and to place less emphasis on understanding old age, a bias evident in the work of Freud, quoted above. Freud seemed to believe that the investment of time, money, and effort in individual psychotherapy for the elderly was not worthwhile (Nemiroff & Colarusso, 1985). Unfortunately, this prevalent anti-aging bias has led directly to insufficient knowledge about mental disorders that affect the elderly population, and to serious underfunding of research studies. Freud's attitudes are ironic in light of his own longevity, his amazing scientific and literary achievements in late life, and his bravery in facing his illness and death (Kahana, 1978).

Mental disorders are of major importance in the elderly population. Some of the serious psychiatric disorders in this age group were

Acknowledgments: Supported, in part, by NIMH grants MH43693, MH45131, MH49671, and by the Department of Veterans Affairs.

described in the previous chapter: dementia, depression, psychoses, delirium, and mania. In addition, alcohol abuse and dependence, hypochondriasis, and posttraumatic stress disorder can seriously impare elderly individuals.

Our own research has focused primarily on the late-life psychoses, so we use this set of diagnoses as a model for understanding the current strengths and limitations of research in late-life disorders as a whole. Although there are a number of clinical differences between the late-life psychoses and other disorders such as dementia and late-life depression, many of the challenges in executing research and treatment of the older population are similar across different psychiatric disorders. It should further be noted that the review below concentrates on biomedical aspects, rather than on other important areas such as psychosocial issues, infrastructure, or health care reform in relation to research in late-life disorders.

CHALLENGES OF RESEARCH ON GEROPSYCHIATRIC DISORDERS

Researchers may feel that the challenges of doing research with older adults are too great, which may result in more effort toward examining psychiatric disorders and their treatment in young adults. To underscore this observation, Jeste and Caligiuri (1991) conducted a Medline search using the keyword "psychosis" and found that for every 16 articles since 1987 pertaining to psychosis in younger adults, only one corresponding article was published on psychosis in late life. Recently, we undertook a survey of research-related experiences and attitudes among members of the American Association of Geriatric Psychiatry (Jeste, Fitten, Clemons, O'Neal, & Harris, 1993). Eighty-five percent of the respondents indicated that geriatric research was important but that there were too many barriers to conducting research. These research barriers include insufficient funding, inadequate research training, and societal bias against aging, as well as certain patient-related factors: increased medical comorbidity, polypharmacy, cognitive impairment and dementia, and increased biological heterogeneity.

Another special issue for research in late-life disorders is the definition of old age. Any fixed age cutoff is necessarily arbitrary. Over the years, different investigators have used different cutoffs. While middle age or late life is often thought to begin at 45 years, the term "elderly" or "geriatric" should be restricted to those over age 65. An elderly person is not simply an "aged younger adult," but a unique entity with many differences from a younger person. These differences can introduce a number of confounding variables. Older adults have an increased number of medical problems that can exacerbate and confuse the clinical picture of a psychiatric illness. The elderly are typically prescribed more medications than younger patients, which can lead to adverse drug interaction effects. Older persons are more likely to have some degree of cognitive impairment or dementia and so may have more difficulty verbalizing their situations. Pharmacokinetics and pharmacodynamics of medications vary considerably among different individuals in the geriatric population. In addition, psychosocial stressors take on more importance. The elderly are susceptible to numerous losses: those of spouse, friends, physical health, job, status, independence, finances, and so forth. There may be social isolation, sensory deprivation, and poverty. All of these factors can exacerbate a preexisting psychiatric disturbance or uncover a new illness in a predisposed person.

Recruiting physically "normal" psychiatric subjects and "healthy" normal comparison groups is therefore difficult. It is also difficult to distinguish between factors representing pathology in the elderly and factors representing normal aging. Further, the issue of measurement presents a particular problem: Most of the standard psychiatric measurement scales have been generated from younger patients, and their validity in the elderly population is unproven. Lastly, long-term follow-up of the elderly is difficult because of institutionalization, physical illness, and death.

However, meaningful solutions to the research problems can be found. For example, difficulties with comorbidity, polypharmacy, and cognitive impairment can be dealt with by using analyses of covariance or stratification variables. Heterogeneity in the older population can be adjusted for with data transformations that allow the use of parametric statistics. Rather than attempting to recruit healthy (and thus nonrepresentative) elderly comparison subjects, it would be more appropriate to have similar medical illnesses in patient and comparison groups. It is thus definitely possible to conduct scientific research in geriatric psychiatry that is as reliable and valid as research in mental disorders in younger adults.

IMPORTANCE OF PSYCHOSES IN LATE LIFE

Psychosis is defined as a disorder associated with personality disintegration and loss of contact with reality (Thomas, 1985). More practically, psychosis is a severe psychiatric disorder characterized by delusions (false, unshakable beliefs that cannot be explained merely on the basis of a person's sociocultural or educational background) or hallucinations (false perceptions in the absence of relevant stimuli). It has been said that chronic psychoses are to the mental health profession what cancers are to the general medical profession. Both psychosis and cancer represent diverse, heterogeneous groups of conditions that are typically malignant and difficult to treat, and the treatments for both often have serious side effects. Both disorders exact a terrible emotional toll on patients and their caregivers, and both result in considerable morbidity and mortality. Certain variants of the two conditions, however, have a much less negative outcome, and on occasion, remissions do occur.

The late-life psychoses are an under-studied yet increasingly important group of conditions. With the overall rise in longevity, there will be an increasing number of new cases of late-life psychosis as well as an increasing number of patients who developed psychosis in adolescence or young adulthood and will be living into old age.

The late-life psychoses are traditionally divided into two major categories according to their presumed etiology: those associated with organic mental syndromes (e.g., dementia) and those associated with syndromes whose etiology is unclear (e.g., schizophrenia). Nearly all types of psychoses that occur in younger persons may also be seen in older persons. The psychotic syndromes most characteristic of older patients are psychosis complicating dementia, late-life delusional disorder, early-onset schizophrenia progressing into older age, and late-onset schizophrenia. Other psychotic conditions that can be present in the elderly but are less specific to this age group are psychoses associated with mood disorders, psychoses secondary to other organic mental syndromes (e.g., drug induced), and psychoses not otherwise specified.

Frequency

Schizophrenia occurs in approximately 1% of the general population and is observed in up to 1% of the elderly population (Gurland & Cross, 1982). Ninety percent of elderly schizophrenic patients experienced onset of illness before age 45. In their literature review, Harris and Jeste (1988) found that 23% of schizophrenic patients on an inpatient psychiatric service were reported to have had the onset of illness after age 40. The frequency of delusional disorder is estimated to be 0.03% (American Psychiatric Association, 1987). Approximately one third of patients with the most common form of dementia (dementia of the Alzheimer's type) suffer from psychosis at some point during the course of their illness (Wragg & Jeste, 1989). About 1.5 million Americans suffer from severe dementia, and an additional 1 to 5 million have mild to moderate dementia (U.S. Congress Office of Technology Assessment, 1987). Most psychotic symptoms appear in patients with moderate to severe dementia. Thus there may be at least 1 million Americans with dementia who develop psychotic symptoms. Based on the frequencies mentioned above, one can therefore conservatively estimate that 1,257,500 people over age 65 have psychosis (including dementia with psychosis, schizophrenia, and delusional disorder). This figure represents represents about 5% of the entire population over the age of 65 and does not even take into account psychosis associated with other disturbances such as mood disorders.

Seriousness

In addition to their high frequency, the late-life psychoses are important because of their negative impact on patient, caregiver, family, and society. Psychotic patients have a higher mortality rate than the general population. This is related to natural causes as well as unnatural ones such as violence and suicide (Allebeck, 1989). There is a high rate of suicide in schizophrenic patients: According to some investigators, up to 50% of schizophrenic patients attempt suicide, and 10% eventually complete suicide (Roy, 1990). In general, elderly persons have the highest suicide rate of all age groups, so it is possible (but not yet demonstrated) that elderly schizophrenic patients have a higher suicide rate than their younger counterparts.

Since physical comorbidity is known to increase with aging, it can be expected that there will be a high prevalence of medical illnesses among older psychotic patients. Unfortunately, psychotic patients do not seem to receive the required care for their illnesses or sensory impairments with the same reliability as nonpsychotic patients, resulting in a higher morbidity. Prager and Jeste (1993) found that the older psychiatric patients in their sample all had more severe corrected-vision and corrected-hearing impairment than normal comparison subjects of similar age, and that schizophrenic patients in particular tended to have visited an eye doctor less recently than normal subjects. Several case series have emphasized that even severe sensory deficits in the elderly population are often overlooked by physicians. Often elderly patients are also financially impoverished, which may limit their access to care. These factors suggest that treatment for medical conditions may be harder to obtain for older psychotic patients because of difficulties in dealing with the health care system.

Psychosis causes extreme psychological distress, and most patients who have experienced psychotic symptoms describe the experience as deeply frightening. One can imagine the sense of loss of control that would accompany the loss of touch with reality. Glantz, Bieliauskas, and Paleologos (1986) noted that a cohort of Parkinson's disease patients had impairment in life functioning as well as increased anxiety, somatization, self-doubt, self-devaluation, social alienation, bizarre feelings, and general dissatisfaction when hallucinations were present. "Quality of life" is a multifactorial concept that includes physical and social functioning as well as emotional health. Patterson et al. (1995) recently completed a study examining the quality of well-being in older patients with psychosis. Psychotic patients were found to be significantly more impaired in terms of quality of well-being than normal comparison subjects and had even a slightly lower quality of well-being than ambulatory patients with AIDS. The greatest loss of quality of well-being derived from positive symptoms (delusions and hallucinations) of schizophrenia.

The psychological impact on caregivers of patients with psychosis has been well described in the literature on psychosis in dementia. Studies have demonstrated that behavioral disturbances resulting from psychosis represent a more important reason for institutionalization than the actual severity of dementia (Ferris, Steinberg, & Shulman, 1985; Rabins, Mace,

& Lucas, 1982). Rabins et al. found that psychotic symptoms were noted by caregivers of patients with Alzheimer's disease as a problem that negatively affected quality of life for both patient and caregiver. Other studies of the demented elderly suggest that even slight improvement in agitation (often resulting from psychosis) may result in substantial gains in function (Shulman & Steinberg, 1985). Patients with Alzheimer's disease with delusions experience significantly more wandering, agitation, family and marital problems, and lack of self-care than patients with Alzheimer's disease without delusions (Rockwell, Jackson, Vilke, & Jeste, 1994).

Persons with late-life psychoses are apt to experience major social difficulties. As a result of their often bizarre, disorganized behavior, they often have great difficulty maintaining a stable living situation and consequently may often have periods of homelessness. These patients may lose touch with family and friends and find themselves increasingly socially isolated. Many patients with psychosis occurring late in life have had preexisting personality styles (schizoid or paranoid) that lead other people to find them eccentric and unapproachable, thus reducing their social networks.

Problems in Management

Though remarkable and exciting breakthroughs have been made to treat those suffering from late-life psychosis, the fact remains that current treatment is largely symptomatic, not curative. The mainstay of care is the antipsychotic (or neuroleptic) medication, which produces improvement in psychotic symptoms and decreases need for psychiatric hospitalization but which is also associated with numerous unpleasant and sometimes dangerous side effects.

Probably the most disturbing side effect of antipsychotic medication is tardive dyskinesia (TD), a potentially irreversible involuntary movement disorder that is among the most serious iatrogenic disorders in psychopharmacology. A number of factors make TD an important problem. In a majority of patients with TD, the disorder persists for longer than 3 months despite discontinuation of medication (Jeste & Wyatt, 1982). There is no consistently effective treatment for persistent TD (Jeste, Lohr, Clark, & Wyatt, 1988), and there has been a growing number of malpractice lawsuits against clinicians and hospitals filed by patients who developed TD (Tancredi, 1988). Concern about TD is especially pronounced among elderly persons, because the risk of the disorder is much higher for them (Jeste et al., in press). TD in the elderly is more likely to be severe and persistent than TD in the young, and if the medication is not withdrawn, the likelihood of remission is low (Kane et al., 1992).

All these factors make late-life psychoses important conditions from a public health policy perspective.

CURRENT KNOWLEDGE BASE

After decades of neglect, considerable research into late-life psychoses has been accomplished in the past 15 to 20 years. It is currently one of the most exciting areas of research in psychiatry.

Schizophrenia in the Elderly

Schizophrenia in the older population can be divided into two types: that first presenting in old age (late onset) and that first presenting in younger age and carrying into older age (early onset). Despite substantial controversy, much evidence suggests that schizophrenic symptoms can arise in middle and late life—the first onset of the disorder is not restricted to young adulthood. Late-onset schizophrenia is generally of the paranoid type. The patients have more positive symptoms (symptoms not seen in "normal" or healthy individuals, such as delusions and hallucinations) than early-onset schizophrenic patients, who tend to have a reduction in positive symptoms and an increase in "negative" symptoms (symptoms characterized by deficits in phenomena that are normally present, such as reduction of affect or social isolation) as they enter middle and old age (Belitsky & McGlashan, 1993). Female gender is a risk factor for late-onset schizophrenia, despite a correction for the relative excess of women in the older population; the excess of female patients has been reported as 2- to 10-fold.

The pathogenesis of late-onset schizophrenia is not yet well understood; however, genetic predisposition and possible perinatal brain lesions seem to be involved (Jeste et al., 1995). A connection has been reported between sensory impairment (deafness or blindness) and the late-onset psychoses. Kay and Roth (1961) found a relationship between visual and hearing impairment and the onset of schizophrenia. Prager and Jeste (1993) suggested that the association might be at least partly a result of insufficient correction of sensory deficits in older patients when compared with normal controls.

An exciting focus in research on these patients has been the use of various structural and functional brain-imaging techniques. Different investigators have noted four structural findings: (a) increased ventricle-to-brain ratio on computer tomography scan or magnetic resonance imaging (Kumar, 1976), (b) areas of subcortical white matter hyperintensities (Lesser, Miller, Boone, Hill-Gutierrez, & Mena, 1991), (c) an increased number of vascular lesions (Flint, Rifat, & Eastwood, 1991), and (d) an increased volume of thalamus (Jeste et al., 1995). The meaning of these structural findings is unclear. Studies of functional brain imaging (single-photon emission computed tomography and positron emission tomography) have revealed lower global cortical uptake in late-onset schizophrenia patients than in comparison subjects (Dupont et al., 1994) and elevated receptor densities for dopamine D_2 receptors in neuroleptic-naive patients with LOS compared to normal controls (Pearlson et al., 1993).

As individuals with schizophrenia of the early-onset type enter old age, the course of illness varies. Neuroleptic withdrawal often worsens the psychosis. Good compliance with medication (often fostered by a reliable doctor-patient relationship) and supportive psychosocial therapy tend to produce the most symptom-free course for these patients. The course of illness may be different in different patient populations. For instance, Davidson et al. (1991) noted that a cohort of chronically institutionalized schizophrenic patients had cognitive deficits that followed a course analogous to that of progressive dementia, whereas Goldberg, Hyde, Kleinman, and Winberger, (1993) and Heaton et al. (1994) found that schizophrenic patients remained cognitively stable but impaired throughout the course of their illness, suggesting a static encephalopathy. Recent studies have noted that the long-term course of schizophrenia may be less bleak overall than had previously been thought. Belitsky and McGlashan (1993) found that nearly a quarter of schizophrenic patients underwent remission and more than a third were left with mild symptoms over the long term.

A recent *New York Times* article (Nasar, 1994) alludes to the potential for dramatic remission from schizophrenia in later life. John Nash was one of the most promising mathematicians when *Forbes* magazine singled him out in 1958 as a pioneer of "New Mathematics." Later that year, he was found to have paranoid schizophrenia. For the next three decades, his life was dominated by delusions, commitment to psychiatric hospitals, periods of roaming around Princeton University writing strange equations on the blackboards, a divorce from his wife, and total alienation from his professional colleagues. Then, in his mid to late 50s, Nash slowly began to improve. The change started with his talking to other mathematicians again and making friends with graduate students. He began to learn how to use a computer and to do mathematics again. Now in his 60s, he is in remission and recently he was awarded the Nobel Prize for work that he had completed as a student in 1949. As pointed out by Belitsky and McGlashan (1993), remission of schizophrenia in old age is not rare but occurs in a sizable minority of patients.

Antipsychotic (or neuroleptic) medications are currently the best available option for treating the symptoms of schizophrenia. Generally, much smaller doses of medication suffice to alleviate symptoms in older patients. The elderly population is much more sensitive to the side effects of these medications; therefore, the guiding principle is to use the lowest effective dose.

A revolution in psychopharmacology is taking place. The newer serotonin–dopamine antagonist antipsychotic medications (clozapine and risperidone) afford increased efficacy against negative symptoms and seem less likely to cause movement disorders. They may also improve some cases of tardive dyskinesia. These medications (which do have their own side effects) are, however, under-studied in the elderly population.

Late-Life Delusional Disorder

Paranoid behavior is a common problem in the elderly. Approximately 4% of the community-living elderly population experience paranoia (Christenson & Blazer, 1984). Paranoia is usually associated with another psychiatric disorder such as schizophrenia, mood disorder, or dementia, but sometimes a chronic, nonbizarre delusional disorder is present that is not attributable to any other psychiatric disorder. Delusional disorder usually presents first in mid to late adulthood. The patient with delusional disorder is often difficult to treat effectively; low-dose neuroleptic medications can be partially effective, but noncompliance is a frequent problem in these patients.

Psychosis Complicating Dementia

Dementia of the Alzheimer's type (DAT) is the most common form of dementia seen in the elderly. About one third of DAT patients have symptoms of psychosis during the course of their illness (Wragg & Jeste, 1989). Simple, persecutory delusions are the most commonly reported symptom of psychosis; they are often stimulated by some environmental stress or change. The pathogenesis of the psychotic symptoms is unknown, although a number of recent neuropsychological and brain-imaging studies have begun to help us better understand the condition (Stern et al., 1994). There is a paucity of well-controlled studies of the treatment of psychotic symptoms in patients with DAT. The available data support the use of low-dose neuroleptic medication for treatment of psychotic symptoms.

Late-Life Psychoses in Special Populations

Gender

Only recently has gender's role in the development or modification of neuropsychiatric illness been investigated. Gender has been shown to influence the risk of some dementias, mood disorders, and psychotic disorders (Giltin & Pasnau, 1989; Harris et al., in press; Henderson, Paganini-Hill, Emanuel, Dunn, & Buckwater, 1994). Yet a literature review examining the occurrence of gender differences in schizophrenia (Wahl & Hunter, 1992) demonstrated that 72% of the studies appearing in four major journals from 1985 to 1989 included more males than females.

Gender differences have been found in various aspects of schizophrenic syndrome, including (a) age of onset of psychosis, (b) symptom presentation, (c) course of illness, (d) results of biochemical and neuroradiological investigations, (e) neuroleptic response, and (f) risk of tardive dyskinesia (for review, see Andia & Zisook, 1991; Harris et al., in press). Briefly, age of onset of the schizophrenic disorder is consistently later for women than for men, and late-onset schizophrenia is 2 to 10 times more common in women than in men. There have been reports of more mood symptoms and paranoia in women; negative symptoms such as amotivational syndrome are more common in men. In addition, the course of schizophrenia has been thought to be less severe in women: Multiple first-admission studies have found that women experience fewer rehospitalizations, shorter hospital stays, better social and work functioning, lower relapse rates, and less severe psychopathological outcomes (Andia & Zisook, 1991).

The gender difference in response to neuroleptics is complex. Some studies report that schizophrenic women require higher doses of neuroleptics; others have found that women respond better than men to such medications. This discrepancy may be explained by hormonal status: Premenopausal women may require lower doses than postmenopausal women. The relationship between hormone levels and neuroleptic responses has not been investigated adequately.

An interaction effect of gender and age also appears for tardive dyskinesia. Prevalence of TD increases with age for women but not for men, suggesting that the hormonal withdrawal during menopause may increase the risk of TD. Gender's relationship to neuroradiological abnormalities and cognition is unclear.

Estrogen and psychosis. There is evidence to suggest a rather complex relationship between estrogen and psychosis (for review, see Seeman & Lang, 1990). Generally (but not consistently), low estrogen levels are associated with an increased risk of psychosis whereas high estrogen levels may reduce vulnerability. Postmenopausal women not undergoing hormone replacement therapy may demonstrate a heightened vulnerability to psychosis.

The development of psychosis in estrogen–depleted states most likely involves an interaction of estrogen and dopamine. Riecher-Rössler et al. (1994) have proposed that estrogen may exert a neuroleptic-like effect. Pearlson et al. (1993) have reported an age-related decrease in the number of dopamine D_2 receptors. Men lose them at a faster rate with increasing age, leaving older women with a relative excess. Riecher-Rössler and colleagues noted a significant relationship between general psychopathologic measures and specific measures of psychosis and serum estrogen levels. There was no correlation between estrogen levels and depression measures, however.

Direct effects of dopamine on estrogen have been demonstrated in animal studies (Becker, 1990). Gender differences in dopamine metabolism have been observed in the basal ganglia in rats, and 17-β-estradiol has been shown to down-regulate rat D_2 receptors. Another study reported gender differences in basal extracellular striatal dopamine levels, with castrated male rats having 20% higher levels than ovariectomized females. Estrogen may be antidopaminergic in humans, thus performing a protective role in the development of schizophrenia in women, but the relationship between psychotic symptoms and estrogen level has yet to be examined.

Estrogen and cognition. The evidence supporting the effects of reproductive hormones on cognition is steadily accumulating. Of particular interest to geriatric psychiatry are studies examining memory in postmenopausal women. Although some noncontrolled studies have found a decreased memory performance in postmenopausal women, others have failed to find any decline. Sherwin (1988) performed a double-blind crossover study of surgical menopausal women, who were randomly assigned to one of five groups: estrogen, androgen, estrogen and androgen, placebo, and surgical control. Dependent variables included two psychometric tests of short-term memory, a test of narrative memory, and a test of abstract reasoning before and after each treatment phase. Performance on all four tasks improved in the groups that received hormones relative to either the placebo or control group. Furthermore, Phillips and Sherwin (1992) reported improved memory performance with estrogen supplementation in surgical menopausal women using the Wechsler Memory Scale–Revised (WMS-R). They found that women who received estrogen demonstrated increased performance on the immediate recall condition of paragraph recall of the WMS-R. No difference was noted in delayed paragraph recall, visual memory, or digit span. Kampen and Sherwin (1994) also reported improved verbal memory in healthy postmenopausal women who were receiving estrogen replacement therapy.

Barrett-Connor and Kritz-Silverstein (1993) concluded that estrogen replacement therapy had no benefit on cognition in postmenopausal women. They noted, however, that there may be some indirect effect of the therapy on cognition in recently menopausal women, which might have been secondary to the amelioration of depression or somatic complaints.

Future directions. Gender differences in course, treatment, and outcome of neuropsychiatric illness have been well documented, but the mechanism by which gender exerts its effects is not yet clear. The role of estrogen is of special interest and will require a multidisiplinary approach to investigate. Such studies will have implications for treatment, quality of life, and cost of caring for postmenopausal women.

Ethnicity

The role of ethnicity in the development of late-life psychoses has not been studied, to our knowledge. In general, few publications have discussed possible ethnic differences in the manifestations of schizophrenia. Two papers have reported a higher incidence of hallucinations among African American patients than among White patients with schizophrenia (Adebimpe, 1981; Vitols, Water, & Keeler, 1963). Another publication found no differences in symptom reporting of schizophrenia between White and Hispanic schizophrenic patients (Randolph et al., 1985). A recent communication by Lawson (personal communication, May 1994) indicated that in a sample of elderly schizophrenic patients, there appeared to be a greater incidence of dementia in African American patients than in White patients.

Some authors have questioned whether African American patients are discriminated against in the diagnosis of psychotic disorders. Lindsey and Paul (1989) contended that African American patients were overrepresented in admissions to public institutions because of their lower socioeconomic status and institutional racial bias. Some studies have found that standardized diagnostic measurements have identified African Caribbean patients as having higher rates of schizophrenia than the general population. A particular concern about whether African Americans are overidentified as having psychosis is that this might result in higher levels of neuroleptic medication usage, and increased exposure might increase the risk of developing TD. Strickland et al. (1991) supported this idea, stating that "black patients tend to receive substantially higher doses of neuroleptics." Sramek, Sayles, and Simpson (1986), however, found no significant differences in the daily neuroleptic dosages prescribed to African Americans, Hispanics, or Whites. Glazer, Morgenstern, and Doucette (1994) reported a higher incidence of TD among African Americans than among Whites in a population of younger and middle-aged adults. Some investigators have suggested that Asian patients may respond to lower doses of neuroleptics than Whites; others have not found this to be true. Patterns of neuroleptic use in Hispanic and Native American populations have been reported inconsistently; it is therefore impossible to draw any conclusions about these data at present.

Few of the above-mentioned studies were done on the elderly. Lacro and Jeste (1995) found a nonsignificantly higher risk for TD among African Americans than among Whites in a sample of middle-aged and elderly patients. Overall, these findings suggest a need for caution in using neuroleptics in African Americans, including the elderly.

Ethnicity represents an important variable that may contribute to both the pathogenesis of psychosis and the variations in drug response (as a result of pharmacogenetics, pharmacodynamics, and pharmacokinetics). The role of ethnicity in late-life psychiatric disorders in general and late-life psychoses specifically is presently under-studied and requires much further exploration.

Nursing Home Population

Nursing home patients represent a special population with a high prevalence of psychiatric illness. Prevalence rates of disorders listed in the revised third edition of the *Diagnostic and Statistical Manual of Mental Disorder* (American Psychiatric Association, 1987) have been estimated to be as high as 94% (Rovner et al., 1986). In a sense, this makes nursing homes comparable to psychiatric institutions. The most common psychiatric disorder is dementia, with a prevalence of approximately one-half to three-quarters of residents (Curlick, Frazier, & Katz, 1991). Alzheimer's disease accounts for about half these cases, with other dementias making up the remainder. Patients with dementia are at a higher risk for neuropsychiatric complications such as delirium, psychosis, and depression. Psychotic symptoms are noted in 25% to 50% of demented patients, and secondary major depression is seen in about 33% (Rovner et al., 1986). This risk of depressive illness is much higher than in the community elderly, perhaps in part because nursing home residents tend to have more medical illnesses and be on more medications that can exacerbate or even cause depression.

Most mental health consultations in nursing homes are for the management of behavioral disturbances resulting from dementia, such as pacing, wandering, shouting, exhibiting physical or verbal aggression, or resisting care (Curlick et al., 1991). The major risk factor for behavioral disturbance in the demented elderly is psychotic symptoms. Rovner et al. (1986) have noted that the association between psychosis and behavioral disturbances persists after controlling for cognitive impairment. For most nursing home patients, the result of agitation is the initiation of neuroleptic medication for behavioral control. It is estimated that 20% to 40% of nursing home residents are taking neuroleptic medication and hence are at a high risk for adverse side effects—especially tardive dyskinesia. Although neuroleptic medications have some efficacy for the control of agitation resulting from psychotic symptoms, they are often used for long periods, at inappropriately high doses, and without proper input from a psychiatrist. There is currently a dearth of data on alternative medication strategies for controlling agitation in the elderly demented patient, but there is some evidence for the possible efficacy of certain antidepressants (e.g., trazodone) and newer antianxiety medications such as buspirone.

Underdiagnosis and undertreatment of depression is also a significant problem in this population, resulting in a need for research to evaluate both psychopharmacologic and psychosocial treatments for this disorder. Because nursing homes are traditionally underserved by mental health professionals, there is a pressing need to develop and evaluate liaison approaches to the delivery of mental health care and models that integrate the services of psychiatry and other mental health professions (Curlick et al., 1991).

DEFICIENCIES IN THE KNOWLEDGE BASE

Etiology and Pathogenesis

It is currently unclear whether the late-life psychoses follow a neurodevelopmental model, in which the brain lesions related to the pathogenesis are of developmental origin and not progressive or degenerative, or whether they follow a neurodegenerative pattern similar to a progressive dementia. How the late-life psychoses may be biologically similar to or different from each other is also unknown. More information is needed to understand the interrelatedness of physical, psychological, and social factors in the pathophysiology of late-life psychoses. The answers to these questions are critical to our understanding of these disorders and to our ability to develop effective interventions to alter their frequently destructive path.

Course and Prognosis

One of the most important under-studied aspects of late-life psychoses is their course and prognosis. It is estimated that nearly a quarter of schizophrenic patients experience remission, and another third have marked improvement in their symptoms. The case of John Nash described above illustrates the potential for chronic cases to experience dramatic remissions in late life. At present, we do not know how to predict the course of the late-life psychoses, nor do we know the factors influencing such a course.

Treatment

The vast majority of studies of the treatment of psychosis have been in younger schizophrenic patients. Information is lacking on the treatment of older patients, including the use of newer antipsychotic agents. It is unclear (a) how long neuroleptic medications need to be continued; (b) how the drug response changes with time; (c) whether prior drug treatment affects subsequent therapeutic response; (d) whether there are gender-related differences in treatment response; (e) how to treat patients who show only a minimal response to medication; (f) how, why, and when to use the newer antipsychotic medications; and (g) what specific

pharmacokinetic and pharmacodynamic changes influence neu͟
fect in the elderly. Even less is known about the specifics ͟
pharmacologic treatments, such as psychotherapy, behavior modifica͟
and cognitive therapy, in the management of the elderly.

Special Populations

Special issues such as gender, ethnicity, and chronic care require much further study in order to understand the specific implications of treating psychoses in special populations of the aged.

Research of the kind recommended above requires multi-disciplinary, comprehensive, longitudinal evaluations of patients, which should include psychiatric, neurologic, medical, neuropsychological, and psychosocial aspects. Because of the large number of variables involved and the unique issues described previously in conducting research on this patient population, the samples must be as large as possible. Cross-cultural comparative studies using similar designs will give information about different treatment strategies in different settings.

We should reemphasize that the discussion above applies to late-life psychoses. There are, of course, various other important deficiencies in the knowledge base for other mental disorders of later life.

The challenges facing research are not insurmountable by any means and need not be barriers to our understanding of psychopathology across the life cycle. In view of the severely limited existing database, it may be appropriate to begin with qualitative research in this area; as experience accumulates, the research can be made more quantitative. As our population continues to age, we hope that there will be a continued recognition of the need for further training of geriatric researchers and clinicians as well as further funding to support these worthwhile areas of investigation.

ISSUES OF COST AND HEALTH CARE SERVICE UTILIZATION

From an economic perspective, mental illness has a great impact on our society as a whole. Mental disorders, particularly psychoses, produce an economic burden that includes direct treatment costs, loss of productivity, expenditures for public assistance, family and caregiver burden, and legal costs (Kaplan & Sadock, 1988).

Schizophrenia is one of the most expensive mental illnesses (Andrews et al., 1985; McGuire, 1991; Rupp & Keith, 1993). The cost of this severe illness has been reported to be more than $33 billion per year (Rice & Miller, 1992). Most published studies of schizophrenia have focused primarily on young adult patients; little information exists on the course of schizophrenia in old age. A recent review on the course of schizophrenia in relation to aging concluded that older patients with schizophrenia suffered less from positive (active) symptoms and more from negative (passive) symptoms (Belitsky & McGlashan, 1993). This suggests that a different type of management might be required for elderly patients, which could dramatically affect the allocation of health care resources for this group. We have found that patterns of health care service utilization in individual schizophrenic patients are quite variable (Halpain, Heaton, Warren, Lacro, & Jeste, 1995). Our recent study found that older schizophrenic patients did not differ from their younger counterparts in the utilization of psychiatric health care resources but did need significantly more general medical health care. Limited work has been done specifically on the cost of schizophrenia in late life (Halpain & Jeste, 1994). Further studies are clearly needed in this area before resource planning and allocation occurs and before public policy is enacted.

There has been considerable recent interest in the use of the newer "atypical" antipsychotic medications, such as clozapine and risperidone, in schizophrenic patients. These medications are considerably more expensive than the "typical" or conventional antipsychotics; however, they have been reported to dramatically reduce the total cost of schizophrenia in limited groups of patients. Clozapine has been reported to result in a mean decrease in the total cost of patient care of approximately $23,000 per year per patient, and risperidone has been reported to produce a 73% reduction in the number of hospital days required by patients (Addington et al., 1993). Relatively little work has explored these atypical neuroleptics specifically in older schizophrenics (Jeste, Lacro, Gilbert, Kline, & Kline, 1993).

Another mental disorder that has a highly significant economic impact in this country is Alzheimer's disease. It has been reported that Alzheimer's disease costs the nation an average of nearly $83 billion per year (Ernst & Hay, 1994) and that the cost of care for patients with Alzheimer's disease nearly doubles when they are institutionalized (Hu, Huang, & Cartwright, 1986). One of the most common reasons for institutionalization is difficulty with behavioral management (Rabins et al., 1982). A large proportion of patients with dementia develop behavior problems at some point during the course of their illness. This issue has obvious implications for resource planning and public policy. Many of these patients become more and more dependent on public assistance over time, requiring allocation of a larger proportion of the limited resources.

Depression also produces a significant economic impact on our society, with an estimated cost of $43.7 billion annually (Greenberg, Stiglin, Finkelstein, & Berndt, 1993). Depression is not an uncommon disorder in late life. It has been associated with greatly increased medical comorbidity in all age groups. This may be a significant factor in late life, when individuals typically experience an increase in physical comorbidity. If one considers this fact in conjunction with the decline in quality of life, depression can have a major impact on the older population.

The disorders mentioned above represent just a few examples of the economic costs that mental disorders place on the health care system. There are several factors that also warrant attention when examining the economic impact of late-life mental illness. Gender and ethnicity can both strongly influence access (financial and physical) to health care, treatment patterns, and other important elements related to outcome. Another important factor is the possible underestimation of cost of illness in late life. Economic models tend to weigh heavily the loss of lifetime earnings, the decrease in productive capacity, and the lost value of potential output. It is generally assumed that individuals over age 65 have markedly reduced ability to earn and produce in our society, a limitation of these models that does not take into consideration factors such as asset base or ability to be productive. Models that are more appropriate for aged persons are needed to calculate illness costs.

More formal research on late-life psychiatric disorders must be conducted as well as research on health care service utilization and cost in older patients. Resource allocation will become a critical issue as the population continues to age, resulting in a larger number of individuals expected to require psychiatric resources over time.

REFERENCES

Addington, D. E., Jones, B., Bloom, D., Chouinard, G., Remington, G., & Albright, P. (1993). Reduction of hospital days in chronic schizophrenic patients treated with risperidone: A retrospective study. *Clinical Therapeutics, 15*, 917-926.

Adebimpe, V. R. (1981). Hallucinations and delusions in Black psychiatric patients. *Journal of the National Medical Association, 73*, 517-520.

Allebeck, P. (1989). Schizophrenia: A life-shortening disease. *Schizophrenia Bulletin, 15*, 81-89.

American Psychiatric Association. (1987). *Diagnostic and statistical manual of mental disorders* (3rd ed., rev.). Washington, DC: American Psychiatric Press.

Andia, A. M., & Zisook, S. (1991). Gender differences in schizophrenia: A literature review. *Annals of Clinical Psychiatry, 3*, 333-340.

Andrews, G., Hall, W., Goldstein, G., Lapsley, H., Bartels, R., & Silove, D. (1985). The economic costs of schizophrenia: Implications for public policy. *Archives of General Psychiatry, 42*, 537-543.

Barrett-Connor, E., & Kritz-Silverstein, D. (1993). Estrogen replacement therapy and cognitive function in older women. *Journal of the American Medical Association, 269*(20), 2637-2641.

Becker, J. B. (1990). Direct effect of 17-β-estradiol on striatum: Sex differences in dopamine release. *Synapse, 5*, 157-164.

Belitsky, R., & McGlashan, T. H. (1993). At issue: The manifestations of schizophrenia in late life: A dearth of data. *Schizophrenia Bulletin, 19*, 683-685.

Christenson, R., & Blazer, D. (1984). Epidemiology of persecutory ideation in an elderly population in the community. *American Journal of Psychiatry, 141*, 1088-1091.

Curlick, S. M., Frazier, D., & Katz, I. R. (1991). Psychiatric aspects of long-term care. In J. Sadavoy, L. W. Lazarus, & L. F. Jarvik (Eds.), *Comprehensive review of geriatric psychiatry* (pp. 547-564). Washington, DC: American Psychiatric Press.

Davidson, M., Powchik, V., Haroutunian, V., Harvey, P. D., Perl, D., Losonczy, M. S., Freske, E., Bierer, L., Mohs, R. C., & Davis, K. L. (1991, December). Dementia-like symptoms in elderly schizophrenic patients [Abstract]. *American College of Neuropharmacology*, p. 67.

Dupont, R. M., Lehr, P., Lamoureaux, G., Halpern, S., Harris, M. J., & Jeste, D. V. (1994). Preliminary report: Cerebral blood flow abnormalities in older schizophrenic patients. *Psychiatry Research, 55*, 121-130.

Ernst, R. L., & Hay, J. W. (1994). The U.S. economic and social costs of Alzheimer's disease revisited. *American Journal of Public Health, 84*(8), 1261-1264.

Ferris, S. H., Steinberg, G., & Shulman, E. (1985). Institutionalization of Alzheimer's patients: Reducing precipitating factors through family counseling. *Archives of the Foundation of Thanatology, 12*, 7.

Flint, A., Rifat, S., & Eastwood, R. (1991). Brain lesions and cognitive function in late-life psychosis [Letter]. *British Journal of Psychiatry, 158,* 866.

Freud, S. (1924). On psychotherapy. In *Collected papers, 1,* 249-263. London: Hogarth Press. Weiner Medizinische Presse, translated by Bernays, J.

Giltin, M. J., & Pasnau, R. O. (1989). Psychiatric syndromes linked to reproductive function in women: A review of current knowledge. *American Journal of Psychiatry, 146,* 1413-1422.

Glantz, R. H., Bieliauskas, L., & Paleologos, N. (1986). Behavioral indicators of hallucinosis in levodopa treated Parkinson's disease. In M. D. Yahr & K. J. Bergmann (Eds.), *Advances in Neurology* (pp. 417-420). New York: Raven.

Glazer, W. M., Morgenstern, H., & Doucette, J. (1994). Race and tardive dyskinesia among outpatients at a CMHC. *Hospital and Community Psychiatry, 45,* 38-42.

Goldberg, T. E., Hyde, T. M., Kleinman, J. E., & Weinberger, D. R. (1993). The course of schizophrenia: Neuropsychological evidence for a static encephalopathy. *Schizophrenia Bulletin, 19,* 797-804.

Greenberg, P. E., Stiglin, L. E., Finkelstein, S. N., & Berndt, E. R. (1993). The economic burden of depression in 1990. *Journal of Clinical Psychiatry, 54,* 405-418.

Gurland, B. J., & Cross, P. S. (1982). Epidemiology of psychopathology in old age: Some implications for clinical services. *Psychiatric Clinics of North America, 5,* 11-26.

Halpain, M. C., Heaton, S. C., Warren, K. A., Lacro, J. P., & Jeste, D. V. (1995). Health care utilization patterns in late-life schizophrenia: Case histories. In M. Bergener, J. Brocklehurst, & S. Kanowski (Eds.), *Aging, Health, and Healing.* New York: Springer.

Halpain, M. C., & Jeste, D. V. (1994). The cost of schizophrenia in late life. *American Journal of Geriatric Psychiatry, 2*(3).

Harris, M. J., & Jeste, D. V. (1988). Late-onset schizophrenia: An overview. *Schizophrenia Bulletin, 14,* 39-55.

Harris, M. J., Lindamer, L. A., Heaton, S. C., Paulsen, J. S., McAdams, L. A., Zisook, S., Heaton, R. K., & Jeste, D. V. (in press). Relationship of gender, age, and subtype to clinical and neuropsychological characteristics of schizophrenia. *Schizophrenia Research.*

Heaton, R., Paulsen, J., McAdams, L. A., Kuck, J., Zisook, S., Braff, D., Harris, M. J., & Jeste, D. V. (1994). Neuropsychological deficits in schizophrenia: Relationship to age, chronicity, and dementia. *Archives of General Psychiatry, 51,* 469-476.

Henderson, V. W., Paganini-Hill, A., Emanuel, C. K., Dunn, M. E., & Buckwalter, J. G. (1994). Estrogen replacement therapy in older women. *Archives of Neurology, 51,* 896-900.

Hu, T., Huang, L., & Cartwright, W. (1986). Evaluation of the costs of caring for the senile demented elderly: A pilot study. *The Gerontologist, 26,* 158-163.

Jeste, D. V., & Caligiuri, M. P. (1991). Biological research in geriatric psychiatry. *Biological Psychiatry, 30,* 855-856.

Jeste, D. V., Caligiuri, M. P., Paulsen, J. S., Heaton, R. K., Lacro, J. P., Harris, M. J., Bailey, A., Fell, R. L., & McAdams, L. A. (in press). Risk of tardive dyskinesia in older patients: A prospective longitudinal study of 266 patients. *Archives of General Psychiatry.*

Jeste, D. V., Fitten, L. J., Clemons, B., O'Neal, S., & Harris, M. J. (1993). A survey of geriatric psychiatrists in the US regarding research. *International Journal of Geriatric Psychiatry, 8,* 13-18.

Jeste, D. V., Harris, M. J., Krull, A., Kuck, J., McAdams, L. A., & Heaton, R. (1995). Late-onset schizophrenia: Clinical and neuropsychological characteristics. *American Journal of Psychiatry, 152,* 722-730.

Jeste, D. V., Lacro, J. P., Gilbert, P. L., Kline, J., & Kline, N. (1993). Treatment of late-life schizophrenia with neuroleptics. *Schizophrenia Bulletin, 19,* 817-830.

Jeste, D. V., Lohr, J. B., Clark, K., & Wyatt, R. J. (1988). Pharmacological treatment of tardive dyskinesia in the 1980s. *Journal of Clinical Psychopharmacology, 8*(Suppl.), 38S-48S.

Jeste, D. V., & Wyatt, R. J. (1982). *Understanding and treating tardive dyskinesia.* New York: Guilford.

Kahana, R. (1978). Psychoanalysis in later life. *Journal of Geriatric Psychiatry, 11,* 37-49.

Kampen, D. L., & Sherwin, B. B. (1994). Estrogen use and verbal memory in healthy postmenopausal women. *Obstetrics and Gynecology, 83,* 979-983.

Kane, J. M., Jeste, D. V., Barnes, T. R. E., Casey, D. E., Cole, J. O., Davis, J. M., Gualtieri, C. T., Schooler, N. R., Sprague, R. L., & Wettstein, R. M. (1992). *Tardive dyskinesia: A task force report of the American Psychiatric Association.* Washington, DC: American Psychiatric Association.

Kaplan, H. I., & Sadock, B. J. (1988). *Synopsis of Psychiatry* (5th ed.). Baltimore: Williams & Wilkins.

Kay, D. W. K., & Roth, M. (1961). Environmental and hereditary factors in the schizo-phrenias of old age ("late paraphrenia") and their bearing on the general problem of causation in schizophrenia. *Journal of Mental Science, 107,* 649-686.

Kumar, B. (1976). Treatment of tardive dyskinesia with deanol. *American Journal of Psychiatry, 133,* 978.

Lacro, J. P., & Jeste, D. V. (1995). The role of ethnicity in the development of tardive dyskinesia. In N. V. P. Nair, R. Yassa, & D. V. Jeste (Eds.), *Neuroleptic-induced movement disorders.* London: Cambridge University Press.

Lesser, I. M., Miller, B. L., Boone, K. B., Hill-Gutierrez, E., & Mena, I. (1991). Brain injury and cognitive function in late-onset psychotic depression. *Journal of Neuropsy-chiatry and Clinical Neurosciences, 3,* 33-40.

Lindsey, K. P., & Paul, G. L. (1989). Involuntary commitments to public institutions: Issues involving the overrepresentation of Blacks and assessment of relevant function-ing. *Psychological Bulletin, 106,* 171-183.

McGuire, T. G. (1991). Measuring the economic costs of schizophrenia. *Schizophrenia Bulletin, 17,* 375-388.

Nasar, S. (1994, November 13). The lost years of a Nobel laureate. *New York Times.* Business Section, p. 1.

Nemiroff, R. A., & Colarusso, C. A. (1985). *The race against time: Psychotherapy and psycho-analysis in the second half of life.* New York: Plenum Press.

Patterson, T. L., Kaplan, R. M., Grant, I., Semple, S. J., Moscona, S., Koch, W. L., Harris, M. J., & Jeste, D. V. (submitted). Quality of well-being in late-life psychosis. *Psychiatry Research.*

Pearlson, G. D., Tune, L. E., Wong, D. F., Aylward, E. H., Barta, P. E., Powers, R. E., Chase, G. A., Harris, G. J., & Rabins, P. V. (1993). Quantitative D2 dopamine receptor PET and structural MRI changes in late onset schizophrenia. *Schizophrenia Bulletin, 19,* 783-795.

Phillips, S. M., & Sherwin, B. B. (1992). Effects of estrogen on memory function in surgically menopausal women. *Psychoneuroendocrinology, 17,* 485-495.

Prager, S., & Jeste, D. V. (1993). Sensory impairment in late-life schizophrenia. *Schizophrenia Bulletin, 19,* 755-772.

Rabins, P. V., Mace, N. L., & Lucas, M. J. (1982). The impact of dementia on the family. *Journal of the American Medical Association, 248,* 333-335.

Randolph, E. T., Escobar, J. I., Paz, D. H., & Forsythe, A. B. (1985). Ethnicity and reporting of schizophrenic symptoms. *Journal of Nervous and Mental Disease, 173,* 332-340.

Rice, D. P., & Miller, L. S. (1992). *The economic burden of schizophrenia.* Paper presented at the Sixth Biennial Conference on the Economics of Mental Health, Bethesda, MD.

Riecher-Rössler, A., Häfner, H., Dutsch-Strobel, A., Oster, M., Stumbaum, M., van Gulick-Bailer, M., & Löffler, W. (1994). Further evidence for a specific role of estradiol in schizophrenia? *Biological Psychiatry, 36,* 492-495.

Rockwell, E., Jackson, E., Vilke, G. & Jeste, D. V. (1994). A study of delusions in a large cohort of Alzheimer disease patients. *American Journal of Geriatric Psychiatry, 2,* 157-164.

Rovner, B. W., Kafonek, S., Filipp, L., Lucas, M. J., & Folftein, M. F. (1986). Prevalence of mental illness in a community nursing home. *American Journal of Psychiatry, 143,* 1446-1449.

Roy, A. (1990). Relationship between depression and suicidal behavior in schizophrenia. In L. E. DeLisi (Ed.), *Depression in schizophrenia* (pp. 39-58). Washington, DC: American Psychiatric Press.

Rupp, A., & Keith, S. J. (1993). The costs of schizophrenia: Assessing the burden. *Psychiatric Clinics of North America, 16,* 413-423.

Seeman, M. V., & Lang, M. (1990). The role of estrogens in schizophrenia gender differences. *Schizophrenia Bulletin, 16,* 185-194.

Sherwin, B. B. (1988). Estrogen and/or androgen replacement therapy and cognitive functioning in surgically menopausal women. *Psychoneuroendocrinology, 13,* 345-357.

Shulman, E., & Steinberg, G. (1985). Emotional reactions of Alzheimer's caregivers in support group settings. [Abstract] *The Gerontologist, 24,* 158.

Sramek, J. J., Sayles, M. A., & Simpson, G. M. (1986). Neuroleptic dosage for Asians: A failure to replicate. *American Journal of Psychiatry, 143,* 535-536.

Stern, Y., Albert, M., Brandt, J., Jacobs, D. M., Tang, M., Marder, K., Bell, K., Sano, M., Devanand, D. P., Bylsma, F., & Lafleche, G. (1994). Utility of extrapyramidal signs and psychosis as predictors of cognitive and functional decline, nursing home admission, and death in Alzheimer's disease: Prospective analyses from the predictors study. *Neurology, 44,* 2300-2307.

Strickland, T. L., Ranganath, V., Lin, K., Poland, R. E., Mendoza, R., & Smith, M. W. (1991). Psychopharmacologic considerations in the treatment of Black American populations. *Psychopharmacology Bulletin, 27,* 441-448.

Tancredi, L. R. (1988). Malpractice and tardive dyskinesia: A conceptual dilemma. *Journal of Clinical Psychopharmacology, 8,* 71S-76S.

Thomas, C. L. (1985). *Taber's cyclopedic medical dictionary* (15th ed.). Philadelphia: Davis.

Tomb, D. A. (1992). *Psychiatry* (4th ed.). Baltimore: Williams & Wilkins.

U.S. Congress Office of Technology Assessment. (1987). *Losing a million minds: Confronting the tragedy of Alzheimer's disease and other dementias* (OTA-BA-323).

Vitols, M. M., Water, H. G., & Keeler, M. H. (1963). Hallucinations and delusions in White and Negro schizophrenics. *American Journal of Psychiatry, 120,* 472-476.

Wahl, O. F., & Hunter, J. (1992). Are gender effects being neglected in schizophrenia research? *Schizophrenia Bulletin, 18,* 313-317.

Wragg, R., & Jeste, D. V. (1989). Overview of depression and psychosis in Alzheimer's disease. *American Journal of Psychiatry, 146,* 577-587.

CHAPTER 4

Stressors and Adaptation
in Late Life

Leonard I. Pearlin and Marilyn McKean Skaff

This chapter has two broad goals: first, to identify the constellations of stressors to which people may be exposed as they move through the ranks of advanced age and, second, to consider the resources and dispositions that enable older people to adapt to the changing demands and conditions of their lives. The conceptual framework for our discussions is detailed below. We use stressors to refer to the hardships, problems, and other circumstances that can affect people's well-being adversely and adaptation to refer to the maintenance of well-being in the face of evolving and difficult circumstances.

Several caveats are necessary at the outset of this discussion. First, although a great deal has been learned about stress and its effects in recent decades, strikingly little of the research has been oriented to learning about the distribution of stressors across the ranks of the old. Particularly lacking are studies that identify the onset and effects of chronic stressors that may be intertwined with aging. Samples in stress studies typically either have been tilted toward younger adults or, when representative of a community population, have contained too few older people for intensive analyses. Related difficulties are the limitations of chronological age itself as a viable construct and the tendency to aggregate multiple ranks of older people, lumping together, for example, all those "65 years and older." This practice masks from view the differences among people who fall within such large age categories.

Partly because of such practices, we know less than we should about the stressors that distinctively impinge on older populations and, indeed, about whether old age is a particularly difficult time of life in comparison to other segments of the life course. The gaps in our knowledge are all the more serious because what is learned from studies of younger people usually cannot be simply extrapolated and applied to older people; the difficulties people face vary across age groups. Moreover, even where potentially stressful conditions are objectively similar, their meaning and, therefore, the way they are experienced may differ with age (Aldwin, 1990; Elder & Liker, 1982; Folkman, Lazarus, Pimley, & Novacek, 1987; Wortman & Silver, 1992). Meaning can be shaped by several factors, including one's position on a life-course trajectory. For example, the loss of a spouse at age 40, when one is still caring for dependent children, will have different consequences than the same loss at age 80. Moreover, the old and the young represent different cohorts, each having roots in a different meaning-shaping historical milieu. Again, the very fact that it is necessary to speculate about issues of this sort underscores both the shaky underpinnings of our knowledge and the need to be cautious in assuming that we can apply what we know of younger people to their elders.

People of the same age do not necessarily face the same stressful circumstances. Not only does the unique biography that each individual brings to old age contribute to this variability, but status within the larger society also underlies the variability of the stress process. For example, exposure to stressors is likely to vary with economic resources, gender, ethnicity, and educational level, and there is no evidence that the importance of such socioeconomic divisions is reduced by advancing age. Both exposure to stressors and the resources to deal with stressors successfully are prominently influenced by one's location within social structural systems, and this is as true among the very old as among younger adults (Pearlin & Schooler, 1978). Any future inquiry into the stress process as it affects people in late life, therefore, must take account of the variability that parallels lines of social and economic demarcation. Again, empirically based knowledge of such variability is currently not sufficiently established.

Finally, turning to the caveat regarding the limitations of reliance on chronological age, the reason for this assertion is that people of the same age can and often do differ widely in the trajectories of their life courses. For example, one 70-year-old might be fully engaged in occupational life and all the associated routine and obligations, while another might have been retired for 5 years and completely restructured life around the absence of occupation. This kind of difference in life-course direction and location, we propose, limits the usefulness of age as an analytic construct in the study of stress. Consequently, we avoid specifying age in numbers of years and instead employ general descriptors such as "early old" or "oldest old." We assume that within these broad categories are people who are dissimilar with regard to their engagement with or disengagement from social roles, expansion or contraction of network activities, and scope of functional health and dependencies.

THE STRESS PROCESS FRAMEWORK

Much of our approach to the discussion of stress and adaptation in late life is organized around the framework of the stress process, and consequently, we will present an overview of some of the features of this framework. The stress process has three major interrelated components: stressors, moderators, and outcomes. Its development was aimed at capturing the actual flow of people's experience as they face serious stressors and was spurred by findings that emerged from longitudinal research allowing the observation over time of people under stress (Pearlin, Lieberman, Menaghan, & Mullan, 1981). In part, too, it was developed in reaction to a predominant paradigm that views stress as a consequence of exposure to one or more life events. The exclusive attention to eventful experience necessarily overlooked the more potent chronic or repeated stressors that may impinge on people.

Stress Proliferation

Equally important, the preoccupation with events overlooked what we subsequently have come to recognize as *stress proliferation*: the tendency for one serious stressor to lead to others. The initial stressors are referred to as *primary stressors*, and those resulting from them are *secondary stressors*. A primary stressor may be an undesired event or a more enduring problem, and the proliferated secondary stressors similarly might be of different types. For example, when a person falls and breaks a hip, it makes shopping for food difficult, creates economic strain, and prevents leisure activities. Additional examples are plentiful, each underscoring that a comprehensive view of the challenges under which people labor requires that we look for constellations of stressors that evolve and change over time. Whether we study young adults or people of advanced age, the potential hardships to which they may be exposed must be seen, first, within the larger contexts of the organization of their lives and, second, as clusters of problems that change and develop over time. Any attempt to understand stress among old people by looking at a limited number of hardships within a limited time frame can be misleading. Ideally, our observations of people should cast a wide net and should enable us to track life-course trajectories over a considerable time.

Moderators

Part of the reason we think of stress as a process, then, stems from the common phenomenon of stress proliferation. Moderators are another component of the stress process that contributes to its dynamic character. Essentially, moderators are conditions that regulate the stressors' impact on well-being. Among the conditions typically treated as moderators in stress research are coping repertoires, social support, and certain elements of self-concept, such as mastery. Moderators such as these help to explain why people are affected differently by what appear to be similar stressors; that is, the same stressors will have different effects when people react to them with different moderating resources (Cohen & Edwards, 1989). However, changes in the configuration of stressors can alter the resources themselves. Continued hardship, for example, can lead to changes in coping strategies, to a burnout of social support, or to an erosion of mastery (Aldwin, 1992; Skaff & Pearlin, 1994). It is also important to note that little information exists about possible normative changes in the possession and use of moderating resources as people move through late life. We shall have more to say about these resources in our later discussion of adaptive mechanisms.

100

Outcomes

The final major component of the stress process framework entails the *outcomes*: the direct and interactive effects of stressors and moderators on people's well-being. Criteria of successful aging, such as life satisfaction, are regarded as outcomes in studies of aging (Ryff, 1989a, b). However, many other outcomes can be drawn from multiple levels of organismic functioning, including psychological and behavioral disorders (e.g., substance abuse, depression, and anxiety) and functional and physical impairments. There is also mounting evidence that the suppression of the immune system is a consequence of exposure to stressors (Kiecolt-Glaser, Dura, Speicher, Trask, & Glaser, 1991). Just as different groups may be exposed to different arrays of stressors and have access to different resources, the ways stress outcomes are manifested by people also may vary with their social and economic characteristics. For example, there is substantial evidence that women are more likely to express distress in depressive affect while men, by contrast, are more likely to manifest it in aggressive behavior or substance abuse (Aneshensel, Rutter, & Lachenbruch, 1991; McCall, 1989; Pearlin, 1989). As yet, no inquiries have examined whether the outcomes of the stress process vary with life stage.

THE UNIVERSE OF STRESSORS IN LATE LIFE

We turn now to examine in closer detail the changing types of stressors people confront as they progress through late life. At the outset it is necessary to shed any assumption that advanced age is necessarily a difficult time of life because of inevitable decline in health and vigor or because people must confront a future that no longer stretches ahead indefinitely. Old age is difficult for many, but the view of old age as a time of stress and despair is unsupported by systematic research (Baltes & Baltes, 1990; Gatz & Hurwicz, 1990; Ryff, 1989b). In this connection, keep in mind our earlier caveat that there is little established empirical knowledge concerning late-life stress. Some of our discussions, therefore, are necessarily based on conjecture, albeit educated conjecture; some on preliminary information emerging from interviews we are currently conducting with older people; and some, though not as many as we would like, on fairly firm evidence. It should also be recognized that although we may single out a particular type of stressor for discussion, the stressor might be only one of many acting on the life of the elder.

Our discussion will focus on two types of stressors, life events and chronic strains. Chronic strains include ambient, role, and quotidian strains, each meriting detailed treatment. However, we shall limit ourselves to a brief description that highlights and illustrates each of them.

Life Events

Life events comprise a large class of stressors that has been at the center of much stress research for the past two decades. The overall relationship between exposure to stressful events and life-course location would suggest the eventful experience is not a dominant source of stress among the old (Dean & Ensel, 1982; Ensel, 1991). In general, there appears to be a negative association between age and the likelihood that people will report having recently experienced stressful life events (Murrell, Norris, & Grote, 1988). The epidemiological distribution of life events may, in fact, be tilted toward younger adults, but some caution is necessary before accepting this notion because of the inventories often used to assess exposure to life events. The types of events included in these inventories tend to tap the earlier part of the life course more thoroughly than the later part, covering events associated with the process of younger people settling into economic, occupational, marital, and parental roles. It is interesting to note in this regard that one inquiry reports that the event most frequently mentioned by old people is a trip out of town (Murrell, Norris, & Hutchins, 1984). We believe that the organization of older people's lives simply exposes them to fewer eventful experiences than is the case for the younger; at the same time, we recognize that researchers have not equally sampled life events representative of different ends of the life course.

Knowing whether in reality older people experience fewer events may be less germane than knowing whether they experience more or fewer events of certain kinds. Following the theoretical lead of Selye (1956), researchers initially assumed that changes brought about by events of all types placed a burden on the adaptive capacities of individuals and were therefore inimical to well-being. Later work, however, revealed that it is largely *unscheduled or undesired* events that are likely to be stressful (George, 1989; Murrell et al., 1984). Scheduled events are those that are linked to the normative transitions of the life cycle—such as marriage, parenthood, the empty nest, and grandparenthood—and can be anticipated and prepared for. In late middle and old age, these events are likely to entail the loss of roles and status; however, some losses, most notably retirement, have been observed to have positive effects on well-being (Aldwin, 1990). At any rate, these kinds of scheduled losses generally do not appear to have deleterious effects (George, 1980).

Health-related events are among the most common events experienced by older persons and, when they occur, appear to have a more depressive effect than many other types of events they experience (Ensel, 1991; Murrell et al., 1988). However, it may be difficult to distinguish the depressive effects of *acute* health events from those of *chronic* problems that result from those events.

The deaths of generational and age peers understandably increase in frequency as one ages. Evidence suggests that network losses involving friends and kin may be most keenly felt by women (Holahan, Holahan, & Belk, 1984; Kessler & McLeod, 1984). The loss of a spouse, on the other hand, may have a depressive effect on men and women alike, an effect that is typically observed to last for about 6 months before it begins to recede (Mullan, 1992). Death may also affect well-being through its impact on moderating resources. Specifically, the loss of a spouse or other person to whom the individual is attached may result in adverse outcomes, not only because of the death itself but also because part of one's network that provided social support may be lost.

The normative loss of older loved ones, then, can have a negative impact on survivors; however, some studies indicate that even such a loss can have positive effects on the individual, including increased social contact and improved self-concept (Calhoun & Tedeschi, 1989; Lopata, 1979; Mullan, 1992; Skaff & Pearlin, 1994; Wortman & Silver, 1992). For example, Lopata reported that widows in her study gained a new sense of independence and competence after the deaths of their husbands. Likewise, in our study of Alzheimer's caregivers, family members reported an increase in both their sense of mastery and the amount of contact they had with other people following the death of the ill relative. Positive effects, however, may be less likely in instances of nonnormative loss events, such as the death of a young loved one. As longevity increases parents are more likely to experience the death of a child. There are indications that this is the most stressful event one can experience (Aldwin, 1990), and we suspect that bereaved parents are often unable to return to an earlier state of well-being.

Both death and health events can set in motion circumstances that lead to secondary stressors, as, for example, when the loss of a spouse results in severe economic strains or a health event leads to increased dependency on others. Attempts to evaluate the importance of a loss, therefore, must look beyond the event itself. Aside from losses and other stressful events in their own lives, older people may be deeply affected by untoward events that impinge on others to whom they are close—"nonegocentric" events (Aldwin, 1990). An injury to a child or grandchild, the breakup of a marriage, or an involuntary job loss in the family can cause pain to the older relative as well as to those more directly involved in the unscheduled event. Aldwin's work suggests that such events may be more painful for those older persons who lack the resources to offer support to the family member or friend who experiences the event directly.

A final observation about the effects of eventful experience in late life concerns differences in their timing and clarity among different social and economic groups. As noted, most scheduled events entail transitions into and, more frequently, out of institutional roles and statuses. The points at which these events occur along the life course and, therefore, their meanings apparently vary among socioeconomic, ethnic, and gender groups. It has been observed that the occurrence of transitional events may be accelerated among some racial and ethnic groups, a phenomenon not explained by the pace of aging or differences in longevity (Barresi, 1987; Gelfand, 1994; Gibson, 1987). Retirement from occupational life is a case in point, since minority members are disproportionately on the margins of mainstream occupations. The employment history of marginalized workers, in turn, influences whether and when they define themselves as retired. If work history includes frequent periods of unemployment, a clear transition may be lacking; as Gibson (1987) points out, the "unretired retired" may continue to work sporadically well into old age. Ambiguity surrounding retirement may also occur for women whose work history includes multiple entrances and exits from the labor force.

Aside from occupational retirement, a number of transitions involving family roles may occur earlier for some ethnic and economic class groups (Gibson, 1987). In groups where parenthood is likely to occur earlier, the emptying of the nest and grandparenthood will be accelerated as well. Indeed, grandparenthood may sometimes be converted to surrogate parenthood, perhaps casting some ambiguity over the transition to grandparental status and potentially interfering with other normative transitions (Minkler & Roe, 1993).

At this time, we cannot be sure whether the timing and finality of transitions themselves constitute stressful conditions. But it is important to recognize that whatever the problems and dislocations that might result from these transitions, their distribution follows the lines of social and economic demarcation. It is also worth repeating what is by now a familiar theme: Whatever the stressful event and regardless of whether it is scheduled or unscheduled, over time it is quite likely to become folded into clusters of other stressful conditions, some of them secondary stressors.

Chronic Strains

The mix of potential stressors that may be intertwined with people's lives includes some that do not necessarily arise discretely in time but, unlike events, surface insidiously and persist. Among stressors that are more recurrent or durable, three types of chronic strains can be distinguished: *ambient, role,* and *quotidian* strains.

Ambient Strains. Ambient strains pertain to the junctures of person-environment interactions that the person finds problematic. It is our impression, supported by an ongoing series of interviews we are conducting with old people, that as people climb the ranks of old age they become increasingly threatened by certain qualities of their community and neighborhood environments. For some, relocation may place them in an unfamiliar environment, among strangers. But even if they remain in the same place, the environment may become unfamiliar. Physical safety, for example, may be a source of stress that for many expands in importance as they age. People may feel more vulnerable to environmental threats even when the presence of such threats has not increased. First, growing physical frailty may leave people feeling that they would be unable to defend themselves should the need arise. Second, in the organic evolution of neighborhoods new faces replace familiar ones. Such changes, which can dramatically alter the composition of a neighborhood in a few years, can leave older residents living among strangers. Finally, if friends and acquaintances are among those replaced, older people may be separated from support networks of people concerned about and protective of their well-being.

Features of the community other than those that reduce the sense of safety and security may also act as stressors. For example, old people are sensitive to the deterioration of housing and to the neatness and orderliness of their communities. A decline in the aesthetics of their surroundings can leave them feeling that they are on a sinking ship with no way to abandon it. Transportation and access to certain amenities can also change dramatically with relocation or changes in the community. The convenience of shopping, proximity to physicians and medical care, and availability of recreational facilities such as senior centers and movie theaters are among the amenities whose absence may constitute ambient stressors.

Role Strains. Role strains are ongoing problems and hardships that may arise within the context of institutionalized social roles, especially those involving family relationships. Families are highly complex institutions, encompassing an intricate web of expectations and obligations, mutual support, and intense emotional attachments. The potential for conflict within these relationships is great. Because family relationships are important to most people, family problems are likely to exert considerable impact.

For several reasons, relationships between older and younger generations may be particularly difficult. For example, by the time people become old they are able to evaluate the developmental trajectories of their adult children. In old age, people must acknowledge the disjuncture between the dreams and values they might have nurtured for their children and their children's actual accomplishments. Their children might not be as successful or driven to achievement as they would like, they might have scorned their religious roots (or have been born again), they might drink too much, or they might not be raising their own children in a way that meets the approval of their parents. We discuss below mechanisms of

106

adaptation, but we can note here that although families may provide important social support to aging persons, when expected support is not forthcoming or is given in a way that diminishes the autonomy or self-respect of the recipient, this itself can be a potent stressor. There is some evidence that among the oldest old, people actually loosen their intense involvement in family affairs and become more oriented to their own inner enrichment (McCarthy, 1994; Neugarten, 1977). It is our guess that some of this emotional separation is a way to avoid the pains of disappointment that can be engendered in the family.

Two other chronic strains commonly found in late life are financial hardship and chronic health problems. Although strictly speaking these are not in themselves role strains, they nevertheless can affect the enactment of institutional roles. The chronic health problems of old age, for example, are particularly likely to proliferate to other areas of life. Financial strains, too, can affect virtually every domain of activity and relationship of older people. On the other hand, there is some evidence that because health problems and financial constraints are normative in late life, they may be less potent sources of stress for older than for younger people (George, 1989; Hughes, Blazer, & George, 1988). As we will discuss later, the meaning of potential stressors can be shaped by the expectations that prevail at a particular stage of life.

One type of role strain, caregiving, has come under a great deal of scrutiny in recent years, and consequently, a great deal is known about it. Caring for an impaired family member is likely to involve people in the late stages of their lives, particularly when the care is being given to a spouse. Elsewhere we have described caregiving as an unexpected role (Pearlin & Aneshensel, 1994). Although the aging of society makes this an increasingly common role, as people contemplate their own life-course trajectories, they typically do not factor in caregiving as something that is likely to occupy them for a significant segment of their later years. However, this role is capable of not only occupying people but engulfing their entire lives (Skaff & Pearlin, 1992).

The stress process outlined above is nowhere better exemplified than in caregiving (Pearlin, Mullan, Semple, & Skaff, 1990). It is possible to observe a panoply of primary stressors directly anchored in caregiving activities. They may include the assistance required by the care recipient to satisfy basic needs, such as feeding and grooming, and difficulties in communicating with and managing the problematic behaviors of the impaired patient. Primary stressors can also be gauged through certain subjective states of the caregiver, such as the sense of being overloaded by an irreducible mountain of responsibilities or the feeling of being a captive of an unwanted role.

Over time, these primary stressors generate a host of secondary stressors. For example, the continued demands of caregiving may be a seedbed of family conflicts (Semple, 1992); they often result in financial strains, and for caregivers having outside employment, severe dilemmas may arise at the junctures of caregiving and occupation. Finally, secondary stressors may also appear in the form of painful intrapsychic strains, such as the sense that absorption into caregiving has resulted in the loss of the caregiver's former identity. Once they are created, all of these secondary stressors become independent sources of stress, often more potent than those that are primary. We cannot emphasize too much that unexpectedly emergent caregiving roles must be included in an attempt to chart the range of stressors to which people may be exposed during late life.

Quotidian Stressors. We employ the construct of quotidian stressors to direct attention to a type of hardship that is distinct from those we have been describing. Whereas ambient stressors reside in conditions within the community and neighborhood environments of people and role strains are conditions embedded in the relationships and activities within the context of major social roles, quotidian stressors are those encountered within the microenvironment. More concretely, they are the ordinary logistical problems people face in the course of their daily activities. Studies of the oldest old who are living independently in the community have focused attention on this class of stressors (Barer, 1993).

There is nothing exotic about quotidian stressors; they overlap somewhat with what others have called "hassles" (Folkman et al., 1987). Stressors of this type may make their first appearance during the early years of old age and grow insidiously to become commonplace among the oldest old. Quotidian stressors may include such ordinary activities as climbing the stairs to reach a bathroom, bending over to remove food from a refrigerator, managing the steps on a bus, seeing the fine print in a telephone book, changing a lightbulb, removing trash for pickup, and so on.

One might judge that these are not stressors but trivial activities that are quickly accomplished and immediately forgotten—a valid observation for most of us. It ceases to be valid, of course, among people of advanced age for whom these simple tasks stand as major obstacles to be overcome each and every day (Barer, 1993). Indeed, for these people it is accurate to characterize such stressors as constituting the salient elements of daily life. For the frail, daily life may be planned and organized around problematic activities to which the younger and healthier would give little or no attention.

We wish to emphasize that whatever its type, the same event or chronic stressor may have very different consequences among people who experience it, including people of the same age. Several factors may explain this variability. One explanation concerns the importance or salience of the area in which stressors arise. Stressors that occur in life domains or social roles that are of central importance to the individual should have more impact on well-being than those residing in a peripheral domain (Krause, 1994). For example, arthritis may be a minor irritation for someone who loves to read but takes on much greater meaning for an artist who is no longer able to paint. Both the salience of the domain in which a stressor occurs and whether a stressor occurs at an expected time can influence sense of control and as a consequence help to shape the meaning of the stressors to the individual.

In an important sense, then, whether a given condition constitutes a stressor depends on one's capabilities for dealing with the condition as well as the value and meaning one gives to that particular domain. More broadly, the effects of life circumstances on the well-being of people typically depend on the moderating resources people are able to mobilize in response to the circumstances. It is to these issues that we now turn.

MECHANISMS OF ADAPTATION

In our judgment, virtually all old people experience at least some stressors that are potentially inimical to their well-being. It is also our judgment that despite such exposure, most old people are able to maintain their well-being and to function at a positive level. To emphasize both elders' exposure to potentially damaging circumstances and their general well-being is less of a contradiction than it might at first appear. The explanation lies in the resources people possess and use. These resources, we shall argue, enable them to be truly adaptive and not merely the passive objects of life exigencies.

The resources considered here include coping, social support, and mastery—one's sense of control. We do regard these resources not as stable attributes of the individual but more as characteristics that ebb and flow as experiences unfold across the later years. Moderating resources have a ubiquitous and dynamic presence in the stress process. Thus, although they are usually thought of only in terms of their capacity to cushion the deleterious effects of stressors, the resources themselves may be enhanced or diminished by exposure to stressors (Skaff & Pearlin, 1994). It is useful, therefore, to think of resources not simply as affecting the stress process from the outside but instead as being embedded in a changing set of interrelationships with the other components of the process. From this perspective, it is simplistic to assume that once one possesses a resource, it remains in some stable form, ready to be called on whatever the changing nature of the stressors one faces.

Coping

With these considerations in mind, we look first at the coping repertoires of old people. *Coping*, of course, refers to the things that people do to avoid being harmed by stressful conditions. Three functions of coping have been distinguished: management of the situations giving rise to the stressors, management of the meaning of the problematic situations, and management of the stresses resulting from the situation (Pearlin & Schooler, 1978). Age differences have been found not only in the numbers of strategies people employ but also in the types of strategies they use. Specifically, older people are less likely to direct their coping efforts toward managing the situation through problem solving. Correspondingly, they employ more strategies for managing meaning and controlling symptoms of stress—functions that are sometimes collectively referred to as *emotion-focused coping* (Chiriboga, 1992; Folkman et al., 1987; Martin et al., 1992; Meeks, Carstensen, Tamsky, Wright, & Pellegrini, 1989; Quayhagen & Quayhagen, 1982).

To the extent that problem-solving behaviors represent a rational and efficacious way to cope with adversity, clinicians and counselors tend to favor them. However, we should not assumee that because they rely more on other strategies elders are not effective copers. Many of the stressors experienced by older people, such as frailty and "irreversible loss" (Pearlin & Mullan, 1992), are relatively intractable and not easily modified by problem solving. This means not that older people necessarily passively resign themselves to overpowering fate but that they turn more to reshaping the meaning of exigencies as a way to reduce their threat. Thus, specific coping responses should not be categorized as universally effective or ineffective for all groups; rather, coping entails an evolving, selective use of skills as one moves across the life course (Kahana, 1992).

Because the management of meaning tends to be more prominent as a coping strategy among older people, it is useful to describe two mechanisms by which it is exercised. One entails the restructuring of priorities and the realignment of the centrality of life domains. Problems arising around activities, relationships, or aspirations that are highly valued and with which one is ego involved can result in considerable distress. One way to minimize the impact of stressors arising within an important life domain is to move the domain to a position of reduced importance or centrality. Such movement, which typically is less purposive than outside one's awareness, is consistent with the suggestion of Brandtstädter and Baltes-Götz (1990) that with aging there is a shift that accommodates the realities of constraints and hardships posed by the aging process. The devaluation of problematic areas of life does not eliminate the problems but may help to render them less onerous.

A second mechanism is positive comparison. Although people of all ages use their own age cohort as a frame of reference for self-evaluation, this is probably most common among people of advanced age. That is, they tend to describe their lives and problems in light of what is to be normatively expected at their location on the life course (Lerner & Gignac, 1992). Friends and family also serve as reference points, giving all of us the opportunity to cast about selectively to find someone who is at least no better off than ourselves, if not actually worse off. At any rate, people confronting hardships are reassured to know that the slings and arrows are aimed not only at themselves but also at others in their networks, especially others of the same age cohort.

Social Support

Perhaps the most important resource people can have in their armory is social support, a moderator that may be particularly beneficial to people facing problems that are resistant to individual coping efforts (Hansson & Carpenter, 1994). Yet while a plethora of studies indicates that social support can cushion the deleterious impact of life problems, the conditions under which this cushioning effect is maximized are far from clear (Artonucci, 1990). However, enough is known to invite the suggestion that the efficacy of social support is enhanced by being able to call on particular kinds of people for particular forms of support while contending with particular types of problems. To clarify this statement, we need to recognize that the rubric of social support subsumes a variety of forms of assistance, the major ones being instrumental and emotional supports (Dean, Kolody, Wood, & Engel, 1989; Pearlin, Aneshensel, Mullan, & Whitlatch, 1995). What we propose is that the efficacy of support depends on who the sources of support are and whether the type of support that is given is appropriate to the problem. The efficacy of social support as a moderator, we submit, depends on its specialized fit with extant stressors.

Evidence for the specialization of fit comes from several sources. For example, it appears that children are not as effective sources of emotional support for their newly widowed mothers (Bankoff, 1983) as other widows are. This raises the hypothesis that support from people who have experienced the same problems is especially efficacious. Further insights into specialization are drawn from our own studies of Alzheimer's caregivers (Pearlin et al., 1995). Thus, without going into possible explanations, we can report that only instrumental help provided by trained personnel was useful in preventing a sense of overload created by the patient's dependences on assistance in such activities as bathing and feeding. By contrast, only instrumental assistance by informal sources—friends and relatives—was effective in reducing the overload that results from the problematic and unruly behavior of the patient. Finally, emotional support, but not instrumental, helped cushion the depressive effects of the stressors of caregiving. The conclusion we can draw from available evidence is that social support helps, but particularly if there is an appropriate meshing of source, form, and problem.

Most research into social support is from the perspective of the recipient. However, Krause and Keith (1989) have demonstrated that giving support may help the donor as well as the recipient. Aldwin (1992) has reported that this is especially salubrious for older people who are able to feel useful when they see themselves as needed. Giving support is an important way to matter to others and to avoid a sense of uselessness and isolation.

We need to remind ourselves that as people age they might increasingly find their support networks contracting. This is clearly evident among the oldest old who might be the sole survivors of their generation of kin or of their age cohort. If we think of aging taking place within a convoy, as it has been described by Kahn and Antonucci (1980), then there are many long-term survivors who can be described as the last ship afloat. However, it is not only death that depletes the network or loosens the attachments within it; factors such as relocation or increasing frailty that reduces or eliminates direct contact also undermine networks and the support they would otherwise provide. On the other hand, it is quite remarkable that even among the oldest old, people replace with new companions those who have been lost by death or relocation. Thus, Johnson and her colleagues (Johnson & Barer, 1992; Johnson & Troll, 1994) found in their sample that nearly half had made a new friend since the age of 85. However, while the loss of the network might be slowed by replacement, we surmise that when loss does occur it can act both as a stressor and as the attrition of a crucial moderating resource.

Sense of Control

The third resource we shall discuss is mastery, the sense people have regarding their ability to exercise control over the important circumstances of their lives. Conventional wisdom would suggest that the level of mastery declines with the frailties and losses that accompany old age. However, it is apparent that many old people are able to maintain a sense of mastery and that it extends into late life as a resource important to well-being (Rodin, 1986).

The sense of control, which Mullan (1992) has described as a general orientation about the self in relation to the world, has been found to be an effective buffer mitigating the impact of stressors (Cohen & Edwards, 1989; Krause & Styker, 1984; Skaff, 1991; Wheaton, 1983). But although the potency of mastery has been repeatedly documented, surprisingly little is known about how it enables people to sustain well-being in the face of hardship. One explanation is that a sense of control by itself helps to reduce the onerousness and threat of difficult life conditions; to the extent that one feels in ultimate control of such conditions, one is less likely to feel helplessly victimized by them. It has also been proposed that the sense of control frees people to cope actively and to mobilize social support in their own behalf (Brandstädter & Baltes-Götz, 1990; Folkman, 1984; Krause, 1986).

While the reasons for the effectiveness of mastery as a stress moderator remain speculative, it is a most crucial resource in the context of stress, no less so for the old than for the young. What is the role of mastery in adaptation to aging? As with coping and social support, mastery can serve as a buffer against the stressors associated with aging and can itself be affected by experiences in late life. For example, in our Alzheimer's caregivers we have found that a strong sense of mastery protects the caregiver against the stressors arising in the daily care of the patient (Skaff, 1991). At the same time, however, the chronic stressors associated with prolonged caregiving have a detrimental effect on the level of caregivers' mastery—an effect, we can note, that is reversed with the death of the Alzheimer's patient and the cessation of caregiving (Skaff & Pearlin, 1994). At any rate, within the stress process, mastery is clearly seen both as a resource that contributes to adaptation and as a consequence of that process (Ryff, 1989a).

Of course, it would be useful to identify the mechanisms by which this important resource can be maintained across the aging process and, presumably, in the face of declining opportunities to experience control. We have learned that social support helps to maintain mastery and that it is positively related to such characteristics as education and income (Skaff & Pearlin, 1994). But beyond this, little is known about the conditions that maintain a sense of mastery. It is likely that the sheer experience of successful control enhances the sense of mastery. For example, Langer and Rodin (1976) have demonstrated that simple manipulations in the environmental choices of nursing home residents affected their sense of control and subsequently their health. In some of our current pilot interviews, too, we have seen indications that elderly persons draw on past experience for evidence of their mastery, even though the conditions from which those experiences stemmed have changed. Additionally, they can selectively pick out specific and usually mundane parts of their daily lives over which they are able to maintain control, and these parts, we believe, replace previous activities as sources of feelings of mastery. To some extent, therefore, the process of adapting to late life may involve staking one's mastery on domains over which one can exert control and yielding it where control is now more difficult.

In conclusion, we view adaptation to aging as a dynamic process in which the aging person confronts the stressors and challenges of aging not as a passive victim but as an actor drawing on resources that may themselves undergo both positive and negative change. There is strong evidence that many of the losses attributed to aging, such as cognitive decline and physical dysfunction, are preventable and even reversible (Rowe & Kahn, 1987). Even the impact of losses that may be irreversible, as in health and social attachments, can be minimized by the restructuring of personal meaning, by the availability of appropriate social support, and by some sense of mastery over the important circumstances of life.

OUTCOMES OF ADAPTATION

Gerontologists and life-course researchers have probably given more attention to what we call "outcomes" than to other aspects of the stress process. We use the term to represent the various attributes of people that indicate the state or level of their well-being. To this point, we have been concerned with the stressful conditions of life that might have a negative effect on well-being and with the resources that help people adapt to these conditions in ways that protect well-being. The question we briefly address now is how well-being in later life and its changes are judged and evaluated; how do we evaluate the adaptations to challenging life conditions? Some of the outcomes of the stress process are very familiar in the literature and relatively specific; they include various indicators of mental health, physical health, and functional capabilities.

However, two related constructs have come under considerable scrutiny and therefore merit special attention: successful aging and life satisfaction.

The term "successful aging" usually refers to the mental and physical health of people and their continued ability to engage in social life. In these respects, the perspectives of the stress process and successful aging converge, but there is also a substantial difference. By and large, scholars concerned with successful aging have focused on the criteria for and the correlates of successful aging but have neglected the social, economic, and experiential conditions that can interfere with successful aging and the resources that might enhance it. We would argue, by contrast, that to understand fully how people age successfully it is necessary to take into account the stressors to which they are exposed and the resources they can call on to cushion the effects of these stressors. We might also add that because many of these stressors are rooted in the social and economic circumstances of the larger society, the understanding of successful aging is inseparable from the understanding of successful societies.

Further, the literature on successful aging seems to suggest that there is a universal set of endpoints that, if achieved, signal that one has aged successfully. That is, it is assumed that if people have the right attitudes and do the right things, they will live long, in good health, and be quite pleased with their lives. Our perspective fits more closely with the view that successful aging is not an endpoint but a dynamic process in which aging individuals are repeatedly called on to confront challenges that face them in an ongoing interaction between themselves and their environments (Featherman, Smith, & Peterson, 1990; George, 1987). Adaptation and successful aging, we submit, are better seen not as products but as an ongoing, interactive process in dynamic relationship with the changes taking place in the structure of lives.

Life satisfaction, as rated by the older individual, is another frequently used outcome. It is related to the notion of successful aging in that it is used as a criterion of success. Indeed, the two constructs share some of the same ambiguities; in neither case can one be sure what the construct subsumes. With life satisfaction, further uncertainty is nurtured by the fact that old people may simultaneously harbor symptoms of psychological disorder or problems of physical health and express a high level of satisfaction with their lives (Baltes & Baltes, 1990). It is likely that in responding

116

to questions about life satisfaction some people are appraising the past while others may be reporting judgments of current life.

However, our reservations about research into life satisfaction and successful aging are based less on methodological than on theoretical grounds. In short, we see little to be gained in understanding the well-being of old people by emphasizing outcome criteria without also examining in detail the conditions that contribute to or stand in their way. We have no quarrel with the constructs of successful aging or life satisfaction except as they are given a life of their own. They will acquire much greater utility as they are placed within a more dynamic framework of challenge and change in the adult life course. Only part of the job is done when adaptive outcomes are judged without knowledge either of the conditions to which people must adapt or of the adaptive resources and mechanisms they employ.

CONCLUSIONS AND POLICY IMPLICATIONS

Future Research

Our discussion of stress and adaptation to late life suggests that we have much to learn about the kinds of things that are stressful to older people, the resources that help protect them, and the impact on their well-being. As stated earlier, we cannot simply extrapolate from what we know about the stress process in earlier adulthood to the conditions of late life; the type of stressors, their meaning, and their potential for management may be significantly different from those in other segments of the life course. There is, however, a thread of continuity that connects earlier experience with the experience of stress in late life. Therefore, we encourage research into stress across the life course, but with increased attention to late life. We need to identify the specific stressors that are most common and most powerful in the lives of older people. Putting aside negative stereotypes about late life, we must also look at the resources and strengths with which people negotiate the challenges of old age. One area in which there is considerable room for advancement is the identification and measurement of the ways older people cope with their problems. As Kahana (1992) admonished us, we need to begin by asking older people about their problems and how they handle them. We will accomplish this goal not by relying on old measurement tools but by developing age-appropriate instruments that accurately tap the experience of older people.

Policy Implications

At a fundamental level, older segments of society do not require public policy different from that for other age segments; that is, policy should minimize threats to security and health for all segments of society. However, policy must consider the unique health and security needs of older people. Because Americans are living longer lives, it becomes increasingly evident that we need to distinguish between implications for the oldest old and the younger old. The younger old, for the most part, live active, involved lives, with needs that differ little from those of younger age groups.

As a group, the oldest old differ from younger age groups, especially in terms of medical care. It is not clear whether geriatric medicine has kept pace with the increasing numbers of the oldest old or with our growing knowledge about them. Although health is a primary source of stress for older people, no policy can prevent all health problems or the encroachment of age and physical limitations. However, prevention programs that promote adequate diet, exercise, and preventive medicine can separate illness from natural aging and prevent or slow debility. Athough much remains to be learned about the nature of the stressors that arise in late life, our understanding of the proliferation of stressors suggests that it is cost efficient in both financial and social terms to approach services from the perspective of dealing with the primary stressor in a way that reduces the likelihood that it will spread to other areas of people's lives. Programs that assist older people in adapting to health problems and disabilities should limit the impact that those problems have on other areas of life such as finances, family relationships, and maintaining independence. In addition, it is crucial that program philosophy reflects the idea that old people have the right to desire well-being.

One group that may be particularly vulnerable to stress proliferation can be found among those who enter late life following a lifetime of economic or social marginality. Assistance with basic needs would greatly decrease their sources of stress. Our pilot interviews have indicated that services such as providing adequate housing can reverse some of the effects of such long-term deprivation among this group. These interviews suggest that even the most vulnerable members of our older population can flourish under the right conditions: relief from ambient threats, stable and adequate housing, and sufficient material resources.

The power of social resources to provide a buffer against the effects of stressors should not be underestimated for older people. Being embedded in a supportive network of friends and family is one of the best protections against the stressors that confront people of any age. Because death of age peers becomes more common with advanced age, new sources of companions and helpers may be needed. For older people who are isolated, programs that provide opportunities to meet other people as well as assistance in removing barriers to social contact—such as lack of transportation, inaccessible meeting places, and cost—could be an essential resource for aging people.

A desideratum arising from our review of the current knowledge in the area of stress and adaptation in late life is to keep people independent and autonomous for as long as possible. For the oldest old, our pilot interviews indicate that programs that provide assistance for logistical needs such as shopping, housekeeping, and transportation allow older people to preserve their independence. Whatever the programs might be, they should not contribute to the shrinkage of people's autonomy. Rather, programs should empower people to maintain a sense of control over their lives.

REFERENCES

Aldwin, C. M. (1990). The elders life stress inventory: Egocentric and nonegocentric stress. In M. A. Stephens, S. E. Hobfall, J. H. Crowther, & D. L. Tennenbaum (Eds.), *Stress and coping in later-life families* (pp. 49-69). New York: Hemisphere.

Aldwin, C. M. (1992). Aging, coping, and efficacy: Theoretical framework for examining coping in life-span developmental context. In M. L. Wykle, E. Kahana, & J. Kowal (Eds.), *Stress and health among the elderly* (pp. 96-113). New York: Springer.

Aneshensel, C. S., Rutter, C. M., & Lachenbruch, P. A. (1991). Social structure, stress, and mental health: Competing conceptual and analytic models. *American Sociological Review, 56,* 166-178.

Antonucci, T. C. (1990). Social supports and social relationships. In R. H. Binstock & L. K. George (Eds.) *Handbook of aging and the social sciences*, 3rd edition, New York: Academic Press.

Baltes, P. B., & Baltes, M. M. (1990). Psychological perspectives on successful aging: The model of selective optimization with compensation. In P. B. Baltes & M. M. Baltes (Eds.), *Successful aging: Perspectives from the behavioral sciences* (pp. 1-34). Cambridge, England: Cambridge University Press.

Bankoff, E. A. (1983). Social support and adaptation to widowhood. *Journal of Marriage and the Family, 45,* 827-839.

Barer, B. M. (1993). *Stressors in late late life: Does race make a difference?* Paper presented at the annual meeting of the Gerontological Society of America, New Orleans, LA.

Barresi, C. M. (1987). Ethnic aging and the life course. In D. E. Gelfand & C. M. Barresi (Eds.), *Ethnic dimensions of aging* (pp. 18-34). New York: Springer.

Brandstädter, J., & Baltes-Götz, B. (1990). Personal control over development and quality of life perspectives in adulthood. In P. B. Baltes & M. M. Baltes (Eds.), *Successful aging: Perspectives from the behavioral sciences.* Cambridge, England: Cambridge University Press.

Calhoun, L. G., & Tedeschi, R. G. (1989). Positive aspects of critical life problems: Recollections of grief. *Omega, 20,* 265-272.

Chiriboga, D. A. (1992). Paradise lost: Stress in the modern age. In M. L. Wykle, E. Kahana, & J. Kowal (Eds.), *Stress and health among the elderly* (pp. 35-71). New York: Springer.

Cohen, S., & Edwards, J. R. (1989). Personality characteristics as moderators of the relationship between stress and disorder. In R. W. J. Neufeld (Ed.), *Advances in the investigation of psychological stress* (pp. 235-283). New York: Wiley.

Dean, A., & Ensel, W. M. (1982). Modeling social support, life events, competence, and depression in the context of age and sex. *Journal of Community Psychology, 10,* 392-408.

Dean, A., Kolody, B., Wood, P., & Ensel, W. M. (1989). The effects of types of social support from adult children on depression in elderly persons. *Journal of Community Psychology, 17,* 341-355.

Elder, G. H., Jr., & Liker, J. K. (1982). Hard times in women's lives: Historical influences across forty years. *American Journal of Sociology, 88*(2), 241-269.

Ensel, W. M. (1991). "Important" life events and depression among older adults. *Journal of Aging and Health, 3,* 546-566.

Featherman, D. L., Smith, J., & Peterson, J. G. (1990). Successful aging in a post-retired society. In P. B. Baltes & M. M. Baltes (Eds.), *Successful aging: Perspectives from the behavioral sciences* (pp. 50-93). Cambridge, England: Cambridge University Press.

Folkman, S. (1984). Personal control and stress and coping processes: A theoretical analysis. *Journal of Personality and Social Psychology, 46*(4), 839-852.

Folkman, S., Lazarus, R. S., Pimley, S., & Novacek, J. (1987). Age differences in stress and coping. *Psychology and Aging, 2,* 171-184.

Gatz, M., & Hurwicz, M. (1990). Are old people more depressed? Cross-sectional data on Center for Epidemiological Studies depression scale factors. *Psychology and Aging, 5,* 284-290.

Gelfand, D. E. (1994). *Aging and ethnicity: Knowledge and services.* New York: Springer.

George, L. K. (1980). *Role Transition in later life*. Monterey, CA: Brooks, Cole Publishing.

George, L. K. (1987). Adaptation. In G. L. Maddox (Ed.), *The encyclopedia of aging* (pp. 5-7). New York: Springer.

George, L. K. (1989). Stress, social support, and depression over the life course. In K. S. Markides & C. L. Cooper (Eds.), *Aging, stress and health* (pp. 241-267). New York: Wiley.

Gibson, R. (1987). Defining retirement for Black Americans. In D. E. Gelfand & C. M. Barresi (Eds.), *Ethnic dimensions of aging* (pp. 224-238). New York: Springer.

Hansson, R. O., & Carpenter, B. N. (1994). *Relationships in old age: Coping with the challenge of transition*. New York: Guilford.

Holahan, C. K., Holahan, C. J., & Belk, S. S. (1984). Adjustment in aging: The roles of life stress, hassles, and self-efficacy. *Health Psychology, 3,* 315-328.

Hughes, D. C., Blazer, D. G., & George, L. K. (1988). Age differences in life events: A multivariate controlled analysis. *International Journal of Aging and Human Development, 27,* 207-220.

Johnson, C. L., & Barer, B. M. (1992). Patterns of engagement and disengagement among the oldest old. *Journal of Aging Studies, 6,* 351-364.

Johnson, C. L., & Troll, L. E. (1994). Constraints and facilitators to friendships in late late life. *The Gerontologist, 34,* 79-87.

Kahana, E. (1992). Stress research and aging: Complexities, ambiguities, paradoxes, and promise. In M. L. Wykle, E. Kahana & J. Kowal (Eds.), *Stress and health among the elderly* (pp. 239-256). New York: Springer.

Kahn, R. L:, & Antonucci, T. C. (1980). Convoys over the life course: Attachment, roles, and social support. In P. B. Baltes & O. G. Brim (Eds.), *Life-span development and behavior, Vol. 3.* New York: Academic Press.

Kessler, R. C., & McLeod, J. D. (1984). Sex differences in vulnerability to undesirable life events. *American Sociological Review, 49,* 620-631.

Kiecolt-Glaser, J. K., Dura, J. R., Speicher, C. E., Trask, O. J., & Glaser, R. (1991). Spousal caregivers of dementia victims: Longitudinal changes in immunity and health. *Psychosomatic Medicine, 53,* 345-362.

Krause, N. (1986). Stress and coping: Reconceptualizing the role of locus of control beliefs. *Journal of Gerontology, 41*(5), 617-622.

Krause, N. (1994). Stressors in salient social roles and well-being in later life. *Journal of Gerontology: Psychological Sciences, 49,* 137-148.

Krause, N., & Keith, V. (1989). Gender differences in social support among older adults. *Sex Roles, 21,* 609-628.

Krause, N. & Stryker, S. (1984). Stress and well-being: The buffering effect of locus of control beliefs. *Social Science Medicine, 18*(9), 783-790.

Langer, E. J., & Rodin, J. (1976). The effects of choice and enhanced personal responsibility for the aged: A field experiment in an institutional setting. *Journal of Personality and Social Psychology, 34,* 191-198.

Lerner, M. J., & Gignac, M. A. (1992). Is it coping or is it growth? A cognitive-affective model of contentment in the elderly. In L. Montada, S. Filipp, & M. J. Lerner (Eds.), *Life crises and experience of loss in adulthood* (pp. 321-337). Hillsdale, NJ: Erlbaum.

Lopata, M. (1979). *Women as widows: Support systems*. New York: Elsevier.

Martin, P., Poon, L. W., Clayton, G. M., Lee, H. S., Fulks, J. S., & Johnson, M. A. (1992). Personality, life events, and coping in the oldest-old. In L. W. Poon (Ed.), *The Georgia centenarian study* (pp. 19-30). Amityville, NY: Baywood.

McCall, M. E. (1989). *Social roles and mental health: Gender differences in sources and forms of mental distress.* Unpublished doctoral dissertation, University of California, San Francisco.

McCarthy, J. L. (1994). *Effects of widowhood on role-related dimensions of satisfaction in midlife.* Paper presented at the annual meeting of the Gerontological Society of America, Atlanta, GA.

Meeks, S., Carstensen, L. L., Tamsky, B., Wright, T. L., & Pellegrini, D. (1989). Age differences in coping: Does less mean worse? *International Journal of Aging and Human Development, 28,* 127-140.

Minkler, M., & Roe, K. M. (1993). *Grandmothers as caregivers.* Newbury Park, CA: Sage.

Mullan, J. T. (1992). The bereaved caregiver: A prospective study of changes in well-being. *The Gerontologist, 32,* 673-683.

Murrell, S. A., Norris, F. H., & Grote, C. (1988). Life events in older adults. In L. H. Cohen (Ed.), *Life events and psychological functioning: Theoretical and methodological issues* (pp. 96-122), Newbury Park, CA: Sage.

Murrell, S. A., Norris, F. H., & Hutchins, G. L. (1984). Distribution and desirability of life events in older adults: Population and policy implications. *Journal of Community Psychology, 12,* 301-311.

Neugarten, B. L. (1977). Personality and aging. In J. E. Birren & K. W. Schaie (Eds.), *Handbook of the psychology of aging* (pp. 626-649), New York: Van Nostrand Reinhold.

Pearlin, L. I. (1989). The sociological study of stress. *Journal of Health and Social Behavior, 30,* 241-256.

Pearlin, L. I., & Aneshensel, C. S. (1994). Caregiving: The unexpected career. *Social Justice Research, 7,* 373-390.

Pearlin, L. I., Aneshensel, C. S., Mullan, J. T., & Whitlatch, C. J. (1995). Caregiving and its social support. In R. Binstock & L. George (Eds.), *Handbook on aging and the social sciences* (4th ed.). San Diego, CA: Academic Press.

Pearlin, L. I., Lieberman, M. A., Menaghan, E. G., & Mullan, J. T. (1981). The stress process. *Journal of Health and Social Behavior, 22,* 337-356.

Pearlin, L. I., & Mullan, J. T. (1992). Loss and stress in aging. In M. L. Wykle, E. Kahana, & J. Kowal (Eds.), *Stress and health among the elderly* (pp. 117-132). New York: Springer.

Pearlin, L. I., Mullan, J. T., Semple, S. J., & Skaff, M. M. (1990). Caregiving and the stress process: An overview of concepts and their measures. *The Gerontologist, 30,* 583-594.

Pearlin, L. I., & Schooler, C. (1978). The structure of coping. *Journal of Health and Social Behavior, 19,* 2-21.

Quayhagen, M. P., & Quayhagen, M. (1982). Coping with conflict: Measurement of age-related patterns. *Research on Aging, 4,* 364-377.

Rodin, J. (1986). Aging and health: Effects of the sense of control. *Science, 233,* 1271-1276.

Rowe, J. W., & Kahn, R. L. (1987). Human aging: Usual and successful. *Science, 237,* 143-149.

Ryff, C. D. (1989a). Happiness is everything, or is it? Explorations on the meaning of psychological well-being. *Journal of Personality and Social Psychology, 57,* 1069-1081.

Ryff, C. D. (1989b). Beyond Ponce de Leon and life satisfaction. *International Journal of Behavioral Development, 12,* 35-55.

Selye, H. (1956). *The stress of life.* New York: McGraw-Hill.

Semple, S. J. (1992). Conflict in Alzheimer's caregiving families: Its dimensions and consequences. *The Gerontologist, 32,* 648-655.

Skaff, M. M. (1991). *Self-concept as a buffer against stress in Alzheimer's caregivers.* Paper presented at the annual meeting of the American Psychological Association, San Francisco, CA.

Skaff, M. M., & Pearlin, L. I. (1992). Caregiving: Role engulfment and the loss of self. *The Gerontologist, 32,* 656-664.

Skaff, M. M., & Pearlin, L. I. (1994). *Transitions in the caregiving career: Effects on sense of mastery.* Paper presented at the annual meeting of the Gerontological Society of America, Atlanta, GA.

Wheaton, B. (1983). Stress, personal coping resources, and psychiatric symptoms. *Journal of Health and Social Behavior, 24,* 208-229.

Wortman, C. B., & Silver, R. C. (1992). Reconsidering assumptions about coping with loss: An overview of current research. In L. Montada, S. Filipp, & M. J. Lerner (Eds.), *Life crises and experience of loss in adulthood* (pp. 341-365). Hillsdale, NJ: Erlbaum.

CHAPTER 5

Importance of Self-Perceptions for Health Status Among Older Persons

Jana M. Mossey

I t is widely appreciated that the perceptions an individual has about different aspects of himself or herself affect behaviors; recently, the link between self-perceptions and health states has received increasing attention from gerontologists and epidemiologists. Researchers have demonstrated that an individual's perceptions of his or her overall health status and emotions affect such health outcomes as the risk of mortality, changes in morbidity, and recovery from illness. Although not as extensively researched, it is also speculated that an individual's attitudes about the aging process and the meaning and purpose of his or her life while growing older have important significance for concurrent and future morbidity and mortality.

Although the research evidence is growing, very little has been translated into the practice of public health, clinical medicine, or personal health habits. This lack of translation into practice is due in part to the equivocal nature of some of the research findings. More important, however, it reflects difficulties in disseminating the findings to educators, policy developers, practicing clinicians, and older persons.

The purpose of this chapter is to facilitate dissemination and implementation of the research findings. It summarizes the findings linking morbidity and mortality to (a) the individual's perceptions of his or her own global health status; (b) the individual's perceptions about his or her emotional health status—specifically, subdysthymic depression; (c) the individual's subjective age and his or her attitudes toward the aging process; and (d) the individual's sense of meaning, purpose, and goals. The chapter also translates the background information into policy recommendations that address issues related to service development and delivery as well as to the expansion of the knowledge base pertinent to the four main topics.

SELF-PERCEPTIONS OF HEALTH

There is an extensive body of literature in which different aspects of health are identified and modeled. It is not the purpose of this chapter to summarize or critique the literature, but before discussing research findings pertinent to self-perceptions of health, a definition of health would serve as an anchoring point for personal self-evaluations.

It is clear that there is no widespread consensus, conceptually or operationally, for a definition of health. There is, however, some agreement on several issues related to defining health. As advocated by the World Health Organization, health is multidimensional, reflecting dimensions of physical, mental, and social well-being. Health is characterized by the presence or absence of specific attributes or states. Health may be understood as a function of both current status and future status or prognosis.

Although many objective indicators of health status are accessible to an observer or reported by an individual, health is perceived phenomenonologically. Subjective health perceptions do not necessarily correspond to the sum of objective indicators. Researchers have begun to ask questions about self-evaluations of health: What are subjective health ratings? What influences subjective health ratings, and by what internal processing mechanisms are evaluations derived? What effect do subjective evaluations have on the current or future health of an individual, and through what mechanisms are the effects realized?

Until recently, pertinent research has relied on data collected for other purposes. Rather than evolving from a conceptual understanding, subjective, self-perceived health has been defined operationally in terms of the measures collected during these other studies. This might be, for

TABLE 1 Distribution of Self-Ratings
of Health in Selected Studies

Excellent	13.8%
Good	48.4%
Fair	28.3%
Poor/Bad	9.5%

NOTE: Data are from the Manitoba Longitudinal Study
on Aging (N = 3533; Mossey & Shapiro, 1982).

example, in response to a single question about global health status. Although there are several question formats, the most common is "How do you rate your health today (or over a defined time period)—excellent, good, fair, poor, or bad?" Most research summarized below uses this global indicator of self-rated health. Skeptics might argue that it is risky to base a body of research on responses to a single question. As will become evident, however, there is compelling evidence both that the subjective construct tapped by the question is a unique phenomenon and that it has important significance for the current and future health of the individual.

Before summarizing the research literature, it is instructive to examine the distribution of self-ratings of health in a sample of elderly persons dwelling in the general community. This is shown in Table 1 for individuals included in several large studies referenced in Table 2. Across studies, the majority of respondents rated their health as good, with the next largest proportion choosing a rating of "fair."

As one would expect, self-rated health does reflect objective conditions. Among individuals who had recently undergone a surgical repair for a fractured hip (Mossey, Knott, and Craik, 1990), 34.6% rated their health as fair and 22.1% as poor.

Model of Subjective, Self-Rated Health

Liang (1986) and Liang, Bennett, Whitelaw, and Maeda (1991) introduced one structural model for self-reported health in adults; Johnson and Wolinsky (1993) introduced another. Both models, although distinct, suggest that an individual conceives of and reports about his or her health in relation to several primary criteria: (a) a disease or a chronic symptom, reflecting physical illness; (b) performance, reflecting physical functioning and role functioning; and (c) a subjective assessment, indicated by a person's self-rated health. Analyses of data from the large sample ($N = 16,148$) of the National Health Interview Survey 1984 Supplement on Aging or the elderly subset of that sample who were followed longitudinally ($N = 5,151$) support the hypothesis that self-perceived health is a function of physical illness and functional status.

Important elements of the models and the main pathways are presented in Figure 1. A dimension labeled "mental health/illness" has been added to encompass components of mental health, mental illness, and psychological functioning. It is included to emphasize the substantial correlation between self-rated health and psychological status, measured primarily in terms of psychological distress or depressive symptoms (Jylhä, Leskinen, Alanen, & Heikkinen, 1986; Mossey et al., 1990; Murray, Dunn, & Tarnopolsky, 1982; Tessler & Mechanic, 1978).

The following summarizes the research findings pertinent to the relationships hypothesized in Figure 1. With few exceptions, analyses in which self-rated health has been treated as a dependent variable are cross-sectional; findings have been fairly consistent. The lack of consensus in the

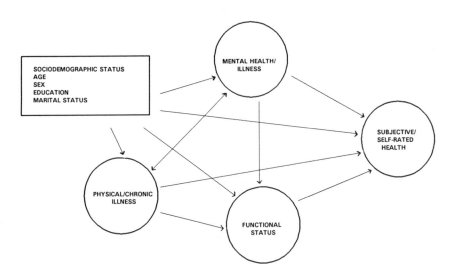

FIGURE 1 Proposed model of subjective/self-rated health.

definition of health status is reflected in the lack of a uniform measure of physical health. The Cumulative Illness Rating Scale, Geriatric Version (under development; Miller et al., 1992), may provide an instrument for systematic assessment of objective health.

Physical Health

Thus far, physician ratings or patient self-reports of symptoms or conditions have been the most commonly reported indicators of the physical health/illness construct. Statistically significant but modest relationships between these variables and self-rated health have consistently been noted. (For physician ratings, see Friedsam & Martin, 1963; LaRue, Bank, Jaruik, & Hetland, 1979; Maddox, 1962; Mossey & Shapiro, 1982; Palmore & Luikart, 1972; Suchman, Phillips, & Streib, 1958. For self-reports of conditions and symptoms, see Fylkesnes & Forde, 1991; Johnson & Wolinsky, 1993; Jylhä et al., 1986; Liang, 1986; Murray et al., 1982; Tissue, 1972; Zonderman, Leu, & Costa, 1986.) Suchman et al. reported significant differences in physician ratings and patient self-ratings in more than one third of the individuals studied. In a large study of elderly dwelling in the general community, Mossey and Shapiro observed that self-rated health and a measure of objective health based on physician diagnoses, self-reports of conditions, and health service utilization correlated to only 0.34.

The modest congruence observed between physician ratings and self-ratings of health prompted researchers to question whether such self-ratings were valid indicators of physical health. As shown in Figure 1, despite inconsistencies, the influence of objective health status on self-ratings is acknowledged; it is also recognized that other factors influence such evaluations. Moreover, while reported objective indicators appear important regardless of age, gender, or race, there is some evidence suggesting that the nature of the association may not be the same for all members of different subgroups.

Controlling for measures of physical health, women are reported to be more optimistic in their ratings than men (Ferraro, 1980; Fillenbaum, 1979). Within the elderly, advancing age also appears to have a positive association with optimism in self-rated health—that is, reporting one's health to be better than indicated by more objective measures (Idler, 1993; Liang et al., 1991; Stoller, 1984).

Functional Status

A consistent positive association between measures of physical function and self-rated health has been observed across studies. These studies include measures of physical performance, such as activities of daily living (ADLs) and instrumental ADLs (Johnson & Wolinsky, 1993; Liang, 1986; Mossey et al., 1990; Tissue, 1972), and measures of physical fitness or physical activity (Fylkesnes & Forde, 1991; Jylhä et al., 1986). As with the measures of reported symptoms and conditions, associations may not be uniform across subgroups. Johnson and Wolinsky (1994), for example, observed gender differences in associations between different types of ADL measures and perceived health.

Age

In most studies, objective measures of health status decrease with age; concurrently, older members of samples studied are consistently more optimistic in their self-ratings of health (Fillenbaum, 1979; Idler, 1993; Liang et al., 1991; Maddox & Douglass, 1973; Murray et al., 1982; Stoller, 1984). Ferraro (1980) noted that among the oldest old (e.g. 75 or older), individuals who rated their health as excellent had about the same disability level as younger elderly individuals who said their health was good. Using longitudinal data from the New Haven Established Populations for Epidemiologic Studies of the Elderly (EPESE) sample, Idler (1993) tested whether the observed optimism in self-assessments of health was predominantly due to changes with age, to cohort effects, or to survivorship. She summarizes her findings as follows:

> We can only say that all the explanations (age, cohort, survivorship effects) appear to play some role in creating the patterns we see. The oldest people in this sample did give better self-assessments than one would expect. The most positive self-assessments were specific to the earliest cohorts. The survivors did have better self-assessments of health than the deceased members of the cohorts. And the oldest survivors' self-assessments did improve over the period of the study. At this point, none of the explanations can be ruled out. (p. S298)

In addition to the observed optimism among older individuals, there are some data indicating that the relationship between objective indicators of physical or emotional health and self-rated health may be age dependent. Jylhä et al. (1986) noted that felt symptoms and an index of physical fitness best explained the self-rated health of the younger members of their male sample. Among middle-aged individuals, the most relevant explanatory variables were symptoms and a measure of psychic well-being; in the oldest group, self-rated health was best explained by chronic diseases, felt symptoms, and a measure of frailty.

Gender

The dependence of self-rated health on gender has not been clearly established. However, as indicated above, gender appears to be associated with self-rated health; females have more positive ratings of self-perceived health than males at a given level of objective health status (Ferraro, 1980; Fillenbaum, 1979; Idler, 1993). Johnson and Wolinsky (1994) also report gender differences in the determinants of perceived health. Specifically, they observed that household ADLs (e.g., house cleaning or meal preparation) were not important determinants of self-perceived health in males, although they were in females. Among Whites, there was a significant effect of advanced ADLs (e.g., managing money) for males but not for females. In contrast, Liang et al. (1991) observed no significant gender effect in either American or Japanese elderly samples. Similarly, of the 12 studies presented in Table 2, only 3 found that the interaction between gender and self-rated health predicted mortality.

Race

The significance of race for self-perceived health has been investigated in several studies. The general conclusion is that the structure of self-assessments of health does not differ substantially by race. Liang et al. (1991) found similar results when they compared American and Japanese elderly. Johnson and Wolinsky (1994), while noting that there were differences in the objective measurement of health between Blacks and Whites, found no differences in the determinants of perceived health.

Gibson (1991) also concluded that the model of self-reported health she tested was similar for Blacks and Whites, although she found that the subjective self-rated health variable was not as valid an indicator of health status for Blacks as it was for Whites. Comparisons of relative optimism or pessimism between Black and White elderly show mixed results. Although Idler (1993) observed no racial differences in her study of community-dwelling elderly in New Haven, Krause (1987a) observed that Blacks reported poorer self-rated health even after controlling for objective measures of health status.

Other Variables

Several other variables examined in relation to self-rated health warrant mention here. Zonderman et al. (1986), using a sample of relatively healthy elderly enrolled in the Baltimore Longitudinal Study on Aging, found that, after controlling for potentially confounding variables, neuroticism was related to self-rated health; higher levels of neuroticism were associated with poorer self-ratings. This research, coupled with findings from other studies that show a subset of individuals with pessimistic ratings (Blazer & Houpt, 1979; Maddox, 1962), lends some support to the notion that self-ratings of health may reflect enduring personality traits.

Life stress and social support variables have also been studied in relation to self-rated health. In one of the few longitudinal studies that has examined self-rated health, Minkler and Langhauser (1988) observed that the social contact variable was the most important predictor of health self-ratings over a 5-year period. In a cross-sectional study, Krause (1987b) reported that satisfaction with social supports, rather than number or frequency of contacts, was significantly related to self-ratings of health. Social participation (Sugisawa, Liang, & Ling, 1994) and the converse, social disconnection (Kaplan & Camacho, 1983), are also associated with self-rated health. Weinberger et al. (1986b), using an older sample, observed statistically significant relationships between life stress variables and self-rated health. In contrast, Krause (1987a) did not find life stress to be predictive of self-rated health for either Whites or Blacks.

Even within cross-sectional studies, the preceding variables have been treated as independent variables affecting self-rated health. The impact of self-rated health on measures of subjective well-being, such as life satisfaction or general well-being, has been studied extensively. Although most of the relevant studies have been cross-sectional, self-rated health has implicitly been viewed as the independent variable (see summaries by Larson, 1978, and Okun, Stock, Haring, & Witler, 1984). This research has consistently demonstrated a strong positive association between measures of subjective well-being and self-rated health, independent of age, gender, or racial background.

Stability of Self-Rated Health

There is limited information dealing with the stability of self-ratings of health over time. However, two not necessarily incompatible trends have been observed. First, self-rated health appears to be sensitive to acute changes in health state. Both Maeland and Havik (1988) and Mossey et al. (1990) obtained retrospective and current ratings of self-perceived health following an acute medical event—myocardial infarction and hip fracture, respectively. In each case, there was a substantial reduction in the proportion of patients reporting their health as excellent or good for the time reference "today" as compared with the time reference "before the event." Maeland and Havik reported that 67% of their sample gave a high global health rating for the time before they sustained a myocardial infarction; at hospital discharge only 21% gave this rating. Over time, there appears to be recovery in self-ratings, suggesting a return to a more enduring perception. The notion of stability in self-rated health is supported by the observation across several studies that the relationship between self-rated health and mortality is the same regardless of whether mortality occurred early on, directly after the rating was obtained, or as many as 4 years later (Idler & Kasl, 1991, Mossey & Shapiro, 1982).

The preceding research findings indicate that subjective self-ratings of health reflect, but are not entirely determined by, a person's physical, functional, and emotional health. Investigators speculate that subjective evaluations are generally grounded in reality but are responsive to other attitudes, perceptions, life experiences, and psychological traits and states. Among the elderly, female and older members tend toward optimism in their ratings. This age effect may reflect both comparisons with others and comparisons with the self at earlier ages. However, considerable additional research is required in order to fully describe the phenomenon and to develop an explanatory model of causation. A large number of studies and analyses concerned with the relationship between self-ratings of health and different causal factors have been based almost entirely on data from studies designed for other purposes.

Predictive Significance of Self-Rated Health

In recent years, considerable attention has been focused on evaluating the predictive significance of self-rated health for mortality. Table 2 summarizes the major studies. Several points are important to bear in mind:

1. With few exceptions, the study samples reflect large, representative samples of defined populations. All but one of the samples is in excess of 500 individuals.

2. In most cases, the studies are limited to older individuals. The three that include younger individuals also include older persons.

3. Ten of the 12 studies include a global rating of health as the independent self-rated health variable under study.

4. In three of the studies, the measure of objective health status that provides the control for physical or medical health status has been derived wholly or partly from physician-generated data rather than solely from respondent self-reports. This feature is critical because control for objective health is a prerequisite for determining the unique contribution of self-perceptions of health to mortality. When physician observations are not available, information on prognostically important health behaviors has been obtained.

5. The studies represent heterogeneous samples derived from different geographic locations; they include individuals of assorted racial and ethnic backgrounds.

6. The studies include, on average, 5 years of follow-up. This permits investigation of whether the influence of self-rated health is ephemeral or enduring.

TABLE 2   Longitudinal Studies on the Predictive Importance of Self-Rated Health for Mortality and Morbidity

Authors	Location	Study Design	Sample	Self-Perceived Health Variable
Singer, Garfinkel, Cohen, & Srole, 1976	Community residence, Manhattan, New York	Longitudinal, 20 years of follow-up	1,660, 20-59, in 1954 Midtown Manhattan Study	Global rating, 4-point scale: excellent, good, fair, poor
Mossey & Shapiro, 1982	Community residence, Manitoba, Canada	Longitudinal, 7 years of follow-up	3,128 adults, 65+, random sample Manitoba Longitudinal Study on Aging	Global rating, 5-point scale: excellent, good, fair, poor, bad
Markides & Pappas, 1982	Community residence, San Antonio, Texas	Longitudinal 4-years of follow-up	460 Mexican Americans and Anglos, 60+, 70% Mexican American, 61% female, predominantly working- or lower-class background	Global rating, 4-point scale: excellent, good, fair, poor
Kaplan & Camacho, 1983	Community residence, Alameda County, California	Longitudinal, 9 years of follow-up	6,928 adults, 16-94, in 1965 human population laboratory	Global rating, 4-point scale: excellent, good, fair, poor
Kaplan, Barell, & Lutzky, 1988	Community residence, Kiryat Ono, Israel	Longitudinal 5-years of follow-up	1,078 adults, 65+, population random sample	4-point rating: Do you consider yourself healthy, fairly healthy, sick, very sick?
Mossey, Knott, & Graik, 1990	Community sample identified during acute care hospital stay	Longitudinal, 1-year of follow-up	219 females, 59+, hospitalized for surgical repair of a fractured hip	Global rating, 5-point scale: excellent, good, fair, poor, bad

Outcome Variables	Control Variables	Results
Mortality (informant and administrative reports)	Age, sex, education, marital status, income, presence of specific health conditions, smoking, drinking behaviors, obesity index, mental health rating, summary health index	Self-rated health predicted mortality after controlling for other variables.
Mortality (administrative records)	Age, sex, education, marital status, income, life satisfaction, urban/rural residence, objective health status (based on physician diagnosis, symptom reports, and health care utilization)	Self-rated health predicted early and late mortality with a dose–response effect. Effects were similar across age, sex, and urban/rural residence groups.
Mortality (informant report)	Age, sex, ethnic background, education, marital status, self-reported conditions, ill-bed days in prior year, hospital days, subjective age	Self-rated health was not an independent predictor of mortality for any age, sex, or ethnic group. Subjective age discriminated survivors from deceased more strongly than age or objective health.
Mortality (death certificates or informant reports)	Age, sex, income, education, physical health status, smoking history, weight, physical activity, alcohol consumption, sleeping patterns, social network participation	Self-rated health predicted all-cause mortality after controlling for other variables. The increased risk of death in persons with fair or poor ratings was present for deaths due to ischemic health disease, to cancer (for males and women under 44 years), and to all other causes.
Mortality (administrative and informant reports)	Age, sex, health conditions, functional health, medication use	Self-health rating predicted mortality independent of control variables.
Mortality (informant), recovery in prefracture physical function	Age, marital status, depressive symptoms, personality, social supports, physical function, reported medical conditions, cognitive status, fracture site, repair type, length of hospital stay	Self-rated health predicted mortality after introducing control variables. Adjusted odds ratios increased as self-ratings decreased. Self-rated health did not predict 12-month recovery in prefracture physical function.

135

TABLE 2 *Continued*

Authors	Location	Study Design	Sample	Self-Perceived Health Variable
Idler & Angel, 1990	Community residence, U.S. probability sample	Longitudinal up to 10 years follow-up	6,440 adults, 25-74, NHANES–1 /NHEFS sample	Global rating, 5-point scale: excellent, very good, good, fair, poor
Idler, Kasl, & Lemke, 1990 (New Haven); Idler & Kasl, 1991 (Iowa)	Community residence, New Haven, Conn.; Iowa and Washington Counties, Iowa	Longitudinal 4-years of follow-up	Adults 65+: 2,812 New Haven EPESE Study Sample; 3,097 Iowa sample	New Haven: Global rating 5 point scale Iowa: Health compared to age mates
Pijls, Feskens, & Kromhout, 1993	Community residence, Netherlands	Longitudinal 5-year follow-up	783 males, 65-85, Zutphen Study	4-point rating: What do you think about your health? Do you feel healthy, rather healthy, moderately healthy, not healthy?
McCallum, Shadbolte, & Wange, 1994	Community residence, Sidney, Australia	Longitudinal, 7 years of follow-up	811 adults, 60+, Aging and the Family Project survey	Global rating, 4-point scale: excellent, good, fair, poor
Schoenfeld, Malmrose, Blazer, Gold, & Seeman, 1994	Community residence, East Boston, Mass.; New Haven, Conn.; Durham, North Carolina	Longitudinal, 3 years of follow-up	1,192 adults, 70-79, MacArthur Field Study of Successful Aging, high functioning cohort	Global rating, 5-point scale: excellent, good, fair, poor, bad

Outcome Variables	Control Variables	Results
Mortality (proxy report or death certificate), survival time	Age, sex, race, education, income, medical diagnosis from physician exam, illness severity index, smoking status, alcohol consumption, inactivity measure, obesity index	After adjustment, self-rated health predicted mortality for middle-aged men, but not for older men or females of any age.
Mortality (proxy reports or death certificate)	Age; sex; race; education; income; marital status; religious preference; physical health status: chronic conditions, functional disability (ADL, performance, mobility), blood pressure; use of cardiovascular medications; health risk behaviors: smoking, alcohol consumption, adiposity index, physical exercise	After adjustment, self-rated health predicts mortality for males and females in both communities with a dose–response effect observed. Predictive ability unrelated to whether death occurred early or late.
Mortality (administrative and informant reports)	Age, education, marital status, family history of chronic diseases; from physician exam: anthropomorphic measures, diagnoses, blood pressure, serum cholesterol, electocardiographic diagnoses, medication use, smoking history, alcohol consumption, physical activity, dietary history	Self-health rating, dichotomized to moderately healthy/not healthy vs. healthy, was a risk factor for cancer mortality and mortality from other causes excluding cardiovascular disease. Self-rated health did not independently predict incidence of chronic diseases.
Mortality (state death records)	Age, sex, marital status, ethnic origin, home ownership, self-reported serious illness or accident, six-month illness bed days, ADL, IADL, depression, social support	Adjusting for measures of objective illness and other control variables, poor self-ratings of health did not differentiate the risk of survival in men or women. For women, only individuals with good or fair ratings were at increased risk of death compared with those with excellent ratings.
Mortality (proxy report or health department record)	Age, sex, race, marital status, education, cognitive status, number of chronic diseases, hospitalization in previous year, smoking behaviors, alcohol consumption	Self-rated health predicted mortality in healthy aged. A dose–response effect was observed. Among the healthiest, adjusted odds ratio for mortality for poor self-rated health compared with excellent self-rated health was 93.51.

TABLE 2 *Continued*

Authors	Location	Study Design	Sample	Self-Perceived Health Variable
Sugisawa, Liang, & Lui, 1994	Community residence, Japan	Longitudinal, 3 years of follow-up	2,200 adults, 60+, stratified random sample	Global rating, 5-point scale: excellent, very good, good, fair, poor

Findings summarized in the Results column of Table 2 show the nature of the association between self-rated health and mortality, controlling for confounding variables such as age, gender, race, and objective measures of health status. In seven of the studies, self-rated health is observed to be an unequivocal predictor of mortality across age and gender. In these studies, the odds ratios for mortality increase, in a dose-response fashion, as the divergence of a person's self-rated health from the "excellent" category increases. In four additional studies, self-rated health predicts mortality only for specific subsets of the sample. In the study reported by Kaplan and Camacho (1983), self-rated health predicted ischemic heart disease deaths in all groups, cancer deaths in men and women under 44 years of age, and deaths in all age and gender groups for other causes. In the study of males resident in the Netherlands (Pijls, Feskens, & Kromhout, 1993), self-rated health predicted cancer mortality and mortality from other causes but not cardiovascular disease mortality. In a third study, in which individuals between the ages of 25 and 74 were included (Idler & Angel, 1990), self-rated health predicted mortality only in middle-aged men. In only one case—the study of Mexican Americans and Anglos reported by Markides and Pappas (1982)—was self-rated health unrelated to mortality in all age, gender, and ethnic groups. Looking carefully at the studies, there is no one particular feature that distinguishes studies in which the association between self-rated health and mortality was unequivocal from studies in which the findings were mixed. Given the diversity in sample, location, measures, and follow-up time frames, the evidence supporting the importance of self-rated health as an independent

Outcome Variables	Control Variables	Results
Mortality (months to death)	Age, sex, education, marital status, social contacts, social participation, feelings of loneliness, social support, number of chronic conditions reported, functional disability, drinking, smoking behaviors	Self-rated health predicted mortality for both males and females after controlling for other variables.

predictor of mortality is compelling. Although specific adjusted odds ratios associated with the different levels of self-rated health are not included in Table 2, they are available in several of the referenced published papers (e.g., Idler & Kasl, 1991; Mossey & Shapiro, 1982; Pijls et al., 1993; Schoenfeld, Malmrosen, Blazer, Gold, & Seeman, 1994). Although there are differences across studies, the most common finding is that the adjusted odds ratio between individuals who rate their health as poor and those who rate it as excellent is about 3. In other words, individuals who rate their health as poor are about three times as likely to die in the follow-up period as those with similar characteristics (e.g., age, gender, race, and objective health status) but a better self-rating.

It is evident from these data that self-rated health is not only a statistically significant predictor of mortality, but also a nontrivial predictor of mortality. Mossey and Shapiro (1982) reported that the risk of death associated with self-perception of health is not too dissimilar from the association of age and health, which generally is one of the strongest predictors of mortality; the adjusted odds ratio for age was 3.82. In the study reported by Schoenfeld et al. (1994), with individuals age 70 to 79 in relatively good objective health, the increased risk of death associated with poor self-rated health was substantially greater than that associated with age. Moreover, there was a significant interaction showing that the effect of poor self-rated health was much greater among those judged by objective measures to be in good health than among those in objectively poorer health.

Although mortality has been the outcome variable most often

related to self-ratings of health, self-ratings have also been examined with regard to course of illness, recovery from illness, and incidence of new disease. Findings from the few prospective studies are mixed. There is some evidence to suggest that self-rated health affects psychosocial outcomes related to illness course and recovery. Garrity (1973) and Brown and Rawlinson (1975, 1976) observed a positive association between self-rated health and morale following a myocardial infarction and open heart surgery, respectively. Garrity (1973) also noted a positive relationship between self-rated health and return to work after a myocardial infarction. However, this relationship was not observed by Maeland and Havik (1987) when they controlled for a variable indicating the individual's self-reported expectation of returning to work. Mossey et al. (1990) found self-rated health to be an important predictor of depressive symptoms but not physical function 12 months after hip fracture. Grand, Grosclaude, Bocquet, Pous, and Albarede (1988) report that self-rated health predicted deterioration in functional ability in a sample of rural French individuals 60 years of age and older. This association held even after controlling for conditions of illness. In contrast, Pijls et al. (1993) found no association between self-rated health and incidence of chronic disease. The contradictory nature of these findings and the limited number of relevant studies reported in the literature suggest the need for further research.

Self-rated health has been examined in relation to use of health services; however, there is a surprising lack of information on this topic. Weinberger et al. (1986a) and Wolinsky, Cullen, Callahan, and Johnson (1994) found, in prospective studies, that self-rated health predicted hospital utilization and nursing home placement. Further studies are needed to clarify the relationship between self-rated health and physician utilization and to evaluate how much the use of specific types of providers or services affects self-rated health.

In summary, there is substantial evidence that self-rated health makes a unique and important contribution to a variety of health outcomes. Death is the most studied outcome. These findings raise several questions: Why does self-perception of health contribute to outcome? What is self-rated health really measuring? What mechanisms operate to affect an individual's risk of dying and other health outcomes? Can a person's self-rated health be intentionally modified? If so, is the individual's risk of mortality also altered? There are a number of hypotheses pertinent to these questions. Results support the hypothesis that self-ratings reflect aspects of a person's physical, mental, and social health, but we do not have adequate information about what data the individual actually uses in making a rating.

Several mechanisms have been proposed for the operation of self-rating:

1. Self-ratings of health do not affect mortality directly; the observed association would disappear if important, yet unmeasured, variables were controlled for. Initially, it was thought that personal health behaviors, such as smoking or alcohol consumption, might account for an observed association; however, such behaviors have been controlled for in a number of studies without diminishing the association between self-rated health and mortality.

2. Self-ratings may affect mortality risk because they are a more sensitive indicator of a person's real health status than other measures that are accessible to the physician. In this context, it is hypothesized that such ratings reflect a prescient understanding by the individual of subtle biological and physiological changes.

3. Positive self-ratings may be protective because optimistic, positive feelings are in themselves protective. Conversely, negative, pessimistic ratings may simply reflect the individual's emotional status, functioning in the same ways as emotional distress by precipitating a stress reaction, such as the stimulation of the hypothalamic-pituitary-adrenocortical axis.

4. Self-ratings of health may be a measure of overall susceptibility that reflects psychophysiological mechanisms not yet understood.

While there is some evidence to refute certain of the above explanations, such as the potential confounding role of health behaviors, there is no clear understanding of which explanation or explanations reflect reality. Mechanisms through which self-ratings operate constitute an area in which research is badly needed. Because of the complexity of the topic, it is unlikely that much progress can be made through continued secondary analyses of existing data sets; rather, it appears critical that self-rated health must be studied in its own right. The need for specifically focused research applies to questions that deal with the modifiability of self-ratings of health and the methods for achieving changes.

JANA M. MOSSEY

Implications of the Research Findings for Current Practice

Despite gaps in our understanding of the meaning of subjective self-ratings of health and the mechanisms through which the observed effects operate, the findings have important implications for current clinical practice, research, and health care planning and evaluation.

Clinical Practice

Self-rated health, even the global rating measured through a single question, is uniformly seen to be an important indicator of subsequent health outcomes. Although Schoenfeld et al. (1994) observed a dramatically increased risk of mortality only among the healthier cohort studied who had poor self-ratings of health, in most studies both positive and negative ratings have prognostic implications.

It would make sense to include assessment of self-rated health as part of any routine clinical work-up in outpatient and inpatient settings. Although it is not yet clear what such ratings actually mean, poor ratings—especially in the individual who otherwise appears to be in objectively good health—identify those for whom further examination by a physician would be warranted. It is important that the examination focus on aspects of both physical and mental health.

Routine monitoring of self-rated health would also permit identification of individuals whose perception of their overall health is deteriorating. Since older individuals tend to have optimistic health ratings, even in the face of declining objective health, deteriorating ratings constitute high-risk profile that should trigger additional examination by the physician or other health care practitioner.

Research

The most obvious recommendation for the researcher is that a global self-rated health question, although convenient and easy to include, is not appropriate as the sole indicator of health and well-being in a study of an individual's objective health. It is not suggested that self-rated health be excluded, but rather that other measures of physical illness, emotional well-being, and functional status need to be included. As noted earlier, instruments such as the Cumulative Illness Rating Scale, Geriatric Version (Miller et al., 1992), are being developed and may be useful for measuring these other indicators.

The global index of self-rated health also should not be considered the only indicator of subjective health. A more inclusive definition should be developed that includes a comparative dimension as well as an evaluation of how health affects performance of desired activities. A research agenda specific to subjective self-ratings of health is required—for example, studies directed toward the meaning of self-health ratings, intergenerational and cross-cultural differences, the mechanisms through which such ratings operate, the methods by which they can be modified, and the consequences of their modification. Relationships between self-rated health and behaviors such as smoking, alcohol and drug use, exercise, use of physician services, and compliance with therapeutic regimens should be evaluated. Additional studies could specifically address whether the pessimistic ratings held by some individuals are, in fact, a result of depression or whether an independent optimistic/pessimistic factor is operating.

It is important that a research agenda pay attention to both large-sample, prospective, epidemiological studies and smaller, in-depth, anthropological studies. A research agenda should also include clinically based studies in which the physician uses information on subjective health ratings to develop a plan for patient care.

Health Care Planning and Evaluation

In any future health care system, it seems likely that accountability in planning for, monitoring, and evaluating service delivery will be critical. To accomplish this, indicators of population health status, potential resource consumption, patient case mix, and individual prognosis will be important. Subjective global self-rated health is one such indicator. Since the distribution of self-rated health in the population has implications for health service resource consumption and survivorship, it can be useful in comparing two populations or one population at two points in time. In planning health services, information on self-health ratings could be important in identifying population subgroups in which high resource use

JANA M. MOSSEY

would be expected. This could facilitate the distribution of scarce resources or permit high-risk groups to be targeted. The trend toward managed care and per capita reimbursement also requires methods for determining the prognostic characteristics of the enrolled population and for evaluating case mix differences. Differential capitation based on self-rated health measures, in combination with other measures of health status and prognosis with safeguards built in for individuals, might be worthy of consideration.

SUBDYSTHYMIC DEPRESSIVE SYMPTOMATOLOGY

In this section, the individual's perceptions of his or her emotional health status are considered. Self-rated health was described in the preceding section as a global composite rating reflecting, at the least, a person's self-perceived physical health, functional status, and mental health. Within the mental health domain, perhaps the most important indicator of self-perceived emotional well-being is self-reported depressive symptomatology. Moreover, there is increasing evidence of a high prevalence of such symptoms among the elderly that do not meet criteria for major depressive disorder or dysthymia but that nonetheless are clinically significant and for which treatment, not now generally offered, may be warranted (Broadhead, Blazer, George, & Tse, 1990; Howarth, Johnson, & Klerman, 1992; Johnson et al., 1991; Judd, Rapaport, Paulus, & Brown, 1994; Mossey et al., 1990; Wells, Burnam, Rogers, Hayes, & Camp, 1989, 1992). Such depressive symptomatology is associated with increased risk of subsequent major depression, medical morbidity, increased use of health services, longer hospital stays, slower or less complete recovery from an illness or injury, and functional disability.

In this chapter, the terms "subdysthymic condition," "subdysthymic depression," and "subdysthymia" are used interchangeably to refer to elevated depressive symptomatology that does not meet criteria for major depression or dysthymia. In the literature, subdysthymic conditions have been referred to by such terms as "elevated depressive symptoms," "subsyndromal depression," "subclinical depression," "mild depression," "subthreshold depression," and "minor depression" (Broadhead et al, 1990; Johnson et al., 1991; Judd et al., 1994; Wells et al., 1989). Judd et al.

144

(1994) recently proposed "subsyndromal symptomatic depression," which may substantially overlap with "minor depressive disorder" as described in the *Diagnostic and Statistical Manual of Mental Disorders,* fourth edition (American Psychiatric Association [APA], 1994), or "minor depression" as indicated by Research Diagnostic Criteria (Spitzer, Endicott, & Robins, 1978).

The following sections describe the epidemiology of the phenomenon, including whether discrete subdysthymic conditions may exist, their natural history and clinical course, and which preventive or treatment strategies may be effective.

Background

The notion is only now becoming more widely accepted that depression warrants treatment as a spectrum disorder, ranging from severe major depression to clinically significant subdysthymic presentations. The limited consensus regarding less severe forms of depression reflects, as well, the fact that distinguishing those with significant levels of depressive symptoms from individuals who are experiencing day-to-day mood fluctuations associated with the human condition involves clinical perceptions that are aesthetic as well as scientific. This difficulty has been heightened by three factors:

1. Until recently, there was limited awareness that such states as depressed mood, feelings of helplessness, or loss of interest in life are not inevitable consequences of "normal aging."

2. There is overlap between symptoms of illness (e.g., disturbed sleep, diminished appetite, weight loss, and fatigue) and the psychomotor retardation characteristic of depressive states.

3. Depressive symptoms frequently present similarly to dementia.

In the absence of a concise definition, it has been difficult for the clinician to appreciate the clinical significance of the milder symptom clusters. It has been difficult, as well, for the researcher to study a condition that is incompletely or ambiguously defined. Available studies tend to be cross-sectional or designed for other purposes, with the definition of subdysthymic depression made after the fact rather than beforehand. Associated methodological weaknesses and idiosyncratic operational definitions have meant that the cross-study comparisons necessary for scientific development and clinical advancement have not been easy.

Over time, two approaches to defining subdysthymic depressions have emerged. In one, subdysthymic depression has been based on a clinical rating; in the other, it is based on self-reporting of symptoms. The category "minor depression" in the Research Diagnostic Criteria (1978) represents attempts to define the phenomenon clinically but within a research perspective. The Beck Depression Inventory (Beck, Ward, Mendelson, Mock, & Enbaugh, 1961), the Center for Epidemiologic Studies Depression Scale (Radloff, 1977), and the Geriatric Depression Scale (Yesavage & Brink, 1983) represent self-rated depression scales. The early research using these scales, however, was limited by the inability to distinguish between persons who had a subdysthymic level of depression and those who met syndromal criteria.

The development of instruments designed to make research-based diagnostic assessments, such as the Structured Clinical Interview for *DSM-III* (Spitzer, Williams, Gibbon, First, 1990) and the Diagnostic Interview Schedule (DIS; Robbins, Helzer, Croughan, & Ratcliff, 1981), have clarified the operational definition of subdysthymia. Two different methods have been used. In one, subdysthymia is defined in terms of the number and structure of depressive symptoms endorsed on the DIS. Studies using the data from the Epidemiologic Catchment Area (ECA) study have used this method (Broadhead et al., 1990; Johnson et al., 1991; Judd et al., 1994). The other method uses two stages: Individuals are first classified according to a self-reported depression screening scale; high-scoring individuals are further evaluated to rule out major depression and dysthymia. Wells et al. (1989) used this method in the Medical Outcome Studies. A depression screening scale developed for the study was used; those individuals who screened high were administered the DIS by telephone.

Incidence and Prevalence

The data from the ECA study indicate a prevalence of 1% to 2% for major depression and about 2% for dysthymia in the elderly population (Blazer, 1989). In further analysis of the ECA study data, Judd et al.

(1994) found a one-year prevalence of "subsyndromal symptomatic depression" to be 11.8%, with a prevalence in the elderly of 14.6%. Using data from the ECA–Duke Piedmont Health Survey, Blazer, Hughes, and George (1987) report a 19% prevalence of subdysthymic levels of depressive symptoms in the sample of persons age 60 and over. Wells et al. (1989) report a 15.9% prevalence of subdysthymia, according to their two-stage definition, among individuals without a chronic condition who had been seen by a general medical provider. Prevalence rates were reported to be higher among those with a chronic condition.

Most other studies that yield prevalence estimates have relied on the self-reported depression measures (e.g., the Center for Epidemiologic Studies Depression Scale [CESD], the Beck Depression Inventory, and the Geriatric Depression Scale). Unpublished data from a study currently in progress by Mossey indicate that the majority of those with self-reported elevated depressive symptoms fall into the subdysthymic category. The studies that rely on self-reported measures find prevalence rates of elevated depressive symptoms in older individuals dwelling in the general community that range between 15% and 30% (Blazer & Williams, 1980; Blazer et al., 1987), with rates among medically ill hospitalized individuals typically ranging from 23% to 40% (Magni, Diego, & Schifano,, 1985; Saravay, Steinberg, Weinshel, Pollack, & Alovis, 1991). Indeed, in the study of recovery from hip fracture (Mossey et al., 1990), 51% of the women reported CESD scores above the cutoff point (16 or greater) when interviewed shortly after hip fracture surgery.

The one thing that is clear from the studies is that subdysthymic depressions are relatively common in the general population and strikingly prevalent in the medically ill. The studies uniformly indicate that the level of morbidity seen with subdysthymia is not as great as that associated with major depression. However, the presence of a large number of affected individuals and the high associated attributable risks make it clear that such depressive symptom levels constitute a significant public health problem (Broadhead et al., 1990; Johnson, Weissman, & Klenman, 1992; Judd et al., 1994; Wells et al., 1989). Judd et al., for example, extrapolate from their 1-year prevalence rate of subsyndromal symptomatic depression to estimate that, in a given year, over 10 million people more than 18 years of age in the United States are suffering from the condition.

Natural History/Clinical Course

There is limited information concerning the epidemiology of subdysthymia because of the paucity of appropriate longitudinal studies. The results of cross-sectional studies indicate that individuals with sub-dysthymia are more likely to be female (Blazer, Burchett, Service, & George, 1991; Blazer et al., 1987; Broadhead et al., 1990; Johnson et al., 1991; Pfifer & Murrell, 1986) but less likely to be married (Broadhead et al., 1990; Judd et al., 1994) or to be from a high social class (Judd et al., 1994). Scores on all measures of health status are poorer; the individuals are more likely to have fair or poor self-rated health (Judd et al., 1994; Blazer et al., 1987), to have a physical dysfunction or impairment (Blazer et al., 1987; Broadhead et al., 1990; Judd et al., 1994; Wells et al., 1992), to report current pain (Judd et al., 1994), and to report more health problems.

Scores on social dysfunction scales also indicate more dysfunction (Johnson et al., 1991; Judd et al., 1994). Individuals with subdysthymia make greater use of health services (Broadhead et al., 1990; Johnson et al., 1991; Wells et al., 1989) and report more disability days and days lost from work (Broadhead et al., 1990). They also are at substantially higher risk of a first episode of major depression (Howarth et al., 1992; Wells et al., 1989). Although older persons were once thought to have higher rates of subdysthymic levels of depressive symptoms, this may be an artifact of the data, due to the inability to control adequately for physical function and medical status. When these variables are controlled for, the rates among the elderly are lower than those among younger age groups (Blazer et al., 1987).

Findings from several longitudinal studies suggest that there may be a number of distinct features related to clinical course. Persistence of symptoms appears to be one important distinction. Over time, elevated depressive symptoms appear to persist in 30% to 40% of cases (Broadhead et al., 1990; Mossey et al., 1990; Thomas, Kelman, Kennedy, Ahn, & Yang, 1992). The clinical significance is not well specified. Thomas et al. reported almost no differences among the variables they measured, except worsening health status, between those whose depressive symptoms persisted and those whose symptoms remitted. Mossey et al. reported significant differences between these two groups in recovery from hip fracture.

Those with persistently elevated scores had a much poorer recovery experience.

Predictive Significance of Depressive Symptoms

The strength and consistency of the associations between physical health, physical disability, and subdysthymic levels of depressive symptoms raise questions of cause and effect. Investigators are aware that the methods used, even if longitudinal, are not adequate to fully address this issue. Most studies reviewed suggest that physical health or physical disability has a strong immediate effect on depression, with depressive symptoms having lagged effects on health status (Aneshensel, Frerichs, & Huba, 1984; Gurland, Wilder, & Berkman, 1988; Harris, Mion, Patterson, & Frangley, 1988). In the study of hip fracture reported by Mossey et al. (1990), however, the importance for recovery of persistent depressive symptoms remained even after controlling for prefracture physical function, the strongest predictor of recovery.

In contrast to the strong, consistent relationship between self-rated health and mortality, the studies that have investigated the question of an association between subdysthymic levels of depressive symptoms and subsequent mortality are inconclusive. Some investigators have observed an association (e.g., Bruce & Leaf, 1989; Kaplan and Camacho, 1983; Murphy, Monson, Oliver, Sobal, & Leighton, 1987; Schekelle et al., 1981). In their 16-year follow-up of residents of Stirling County, Nova Scotia, Murphy et al. observed an increased risk of death among individuals who had subdysthymic symptoms of affective disorder during the first interview wave. Bruce and Leaf (1989) also reported that excess mortality associated with elevated depressive symptoms identified by the DIS persisted even after controlling for age, gender, and baseline physical health status. Other investigators, however, have reported that when controls for physical health status have been introduced, any observed zero-order associations disappear (Thomas et al., 1992).

Treatment Approaches

Unlike self-rated health, some research pertinent to the treatment of subdysthymic levels of depressive symptoms has been undertaken. Moreover, it is widely believed—and is beginning to be substantiated by research data (Sireling, Paykel, Freeling, Raon, & Patel, 1985)—that there are many older individuals with subdysthymic levels of depression who are currently being treated for their depressive symptoms in the primary care setting. From a review of the clinical and research literature, two trials have been identified that include individuals with depressive symptoms at the subdysthymic level, and a third trial, directed toward medically ill elderly with subdysthymic depressive symptoms, is in progress.

Klerman et al. (1987) reported good results with interpersonal counseling (IPC), a derivative of interpersonal psychotherapy for depression (Klerman, Weissman, Rounsaville, & Chevnon, 1984), in a study involving middle-aged enrollees of a large health maintenance organization in New England. They observed a reduction in General Health Questionnaire scores among those receiving IPC.

Paykel, Hollyman, Freeling, and Sedgwick (1988) reported on another study in which they used amitriptyline (vs. placebo) with individuals they identified as being in the "mild" symptom range. Contrary to Klerman et al. (1987), they observed no positive benefit from treatment among those with mild depressive symptoms. Because of the differences in case definition and the treatments studied, it is difficult to draw comparative conclusions between the studies.

Mossey and her colleagues are completing a randomized intervention trial using IPC with an elderly medically ill sample recruited during a hospital stay. Unpublished data from the first 6 months of follow-up show a reduction in depressive symptom scores and an improvement in self-rated health among the treated group but no change in measures of physical function that can be attributed to treatment.

Implications of the Research Findings for Current Practice

The research findings above indicate subdysthymic levels of depression to be quite prevalent and associated with substantial morbidity. Implications for clinical practice, research and health care policy and evaluation are summarized below.

Clinical Practice

Apparent reasons that clinicians have not given greater attention to subdysthymic depressive symptom levels include the absence of a consensus regarding definition and measurement and the lack of agreement concerning who should be treated and under what circumstances. While these issues are being addressed, it makes sense to treat subdysthymic depression, at the least, as a risk factor that warrants further evaluation. Among individuals who are medically ill, screening for depressive symptoms in particular should be actively initiated by health care providers in both the inpatient and the outpatient settings. Self-reported screening scales such as the Geriatric Depression Scale would be appropriate for this purpose.

Research

Considerably more must be learned about subdysthymic levels of depressive symptoms in terms of etiology, clinical course, and impact on the course of and recovery from medical illness. It is particularly important to investigate the relationship between subdysthymic depression and more severe syndromal depression. For example, Howarth et al. (1992) and Wells et al. (1992) have found some support for the hypothesis that subdysthymic presentations may represent the waxing and waning of major depression or dysthymia. Greater clarification is also required on the relationships between depressive symptoms and such variables as self-rated health, physical function, personality, and use of health services. The degree of association and the direction of causal relationships need to be identified so that appropriate variables may be targeted for prevention or intervention efforts. As with recommendations pertinent to self-rated health, it is important that research be designed to address hypotheses related to subdysthymia. Here, in particular, in-depth retrospective studies are required in order to obtain data on lifetime history and on the meaning of specific symptom endorsement. There is considerable need for more intervention-related research evaluating different treatment approaches. Medications, alone or in combination with psychosocial or behavioral interventions, need to be investigated. Treatments, with and without a maintenance component, are required. Alternative programs that take into account the reluctance of members of the older cohorts to acknowledge their depression or to seek help from mental health practitioners also need to be implemented and evaluated.

Health Care Policy and Development

Health care planning, delivery, and financing in the United States are predominantly focused on physical health. To be responsive to individuals with subdysthymic levels of depression (as well as to those with syndromal depression), mental and physical health care services need to be actively integrated and coordinated. For example, individuals need to have the same access to mental health services that they have to physical health care. Reimbursement policies that typically favor physical care need to change so that there is parity between mental and physical health care in such aspects as copayments, limitations to services, and insurability. Moreover, the educational systems need to better integrate mental and physical components into the curricula for physicians and other health care providers.

SUBJECTIVE AGE

In addition to those of overall health status and subdysthmic depressive symptomatology, another set of self-perceptions concerns subjective age. Similar to the coexistence of objective and subjective ways of perceiving health status, individuals think of themselves in terms of both chronological age and subjective age. Subjective age is defined as the age an individual perceives himself or herself to be. Like other perceptions, it is thought to be multidimensional; however, a concise, uniform conceptual or operational definition has not been developed. The initial work of Kastenbaum, Derbin, Sabatini, and Artt (1972) provides the most frequently observed operational definition: Subjective or personal age is defined in terms of how old the individual feels he or she is, how old he or she looks to himself or herself, and the age level of the interests and activities he or she has. Although considerable research has been conducted to describe the relationship between chronological age and this definition of subjective age, only a few studies were identified that examined subjective age in relationship to indicators of health status.

Descriptive studies of the relationship of subjective age to chronological age have consistently demonstrated the presence of a youthful bias, with individuals reporting their subjective age to be younger than their chronological age. Contrary to initial expectations, the magnitude of the bias is seen to increase with advancing age. Staats et al. (1993) report that it is even observed among individuals whose health status appears to be declining. Indeed, they found only modest correlations between measures of subjective age and health status. Other investigators have observed that the youthful bias was greater in women than in men and that the discrepancy between chronological age and subjective age was associated with personal fears of aging and life satisfaction (Montepare & Lachman, 1989). Staats et al. also examined the relationship between the different dimensions of subjective age and present and expected quality of life. They found youthful interests were important predictors of expected quality of life.

These findings raise questions concerning the protective health benefits associated with youthful, optimistic perceptions of subjective age. Except for a study reported by Markides and Pappas (1982), described in Table 2, there is almost nothing in the literature. Markides and Pappas observed that, after controlling for objective health variables and socio-demographic factors, older subjective age predicted mortality. Self-rated health did not predict mortality in their study.

It makes intuitive sense that youthful age perceptions might be protective to the individual; more research, however, is needed to determine what constitutes productive youthful bias as opposed to potentially harmful denial. Moreover, the relationship between subjective age and self-perceptions of health requires further study. In a small study of Black elderly, Smith, Plaweki, Houser, Carr and Plawecki (1991) observed that those who reported feeling younger had more positive self-ratings of health.

It is important to determine whether the observed association between self-rated health and mortality is affected by perceptions of subjective age. The lack of data on this topic is due largely to the fact that subjective age has not been measured in the longitudinal studies, such as those included in Table 2, where data on mortality have been obtained.

The recommendations for clinical practice, research, and health care planning and evaluation pertinent to the potential meaning and significance of subjective age are similar to those identified earlier with respect to self-perceptions of health. A pessimistic, older perception of one's age may represent an indicator of risk warranting further evaluation.

PURPOSE AND MEANING IN LIFE

Another set of self-perceptions involves an individual's views of his or her purpose and meaning in life, the goals an individual determines are important, and the self-perceived ability of the individual to achieve specific goals. Although changes in health status may affect one's perceptions and expectations about life's purpose, such perceptions and expectations are also thought to have an impact on the individual's health. Review of the epidemiological literature, however, reveals almost no studies in which an individual's perceptions of the purpose and meaning of his or her life, other than the extreme situation of anhedonia in the context of depression, were specifically examined in relation to morbidity and mortality.

Hooker and Seigler (1993) studied the relationships between life goals, satisfaction, and self-rated health. Individuals who reported greater achievement in life goals and those who rated recreational activities as important were more likely to have a better self-rated health. In a study by Grand et al. (1988), purposelessness, as indicated by feeling useless and having no projects, was observed to predict deteriorating health, independent of other factors such as age. In the absence of other studies, the following brief discussion outlines several issues pertinent to this topic that appear important for clinical practice and research.

Gerontologists have written extensively on the existence and importance of a sustained purpose and meaning to the lives of older individuals. Increasingly, it is recognized that, despite losses in terms of physical health and functioning, social roles, and interpersonal relationships, maintenance of optimistic engagement in life is normative. (See Carstensen & Freund, 1994, for a particularly salient discussion of resilience in aging; see Rapkin & Fischer, 1992a, 1992b, for a discussion of the personal goals of older adults.) One of the objectives, therefore, of clinical practice should be to protect and foster an individual's ability to remain actively engaged. Individuals who manifest a sustained loss of interest or pleasure in activities or pursuits should not be dismissed as "sick" or "just getting older." Their symptoms should be evaluated as potentially indicative of a depressive disorder that could warrant treatment.

There are many research questions pertinent to the relationships of the perception of meaning and purpose to the multiple dimensions of health status. Of particular interest are the reasons some individuals, but not others, remain optimistic, goal oriented, and actively engaged and how and through which mechanisms these attributes influence and reflect health status and survivability. As with the other perceptions discussed here, it is important to determine whether and how a person's sense of meaning and purpose in life can be modified. Moreover, because depressive symptoms can be treated, it is especially critical to determine whether the absence of a sense of meaning and purpose is simply a manifestation of depression.

CONCLUSIONS AND RECOMMENDATIONS

Conclusions

1. Self-perceptions, in terms of subjective health ratings and depressive feelings, have a significant effect on an individual's health and use of health services. Though less well documented, there are some data suggesting that a person's perception of his or her age and his or her perceptions of meaning and purpose in life also affect health status and health outcomes.

2. Despite losses in terms of decline in health status and physical functioning, social roles, and interpersonal relationships, older individuals tend to have optimistic self-perceptions. They rate their health more favorably than that indicated by more objective markers, they have a youthful bias when indicating their subjective age, and they see life as having purpose and meaning. Although subdysthymic levels of depressive symptoms are not uncommon, the majority of older individuals report low levels of depressive symptoms. Optimistic perceptions appear normative and protective. For example, among individuals with objectively poor health status, discrepant but positive self-rated health is associated with a more favorable survival experience than congruent but poor ratings are.

3. Pessimistic, negative perceptions constitute a risk factor for poor health outcomes and far more frequent use of health services. This is observed even if the negative perceptions appear congruent with reality. As noted by one study (Schoenfeld et al., 1994), pessimistic self-evaluations in the face of objectively good circumstances may indicate a particularly high risk.

4. The tendency for optimism or pessimism appears to be correlated with age, gender, and race. Though not well documented, the presence of cohort and cross-cultural effects is suspected.

5. Although there is considerable evidence demonstrating that pessimistic self-evaluations increase an individual's health risk, there is little indication that the information has been translated into clinical practice.

Recommendations

1. The most important recommendation for research emerging from a review of the literature is to develop research agendas designed to investigate the meaning and significance of an individual's perceptions of his or her health, his or her emotional status in terms of depressive symptoms, his or her age, and the purpose and meaning of life. In addition, studies are needed that explore further the interactions between these variables and health status and health behaviors, including use of health services.

Although there is substantial evidence that self-rated health is an independent predictor of mortality, research is required that will permit identification of the mechanisms by which such evaluations affect survivability. It makes intuitive sense that subjective age and a person's sense of meaning and purpose of life would affect health status; this and related hypotheses require further evaluation. The findings observed through analyses of data collected for other purposes are too provocative to allow further investigation to be left to chance. It should be stressed here that the association between self-rated health and mortality is not trivial; it appears similar to that associated with chronological age.

Furthermore, the epidemiology and treatability of subdysthymic levels of depressive symptoms require further clarification. This is particularly important because of the public health burden associated with such levels of depressive symptoms. Depression can be treated successfully—unlike many of the problems experienced by older individuals.

2. Despite the gaps in understanding the meaning and particularly the modifiability of self-perceptions of health and age, self-rated health and depressive symptom levels are risk indicators that are easy to measure. Screening procedures should be built into routine clinical evaluations in both the inpatient and outpatient settings. Currently there are sufficient data to justify using the information to identify individuals for whom additional evaluation would be warranted.

3. There is limited understanding of the factors that influence why an individual has an optimistic or pessimistic outlook to evaluations of health, age, and meaning in life. Is the tendency to pessimism a personality trait that is relatively stable over the life course? Is it a symptom of depression that would change if the depression were treated? Questions of this sort need to be answered to determine whether it is possible to develop ways to foster an optimistic outlook or to modify an individual's tendency to pessimism.

4. Education of health care providers—physicians as well as others—is required. Both the practitioner in training and the individual in clinical practice should be targeted. Specific information about the risk factor status of self-perceptions and depressive symptoms should be included. More important, the education program should focus on dispelling the discomfort of health care practitioners regarding mental health issues and needs.

5. Changes that would foster the collection and clinical use of psychosocial and psychiatric information in the medical and primary care settings are needed in the system of health care delivery. One way to achieve this would be through greater integration of the mental and physical health delivery systems. In the hospital setting, routine screening of self-rated health, depressive symptoms, and subjective age could accompany the admission work-up. Psychiatric nurses might be particularly appropriate to work with the medical patients and the nursing and medical staffs.

REFERENCES

American Psychiatric Association. (1994). *Diagnostic and statistical manual of mental disorders* (4th ed.). Washington, DC: Author.

Aneshensel, C., Frerichs, R., & Huba, G. (1984). Depression and physical illness: A multi-wave nonrecursive causal model. *Journal of Health & Social Behavior, 25,* 350-371.

Beck, A. T., Ward, C. H., Mendelson, M., Mock, J., & Erbaugh, J. (1961). An inventory for measuring depression. *Archives of General Psychiatry, 4,* 53-63.

Blazer, D., 1989. Depression in the elderly. *New England Journal of Medicine. 267,* 1478-1483.

Blazer, D., Burchett, B., Service, C., & George, L. K. (1991). The association of age and depression among the elderly: An epidemiologic exploration. *Journal of Gerontology, 46,* M210-M215.

Blazer, D. C., & Houpt, J. L. (1979). Perception of poor health in the healthy older adult. *Journal of the American Geriatrics Society, 27,* 330-334.

Blazer, D., Hughes, D. C., & George, L. K. (1987). The epidemiology of depression in an elderly community population. *The Gerontologist, 27,* 281-287.

Blazer, D., & Williams, C. D. (1980). Epidemiology of dysphoria and depression in an elderly population. *American Journal of Psychiatry, 137,* 439-444.

Brown, J. S., & Rawlinson, M. (1975). Relinquishing the sick role following open-heart surgery. *Journal of Health & Social Behavior, 16,* 12-19.

Brown, J. S., & Rawlinson, M. (1976). The morale of patients following open-heart surgery. *Journal of Health & Social Behavior, 17,* 134-137.

Broadhead, W. E., Blazer, D. G., George, L. K., & Tse, C. K. (1990). Depression, disability days, and days lost from work in a prospective epidemiologic survey. *Journal of the American Medical Association, 264,* 2524-2528.

Bruce, M. L., & Leaf, P. J. (1989). Psychiatric disorders and 15-month mortality in a community sample of older adults. *American Journal of Public Health, 79,* 727-730.

Carstensen, L. L., & Freund, A. M. (1994). The resilience of the aging self. *Developmental Review, 14,* 81-92.

Ferraro, K. F. (1980). Self-ratings of health among the old and the old-old. *Journal of Health and Social Behavior, 21,* 377-383.

Fillenbaum, G. G. (1979). Social context and self-assessments of health among the elderly. *Journal of Health and Social Behavior, 20,* 45-51.

Friedsam, H., & Martin, H. W. (1963). A comparison of self and physicians' rating in an older population. *Journal of Health and Social Behavior, 4,* 179-183.

Fylkesnes, K., & Forde, O. H. (1991). The Tromso study: Predictors of self-evaluated health—Has society adopted the expanded health concept? *Social Science and Medicine, 32,* 141-146.

Garrity, T. F. (1973). Vocational adjustment after first myocardial infarction: Comparative assessment of several variables suggested in the literature. *Social Science and Medicine, 7,* 705.

Gibson, R. C. (1991). Race and the self-reported health of elderly persons. *Journal of Gerontology, 46,* S235-S242.

Grand, A., Grosclaude, P., Bocquet, H., Pous, J., & Albarede, J. L. (1988). Predictive value of life events, psychosocial factors, and self-rated health on disability in an elderly rural French population. *Social Science and Medicine, 27,* 1337-1342.

Gurland, B. J., Wilder, D. E., & Berkman, C. (1988). Depression and disability in the elderly: Reciprocal relationships and changes with age. *International Journal of Geriatric Psychiatry, 3,* 163-179.

Harris, R. E., Mion, L. C., Patterson, M. B., & Frengley, J. D. (1988). Severe illness in older patients: The association between depressive disorders and functional dependency during the recovery phase. *Journal of the American Geriatrics Society, 36,* 890-896.

Hooker, K., & Siegler, I. C. (1993). Life goals, satisfaction, and self-rated health: Preliminary findings. *Experimental Aging Research, 19,* 97-110.

Howarth, E., Johnson, J., Klerman, G., et al. (1992). Depressive symptoms as relative and attributable risk factors for first-onset major depression. *Archives of General Psychiatry, 49,* 817-823.

Idler, E. L. (1993). Age differences in self-assessments of health: Age changes, cohort differences, or survivorship? *Journal of Gerontology, 48,* S289-S300.

Idler, E. L., & Angel, R. J. (1990). Self-rated health and mortality in the NHANES-1 epidemiologic follow-up study. *American Journal of Public Health, 80,* 446-452.

Idler, E. L., & Kasl, S. (1991). Health perceptions and survival: Do global evaluations of health status really predict mortality? *Journal of Gerontology, 46,* S55-S65.

Idler, E. L., Kasl, S., & Lemke, J. H. (1990). Self-evaluated health and mortality among the elderly in New Haven, Connecticut, and Iowa and Washington Counties, Iowa, 1982–1986. *American Journal of Epidemiology, 82,* 91-103.

Johnson, J., Weissman, M. M., & Klerman, G. L. (1991). Service utilization and social morbidity associated with depressive symptoms in the community. *Journal of the American Medical Association, 267,* 1478-1483.

Johnson, R. J., & Wolinsky, F. D. (1993). The structure of health status among older adults: Disease, disability, functional limitation, and perceived health. *Journal of Health and Social Behavior, 34,* 105-121.

Johnson, R. J., & Wolinsky, F. D. (1994). Gender, race, and health: The structure of health status among older adults. *The Gerontologist, 34,* 24-35.

Judd, L. L., Rapaport, M. H., Paulus, M. P., & Brown, J. L. (1994). Subsyndromal symptomatic depression: A new mood disorder. *Journal of Clinical Psychiatry, 55*(Suppl. 4), 18-28.

Jylhä, M., Leskinen, E., Alanen, E., Leskinen, A. L., & Heikkinen, E. (1986). Self-rated health and associated factors among men of different ages. *Journal of Gerontology, 41,* 710-717.

Kaplan, G., Barell, V., & Lutzky, A. (1988). Subjective state of health and survival in elderly adults. *Journal of Gerontology and Social Science, 43,* 114-120.

Kaplan, G. A., & Camacho, T. (1983). Perceived health and mortality: A nine year follow-up of the human population laboratory cohort. *American Journal of Epidemiology, 117,* 292-304, 1983.

Kastenbaum, R., Derbin, V., Sabatini, P., & Artt, S. (1972). "The ages of me": Toward personal and interpersonal definitions of functional aging. *Aging and Human Development, 3,* 197-211.

Klerman, G. L., Budman, S., Berwick, D., Weissman, M. M., Damico-White, J., Demby, A., & Feldstein, M. (1987). Efficacy of a brief psychosocial intervention for symptoms of stress and distress among patients in primary care. *Medical Care, 25,* 1078-1088.

Klerman, G. L. L., Weissman, M. M., Rounsaville, B. J., & Chevron, E. S. (1984). *Interpersonal psychotherapy of depression.* New York: Basic Books.

Krause, N. (1987a). Satisfaction with social support and self-rated health in older adults. *The Gerontologist, 27,* 301-308.

Krause, N. (1987b). Stress in racial differences in self-reported health among the elderly. *The Gerontologist, 27,* 72-76.

Larson, R. (1978). Thirty years of research on the subjective well-being of older Americans. *Journal of Gerontology, 33,* 109-125.

LaRue, A., Bank, A., Jarvik, L., Hetland, M. (1979). Health in old age: How do physicians' ratings and self-ratings compare? *Journal of Gerontology, 34,* 687-691.

Liang, J. (1986). Self-reported physical health among aged adults. *Journal of Gerontology, 41,* 248-260.

Liang, J., Bennett, J., Whitelaw, N., & Maeda, D. (1991). The structure of self-reported physical health among the aged in the United States and Japan. *Medical Care, 29,* 1161-1180.

Maddox, G. L. (1962). Some correlates of differences in self-assessments of health status among the elderly. *Journal of Gerontology, 17,* 180-185.

Maddox, G. L., & Douglas, E. B. (1973) Self-assessment of health status: A longitudinal study of elderly subjects. *Journal of Health and Social Behavior, 14,* 89-93.

Magni, G., Diego, D. L., & Schifano, F. (1985). Depression in geriatric and adult medical inpatients. *Journal of Clinical Psychology, 4,* 337-344.

Markides, K. S., & Pappas, C. (1982) Subjective age, health, and survivorship in old age. *Research on Aging, 4,* 87-96.

Maeland, J. G., & Havik, O. E. (1987). Psychological predictors for return to work after a myocardial infarction. *Journal of Psychosomatic Research, 31,* 471-481.

Maeland, J. G., & Havik, O. E. (1988). Self-assessment of health before and after a myocardial infarction. *Social Science and Medicine, 27,* 597-605.

McCallum, J., Shadbolt, D., & Wang, D. (1994) Self-rated health and survival: A 7-year follow-up study of Australian elderly. *American Journal of Public Health, 84,* 1100-1105.

Miller, M. D., Paradis, C. F., Houck, P. R., Mazumber, S., Stack, J. A., Rifai, A. H., Mulsant, B. & Reynolds, C. F. (1992). Rating chronic medical illness burden in geropsychiatric practice and research: Application of the Cumulative Illness Rating Scale. *Psychiatry Research, 41,* 237-248.

Minkler, M., & Langhauser, C. (1988). Assessing health differences in an elderly population: A five year follow-up. *Journal of the American Geriatrics Society, 36,* 113-118.

Montepare, J. M., & Lachman, M. E. (1989). "You're only as old as you feel": Self-perceptions of age, fears of aging, and life satisfaction from adolescence to old age. *Psychology and Aging, 4,* 73-78.

Mossey, J. M., Knott, K., & Craik, R. (1990). The effects of persistent depressive symptoms on hip fracture recovery. *Journal of Gerontology, 45,* M163-M168.

Mossey, J. M., & Shapiro, E. (1982). Self-rated health: A predictor of mortality among the elderly. *American Journal of Public Health, 72,* 800-808.

Murphy, J. M., Monson, R., Oliver, D. C., Sobal, A. M., & Leighton, A. H. (1987). Affective disorders and mortality. *Archives of General Psychiatry, 44,* 473-480.

Murray, J., Dunn, G., & Tarnopolsky, A. (1982). Self-assessment of health: An exploration of the effects of physical and psychological symptoms. *Psychological Medicine, 12,* 371-378.

Okun, M. A., Stock, W. A., Haring, M. J., & Witler, R. A. (1984). Health and subjective well-being: A meta-analysis. *International Journal of Aging and Human Development, 10,* 111-132.

Palmore, E., & Luikart, C. (1972). Health and social factors related to life satisfaction. *Journal of Health and Sociological Behavior, 13,* 68-80.

Paykel, E. S., Hollyman, J. A., Freeling, P., & Sedgwick, P. (1988). Predictors of therapeutic benefit from amitriptyline in mild depression: A general practice placebo-controlled trial. *Journal of Affective Disorders, 14,* 83-95.

Pijls, L. T., Feskens, E. J., & Kromhout, D. (1993). Self-rated health, mortality, and chronic diseases in elderly men: The Zutphen study, 1985–1990. *American Journal of Epidemiology, 138,* 840-848.

Radloff, L. S. (1977). The CES-D Scale: A self-report depression scale for research in the general population. *Applied Psychology Measurement, 1,* 385-401.

Rapkin, B. D., & Fischer, K. (1992a). Framing the construct of life satisfaction in terms of older adults' personal goals. *Psychology and Aging, 7,* 138-149.

Rapkin, B. D., & Fischer, K. (1992b). Personal goals of older adults: Issues in assessment and prediction. *Psychology and Aging, 7,* 127-137.

Robins, L. N., Helzer, J. E., Croughan, J., & Ratcliff, K. S. (1981). National Institute of Mental Health Diagnostic Interview Schedule: Its history, characteristics, and validity. *Archives of General Psychiatry, 38,* 381-389.

Saravay, S. M., Steinberg, M. D., Weinshel, B., Pollack, S., & Alovis, N. (1991). Psychological comorbidity and length of stay in the general hospital. *American Journal of Psychiatry, 148,* 324-329.

Schoenfeld, D. E., Malmrose, L. C., Blazer, D. G., Gold, D. T., & Seeman, T. E. (1994). Self-rated health and mortality in the high-functioning elderly—A closer look at healthy individuals: MacArthur field study of successful aging. *Journal of Gerontology, 49,* M109-M115.

Shekelle, R. B., Raynor, W. J., Ostfeld, A. M., Garron, D. C., Bieliauskas, L. A., Liu, S. C., Maliza, C., & Paul, O. (1981). Psychological depression and 17-year risk of death from cancer. *Psychosomatic Medicine, 43,* 117-125.

Singer, E., Garfinkel, R., Cohen, S. M., & Srole, L. (1976). Morality and mental health: Evidence from the midtown Manhattan restudy. *Social Science and Medicine, 10,* 517.

Sireling, L. I., Paykel, E. S., Freeling, P., Rao, B. M., & Patel, S. P. (1985). Depression in general practice: Case thresholds and diagnosis. *British Journal of Psychiatry, 147,* 113-119.

Smith, M. A., Plawecki, H. M., Houser, B., Carr, J., & Plawecki, J. A. (1991). Age and health perceptions among elderly Blacks. *Journal of Gerontological Nursing, 17,* 13-19.

Spitzer, R. L., Endicott, J., & Robins, E. (1978). Research diagnostic criteria: Rationale and reliability. *Archives of General Psychiatry, 35,* 773-782.

Spitzer, R. L., Williams, J. B. W., Gibbon, M., & First, M. D. (1990). *SCID user's guide for the Structured Clinical Interview for DSM-III-R*. Washington, DC: American Psychiatric Press.

Staats, S., Heaphey, K., Miller, D., Partlo, C., Romine, N., & Stubbs, K. (1993). Subjective age and health perceptions of older persons: Maintaining the youthful bias in sickness and in health. *International Journal of Aging and Human Development, 37*, 191–203.

Stoller, E. P. (1984). Self-assessments of health by the elderly: The impact of informal assistance. *Journal of Health and Social Behavior, 25*, 260–270.

Suchman, E. A, Phillips, B. S, & Streib, G. F. (1958). An analysis of the validity of health questionnaires. *Social Forces, 36*, 223–232.

Sugisawa, H., Liang, J., & Liu, X. (1994). Social networks, social support, and mortality among older people in Japan. *Journal of Gerontology, 49*, S3–S13.

Tessler, R., & Mechanic, D. (1978). Psychological distress and perceived health status. *Journal of Health and Social Behavior, 19*, 254–262.

Thomas, C., Kelman, H. R., Kennedy, G. J., Ahn, C., & Yang, C. (1992). Depressive symptoms and mortality in older persons. *Journal of Gerontology, 47*, S80–S87.

Tissue, T. (1972). Another look at self-rated health among the elderly. *Journal of Gerontology, 27*, 91–94.

Weinberger, M., Darnell, J. C., Tierney, W. M., Martz, G. L., Hinger, S. L., Barker, J., & Neill, P. J. (1986a). Self-rated health as a predictor of hospital admission and nursing home placement in elderly public housing tenants. *American Journal of Public Health, 76*, 457–459.

Weinberger, M., Darnell, J. C., Martz, B. L., Hiner, S. L., Neill, P. C., & Tierney, W. M. (1986b). The effects of positive and negative life changes on the self-reported health status of elderly adults. *Journal of Gerontology, 41*, 114–119.

Wells, K. B., Burnam, A., Rogers, W., Hays, R., & Camp, P. (1992). The course of depression in adult outpatients: Results from the Medical Outcomes Study. *Archives of General Psychiatry, 49*, 788–794.

Wells, K. B., Steward, A., Hays, R. D., Burnam, M. A., Rogers, W., Daniels, M., Berry, S., Greenfield, S., & Ware, J. (1989). The functioning and well-being of depressed patients: Results from the Medical Outcomes Study. *Journal of the American Medical Association, 262*, 914–919.

Wolinsky, F. D., Culler, S. D., Callahan, C. M., & Johnson, R. J. (1994). Hospital resource consumption among older adults: A prospective analysis of episodes, length of stay, and charges over a seven-year period. *Journal of Gerontology, 49*, S240–S252.

Yesavage, J. A., & Brink, T. L. (1983). Development and validation of a geriatric depression scale: A preliminary report. *Journal of Psychiatric Research, 17*, 37–49.

Zonderman, A. B., Leu, V. L., & Costa, P. T. (1986). Effects of age, hypertension history, and neuroticism on health perceptions. *Environmental Gerontology, 21*, 449–458.

CHAPTER 6

Prevention and Early Intervention for Mental Disorders of the Elderly

Michael A. Smyer

This chapter summarizes some of the current strengths and weaknesses of the research literature on prevention and early treatment of older adults' mental disorders. The initial section focuses on a conceptual framework for prevention and early intervention recently developed by the Institute of Medicine (IOM; Mrazek & Haggerty, 1994). This framework includes assumptions about causality of mental disorders, methods of identifying cases with a disorder, and appropriate measures of success or failure following an intervention.

With the framework as a guide, the chapter briefly reviews the research literature on three categories of preventive interventions: universal, selective, and indicated. These categories move from the most general to the most specific targets for intervention, based on the risk for a disorder.

Within the indicated preventive interventions, two illustrative disorders are emphasized: (a) dementias and cognitive impairment and (b) depression. These are highlighted because of their relative frequency for older adults. In data from the Epidemiological Catchment Area (ECA) studies of the National Institute of Mental Health (NIMH), cognitive impairment, depression, and anxiety disorders are among the most frequent problems of community-dwelling elderly (Rabins, 1992). A similar pattern emerges in the nursing home setting (Lair & Lefkowitz, 1990). The intervention research literature on each disorder is reviewed briefly, with attention to two elements: What do we know about effective early interventions, and what do we need to know?

The final section of the chapter provides suggestions for future research investigations and recommendations for improving our understanding of the elements that contribute to effective prevention and early intervention. Throughout the chapter, the literature review is designed to be illustrative—pointing out studies that embody larger themes from the literature—rather than exhaustive.

In addition to the IOM report, three documents have been useful in preparing this summary. The first is the report of an interdisciplinary coordinating group on mental health and the elderly (Finkel et al., 1993). This document was commissioned by NIMH and was designed to assess progress in a variety of areas (including prevention and research) since the last White House Conference on Aging in 1981. The second document, *Vitality for Life* (Park, Cavanaugh, Smith, & Smyer, 1993), was developed as part of the Human Capital Initiative, an effort sponsored by the American Psychological Society and the American Psychological Association to outline research priorities in the social and behavioral sciences. *Vitality for Life* focuses on psychological research for productive aging. Finally, Gatz, Kasl-Godley, and Karel (in press) have provided a very useful overview of aging and mental disorders for the forthcoming *Handbook of the Psychology of Aging*. Their review contributed substantially to the argument presented here.

Two cautionary notes are important: Mental illness is not a part of normal aging, and when it occurs, it has a significant emotional and economic impact (Ernst & Hay, 1994; Hay & Ernst, 1987; Park et al., 1993). Approximately 22% of the elderly have a mental disorder (Gatz & Smyer, 1992; Park et al., 1993), with the highest rates (typically 50% or more) among the institutionalized elderly (Burns et al., 1988; Rovner et al., 1990). Nearly a quarter of hospital costs for older adults are for treatment of mental disorders (Park et al., 1993). Similarly, it has been estimated that $12.4 billion per year is spent on nursing home care for older adults with a primary diagnosis of a mental disorder (Shea, 1994). This estimate does not include what it would cost to provide mental health services for these older adults—costs that are estimated at between $311 million and $1.34 billion per year (Shea, Smyer, & Streit, 1993). In short, the emotional and economic impact of successful preventive interventions can be profound for older adults and an aging society.

PREVENTION AND EARLY INTERVENTION: A CONCEPTUAL FRAMEWORK

Research and practice activities are shaped by and contribute to the dominant conceptual frameworks regarding prevention and treatment of mental illness. For some time, those concerned with mental illness have adapted a public health perspective, outlining the distinctions among primary, secondary, and tertiary prevention (e.g., Caplan, 1964; Smyer & Gatz, 1986). Recently, however, a new scheme has been suggested that takes into account two limitations of earlier efforts: the difficulty of defining a "case" in mental illness, in contrast to physical diseases (Mrazek & Haggerty, 1994; Murray, 1992), and our understanding of the important role that social context plays in the prevention or presentation of a mental disorder (e.g., Dohrenwend, 1986; Kellam & Werthamer-Larsson, 1986).

At the request of Congress, IOM recently developed a set of recommendations for a prevention research agenda on mental disorders (Mrazek & Haggerty, 1994). As part of that effort, IOM suggested a new spectrum of mental health intervention for mental disorders (see Figure 1). The spectrum includes three major classes of intervention: prevention, treatment, and maintenance.

Three types of preventive efforts are identified: *universal* prevention, *selective* intervention, and *indicated* prevention. Risk for disorders is a key factor in distinguishing the targets of each type of intervention:

> In the mental health intervention spectrum, *universal preventive interventions* are targeted to the general public or a whole population group that has not been identified on the basis of individual risk. . . . *Selective preventive interventions* for mental disorders are targeted to individuals or a subgroup of the population whose risk of developing mental disorders is significantly higher than average. . . . *Indicated preventive interventions* for mental disorders are targeted to high-risk individuals who are identified as having minimal but detectable signs or symptoms foreshadowing mental disorder, or biological markers indicating predisposition for mental

165

Treatment

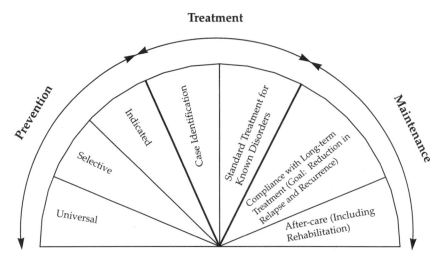

FIGURE 1 The mental health intervention spectrum for mental disorders. SOURCE: From P. Mrazek and R. Haggerty (Eds.), *Reducing Risks for Mental Disorders,* Copyright 1994 by the National Academy of Sciences. Courtesy of the National Academy Press, Washington, DC.

> disorder, but who do not meet DSM-III-R diagnostic levels at the current time. . . . Indicated preventive interventions are often referred to by clinicians as *early intervention* or an early form of treatment. (Mrazek & Haggerty, 1994, pp. 24–25)

These three categories—universal, selective, and indicated—will be used as a framework for reviewing the preventive research literature.

A Theoretical Framework: Diathesis–stress

The IOM conceptual framework on preventive intervention is necessary, but not sufficient, for the development of an effective program of research on preventive interventions. A second necessary component is a theoretical framework that reflects the interaction of the individual and his or her environment in producing a profile of risk for the development of mental disorders.

Gatz, Kasl-Godley, and Karel (in press) have recently suggested the usefulness of extending the diathesis–stress perspective into later adulthood. Zubin and Spring (1977) first developed this model to account for the etiology of schizophrenia. Their work suggested that two dimensions were important: *diathesis*, or the individual's level of vulnerability, and *stress*. Diathesis encompasses genetic influences, acquired biological vulnerabilities, and psychological factors that affect the individual's risk for a disorder. Stress incorporates psychosocial stress (such as the death of a loved one) and environmental stress (such as physical toxic substances). The assumption underlying this model is that greater vulnerability or greater stress or both affect the individual's risk of developing a disorder.

Implicit in the discussion is the importance of the interaction between the individual's vulnerability and the environment, including interpersonal, societal contexts as well as the physical environment. This conceptualization is congruent with the broad outlines first proposed by Lewin (1935) in his equation $b = f(p/e)$. This perspective is also consistent with Lawton's suggestions (1980, 1982) regarding the important interactive role that environmental characteristics and the individual's vulnerability may play in the development of disorders.

Gatz, Kasl-Godley, and Karel (in press) note a third element in considering risks and probabilities of developing a mental disorder: protective factors, whether biological, psychological, or social. The combination of risk and protective factors affects the individual's susceptibility to development of mental disorders. For example, using depressive symptomatology across the life span, Gatz and her colleagues have suggested a hypothetical distribution of biological vulnerability, psychological diathesis, and stressful life events (see Figure 2).

Developmental psychiatric epidemiology can be helpful in understanding these differential pathways. To date, however, such approaches have not been widely used in the latter part of the life span. For example, Kellam and Rebok (1992) have outlined epidemiologically based preventive intervention trials focused on children who are at risk for adverse outcomes later in life because of adjustment problems in school. Kellam and Rebok summarize the purpose of a "developmental epidemiological perspective":

> To allow the mapping of developmental paths within representative samples from a defined community population over significant portions of the lifecourse . . . community epidemiology allows study of the developmental paths of specific cohorts of children who develop toward

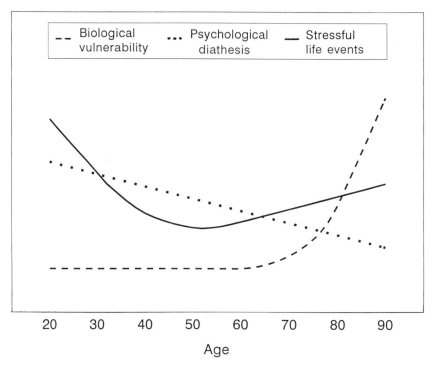

FIGURE 2 Depiction of developmental changes in the magnitude of influence on depressive symptomatology exerted by biological vulnerability, psychological diathesis, and stressful life events. SOURCE: From Gatz et al. (in press). Copyright by Academic Press, Inc. Reprinted with permission of the publisher.

> disorders compared to those in the same community and cohort who do not. . . . From a developmental epidemiological perspective our effort is to explain variation in developmental paths, including antecedents, moderators, and outcomes, within or across neighborhoods or other fairly small populations. (p. 165)

Kellam and Rebok have used such approaches to design, implement, and evaluate preventive interventions focused on children at risk. Similar efforts in the latter part of the life span have not yet been developed.

With this brief introduction to the IOM model, and with a complementary theoretical framework, the three types of preventive interventions will be used to illustrate current strengths and limitations in the preventive research literature.

Universal Preventive Interventions

Universal preventive interventions target all members of an eligible group—for example, all elderly. The assumption is that the intervention is desirable for all individuals, not solely those who have been identified by a specific risk factor. The applicability of this approach to later life is reflected in a segment of *Vitality for Life*:

> The stresses of later life include changing physical and mental abilities, changing social roles, changing family roles, and changing economic resources. . . . Individual adaptation in later life requires individual initiative in the self-maintenance of mental, physical, and social functioning. In addition to individual efforts, social resources (e.g., family members and friends) can act as buffers and moderators of the stresses of later life. Equally important, there are ethnic and gender differences in coping approaches and coping effectiveness. In short, there is no single way to effectively respond to the normal stresses of later life. (Park et al., 1993, p. 12)

Although the need for universal preventive interventions in later life is apparent, there are no major empirical investigations of such interventions. The recent IOM review of intervention research programs reiterated the observation that most prevention programs are directed at infants, preschoolers, elementary-age children, and adolescents (Mrazek & Haggerty, 1994). There is a striking absence of prevention research programs targeted to the needs of adults, including the elderly.

What could researchers contribute to our understanding of effective universal prevention efforts? Again, *Vitality for Life* offers helpful observations:

> Although the descriptive literature on effective responses to later life stress has increased during the last decade there has been relatively little investigation of the effects of organized interventions to support such effective responses. For example, we need to understand the elements of effective coping that can be applied to programmatic interventions for a number of normal, developmental issues of later life: working through life-transition stresses (e.g., retirement, widowhood, etc.); coping with developmental crises; memory training; attacking the loneliness of later life; decision-making skills; and developing new skills. In addition, we need to understand the influence of adaptation across the life course: what is the impact of mid-life responses to stress on adaptation in later

life? What are the unique challenges to mental health among the oldest-old (80+), the fastest growing portion of the older age groups? How does the interaction of the physical, mental, social, and economic determinants of positive mental health change in later adulthood, particularly among the oldest old? (Park et al., 1993, p. 12)

Two themes are important in this statement. First, there is an essential link between research on basic coping processes and the development and implementation of effective preventive intervention programs. We must develop a comprehensive understanding of the elements of effective coping that can be applied to programmatic interventions for a number of normal, developmental issues of late life, such as retirement or chronic illness (see Aldwin, 1994; Baltes & Danish, 1980; Brim & Ryff, 1980).

Second, it is important to understand the influence of adaptation across the life span (e.g., the impact of midlife response to stress on adaptation in later life) and its implications for preventive interventions. Gatz, Kasl-Godley, and Karel (in press) note that mental disorders in late life may be a result of three patterns of development: an individual may develop a mental disorder early in life and grow old; an individual may grow old and develop a mental disorder; or an individual may be exposed to a variety of stressors earlier in life that eventually lead to the development of a mental disorder in later life. Their argument is an expansion of an earlier compilation developed by Kahn (1975).

Selective Preventive Interventions

Selective preventive interventions are focused on individuals at risk for the development of a mental disorder. These interventions build on a basic research base regarding the etiology and course of mental disorders. Thus, to be most effective, research on these preventive interventions must be viewed within a cycle of research development and implementation as outlined in Figure 3, taken from the recent IOM report (Mrazek and Haggerty, 1994).

The research base on selective preventive interventions with older adults is virtually in its infancy. A recent review of research needs in this area suggests several priorities for investigation. First, we need to under-

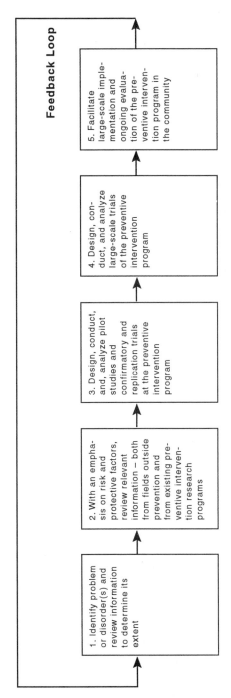

FIGURE 3 The preventive research cycle. Preventive intervention research is represented in Boxes 3 and 4. Note that information from many fields in health research, represented in Boxes 1 and 2, is necessary to the cycle depicted here. However, it is the review of this information, rather than the original studies themselves, that is considered part of the preventive intervention research cycle. Likewise, for Box 5, it is the investigator's facilitation of the shift from research project to community service program with ongoing evaluation, rather than the service program itself, that is part of the preventive intervention research cycle. Although only one feedback loop is represented here, the exchange of knowledge among researchers and between researchers and community practitioners occurs throughout the cycle. SOURCE: From P. Mrazek and R. Haggerty (Eds.), *Reducing Risks for Mental Disorders*, Copyright 1994 by the National Academy of Sciences. Courtesy of the National Academy Press, Washington, DC.

stand individual differences among older adults in responding to the stresses and challenges of late life. Why do many older adults at risk for psychopathology not develop problems? And what are the implications of their coping processes for preventive interventions? Second, what are the unique risks and challenges among the oldest old? And what are the implications for the development and implementation of preventive interventions for this target group?

Indicated Preventive Interventions

Indicated preventive interventions are what might be called early intervention. They focus on prompt treatment of individuals with a diagnosable mental disorder. Here too, recent reviews of the research literature suggest that there is much work to be done. As a general goal, it will be important to identify the biological, social, and psychological markers for risk of mental disorders in late life, as well as the optimal combination of biological, social, and psychological factors for effective preventive interventions and prompt treatment protocols. As discussed below, progress toward this goal has been achieved differentially across several mental disorders.

DEMENTIAS

Alzheimer's disease, or senile dementia of the Alzheimer's type, and other dementias are perhaps the most feared mental disorders of later life. The rate of cognitive disorders increases with age; as many as 29% of those over age 90 may be afflicted, depending on the definition of the disorder, the assessment methods used, and the sample frame used (Ritchie, Kildea, & Robine, 1992).

The development, implementation, and evaluation of selective preventive interventions and indicated preventive interventions require both the identification of groups at risk and an understanding of the course of the disorder. For example, Mortimer (1995) and Gatz, Lowe, Berg, Mortimer, and Pedersen (1994) argue that there is an analogy between our understanding of chronic diseases and preventive efforts focused on Alzheimer's disease and other dementing disorders. In an extension of a diathesis–stress model, they highlight both environmental factors and genetic susceptibility as important elements in the development and expression of dementia. As they point out, it is unlikely that Alzheimer's disease reflects a single underlying cause. Instead, genetic factors—in particular, family history—constitute a notable risk for the disorder (Breitner, Silverman, Mohs, & Davis, 1988). At the same time, environmental factors, such as toxic substances and chemicals, that affect the nervous system may contribute to a variety of dementias. Similarly, lifestyle elements, such as smoking or alcohol abuse, and other environmental insults, such as head trauma, may also contribute to the development of a dementia (Mortimer, 1995).

Selective Preventive Interventions

The implications of the combination of stresses and individual predisposing factors are apparent in a recent set of recommendations for prevention of cognitive impairment with age. As Nolan and Blass (1992) point out, the aim of the steps is fairly straightforward: to maximize brain reserve and minimize brain damage. To achieve these simple goals, they suggest the following preventive interventions:

1. Effective prenatal and perinatal care, including nutrition, to ensure that as many individuals as possible start life with the best neurologic substratum that their genetic endowments allow.

2. Effective education, so that most people enter adult life with a maximal level of knowledge, including the skills to continue learning.

3. Healthy lifestyles, including good nutrition and the avoidance of trauma and of excessive exposure to alcohol or other chemicals that can damage the brain.

4. Prevention of disease, specifically vascular disease.

5. Prompt and effective medical care for infections and other treatable diseases that stress the aging body.

6. Social organization, including living conditions, that minimize dysphoric reactions and other psychiatric disabilities that impair cognitive performance.

Thus far, there have been no systematic investigations of the long-term effects of such interventions.

Indicated Preventive Interventions

We have a relatively good understanding of the progression of cognitive dysfunction associated with Alzheimer's disease, and the behavioral and emotional effects of Alzheimer's disease are beginning to be better described. Neuropsychological testing and neuroimaging techniques permit increasingly accurate diagnosis of different types of dementia, and we have an increasingly sophisticated understanding of the basic mechanisms of cognitive and behavioral decline in these disorders. Intervention is indicated by the discovery of reversible factors that account for cognitive dysfunction. Even in persons with irreversible progressive dementia, some treatment techniques, such as behavior training, can nonetheless be helpful (Bäckman, 1992).

However, the implications for preventive intervention of our descriptive knowledge of the development and course of Alzheimer's and other dementias are not clear. For example, advances in diagnostic tests are greeted with interest and acclaim (e.g., Scinto et al., 1994; Barinaga, 1994); however, there have been few examples of effective indicated preventive interventions with older adults suffering from Alzheimer's disease or other dementias. Park et al. (1993) capture the progress in this area:

> *What We Need to Know. It is urgent that better strategies be developed to differentiate various forms of dementia, early stages of dementia, and to differentiate dementia from depression.* The goal is to develop an effective and efficient set of assessment strategies and improve diagnostic accuracy. To accomplish this, studies need to be conducted that document relationships among non-invasive psychophysiological, neuropsychological, and behavioral indicators to determine how these relate to one another. Similarly, research on the behavioral psychopharmacology of medications commonly prescribed for older adults can help develop safe and effective medication treatment while avoiding the unwanted side effects (e.g., confusion and disorientation) that are common among older adults. In addition, basic research on the neuropsychological underpinnings of dementia should continue. Interventions for dementia are needed on a number of fronts, including therapeutic interventions to assist the recently diagnosed individual in early stages, who may be in great distress, because most research has focused on the family. Appropriate support and interventions for both the individual and the family also must be developed for later stages of the disease. In particular, the non-cognitive mental health aspects of dementia have been understudied, both in terms

of basic descriptive research and intervention. Also, little is known about appropriate support interventions for members of different minority ethnic groups who often use established mental health services less frequently than do members of other groups. Different traditions and different understandings regarding dementia may require different intervention techniques to be effective. (p. 13)

DEPRESSION

A recent National Institutes of Health (NIH) Consensus Panel on depression in late life noted that "depression in the aging and the aged is a major public health problem" (NIH Consensus Development Panel on Depression in Late Life, 1992). In considering indicated preventive interventions for depression, an initial concern is what is meant by the term "depression." For example, estimates of the prevalence of depression in the elderly vary widely, depending on the criteria used to define a case. For our discussion, perhaps the most useful definition is that adopted by the NIH Consensus Development Panel: "Depression is used in the broad sense to describe a syndrome that includes a constellation of physiological, affective and cognitive manifestations" (p. 1019).

Blazer (1993) summarized epidemiological studies of the prevalence of dysthymia and major depression in community samples of older adults: A consistent finding from the literature is that in community samples, the prevalence of major depression is much lower than the prevalence of depressive symptoms. With this finding in mind, it is estimated that depressive symptoms occur in approximately 15% of community residents over the age of 65 but that major depression occurs in less than 3% of the elderly population. Rates can vary, however, depending upon the location of the sample (Blazer, 1993). For example, primary care settings have reported rates of major depression as high as 11.5% (Koenig, Meador, Cohen, & Blazer, 1988), and nursing homes have reported rates between 12% (Parmelee, Katz, & Lawton, 1989) and 23% (Burns et al., 1988).

From a preventive perspective, it is important to highlight the risk factors for depression that are at work with older adults. For the most part, the social and demographic risk factors are similar to those in younger adults: being female, being unmarried (particularly widowed), stressful life events, and the absence of a supportive social network. In older adults, there is additional emphasis on the co-occurrence of certain physical conditions (e.g., stroke, cancer, dementia) and depression. Depression may be an effect of these disorders; depression might also increase vulnerability to these illnesses.

Selective Preventive Intervention

Perhaps the best example of selective preventive interventions is the work of Thompson and Gallagher-Thompson in their psychoeducational approach to depressive symptoms among older adults (Gallagher & Thompson, 1981, 1983). Their approach is based on the theoretical model of depression developed by Lewinsohn and his colleagues (Lewinsohn et al., 1986). Their target group comprises older adults with mild to moderate symptoms of depression who are at risk for developing major depressive disorders. In a series of studies, Thompson and Gallagher-Thompson have explored an effective group intervention that uses a classroom approach for teaching skills in coping with depression or managing moods (Thompson, Gallagher, & Steinmetz–Breckenridge, 1987; Thompson et al., 1991). The results have been impressive in establishing the effectiveness of the psychoeducational approach and in documenting the similar effectiveness of paraprofessional and professional trainers in the program.

Indicated Preventive Interventions

In contrast to the area of dementia, there is a considerable body of literature on the efficacy of indicated interventions for depression in elderly people. Two major approaches have been investigated: biological therapies (including pharmacotherapy and electroconvulsive therapy) and psychotherapy (see Schneider, this volume). The NIH Consensus Panel report notes that there are several limitations to the current knowledge base, including little information on treatment of depression in the very old (those over age 80) and little information on effective treatments for medically ill, depressed elderly people. Psychotherapy approaches have received more attention than biological therapies in the research literature (e.g., Gallagher & Thompson, 1983; Mintz, Steuer, & Jarvik, 1981; Moberg and Lazarus, 1990; Thompson, Gallagher, & Steinmetz-Breckenridge, 1987). Despite advances, there are still gaps in our knowledge. Most notably, there is more to be learned about the efficacy of cognitive behavior therapy, behavior therapy, interpersonal therapy, and short-term psychodynamic therapy with elderly people, especially the very old and the medically ill.

The impact of our inadequate research base and indicated intervention approaches can perhaps best be seen in the rates of suicide in late life. Older adults commit suicide at disproportionate rates. Although they represent 12% of the population, they account for 21% of suicides (Park et al., 1993). The group at highest risk comprises white males age 80 to 84; their rate of suicide is 6 times the nation's age-adjusted rate (Conwell, 1994). Older adults are more successful in completing suicide than any other age group, and depression in older adults is closely linked to suicide among the elderly (Conwell, 1994). Suicide among the elderly is associated with diagnosable psychopathology (most often affective disorders) in approximately 90% of cases (Conwell, 1994). The majority of victims have seen their primary care physicians within the month prior to suicide (Conwell, 1994). Unfortunately, primary care physicians are generally not skilled in diagnosing and treating geriatric depression. Thus, in primary care, there is need for better preparation of physicians for screening and treatment, as well as for better screening and prevention in older adults at risk for suicide (Conwell, 1994; NIH Consensus Panel, 1992). It is in the clinical setting that the absence of well-developed screening procedures and effective treatment protocols has its most direct impact.

DISCUSSION AND CONCLUSIONS

This chapter has outlined a framework for consideration of interventions to prevent mental disorders among older adults. Two themes have received emphasis: (a) Preventive efforts designed for older adults and their families should be considered case examples of the larger themes of prevention theory and research across the life span; and (b) there is much work still to be done in targeting the concerns of older adults.

To be most effective, recommendations to improve prevention research targeting older adults must be part of a larger emphasis on prevention of mental disorders across the life span. Fortunately, the recent IOM report has outlined an agenda for future efforts, highlighting three interrelated aspects: (a) building the infrastructure to coordinate research and service programs and to train and support new investigators, (b) expanding the knowledge base for preventive interventions, and (c) conducting well-evaluated preventive interventions (Mrazek & Haggerty, 1994). In offering suggestions for future action, it will be helpful to use the IOM suggestions as a framework in two ways: (a) to include older adults and their concerns in any structures developed, and (b) to include preventive efforts in any aging-oriented research and service initiatives. The recommendations below are revisions of a larger agenda developed and promulgated recently by the IOM (Mrazek & Haggerty, 1994).

Building an Enhanced Infrastructure

It is essential that federal departments coordinate their research and services in prevention of mental disorders. At the same time, older adults and their concerns should be included in plans for prevention. One simple step toward integrating aging and prevention, for example, could focus on ensuring that the national advisory councils of NIMH, the National Institute of Alcohol Abuse and Alcoholism, The National Institute of Aging (NIA), and the National Institute on Drug Abuse include prevention researchers with gerontological expertise.

Federal agencies can play an important role in ensuring that additional researchers are available to carry out prevention research. For example, current research training mechanisms could be exploited to include research on prevention efforts as well as training in clinical trials and basic research. Similarly, a modest expansion of training slots available for research training from NIMH and NIA could be targeted for expansion of prevention efforts.

State-level initiatives are also important. For example, state-level offices for prevention of mental disorders could collaborate with state-level aging networks to address the mental health needs of each state's aging population.

Expanding the Knowledge Base

Our understanding of modifiable risk and protective factors for the development of mental disorders in late life must be expanded. Several different strategies might be helpful. For example, some efforts might build on already-existing data from at-risk groups followed earlier in the life span (e.g., Women, Infant, and Children program or Head Start databases). Other efforts might focus on conducting longitudinal studies across the life span, expanding our understanding of how risk factors and developmental transitions interact to influence the development and trajectory of psychopathology in late life. Finally, other efforts might emphasize the risk and protective factors associated with the major mental disorders of late life. In short, several approaches are needed to expand the nascent knowledge base.

Conducting Well-Evaluated Interventions

Risk reduction—targeting known risk and protective factors—is the best available theoretical model for the development, implementation, and evaluation of interventions to prevent the onset of mental disorders in late life. Unfortunately, few well-developed preventive intervention studies have been carried out.

Future intervention studies should give priority to proposals that focus on well-validated biological, psychological, and social risk and protective factors. In addition, the interaction between mental and physical illness in late life is a particular concern. Similarly, cultural diversity and ethical considerations must be integrated into the development, implementation, and evaluation of preventive intervention research. In short, well-evaluated interventions must build on and, in turn, contribute to the knowledge base of the etiology and course of mental disorders in later life.

Several mechanisms can help to achieve these ambitious goals. For example, coordination of federal and state initiatives in the Medicaid and Medicare programs could be linked to research priorities and evaluation efforts. Similarly, emphasis in research funding could be expanded to include greater use of secondary data archives from Medicare and Medicaid as tools for evaluating current and future intervention efforts. Achieving these goals, however, may require a specialized prevention research center sponsored through an interagency agreement among NIMH, NIA, and other federal agencies. Regardless of the specific mechanisms chosen, the goal should be clear: to link our understanding of risk and protective factors for mental disorders in late life to effective preventive intervention strategies.

REFERENCES

Aldwin, C. M. (1994). *Stress, coping, and development.* New York: Guilford.

Bäckman, L. (1992). Memory training and memory improvement in Alzheimer's disease: Rules and exceptions. *Acta Neurologica Scandinavica, 139*(Suppl.), 84-89.

Baltes, P. B., & Danish, S. J. (1980). Intervention in life-span development and aging: Issues and concepts. In R. R. Turner & H. W. Reese (Eds.), *Life-span developmental psychology: Intervention* (pp. 49-78). New York: Academic Press.

Barinaga, M. (1994). Possible new test found for Alzheimer's disease. *Science, 266,* 973.

Blazer, D. G. (1993). *Depression in late life* (2nd ed.). St. Louis, MO: Mosby.

Breitner, J. C. S., Silverman, J. M., Mohs, R. C., & Davis, K. L. (1988). Familial aggregation in Alzheimer's disease: Comparison of risk among relatives of early- and late-onset cases, among male and female relatives in successive generations. *Neurology, 38,* 207-212.

Brim, O. G., & Ryff, C. D. (1980). On the properties of life events. In P. B. Baltes & O. G. Brim (Eds.), *Life-span development and behavior* (pp. 368-388). New York: Academic Press.

Burns, B. J., Larson, D. B., Goldstrom, I. D., et al. (1988). Mental disorders among nursing home patients: Preliminary findings from the National Nursing Home Survey. *International Journal of Geriatric Psychiatry, 3,* 27-35.

Caplan, G. (1964). *Principles of preventive psychiatry.* New York: Basic Books.

Conwell, Y. (1994). Suicide in elderly patients. In L. S. Schneider, C. F. Reynolds, B. D. Lebowitz, & A. J. Friedhoff (Eds.), *Diagnosis and treatment of depression in late life: Results of the NIH Consensus Development Conference* (pp. 397-418). Washington, DC: American Psychiatric Press.

Dohrenwend, B. P. (1986). Social stress and psychopathology. In M. Kessler & S. E. Goldston (Eds.), *A decade of progress in primary prevention* (pp. 87-114). Hanover, NH: University Press of New England.

Ernst, R. L., & Hay, J. W. (1994). The U.S. economic and social costs of Alzheimer's disease revisited. *American Journal of Public Health, 84,* 1261-1264.

Finkel, S., Dye, C., Garcia, A., Gatz, M., Greene, R., Hay, D., & Smyer, M. (1993). *Report of the Interdisciplinary Coordinating Group on Mental Health and the Elderly.* Washington, DC: American Psychiatric Association.

Gallagher, D., Thompson, L. W. (1981). *Depression in the elderly: A behavioral treatment manual.* Los Angeles: University of Southern California Press.

Gallagher, D. E., & Thompson, L. W. (1983). Effectiveness of psychotherapy for both endogenous and non-endogenous depression in older adults. *Journal of Gerontology, 18,* 707-712.

Gatz, M., Kasl-Godley, J., & Karel, M. (in press). Aging and mental disorders. In J. E. Birren & K. W. Schaie (Eds.), *Handbook of the psychology of aging* (4th ed.) San Diego: Academic Press.

Gatz, M., Lowe, B., Berg, S., Mortimer, J., & Pedersen, N. (1994). Dementia: Not just a search for the gene. *The Gerontologist, 34,* 251-255.

Gatz, M., & Smyer, M. (1992). The mental health system and older adults in the 1990s. *American Psychologist, 47,* 741-751.

Hay, J., & Ernst, R. (1987). The economic costs of Alzheimer's disease. *American Journal of Public Health, 77,* 1169-1175.

Kahn, R. L. (1975). The mental health system and the future aged. *The Gerontologist, 15*(2), 24-31.

Kellam, S. G., & Rebok, G. W. (1992). Building developmental and etiological theory through epidemiologically based preventive intervention trials. In J. McCord & R. E. Tremblay (Eds.), *Preventing antisocial behavior: Interventions from birth through adolescence* (pp. 162-192). New York: Guilford.

Kellam, S., & Werthamer-Larsson, L. (1986). Developmental epidemiology: A basis for prevention. In M. Kessler & S. E. Goldston (Eds.), *A decade of progress in primary prevention* (pp. 154-180). Hanover, NH: University Press of New England.

Koenig, H. G., Meador, K. G., Cohen, H. J., & Blazer, D. G. (1988). Depression in elderly hospitalized patients with medical illness. *Archives of Internal Medicine, 148,* 1929-1936.

Lair, T., & Lefkowitz, D. (1990). *Mental health and functional status of residents of nursing and personal care homes* (DHHS Publication No. [PHS]90-3470). Washington, DC: U.S. Department of Health and Human Services.

Lawton, M. P. (1980). *Environment and aging.* Pacific Grove, CA: Brooks/Cole.

Lawton, M. P. (1982). Competence, environmental press, and the adaptation of old people. In M. P. Lawton, P. G. Windley, & T. O. Byerts (Eds.), *Aging and the environment: Theoretical approaches* (pp. 33-59). New York: Springer.

Lewin, K. (1935). *A dynamic theory of personality.* New York: McGraw-Hill.

Lewinsohn, P. M., Munoz, R. F., Youngren, M. A., Zeiss, A. (1986). *Control your depression* (rev. ed.). New York: Prentice-Hall.

Mintz, J., Steuer, J., & Jarvik, L. (1981). Psychotherapy with depressed elderly patients: Research considerations. *Journal of Consulting and Clinical Psychology, 49,* 542-548.

Moberg, P. J., & Lazarus, L. W. (1990). Psychotherapy of depression in the elderly. *Psychiatric Annals, 20,* 92-96.

Mortimer, J. A. (1995). Prospects for prevention of dementia and associated impairments. In L. A. Bond, S. J. Cutler, & A. Grams (Eds.), *Promoting successful and productive aging* (pp. 131-147). Thousand Oaks, CA: Sage.

Mrazek, P. J., & Haggerty, R. J. (Eds.). (1994). *Reducing risks for mental disorders: Frontiers for preventive intervention research.* Washington, DC: National Academy Press.

Murray, J. (1992). Prevention and identification of high risk groups. *International Review of Psychiatry, 4,* 281-286.

National Institutes of Health Consensus Development Panel on Depression in Late Life. (1992). Diagnosis and treatment of depression in late life. *Journal of the American Medical Association, 268,* 1018-1024.

Nolan, K. A., & Blass, J. P. (1992). Preventing cognitive decline. *Health Promotion and Disease Prevention, 8,* 19-34.

Park, D., Cavanaugh, J., Smith, A., & Smyer, M. (1993). *Vitality for life: Psychological research for productive aging.* Washington, DC: Public Policy Office, American Psychological Association.

Parmelee, P. A., Katz, I. R., & Lawton, M. P. (1989). Depression among institutionalized aging: Assessment in prevalence estimation. *Journal of Gerontology, 44,* M22-M29.

Rabins, P. V. (1992). Prevention of mental disorder in the elderly: Current perspectives and future prospects. *Journal of the American Geriatrics Society, 40,* 727-733.

Ritchie, K., Kildea, D., & Robine, J. M. (1992). The relationship between age and the prevalence of senile dementia: A meta-analysis of recent data. *International Journal of Epidemiology, 21,* 763-769.

Rovner, B., German, P., Broadhead, J., et al. (1990). The prevalence and management of dementia and other psychiatric disorders in nursing homes. *International Psychogeriatrics, 2,* 13-24.

Scinto, L. F. M., Daffner, K. R., Dressler, D., Ransil, B. I., Rentz, D., Weintraub, S., Mesulam, M., & Potter, H. (1994). A potential noninvasive neurobiological test for Alzheimer's disease. *Science, 266,* 1051-1054.

Shea, D. G. (1994). *Nursing homes and the costs of mental disorders.* Manuscript submitted for publication.

Shea, D. G., Smyer, M. A., & Streit, A. (1993). Mental health services for nursing home residents: What will it cost? *Journal of Mental Health Administration, 20,* 223-235.

Smyer, M. A., & Gatz, M. (1986). Intervention research approaches. *Research on Aging, 8,* 536-558.

Thompson, L. W., Gallagher, D., & Steinmetz-Breckenridge, J. (1987). Comparative effectiveness of psychotherapies for depressed elders. *Journal of Consulting and Clinical Psychology, 55,* 385-390.

Thompson, L. W., Gantz, F., Florsheim, M., DelMaestro, S., Rodman, J., Gallagher-Thompson, D., & Bryan, H. (1991). *New techniques in the psychotherapy of older adults* (3–19). Washington, DC: American Psychiatric Press.

Zubin, J., & Spring, B. (1977). Vulnerability: A new view of schizophrenia. *Journal of Abnormal Psychology, 86,* 103-126.

CHAPTER 7

Let's Not Wait Till It's Broke: Interventions to Maintain and Enhance Mental Health in Late Life

Elinor Waters

Discussion of mental health in late life requires a shift in perspective away from problems and what can be done to fix them (Sherman, 1993). As Cohen (1993) urges, it is necessary to assess strengths, not just weaknesses. Similarly, Kivnick (1993) challenges us to look for "vital involvement." The board of directors of the American Association of Retired Persons (AARP) recommends that we "view mental health care—just as we view physical health care—along a continuum from promotion of good mental health to treatment of serious illness" (AARP, 1994a, p. 2). These statements reflect the philosophical underpinnings for this chapter: a belief that the goal of preventive mental health interventions is to help older adults find pleasure and meaning in their lives, use appropriate supports, and retain or assume as much control over their lives as possible.

The chapter begins with a discussion of the construct of positive mental health in old age and of settings in which it can be promoted. Following this, programs designed to promote mental health in older adults are described. The emphasis is on activities "to enhance competence, self-esteem, and a sense of well-being rather than to prevent a disorder" (Mrazek & Haggerty, 1994, p. 28).

The variety of settings considered reflects a basic belief about the best place to offer such interventions—anywhere we can. The programs described reflect a broad range of normative challenges older adults face: maintaining wellness, reviewing one's life, grieving, caregiving, and retiring. The chapter concludes by looking at some trends that will affect mental health promotion among older adults and by providing some recommendations about the services needed, including suggested sites and modes of delivery.

Outcome data are available on some of the programs described here; for others, evaluation is anecdotal or informal. Because many of these programs and techniques have been developed and implemented by clinicians and self-help organizations rather than social science researchers, evaluation is not always a priority. Where data are available, they are included, but it seems unwise to exclude programs reported to be effective simply because they lack stringent evaluation.

REVIEW OF THE LITERATURE

This section examines several views of mental health and provides a cursory listing of concepts that may be helpful in thinking about what constitutes good mental health in old age. Schlossberg (1993) suggested that we all need "a mental health portfolio" that can help us develop or maintain a sense of hope and optimism, a belief that we matter to other people, and a set of coping skills to deal with the traumas and inconveniences of life. Her definition suggests that practitioners can benefit from using Seligman's concept (1991) of learned optimism and of the ideas of Folkman et al. (1991) on coping styles.

In a similar vein, Dychtwald (1986) talked of people's need to grow older with the highest levels of health, vitality, and independence possible. Solomon (1992) identified several dimensions of successful aging: psychological (flexibility and adaptability), environmental (access to organizational and social resources), interpersonal (ability to maintain autonomy and control), and spiritual (ability to see meaning in one's life). While Solomon's dimensions are useful, they may not fit for all groups. Burton, Dilworth-Anderson, and Bengtson (1991) urged us to develop new paradigms for studying aging and diversity and for providing culturally relevant assistance. They suggest that art, music, dance, literature, and folklore may help practitioners interpret important themes in the lives of ethnic minority elderly and note that some ethnic minority elderly may "perceive aging not as a series of adjustments but rather as a process of survival" (p. 69).

Given that older adults experience a variety of losses and other transitions, an important question is why some survive and cope more effectively than others. One possible explanatory factor is the presence or absence of "hardiness." According to Kobasa, Maddi, and Kahn (1982), hardiness includes commitment, control, and challenge. People with hardiness, then, are more likely to involve themselves fully in what they are doing, to see themselves as influential rather than helpless in the course of their lives, and to see changes as challenging rather than threatening. This definition is consistent with Ryff's findings (1989) that, in the view of older adults, successful aging is marked by the ability to accept change as well as by a sense of humor, an enjoyment of life, and positive relations with others.

Wykle and Musil (1993) document the strong association of both instrumental and emotional support with mental well-being. Perception of support seems to contribute to life satisfaction, although sources of support may differ among ethnic groups. For elderly Blacks, for example, church-related support seems to be particularly important (Walls & Zarit, 1991).

All of the approaches to examining a person's support system can be used diagnostically both to recognize and appreciate existing supports and to pinpoint needed additions. Using Kahn and Antonucci's now classic "convoy" of social support (1980), a counselor can help an older adult identify types of support that are present and missing. Cantor's model (1991) of the social care system of the elderly graphs the relationships of informal and formal supports, thus putting informal supports into an environmental context. Pearson (1990) suggests that when inadequate support seems to be contributing to client difficulties, a first step is to decide whether the difficulties are client based or externally based. Appropriate diagnosis can help service providers tailor interventions to restore a balance of independence and necessary dependence, which in turn may contribute to good mental health.

It is instructive to study how people over age 85 living in the general community maintain independence. For example, in their report on African Americans in a San Francisco study, Perry and Johnson (1994) talked of the strength of the Black family in terms of "its flexibility in molding a family and support network suited to the individual's needs at a given time. Unlike the Whites in this study . . . African Americans have relatives who are substitutes in the absence of children" (p. 47).

Writing about White families in the same study, Johnson (1994) noted that a major risk for this predominately female group is that its members may have outlived their families as well as contemporaries. "Nevertheless . . . a majority of the very old tend to report that their health is good or excellent, a perceived health status that is much more optimistic than their actual level of disability would indicate" (p. 3). Johnson suggested that we may want to rethink our ideas about the value of activity and control when looking at the oldest old, whose level of disability and shrinking social network may make exercising control and socializing exceedingly difficult. Part of their adaptability may include welcoming a degree of detachment or disengagement from some people and activities.

Johnson's suggestions fit with Gatz's caution (1986) that in our efforts to debunk myths of aging, we must not create countermyths that establish too optimistic an expectation. "The implication for mental health education is to guard against promulgating either myth or countermyth" (p. 159). Similarly, Rodeheaver and Datan (1988) warn us not to define mental health in terms of activity and achievement. They observe that "most elders are psychologically robust despite the social, economic, and physical barriers they face" (p. 652). We can use our understanding of this history to help older adults see their longevity not in association with rigidity but rather as a track record of coping skills. We also can acknowledge what Jacobson (in press) said: "Working to come to terms with finitude is neither morbid nor eccentric but necessary to good mental health as we become old."

We need to keep these various components of mental health in mind when considering where to offer preventive services and what kinds of services are most effective in promoting positive mental health. Although many older adults do experience a barrage of losses, most such losses do not result in clinical depression. During tough times, older adults typically rely on friends, family, and other informal supports. If they visit a professional, it is much more likely to be a physician than a mental health professional (Gatz & Smyer, 1992; Phillips & Murrell, 1994). Because older adults are "more likely to conceptualize problems in terms of physical health and adverse life experiences rather than in terms of psychological deficits" (Heller, 1993, p. 124), the settings in which help is provided can be crucial.

ALTERNATIVE SETTINGS FOR PROVIDING MENTAL HEALTH SERVICES

There is ample documentation that most older adults do not use traditional mental health settings, in part because of the stigma many older adults attach to mental health care (Gatz & Smyer, 1992; Kent, 1990). Therefore, this chapter focuses on provision of services in such alternative settings as health care clinics, neighborhood centers, senior centers, community organizations, and religious or educational institutions. People in need of help can visit such facilities without identifying themselves as depressed or as having trouble. Rather, they can define themselves as going to the doctor, attending a class, getting information on community services, or participating in a support group about a specific issue.

One useful model of combining mental and physical health care is provided by the Pike Market Medical Center in Seattle, which has a social worker on its staff. In the examining room, the physician introduces the mental health counselor to the patient and explains the kind of services the counselor can provide. Lustbader (1990) stated,

> The realization that one does not have to be "crazy" to see a counselor is an essential aspect of this introductory contact. The physician conveys this message through the very inclusion of the counselor on the medical team and the jargon-free delineation of concrete goals. (p. 22)

By their nature as community focal points, senior centers also can be a relatively comfortable place for older adults and their families to seek preventive services. The programs offered can help adults develop social skills and expand their social networks, which in turn can contribute to positive mental health. Center participants tend to trust the staff so that "an available staff counselor can utilize nontraditional counseling models" (Grady, 1990, p. 15).

As part of their jobs, senior center staff provide a variety of concrete services, such as arranging for a home care aide or working with a job seeker to improve a resumé. Such services can help older adults develop trust in the helping process and can serve as a precursor to "by-the-way counseling." This term, discussed by Waters and Goodman (1990), reflects the casual manner in which counseling contacts can be initiated. An older person may call or stop by the office of a staff member to ask for information. Once the question has been answered, the person may, with a "while you're up" tone, ask for help with a personal problem. It is virtually impossible to assess the extent and effectiveness of such by-the-way counseling, but we must remember it as a vehicle for delivery of services in nontraditional settings and as a possible point of entry to more conventional modalities.

Community-based programs can be particularly important for members of minority groups. For example, neighborhood services, staffed by people who are bilingual and bicultural, are highly recommended for Chinese elderly living in the United States. According to Cheung (1989), most Chinese elderly go everywhere on foot. If they can walk to a site, preferably in a Chinatown, they are able to control their mobility. This, in turn, may be a boost to self-esteem.

ILLUSTRATIVE PROGRAMS TO ENHANCE SELF-ESTEEM AND INTERPERSONAL RELATIONSHIPS

The literature described earlier noted that key aspects of mental health for older adults involve autonomy and self-esteem as well as relationships and social support—areas that are related to many of the normative issues facing most older adults. The programs described below illustrate community-based programs that address these areas. Professionally led programs as well as self-help and peer counseling programs are included.

Wellness Programs

One well-known program, Alert and Alive, was piloted in senior centers in different ethnic neighborhoods of New York City. Perlstein (1992) stated that "mental wellness programs for older adults are succeeding today . . . helping older Americans acquire the skills and knowledge necessary to cope with and adjust to the changes, losses and transitions that accompany the aging process" (p. 1).

Alert and Alive is a two-part model consisting of a course in mental health education, followed by leadership training for older volunteers. It represents a "holistic approach to growing older: integrating mind, body and emotional needs. Program participants learn how to think creatively, relieve stress, exercise their bodies, and work comfortably with their emotional concerns" (Perlstein, 1992, p. 2). In Perlstein's view, the safety of the peer environment helps participants discover commonalities, receive support, and begin to "redo" life patterns.

Programs are conducted at senior centers in order to reach healthy elderly and provide a base of continuity. Alert and Alive represents an interesting collaboration between professionals and volunteers. Each of the 12 sessions includes a presentation by a professional guest speaker and a discussion facilitated by the volunteers, as well as a physical and mental wellness warm-up and a healthy snack. Besides presenting valuable information, a major role of the professional speakers is to explain the services of their agencies and to help seniors become more comfortable with the idea of using such services.

"Emphasizing coping skills rather than clinical applications is key to both the theory and the practice of the mental wellness course" (Perlstein, 1992, p. 4). In line with the program goal of helping older adults take charge of their own emotional well-being, the topics for the workshops are chosen on the basis of a survey of senior center members.

A publication listing organizations that promote mental health and wellness, of the National Resource Center on Health Promotion and Aging (1991), briefly describes several programs—for example, Growing Wiser, a comprehensive mental wellness program developed by Healthwise in Boise, Idaho. The Realizing Opportunities for Self Exploration (ROSE) program developed by Share DeCroix Bane (n.d.) is another example of a holistic program suitable for community living or institutionalized older adults.

Among the most common health-promotion groups are those designed to help older adults cope with transitions and losses. We focus here on life review and bereavement groups.

Life Review Groups

Since Robert Butler (1963) first articulated the concept of life review, such groups have become an increasingly popular counseling intervention (Capuzzi, Gross, & Friel, 1990; Moody, 1988; Waters, 1990). In a delightful article, "Mint, Garlic, and the Secret Heart of Time," Kastenbaum (1993) reviewed six books published in 1991 and 1992, all dealing with autobiographical memories—how to encourage them, study them, and use them therapeutically. Singer, Tracz, and Dworkin (1991) found that life review groups can encourage socialization, lead to a sense of self-worth and life satisfaction, and help alleviate loneliness, hopelessness, and depression. Topic-centered groups that added a focus on feelings were found to improve the emotional quality of participants' lives more than groups that dealt just with the topics. "Not only did they report that the present was enlivened by their memories, but for most there appeared to be a newer, more open, and accepting or integrative attitude toward the past" (Sherman, 1987, p. 572).

Life reviews can be done individually or in groups and can be initiated in a variety of ways. Leaders of life review groups can help participants gain a sense of pride from thinking of the people they have influenced and the crises they have weathered. Reviewers can be encouraged to identify past coping strategies and survival skills and to consider how they can be applied to present situations.

Many organizations have developed programs for stimulating life reviews. For example, Bi-Folkal Productions (n.d.) has developed a series of reminiscence packages to stimulate memory sharing. The packages, available in many public libraries, include photographs, music, stories, and old household items to use as triggers for reminiscences.

Disch's 1988 volume marking 25 years of the life review describes some unusual life review groups, including one that took the form of a theatrical presentation (Perlstein, 1988). Haight (1991) reviewed 30 years of literature on reminiscing and life review and reported that the majority of evaluations indicated positive results on such variables as self-esteem and depression. She developed the Life Review and Experiencing Form (LREF) as the basis for a structured process of individual life review. The process involves six 1-hour interviews, plus pre- and posttesting sessions to assess psychological well-being and psychological illness (National Mental Health Association Prevention Clearinghouse, n.d.).

A special use of reminiscence to prevent further problems for chemically dependent older persons was described by Manderfield (1994). Designed to help patients identify coping mechanisms from the past that would help them in recovery, the program proved more helpful with late-onset than with early-onset patients.

Reviewing their lives reminds almost everybody of significant people who are no longer living. Discussing these memories as part of the life review sometimes provides all the help people need. At other times, they may seek out a bereavement group.

Bereavement Groups

While we experience losses and grieve over them throughout our lives, old age differs in that we are likely to encounter more losses and must deal with their cumulative effect. It is also the period of life when we are most likely to lose a long-term partner. Such a loss, combined with the loss of social supports, which are often couple related, can constitute a threat to mental health.

Summarizing research on bereavement, Stroebe, Hansson, and Stroebe (1993) reported that a major theme that emerged was "that grief is not a simple, universal process, with a progression of fixed stages [and that we need] a greater understanding of the heterogeneity of individual responses to loss" (p. 462). They also noted that differences in the reported duration and intensity of grief depend on how grief is defined. For example, a longitudinal study of bereaved men and women over age 55 in the Los Angeles area showed that spousal bereavement does indeed have implications for mental health and for possible interventions (Gallagher-Thompson, Futterman, Farberow, Thompson, & Peterson, 1993). Two months after being widowed, both men and women showed significantly higher levels of distress and depressed mood than comparison groups. While symptoms of general distress and depression diminished to normal levels after two and a half years, grief behaviors such as yearning for the spouse stayed high throughout this period.

191

Interventions at the individual, group, and community levels are described in the *Handbook of Bereavement* (Stroebe et al., 1993). Summarizing the interventions, the editors stated that there is much evidence for the efficacy of support, but that more methodologically sound research is needed. In his study of bereavement self-help groups, Lieberman (1993) wrote that published reports from several nations indicate that self-help groups are seen as a viable alternative to professional help:

> The empirical research supporting their efficacy provides some bases for expecting that a large segment of the bereaved can meet their social and psychological needs in self help groups. . . . However the variability of the research and the lack of consistency among studies . . . make it well nigh impossible to develop precise statements about what kind of bereavement and at what points in their grief such groups would be helpful. (p. 426)

Based on their study of spousal bereavement, Gallagher-Thompson et al. (1993) suggested a variety of intervention strategies. For example, their finding that increased mortality rates for men seemed to correlate with an impoverished social network "argues strongly for intervention providing for network enrichment with older males, who are somewhat isolated very early in the bereavement process" (p. 238). This is consistent with Fiske and Chiriboga's observation (1990) that "losing a spouse is often more traumatic for men than for women" (p. 255). When a man's wife dies, he often loses his best friend and the person who was responsible for his social life.

The Widowed Persons Service (WPS), sponsored by AARP, uses the self-help model with professional supervision. WPS, which now operates in more than 220 communities nationwide, served approximately 98,000 people in 1993 in one-to-one and group contacts. More than 5,000 volunteers were involved in these efforts (AARP, 1994b). WPS's approach was based on research by Silverman, Mackenzie, Pettipas, and Wilson (1974), which indicated that grieving people were best helped by others who have rebuilt their lives after suffering similar losses. An admirable feature of this program is that it is conducted under the auspices of an organization, AARP, that recruits, selects, and trains widowed persons to serve as volunteers and then exercises oversight through provision of technical assistance and in-service training.

Vachon and colleagues carried out research on the WPS program as it was replicated in Canada. Summarizing this research, Mrazek and Haggerty (1994, pp. 345-347) reported that widows who participated in the intervention group were more likely than those in the control group to have begun new relationships and activities and experienced fewer depressive symptoms. Control group members recovered more slowly.

Programs for Caregivers

The risk to the physical and mental health of caregivers has been well documented (e.g., Brody, 1990; Silverstone, 1994), but less attention has been paid to the positive aspects of caregiving. Lustbader and Hooyman (1994) discussed a variety of risks to caregivers and suggested strategies that can help caregivers take care of themselves as well as their frail family members.

As the title implies, several authors in the comprehensive book *Caregiving Systems: Informal and Formal Helpers* (Zarit, Pearlin, & Schaie, 1993), discussed the importance of integrating formal and informal support systems. Facilitating such integration and helping caregivers to feel comfortable about accepting outside help can be major roles in preventive intervention. This may mean referring caregivers to individual or group counseling or to a support group.

A recent review of research on interventions with caregivers (Knight, Lutzky, & Macofsky-Urban, 1993) found that caregiver distress was indeed reduced, to varying degrees, by individual and group psychosocial interventions and by respite care programs. They concluded that "the appropriate question now is not whether interventions work but rather what interventions work best at what levels of strength with which kinds of caregivers caring for relatives with specific kinds of impairments" (p. 247).

Mrazek and Haggerty (1994) cited research by Toseland and his associates on peer-led and professionally led support groups for caregivers. Both peer and professional leaders encouraged venting of feelings, expressions of support and understanding, and affirmation of the ability of members to cope. The professionally led group included more education and problem-solving training. Both treatment groups demonstrated lower levels of psychiatric symptoms, including anxiety and depression, and better coping skills than a control group that received only respite care. However, the investigators believe that individual interventions may be more effective for caregivers at the highest risk of developing psychiatric symptoms.

Anecdotal reports to program sponsors suggest that efforts oriented toward education and problem solving, rather than just support and affirmation, more effectively reduce the likelihood of caregivers reaching levels of distress that place them at high risk. If this is true, it makes sense to consider caregiver support groups a billable service when the groups are conducted by a mental health professional in any setting. At present, agencies can bill for group therapy only if caregivers in the group are given a formal diagnosis from the *Diagnostic and Statistical Manual of Mental Disorders*, fourth edition (American Psychiatric Association, 1994). But giving such a diagnosis and conducting groups from a pathological model are likely to alienate many of the people we want to attract.

As a part of education-oriented efforts, excellent print resources for caregivers now exist, including *A Path for Caregivers* (AARP, 1987) and books designed for family members and professionals. For example, Lustbader and Hooyman (1994) address both practical and emotional issues, provide helpful information, and suggest additional resources. Included in their book are user-friendly worksheets, such as a "Family Plan for Task Delegation" (p. 77), that can be the focus of a family meeting. A new resource will be available soon as an outgrowth of a forum on empowering caregivers held in March 1994 to highlight community, state, and federal programs that address the mental health needs of informal caregivers. Conference organizers plan to produce a national directory of innovative and promising programs, particularly those that may reduce the incidence of substance abuse among caregivers.

As we attempt to follow the suggestions of Zarit et al. (1993) to bring informal and formal caregivers together, it is important to be aware of the cultural and ethnic backgrounds of the caregivers. Talking of needs of rural minority elderly, DeCroix Bane (1991) noted that "if we combine the disadvantages of rural living and being a member of an ethnic minority group or Native American tribe, a case can be made for triple or even quadruple jeopardy" (p. 63). In her view, it is vital that rural minority aging programs support the natural network available . . . rather than create new programs that do not fit the orientation of the community. The historical past of the churches and the rural ministers must be taken into account. (p. 65)

Lockery (1991) advised that in thinking about the caregiving needs of minority elders, we must consider generational as well as ethnic differences. He noted that while many ethnic groups have a tradition of filial piety, this may be strained in a different culture:

For example, elderly Korean immigrants follow their children to this country in an attempt to maintain the traditional value system of the extended family. . . . However, once here, many of the older immigrants find that they actually have fewer kinship supports than they anticipated. (p. 60)

Interventions may be helpful here to deal with the tensions likely to be created by different expectations.

Potential new sites for preventive interventions to support caregivers include the workplace—a convenient site for older adults and their family members to get a variety of information and support.

Scharlach (1994) reported that the percentage of major corporations in the United States that offered any kind of elder care program or benefit increased from 3% in 1987 to 28% in 1992. He discussed the impact of organizational cultures on the types of elder care programs a particular company is likely to sponsor. To illustrate the importance of titles or images, he described a highly successful caregiver support group, at a traditional male-dominated engineering company, that called itself a "technical advisory group" (p. 379).

While giving the support group a businesslike name may have made it socially acceptable for men at that company to attend, it may not work everywhere. Studying males caring for Alzheimer's patients, Harris (1993) found that many men would not attend any type of support group. He therefore recommended other types of support, such as caregiver network programs or special male computer bulletin boards. Noting that many of the men relied on clergy for their support, he recommended efforts to educate the clergy. He also recommended that information about Alzheimer's disease be included in retirement planning programs.

Although family care issues are just coming to many collective bargaining tables, some unions already offer a variety of programs. For example, the International Ladies Garment Workers Union has been providing respite care for 25 years.

Programs That Address Work and Retirement Issues

The role of work itself must be considered in addressing mental health issues. For many, if not most, people, feeling useful and productive is an important aspect of mental health. Although we can clearly be useful and productive without having a paid job, work in the traditional sense is important to many people.

The dilemma of many older people is expressed poignantly in Barclay and McDougall's question (1990): "If who we are is what we do, what happens to our identity when we don't do that anymore?" (p. 53). Because of the salience of the work role, policies and practices related to work and retraining for older workers, as well as retirement, have an important place in preventive mental health services. Productive activity, whether paid or unpaid, can play a role in maintaining self-esteem and providing a sense of self-efficacy among older adults. Toward that end, older worker programs, such as Project Able, can be extremely valuable. Project Able is a national network of organizations that promotes employer and public awareness of the qualities of older workers. In working with older workers themselves, project staff provide individualized client assessment, skill training, opportunities for on-the-job training, job leads, and workshops on job-seeking techniques (Barclay & McDougall, 1990).

Safford (1988) saw the workplace as a convenient site for preventive programs to help middle-aged and older workers deal with anxiety about aging and learn preventive mental and physical health techniques. She expressed particular concern for older employees whose identity was closely tied to their work roles. In her view, they represent an at-risk population for retirement difficulties, and social workers should engage them in preparatory experiences for retirement.

Retirement counseling can be an excellent vehicle for preventive mental health interventions. Reiss and Gold (1993) noted that "retirement can provide a late-life opportunity for further self-development and the achievement of life satisfaction" (p. 261). They also suggested that retirement counseling could be improved by borrowing some of the approaches of career counseling, which "involves a wide range of explorations of the inner person and the situation to make plans and set goals . . . by incorporating standardized measures of relevant psychological traits or skills" (p. 275).

SELF-HELP GROUPS

The last half of the twentieth century has been described as the era of the self-help or mutual aid group (Self-help Groups, 1993). The same belief, that such groups represent a major societal trend, is reflected in the title of a recent book, *Sharing the Journey: Support Groups and America's New Quest for Community* (Wuthnow, 1994). The author summarized divergent opinions about the value of such groups, which proponents see as a way of saving American society and critics see as "contributing more to a narcissistic obsession with self than to a more responsible society" (p. ix).

In a review of several types of peer-paraprofessional programs for older adults, Gatz (1986) found that program directors often emphasized psychological benefits to the helper, who "was being given a role where she might feel useful and gain social contacts" (p. 161). In summarizing results of several studies, Gatz pointed to the success of some interventions in helping older adult peer counselors gain a sense of internal control and develop more self-efficacious behavior. She also warned that "programs whose major aim is to increase socialization may be limited, and inadvertently patronizing," and she recommended that "programs should be cautious about over-reliance on peer counselors and other paraprofessionals, to the exclusion of appropriate use of professionals" (p. 163).

To avoid such exclusion, mental health professionals can play a variety of roles in relation to self-help groups. Wax (1985) suggested provision of logistical support, start-up assistance, consultation, referrals, and help with organization and group development issues, and with political action, advocacy, and public education. The support groups sponsored by the Alzheimer's Association are good examples of interaction with professionals, in that professionals provide consultation to groups facilitated by lay leaders (Barnhill, 1994). Counselors can refer their own clients to self-help groups as an adjunct to individual counseling or as a source of support when they terminate a client. Counselors can also help with recruiting. For example, mental health professionals who give public talks or present workshops on such topics as mental health, bereavement, or stress management can give participants a list of recommended support groups.

Probably the most widely replicated peer counseling program is the one developed in Santa Monica. A key to its success may be found in its rigorous preservice and in-service training. Bratter and Freeman (1990) suggested procedures to minimize attrition of peer counselors, which included careful interviewing and selection of trainees and establishment of a clear commitment. They also talked about the importance of careful selection of the trainer-supervisor and noted that "a trainer conducting classes in a 'participatory learning' model exemplifies a nonauthoritarian figure and thus provides an important role model" (p. 50).

ALTERNATIVE MODALITIES AND TECHNIQUES TO USE IN WORKSHOPS

In thinking of preventive mental health workshops, it is easy to focus on lectures and exercises, but other approaches may reach participants at a deeper level. Sometimes poetry or fiction can be simultaneously poignant, profound, and humorous. For example, some of Elise Maclay's poems in *Green Winter: Celebrations of Old Age* (1977) can be inspiring supplements to workshops that focus on fears of aging or intergenerational communication. *When I Am an Old Woman I Shall Wear Purple* (Martz, 1991) can be used to encourage listeners to express their creativity in various ways, and *A Practical Guide to Creative Senility* (Donovan, 1988) uses a whimsical story of an intergenerational friendship as the medium to poke fun at the limiting stereotypes of aging. Kalish's (1985) parable of "The Horse on the Dining Room Table" uses metaphor to underline the importance and value of talking about difficult subjects, such as death.

Edwards (1990) discusses the value of poetry in provoking thought, stimulating life review, and bringing out a sense of creativity. McCloskey (1990) uses music to establish rapport and encourage reminiscing. Various groups around the country employ theater as a stimulus for discussions. For example, the Improbable Players' Next Generation is a troupe of actors over 60 who are in recovery from alcoholism and other drug abuse. An undated flyer about the group explains that "the actors draw on their own experience, sometimes humorous, always poignant, to reenact the devastation of the disease on individuals and families, the power of intervention and the hope of recovery."

OUTREACH

Outreach activities are important in educating older adults, their family members, and the general public. In a heartwarming article, "Mental Health and Aging: A Decade of Progress," Finkel (1993) charted positive trends and identified future challenges. He noted that

> education, public information, and prevention were principal themes in the 1981 White House Conference on Aging. We have seen many advances in these areas over the past decade. Many volunteer and lay organizations have taken an active role in educating older people and their family members on a host of topics related to mental health and aging: [The National Institute on Aging] has put out an Age Page; [The National Institute of Mental Health] has produced Fact Sheets on several issues; . . . AARP has developed a variety of reports . . . and the [National Council on the Aging] has offered many programs to enhance the quality of life." (p. 28)

Outside the aging network itself, many popular magazines carry articles about the aging of the population and the resulting problems for the so-called sandwich generation. Such articles help spread the message that the mental health needs of older adults affect everyone. Some pharmaceutical companies are publishing materials dealing with older adults and depression; these materials may help focus attention on prevention or early intervention.

Other kinds of outreach can be important in targeting socially isolated individuals. Telephone reassurance programs that involve daily check-ins can keep people in touch. Sometimes it is the older person whose welfare is being checked on; at other times, as in programs such as Grandma Please for latch-key children, the older person may be the person providing the reassurance rather than the person being reassured. Friendship lines—electronic or telephone support group—may bring together older adults in similar situations.

The *New York Times* (March 8, 1994, pp. A1, C18) carried an interesting obituary of a man who "was mourned by his family and grieving friends. . . . in the electronic community called cyberspace . . . [who held] an on-line wake that lasted weeks." The article went on to discuss a wide array of computer-based relationships formed by people who seek both information and emotional support from their networks. Sparks (1992) discussed the value of electronic support groups in which participants "share problems, solutions, miracles and miseries" (p. 63). While they lack face-to-face contact, these groups offer more privacy and the opportunity for contact at any time. Using less sophisticated technology, some isolated older adults can benefit from conference-call support groups (Rounds, Galinsky, & Stevens, 1991). Although conference calls can serve only a limited number of people, they represent a way of reaching individuals who might otherwise be groupless.

The award-winning Gatekeepers program in Spokane (Raschko, 1985) uses nontraditional referral sources to locate elderly persons who are at risk. By forming partnerships with business firms, the program has trained groups as diverse as meter readers, bank tellers, letter carriers, and property managers to report any unusual behavior or warning signals that an older person who lives alone may be in trouble.

Ethnically appropriate outreach may be particularly helpful. For example, Neighborhood House in Seattle has a program in which outreach workers of the same ethnicity as potential clients go door to door. They offer help in obtaining services such as home repair, home health care, and assistance with utility bills. While visiting the home and facilitating referrals, they hear all about the person's troubles with depression, mobility, finances, and family issues. In this way, people from underserved groups are bridged into services and receive counseling in an acceptable form. This approach is an example of the potential of by-the-way counseling discussed earlier.

In addition to describing the Seattle program, Lustbader (personal communication, December 1994) mentioned the frustration of program managers who complain that funding is offered to study the effectiveness of ethnically appropriate outreach but not for the ongoing provision of such outreach. The lack of funding to sustain alternative services and settings is a matter of substantial concern for those seeking to maintain and enhance mental health in older adults.

CURRENT AND EMERGING TRENDS

Trends in prevention efforts can be identified in terms of the status of prevention activities, the impact of the aging of the population, the caliber of research conducted, and the changed and changing roles of mental health professionals.

In recent years, the American public has received considerable information on the value of preventive health care. In response, many of us are becoming more health conscious; we exercise and pay attention to our diets. Unfortunately, the emphasis on prevention in the physical health arena has not led to a corresponding effort for mental health. Neither public acceptance nor financial support has been widespread.

The elderly population is becoming older and more diverse. Studies of persons over age 85 indicate that we may have to attach some cautions to urgings of continued activity and involvement. In efforts to debunk myths of aging, we must not create unrealistic countermyths. The percentage of minority elderly is increasing dramatically; people of color may become the majority of older adults in some parts of the country. *Serving Elders of Color: Challenges to Providers and the Aging Network* (American Society on Aging, 1992) documents the need to capture the strengths of various ethnic groups and involve minority elderly in the development of culturally appropriate services—for example, the use of culturally matched outreach workers.

Research on prevention activities is at once woefully lacking and becoming more sophisticated. Because they are sponsored by clinicians and activists rather than social scientists, few educational interventions are systematically evaluated. The reluctance of busy practitioners to conduct research, while understandable, makes accountability difficult. The lack of good research also makes it harder to argue for institutionalization of seemingly successful model programs. At the same time, large studies such as the Bereavement Research Study in Los Angeles and the longitudinal studies on the oldest old in San Francisco, both cited above, have provided excellent data (Stroebe, Hansson, & Stroebe, 1993; Johnson, 1994).

It is difficult to say how much research is required and how stringent it should be. An example of this problem was provided by the Institute of Medicine's Committee on Prevention of Mental Disorders, where Kraemer and Kraemer (1994) raised the question of the value of trials of prevention programs. Their conclusion was that "trials are essentially necessary when the programs are highly costly, entail some risks, and are of questionable efficacy. Then there is no substitute for a trial to document whether or not that program is worth further consideration" (p. 502). Practitioners who are impatient about responding to the needs that they see, and researchers who want clear outcome data, may have to struggle together to decide which programs fit the criteria outlined by Kraemer and Kraemer and which alternative forms of evaluation make sense.

Mental health practitioners have begun to broaden their job definitions well beyond the individual and group counseling for which most were trained. Some counselors now design programs in senior centers and congregate living facilities, while others walk the halls of legislatures as lobbyists. Some offer elder care workshops to company employees on their lunch hours; still others make presentations on preventive mental health on talk shows. All activities can serve the stated goal of enhancing and maintaining the mental health of older adults and their families.

RECOMMENDATIONS

Based on the review of the literature and on identification of trends, it is possible to make recommendations about needed services, sites, and modes of delivery. Making services available can include many different actions:

1. *Offering preventive mental health services of an educational nature in a variety of settings, including doctors' offices, senior centers, neighborhood or community centers, and religious organizations or educational institutions.* Because a limited number of older adults are served in community mental health centers and other traditional mental health settings, services must be made available in locations where older adults and their families normally go. It is important that mental health professionals who offer individual and

group counseling in alternative settings be able to bill for their services, just as they would if the services were offered in a community mental health center.

2. *Encouraging preventive visits to mental health professionals.* Goodman (1992) recommended the dental model for counseling, whereby adults go in for periodic routine checkups. Such an approach might go a long way toward reducing the stigma frequently associated with the use of mental health services.

3. *Offering educational workshops that discuss transitions such as retirement, widowhood, and changes in health status.* When such workshops are presented by mental health professionals, they increase receptivity to the use of mental health services. We need to think carefully about names given to programs. Many older people are more comfortable attending— and telling other people they are attending—discussions, workshops, or meetings such as those described above, rather than saying they are going to counseling. As long as counselors are straightforward about what will happen in such programs, such title adaptations can be helpful and appropriate.

4. *Increasing opportunities for meaningful paid and unpaid work.* Because feeling useful and productive contributes to mental health, policies and practices related to work and retraining for older workers, as well as retirement planning, can have an important impact. Phased retirement, which is more common in Europe than in the United States, may be an attractive alternative for many older adults. Given the demographics that will characterize the population in the near future, phased retirement may also be attractive for employers and may contribute to sound public policy. We should give serious consideration to Dychtwald's proposal (1994) to create an Elder Corps similar to a domestic Peace Corps.

5. *Strengthening ties or establishing linkages between the aging network and mental health agencies.* The Building Ties program in Michigan and the Geriatric Services program in Baltimore County are examples of such ties and linkages. In Florida, the Council for Community Mental Health has developed a continuum of mental health services that includes a variety of preventive approaches. In Oregon, the model plan for senior mental health services is a joint undertaking of people from mental health, aging, and substance abuse units of state government (Davis, 1992).

6. *Encouraging joint efforts of physical and mental health care providers.* The Pike Street Market Clinic (Lustbader, 1990) is a good example of combined services. Physicians, nurses, and other health care workers can be trained not only to spot possible signs of mental illness, but also to routinely recommend preventive mental health interventions.

7. *Giving service providers in settings such as senior centers, congregate living facilities, and nutrition sites training in basic communication and helping skills.* Many applied training programs are available to improve the skills of those who provide direct services. Paraprofessionals and volunteers typically have more contact with older adults than professionals do. They can provide support and challenge and are often in an excellent position to notice behavioral changes that may be a sign of problems. They, like the Gatekeepers in Spokane, Washington, can perform valuable "spotting" services.

8. *Strengthening public education campaigns in mental health.* AARP has made significant strides in this area through its distribution of fact sheets, pamphlets, brochures, and material for the broadcast media. Broadcast media often want local experts in order to give national and international news stories a local tie-in. It is therefore helpful to have a cadre of people who can provide information about the value of mental health interventions.

9. *Providing opportunities for older adults to have a major voice in developing their own programs.* This can be done by including representatives of the population to be served on advisory committees at the policy level and on working committees at the action level. In addition, we need to support programs that use older adults themselves as part of the service delivery system.

10. *Supporting the efforts of self-help groups.* The literature has pointed to many benefits and some limitations of self-help groups. Many support groups for older adults, their families, and caregivers provide welcome services in a more acceptable and less expensive manner than professional group counseling. However, such groups need professional backup. If we forge appropriate alliances, the efforts of professionals and paraprofessionals can be mutually enhancing. Working together, we can develop systems for mutual referrals.

11. *Tailoring interventions to fit the context of the individuals and groups*

with whom we work. This means developing programs that are culturally appropriate, not just translated into another language. Many ethnic groups are better reached through churches and community centers than through mental health centers.

REFERENCES

American Association of Retired Persons. (1987). *A path for caregivers.* Washington, DC: Author.

American Association of Retired Persons. (1994a). *Issue paper: Better mental health care for all generations.* Washington, DC: Author.

American Association of Retired Persons. (1994b). *Widowed Persons Service: 1993 annual report.* Washington, DC: Author.

American Psychiatric Association. (1994). *Diagnostic and statistical manual of mental health disorders.* (4th ed.). Washington, DC: Author.

American Society on Aging. (1992). *Serving elders of color: Challenges to providers and the aging network.* San Francisco: Author.

Barclay, T., & McDougall, M. (1990). Older-worker programs. *Generations, 14*(1), 53-54.

Barnhill, W. (1994). Self-help groups bolster Alzheimer's families. *AARP Bulletin, 35*(3), 1, 15-17.

Bratter, B., & Freeman, E. (1990). The maturing of peer counseling. *Generations, 14*(1), 49-52.

Brody, E. M. (1990). *Women in the middle: Their parent-care years.* New York: Springer.

Burton, L. M., Dilworth-Anderson, P., & Bengtson, V. L. (1991). Creating culturally relevant ways of thinking about diversity. *Generations, 15*(4), 67-72.

Butler, R. (1963). The life review: An interpretation of reminiscence in the aged. *Psychiatry, 26,* 65-76.

Cantor, M. H. (1991). Family and community: Changing roles in an aging society. *The Gerontologist, 31,* 337-346.

Capuzzi, D., Gross, D., & Friel, S. E. (1990). Recent trends in group work with elders. *Generations, 14*(1), 43-48.

Cheung, M. (1989). Elderly Chinese living in the United States: Assimilation or adjustment? *Social Work, 34,* 457-461.

Cohen, G. (1993). Comprehensive assessment: Capturing strengths, not just weaknesses. *Generations, 17*(1), 47-50.

Davis, J. A. (1992). *Model system plan for senior mental health care in Oregon: A vision for the future.* Salem, OR: Governor's Commission on Senior Services.

DeCroix Bane, S. (1991). Rural minority populations. *Generations, 14*(4), 63-66. Bethesda, MD: National Institute of Mental Health.

DeCroix Bane, S. (n.d.). *ROSE (Realizing opportunities for self exploration).* Kansas City, MO.

Disch, R. (Ed.). (1988). *Twenty-five years of the life review: Theoretical and practical considerations.* New York: Haworth.

Donovan, B. (1988). *A practical guide to creative senility.* Nevada City, CA: Blue Dolphin.

Dychtwald, K. (1986). *Wellness and health promotion for the elderly.* Rockville, MD: Aspen.

Dychtwald, K. (1994). "Old" isn't what it used to be. *The Director, 3,* 5-6.

Edwards, M. (1990). Poetry: Vehicle for retrospection & delight. *Generations, 14*(1), 61-62.

Finkel, S. I. (1993). Mental health and aging: A decade of progress. *Generations, 17*(1), 25-30.

Fiske, M., & Chiriboga, D. A. (1990). *Change and continuity in adult life.* San Francisco: Jossey-Bass.

Folkman, S., Chesney, M., McKusick, L. Ironson, G., Johnson, D. S., & Coates, T. J. (1991). Translating coping theory into an intervention. In J. Eckenrode (Ed.), *The Social Context of Coping* (pp. 239-260). New York: Plenum.

Gallagher-Thompson, D., Futterman, A., Farberow, N., Thompson, L. W., & Peterson, J. (1993). The impact of spousal bereavement on older widows and widowers. In M. S. Stroebe, W. Stroebe, & R. O. Hansson (Eds.), *Handbook of bereavement: Theory, research and intervention* (pp. 227-239). Cambridge, England: Cambridge University Press.

Gatz, M. (1986). *Prevention and aging: Community programs.* Resource papers to the report of the National Mental Health Association. Commission on the Prevention of Mental-Emotional Disabilities. Alexandria, VA: National Mental Health Association.

Gatz, M., & Smyer, M. A. (1992). The mental health system and older adults in the 1990s. *American Psychologist, 47,* 741-751.

Goodman, J. (1992). The dental model for counseling. *American Counselor, 1,* 27-29.

Grady, S. (1990). Senior centers: An environment for counseling. *Generations, 14*(1), 15-18.

Haight, B. K. (1991). Reminiscing: The state of the art as a basis for practice. *International Journal of Aging and Human Development, 33,* 1-32.

Harris, P. B. (1993). The misunderstood caregiver? A qualitative study of the male caregivers of Alzheimer's disease victims. *The Gerontologist, 33,* 551-556.

Heller, K. (1993). Prevention activities for older adults: Social structures and personal competencies that maintain useful social roles. *Journal of Counseling and Development, 72,* 124-130.

Jacobson, S. (in press). Overselling depression to the old folks. *Atlantic Monthly.*

Johnson, C. L. (1994). Introduction: Social and cultural diversity of the oldest-old. *International Journal of Aging and Human Development, 38,* 1-12.

Kahn, R. L., & Antonucci, T. C. (1980). Convoys over the life course: Attachment, roles, and social support. In P. B. Baltes & O. C. Brim (Eds.), *Life-span development and behavior, 3,* (pp. 253-286). New York: Academic Press.

Kalish, R. A. (1985). *Death, grief, and caring relationships* (2nd ed.). Monterey, CA: Brooks/Cole.

Kastenbaum, R. (1993). Mint, garlic, and the secret of time. *The Gerontologist, 33,* 275-277.

Kent, K. (1990). Elders and community mental-health centers. *Generations, 14*(1), 19-21.

Kivnick. H. Q. (1993). Everyday mental health: A guide to assessing life strengths. *Generations, 17*(1), 13-20.

Knight, B. G., Lutzky, S. M., & Macofsky-Urban, F. (1993). A metaanalytic review of interventions for caregiver distress: Recommendations for future research. *The Gerontologist, 33,* 240-249.

Kobasa, S. C., Maddi, S. R., & Kahn, S. (1982). Hardiness and health: A prospective study. *Journal of Personality and Social Psychology, 42,* 168-177.

Kraemer, H. M., & Kraemer, K. L. (1994). Design and analysis issues for trials of prevention programs in mental health research. In P. J. Mrazek & R. J. Haggerty (Eds.), *Reducing risks for mental disorders: Frontiers for preventive intervention research.* Washington, DC: National Academy Press.

Lieberman, M. A. (1993). Bereavement self-help groups: A review of conceptual and methodological issues. In M. S. Stroebe, W. Stroebe, & R. O. Hansson (Eds.), *Handbook of bereavement: Theory, research, and intervention* (pp. 411-426). Cambridge, England: Cambridge University Press.

Lockery, S. A. (1991). Family and social supports: Caregiving among racial and ethnic minority elders. *Generations, 14,* 58-62.

Lustbader, W. (1990). Mental health services in a community health center. *Generations, 14*(1), 22-23.

Lustbader, W., & Hooyman, N. R. (1994). *Taking care of aging family members: A practical guide.* New York: Free Press.

Maclay, E. (1977). *Green winter: Celebrations of old age.* New York: Readers Digest Press.

Manderfield, S. (1994). *Using reminiscence with the older adult who is chemically dependent.* Unpublished report, Senior Helping Hands Program, St. Cloud Hospital, St. Cloud, MN.

Martz, S. (Ed.). (1991). *When I am an old woman I shall wear purple* (2nd ed.). Watsonville, CA: Papier-Mache.

McCloskey, L. J. (1990). The silent heart sings. *Generations, 14*(1), 63-65.

Moody, H. R. (1988). Twenty-five years of the life review: Where did we come from? Where are we going? In R. Disch (Ed.), *Twenty-five years of the life review: Theoretical and practical considerations.* (pp. 7-21). New York: Haworth.

Mrazek, P. J., & Haggerty, R. J. (Eds.). (1994). *Reducing risks for mental disorders: Frontiers for preventive intervention research.* Washington, DC: National Academy Press.

National Resource Center on Health Promotion and Aging. (1991). *Mental health and wellness and older adults* (Publication No. 558). Washington, DC: American Association of Retired Persons.

Pearson, R. E. (1990). *Counseling and social support: Perspectives and practice.* Newbury Park, CA: Sage.

Perlstein, S. (1988). Life review and communal theater. In R. Disch (Ed.), *Twenty-five years of the life review: Theoretical and practical considerations.* (pp. 137-148). New York: Haworth.

Perlstein, S. (1992). *"Alert and alive": A mental wellness program for older adults.* New York: New York City Department for the Aging.

Perry, C. M., & Johnson, C. J. (1994). Families and support networks among African American oldest-old. *International Journal of Aging and Human Development, 38,* 41-50.

Phillips, M. A., & Murrell, S. A. (1994). Impact of psychological and physical health, stressful events, and social support on subsequent mental help seeking among older adults. *Journal of Consulting and Clinical Psychology, 62,* 270-275.

Raschko, R. (1985). Systems integration at the program level: Aging and mental health. *The Gerontologist, 25,* 460-463.

Reiss, M., & Gold, D. P. (1993). Retirement, personality, and life satisfaction: A review of two models. *Journal of Applied Gerontology, 12,* 261-282.

Rodeheaver, D., & Datan, N. (1988). The challenge of double jeopardy: Toward a mental health agenda for aging women. *American Psychologist, 43,* 648-654.

Rounds, K. A., Galinsky, M. J., & Stevens, L. S. (1991). Linking people with AIDS in rural communities: The telephone group. *Social Work, 36,* 13-19.

Ryff, C. D. (1989). In the eye of the beholder: Views of psychological well-being among middle-aged and older adults. *Psychology and Aging, 4,* 195-210.

Safford, F. (1988). Value of gerontology for occupational social work. *Social Work, 33,* 42-45.

Scharlach, A. E. (1994). Caregiving and employment: Competing or complementary roles? *Gerontologist, 34*(3), 378-385.

Schlossberg, N. K. (1993, March). *Developing a mental health portfolio.* Keynote speech to the American Counseling Association, Dallas, TX.

Self-help groups—Part I. (1993). *Harvard Mental Health Letter, 9*(9), 1-3.

Seligman, M. (1991). *Learned optimism.* New York: Knopf.

Sherman, E. (1987). Reminiscence groups for community elderly. *The Gerontologist, 27,* 569-572.

Sherman, E. (1993). Mental health and successful adaptation in later life. *Generations, 17*(1), 43-46.

Silverman, P., Mackenzie, D., Pettipas, M., & Wilson, E. (1974). *Helping each other in widowhood.* New York: Health Sciences Publishing.

Silverstone, B. (1994, March). *You and your aging parent revisited: A 20-year retrospective on family caregiving.* Lecture presented at the 40th annual meeting of the American Society on Aging, San Francisco.

Singer, V. I., Tracz, S. M., and Dworkin, S. H. (1991). Reminiscence group therapy: A treatment modality. *Journal for Specialists in Group Work, 16,* 167-171.

Solomon, R. (1992). Curriculum for clinical practice. In M. J. Mellor & R. Solomon (Eds.), *Geriatric Social Work Education,* (pp. 101-117). New York: Haworth.

Stroebe, M. S., Hansson, R. O., & Stroebe, W. (1993). Contemporary themes and controversies in bereavement research. In M. S. Stroebe, W. Stroebe, and R. O. Hansson (Eds.), *Handbook of bereavement: Theory, research and intervention* (pp. 457-475). Cambridge, England: Cambridge University Press.

Walls, C., & Zarit, S. (1991). Informal support from Black churches and well-being of elderly Blacks. *The Gerontologist, 31,* 490-95.

Waters, E. B. (1990). The life review: Strategies for working with individuals and groups. *Journal of Mental Health Counseling, 12,* 270-278.

Waters, E. B., & Goodman, J. (1990). *Empowering older adults: Practical strategies for counselors.* San Francisco: Jossey-Bass.

Wax, J. (1985). Self-help groups. *Journal of Psychosocial Oncology, 3,* 1-3.

Wuthnow, R. (1994). *Sharing the journey: Support groups and America's new quest for community*. New York: Free Press.

Wykle, M. L., & Musil, C. M. (1993). Mental health of older persons: Social and cultural factors. *Generations, 17*(1), 7-12.

Zarit, S. H., Pearlin, L. I., & Schaie, K. W. (1993). *Caregiving systems: Informal and formal helpers*. Hillsdale, NJ: Erlbaum.

CHAPTER 8

Family Involvement in Mental Health Care for Older Adults: From Caregiving to Advocacy and Empowerment

Roberta R. Greene

T he full promise of professionals and family members of older adults with mental illness participating as partners in care, thereby encouraging maximum functioning of older adults, has yet to be realized. A critical question is why many older adults do not make use of existing mental health services, whereas others do not have the services they desire (Speer, Williams, West, & Dupree, 1991). At the same time, elderly mentally ill people in family settings—especially the many families who are primary caregivers—have serious unmet needs. Research can give further clarity to mental health caregiving in a family context and to involvement of families as advocates in increasing access to mental health services.

Although the family's Herculean role in providing care to elderly family members is well recognized, more must be done to ensure that families have a formal role in the health care system (Pfeiffer, 1990). Without sufficient community-based treatments, adult children—who provide most of the daily instrumental care such as cooking or bathing for their older parents—are providing more care, more difficult care, and over much longer periods, often leading to caregiver burden. Clearly, the grow-

The author thanks Mary Stanley, research librarian, for her assistance.

ing number of elderly people, in combination with an increase in the need for mental health services, calls for the development of a meaningful national mental health agenda for elderly people. This chapter addresses how to involve family members as partners of mental health professionals in aiding mentally ill family members, and how to ensure that families are a vital part of the continuum of care.

CAREGIVER BURDEN

Caregiving systems for older adults are both formal and informal. More seems to be known about the nature of informal caregiving than about the fundamental question of the integration of informal and formal services—that is, how families and service providers work together, or fail to do so, and the implications of current policies for the coordination of their efforts (Zarit & Pearlin, 1993).

For example, the U.S. House of Representatives Select Committee on Aging (1987) reported that the average woman in the United States can expect to spend 18 years of her life helping a parent with health impairments. By analyzing a national database, Stone and Kemper (1989) estimated that the odds were 1 in 6 that adults aged 45 to 54 years would have to care for a parent or aged spouse.

Gerontologists have long argued that aged people must be considered family members (Spark & Brody, 1972). At least since the 1980s, this seemingly undebatable notion has become more accepted, and there has been a fuller understanding of the family as a system in which the well-being of any one member affects all (Blenkner, 1965; Brody, 1981, 1986; Cantor, 1983; Greene, 1986, 1989; Shanas, 1979; Silverstone & Burack-Weiss, 1983).

Gerontologists and those theorists interested in the caregiving role of families have learned much about the cumulative social and emotional stress of caregiving and its effect on the family's coping capacity (Brody, 1989). In a seminal Kent Memorial Lecture, Brody (1986) argued that parent care has become a normative family stress for individuals and families. In the intervening decades between 1970–1990, the stressful effects on family caregivers of persons with Alzheimer's disease have increasingly been brought to public attention by such advocates as the Alzheimer's

Association. This awareness has brought about further understanding of the family as client or consumer (Greene, 1986; Light, Niederehe, & Lebowitz, 1994)

Research has also documented that caregiving is embedded in a "life event web" that has ripple effects throughout the family system (Pruchno, Blow, & Smyer, 1984). Major life events, such as the health crises of older family members, have effects that radiate throughout the family system, whether or not a particular family member is directly involved in caregiving (Mellins, Blum, Boyd-Davis, & Gatz, 1993). It is well known that the members of the family who have primary responsibility for caring for older adults are usually female. According to the Family Caregiver Alliance (1992b), approximately 72% of caregivers are wives, daughters, or daughters-in-law. The largest proportion of parent caregiving is provided by daughters in their 50s who may also have multiple family and work demands and may have "finished" their child care roles. Thus for most women, family care is not a single, time-limited episode in the life course (Brody, 1986).

Although one primary family member usually provides care to older adults with health impairments, caregiving actually involves all family members to some extent, making the experience truly intergenerational (Mellins et al., 1993). For example, Creasey and Jarvis (1989) found that children had less supportive relationships with their fathers when their mothers were experiencing the burden of caring for a grandparent. Still another important consideration is that many caregivers are themselves elderly. For some caregivers, particularly those who have been the primary support for a chronically mentally ill child, there is heightened concern about what will happen with their own increasing frailty or death (Lefley, 1987).

Some families report positive changes in their family system with caregiving, such as increased closeness and social support, but other families experience negative effects on some members, particularly emotional distress. Not only do studies indicate that caregiving burdens may lead to clinical depression, but such burdens may cause other physical and financial hardships (Brody, 1989; Connell, 1994; Family Caregiver Alliance, 1992a; Light & Lebowitz, 1991; Parks & Pilisuk, 1991). Further, Smyer and Birkel (1991) suggested that families of elderly people who are chronically mentally ill may be more stigmatized than families of elderly people with physical health impairments.

Relatively little attention has been paid to caregiving situations in which the elderly person has a chronic mental illness other than dementia. In patients with dementia, it is understood that disruptive behavior is a strong predictor of caregiver burden (Lawton, Brody, & Saperstein, 1989). Much less is known about caregiver burden in families of older adults with depression or with schizophrenia. Liptzin, Grob, and Eisen (1988) compared perceived burden among family caregivers for elderly patients with depressive disorder and with dementia. Burden was equal in the two groups, emphasizing that caregiving burden is not restricted to any one diagnostic category.

The past decade has seen a marked increase in interest in families of chronically mentally ill adults and young adults and in their families' caregiving role (Hatfield & Lefley, 1987). One quarter to one third of people with disabling mental illness live with family members, and as many as 65% of all people discharged from inpatient facilities return to live with a relative for some time. According to the National Alliance for the Mentally Ill (NAMI), 42% of people with mental illness live with families (Skinner, Steinwachs, & Kasper, 1992). In one of the few investigations of elderly psychiatric patients, Meeks, Carstensen, Stafford, and Brenner (1990) found that two-thirds were living in the community and were relying on family support.

CAREGIVER NEEDS

Research conducted on families with younger members who experience mental illness have documented needs for assistance with crisis management, community living skills, personal care, managing relationships, and engaging in productive activities (Kasper, Steinwachs, & Skinner, 1992). Families with mentally ill older members may perceive a need for help not only with this set of problems but also with the problems they have in common with families caring for members with physical illness, such as assistance with activities of daily living, supportive housing, and transportation.

Difficulties in caregiving for a person with mental illness at any age may involve management of medication; seemingly bizarre, aggressive, or antisocial behaviors; social withdrawal and isolation; poor hygiene and unusual appearance; and self-destructive or suicidal behaviors (Spaniol, 1987; Spaniol & Zipple, 1988). Among family members providing support for elderly psychiatric patients, Pearson, Verma, and Nellett (1988) found that the patient's disruptive behaviors were the most important predictor of burden. While these researchers found that depressed mood was not a significant predictor of burden, severe depression in older adults can often be associated with very troubling behavior. Warren and Levy (1991) highlighted the importance of the family caregiver by documenting the family's pivotal role in decisions about which treatments to use in dealing with an elderly relative's depression—specifically, when to consent to electroconvulsive therapy.

In the past decade, the literature on treatment and rehabilitative services for families with mentally ill members has broadened. Except for research on caring for patients with dementia, most of these studies have involved samples of younger families. The current trend in the treatment of severely psychiatrically impaired people, particularly with the nonelderly population, emphasizes community-based treatment and often enlists the family as a valuable resource in aftercare (Spaniol, June, Zipple, & Fitzgerald, 1987). The literature suggests that most families prefer to give day-to-day care to ill relatives and combine that care with ongoing community support (Kent, 1990; Spaniol, Zipple, & Lockwood, 1993).

Spaniol et al. (1993) have proposed that the key to improving clinical collaboration between mental health professionals and families with mentally ill members is for clinicians to appreciate that the onset of mental illness in the family, or coping with the long-term effects of chronic illness, changes major roles in the family (Hatfield, 1987). In addition, the myth of family causation of mental illness often has deterred families of mentally ill people from seeking collaboration with professionals (NAMI Training Matters, 1991). Helping family members deal with normal feelings of shock, anger, denial, depression, acceptance, coping, final affirmation, and often advocacy for their mentally ill member facilitates family and patient adjustment (Spaniol et al., 1993).

Gerontologists also have offered suggestions for alleviating caregivers' burden that share some of these elements. The research on older families suggests that caregivers in individual and family counseling were more likely to have successful outcomes (Whitlatch, Zarit, & von Eye, 1991; Zarit, Anthony, & Boutselis, 1987). Zarit, Orr, and Zarit (1985) have proposed a three-prong approach in intervening with caregivers of patients with dementia: providing information about the disease, providing social support, and exchanging ideas about how to manage behavior difficulties. They also suggest that the prime purpose of intervention is to reduce the caregiver's perception of stress. Yet another special population is aging parents who serve as caregivers for mentally ill adult children. Lefley (1987) has suggested that an important element in service design for this group of caregivers is to support the parenting role through education, support, and training. She cautioned that, although the aging parent is considered the primary caregiver, care must be taken to retain needed government-sponsored programs.

With the changing demographics of the family—smaller size, increased divorce rates, variability in the age of childbearing, women's commitment to the workforce, and the prevalence of three and four generations—more needs to be understood about the family caregiving context for elderly people who experience mental illness (Gatz & Smyer, 1992). Relationships among generations of family members and among age groups in society will continue to have important implications for psychological well-being among elderly people. More needs to be understood about the perspectives that shape attitudes toward care, about the interlocked progress—a shared future—of several generations, and about inter-generational exchanges that affect policy and service provision (Gatz, 1993).

DIVERSITY OF OLDER FAMILIES

Because U.S. families are diverse, they may vary on a number of dimensions, including size of household, intergenerational contacts, and family support exchanges. In addition, a number of cultural factors, including gender, cohort group, socioeconomic status, social supports, and race and ethnicity, appear to affect the mental health and well-being of older people and to influence whether formal or informal services are used (Jackson, Antonucci, & Gibson, 1990; Starrett, Decker, & Redhorse, 1984).

An area for particular attention is how families from different ethnic groups use outpatient mental health services (Padgett, Patrick, Burns, & Schlesinger, 1994). Available information (Sotomayor, 1991; U.S. House of Representatives, Select Committee on Aging, 1988) has suggested that minority elderly people are more likely to experience psychological stressors than the elderly population as a whole (Roybal, 1988) and urged the importance of culturally sensitive services. For example, the Select Committee on Aging, in a hearing that examined the mental health needs of African American and Latino elderly people in the New York area, heard all witnesses agree on the need for a comprehensive approach to health care delivery that used client-specific social support networks. Similar hearings in Colorado indicated that American Indian elders preferred community-based services delivered by bilingual staff who understand cultural barriers between generations (U.S. House of Representatives, Select Committee on Aging, 1988).

Insufficient attention to racial and ethnic minority concerns appears to contribute to the underuse of mental health services by minority older adults (Carter, 1978; Roybal, 1988; Sanchez, 1992). A particularly salient concern among minority elderly people may be the feeling that there is a stigma in seeking mental health services (Sanchez, 1992). Reluctance to use a delivery system staffed primarily by English-speaking White professionals or a preference for alternative healers or clergy more in tune with the client's culture may reflect this factor (Padgett et al., 1994).

Further information is still needed on how minority elders use existing services so that this information can inform the development of new service models. For example, what is the degree of acceptance of mainstream treatments among family members? Does acceptance vary with the generation or cohort and knowledge of entitlement programs (American Psychiatric Association, 1994; Antonucci & Cantor, 1991)?

A major explanation for underuse of mental health services is the erroneous assumption that older adults and their families comprise a homogeneous population. In addition to minority status, there are numerous other client situations that must be considered in service design, including whether the elderly client lives in a rural setting (Buckwalter, McLeran, Mitchell, & Andrews, 1988; Buckwalter, Smith, Zevenbergen, & Russell, 1991; Menolascino & Potter, 1989) and how best to serve developmentally disabled elderly people (Gibson, Rabkin, & Munson, 1992; Howell, 1986).

In short, if access to services is to increase, more information is needed about mental health issues among a diverse constituency of elderly people, and professionals trained in geriatrics and gerontology will need further preparation to work with diverse populations.

BARRIERS AND THE ROLE OF FAMILIES IN ACCESS

It is generally accepted that most elders use mental health services less than their proportion in the general population would suggest (Speer et al., 1991). For older adults with mental illness who live with family and receive community-based care, families must be included in considerations of access and utilization.

A poorly developed continuum of care is among the reasons for underuse of community-based health services. Several surveys confirm that community mental health centers that develop geriatric programs are able to lower access barriers (Colenda & van Dooren, 1993). In many areas of the country, however, there continues to be little or no cooperation across components of the mental health and aging systems (Coyne & Gjertsen, 1993; Kane, 1989; Lebowitz, 1993). Elderly people who need mental health care do not self-refer, and families often do not seek services until nursing care appears to be the only alternative for their elderly member (Kent, 1990; Rovner, German, Burton, & Clark, 1993).

When older adults do seek help, they usually present their mental health symptoms to primary care physicians, who may not be prepared to link the patient to mental health care (Smith, 1985). For example, depressed older adults who are suicidal frequently see a physician about their physical health, not a mental health specialist about their mental health (Rabins, 1992).

An issue that has not been sufficiently explored is how families may play a role in access. Often the difficulties that may result from insufficient coordination of professional services fall to the family, who may be unequipped to deal with the barriers of a poorly coordinated service system.

FROM CAREGIVERS TO ADVOCATES

Ecological and advocacy models offer a means for mental health practitioners to reconceptualize family roles. Therefore, such practitioners are increasingly turning to an ecological model of assessment and treatment that addresses the coping strategies of the chronically mentally ill person and his or her family, and the extent of social environmental supports available to that family (Beckett & Coley, 1987; Hatfield, 1987; Terkelson, 1987a, 1987b). Because the ecological approach promotes the use of resources that may occur naturally in the client's environment, it is viewed as a means of improving client competence and social functioning (Sullivan, 1992). Ecological approaches structure the helping process so that it builds on client strengths and the client is principal director of his or her care (Rapp, 1992; Scogin, Hamblin, & Beutler, 1987; Weick & Pope, 1990).

The ecological model requires a different way of thinking about the older adult who is mentally ill. The client's family is recognized as a partner in care, and a prevention model is used in that client's are empowered to use information about their own aging process and that of their peer group (Greene, 1993). Hatfield (1987) has argued that the ecological model also requires a new way of thinking about families that involves a significant shift from the thinking of the past, when professionals often were alienated from the families of chronically mentally ill people. Rather, it features a different alignment of partnership between professional and consumer care (Freund, 1993; Sherman & Porter, 1991).

An ecological coping and adaptation paradigm examines the meaning of individual and family distress, emphasizes the family's role in rehabilitation, and views the family as a component in developing a continuum of care for people who are elderly and mentally ill (Bernstein & Jenkins, 1991; Rapp, 1992). As the family's capacity to cope with a mentally ill elderly member is enhanced, family members may shift their attention to individual, organizational, and legislative advocacy to increase access to mental health care for their relatives (Havel, 1992; National Aging Dissemination Center, 1992; Rickards, 1992; Ross, 1992; Zipple & Spaniol, 1987).

This empowerment stance among families with mentally ill members has evolved over time as a psychiatric rehabilitation response to the need created as mentally ill people were discharged from mental hospitals. The empowerment approach centers on improving consumers' relatedness to society so that they can further act in their own behalf, remaining as independent in the community as is consistent with humane care (Freund, 1993; Kisthardt, 1992; Rappaport, 1985). This approach to advocacy promotes client self-determination in psychosocial rehabilitation (Moxley & Freddolino, 1990) and is a "client-driven" model of service delivery (Freddolino & Moxley, 1992, p. 337; Piazza, 1989).

Over the past two decades, families, particularly those with younger mentally ill members, have assumed a more direct role in advocating for services and for changes in service delivery systems. For example, family members who act as mental health advocates have worked as members of the mental health system. Approximately 80% of state mental health agencies provide financial resources to consumer-run and family-run programs (National Association of State Mental Health Program Directors [NASMHPD], 1993). Another example of community and family advocacy is the NAMI. Founded in 1979, NAMI currently has more than 1,000 affiliate groups in all 50 states. The NAMI project on combating clinical depression specifically targets older Americans (NAMI, 1993).

As a result of such advocacy efforts, family members are more often seen as partners or members of a psychiatric rehabilitation team (Bernheim, 1987; Ooms, Hara, & Owen, 1992). However, professionals, especially those who work with older adults, can expand collaboration with the family in psychiatric rehabilitation by responding to family members' feelings, clarifying family roles, working as a team with family members, educating families and consumers, forming local support groups, acknowledging diverse beliefs, building on family strengths, and including families in care planning (Spaniol et al., 1993). For example, Knight (1994) has indicated that providing clinical interpretations to older clients and their families educates and prevents common problems. Being an advocate often involves finding ways for families to share power with professional caregivers (Spaniol, Zipple, & Fitzgerald, 1984). Stockdill (1992) has argued that growth of the family movement, with families acting as strong supporters for improving quality of care, accounts for many of the improvements in the mental health delivery system.

Gerontologists have already witnessed advocacy successes among family caregivers of persons with Alzheimer's disease. Such families have been unpaid caregivers and spokespersons for relatives unable to care for themselves and have demonstrated the power of consumer-driven and agency-supported care services. This reconceptualization of the role of family members in mental health care and how it can affect access for older adults needs to be better understood and viewed as an opportunity to find avenues to improve care. It is a critical aspect of a national agenda to increase access to mental health services for older adults.

CONTINUUM OF CARE

The continuum-of-care concept is seen as an answer to the interrelated physical, cognitive, emotional, social, economic, and support system needs of older adults (Dyck & Florio, 1994; Hagebak & Hagebak, 1980; Raschko, 1994). The concept further recognizes that providing services piecemeal deters access to good mental health care for older adults. The usual solution for older adults has been to call for an increased use of assertive case management as a means of reducing hospitalizations and increasing effective community-based care (Rose, 1992; Witheridge, 1992). Assertive case management programs usually develop strong outreach or gatekeeping components, view the client as consumer, focus on home visits, assist the client with concrete tasks that improve daily functioning, teach interpersonal skills, develop and enlist community supports, and advocate and broker for interagency services (Dyck & Florio, 1994; Intagliata, 1992; Ooms et al., 1992; Witheridge, 1992).

An increasingly popular idea for improving access to mental health services for older adults is the further incorporation of consumer and family involvement as part of the continuum-of-care design. Over the past decade, numerous organizations have sponsored public awareness and involvement programs. A survey conducted by the NASMHPD (1993) revealed that approximately 80% of state mental health agencies provide financial resources to consumer-run and family-run programs. Most states involve consumers and family members in policy formation and program development. Consumers and family members also serve on boards of directors, provide mutual support, and promote positive public attitudes.

Participation in the continuum of care among younger populations has already been shown to sustain family involvement by achieving a fit between health and social service providers, and partnerships among professionals, families, and communities. Community institutions such as

220

churches, synagogues, and mosques have also come into play in defining such a continuum (Filinson, 1988).

The continuum-of-care components already in use in some communities include outreach, prevention, and education programs. Health education is increasingly seen as a basis of social support and a critical component of the mental health continuum of care (Campbell & Chenoweth, 1981; Greene, 1993). Psychoeducational programs often have a family-centered design and explore new roles for clients, helping professionals, and family members (Libassi, 1992). For example, because there is a range of mental health problems in elderly people, the family may have difficulty distinguishing between normal and abnormal behavior (Barry & Moskowitz, 1988; McLean, 1987). Family members can learn the progression of mental disease and work with professionals to assist in early diagnosis. Families have to know that dementia can coexist with other disorders such as depression and psychosis (Rubin, Zorumski, & Bourke, 1988; Wragge & Jeste, 1989). Armed with such knowledge, families can better understand where to turn for help (Tennessee Alliance for the Mentally Ill, 1994). This type of partnership between professionals and family providers, central to continuity of care, is an important response to the problem of poor accessibility and fragmented services (Grady & Maynard, 1987).

SPECIAL NEEDS OF NURSING HOME RESIDENTS

Meeting the mental health needs of older adults who reside in nursing homes is another arena where advocacy efforts may enhance the delivery of services (Borson, Liptzin, Nininger, & Rabins, 1989; Crose, Duffy, Warren, & Franklin, 1987; Institute of Medicine, 1986; Koyonagi, 1988; Rubenstein & Pepper, 1993). Advocacy efforts may build on the Nursing Home Reform Amendments to the Social Security Act (under the Omnibus Budget Reconciliation Act, December 22, 1987, regulated by the Health Care Financing Administration) that requires screening at admission to determine whether a nursing home placement is appropriate (Allen, 1994; Rubenstein, Rovner, & Pepper, 1992). Among the better known advocacy groups working to ensure compliance with such regulations is the Mental Health and Law Project at the Bazelon Center, formerly known as the Mental Health Law Project (Rubenstein & Pepper, 1993). The center has outlined what federal law requires for nursing home residents' psychological well-being and makes this information available in the form of advocacy guides. Advocates, often family members and community volunteers, are asked to play a role in shaping a range of professional treatment approaches and services according to residents' preferences and choices. Materials caution that people with serious mental illness, mental retardation, or related mental disability are often referred to nursing homes when nursing home care is not really needed.

NATIONAL AGENDA FOR EMPOWERING FAMILY CAREGIVERS

Clearly, the growing number of older adults in combination with an increased need for mental health services calls for the development of a meaningful national agenda for the mental health of elderly people, an agenda that addresses difficulties in access. Table 1 presents suggested policy and research efforts that should be important parts of that agenda. A review of the literature suggests that, although there has been expanded attention to certain syndromes such as Alzheimer's disease and depression, there is a compelling need for comprehensive leadership and direction in the area of geriatric mental health. That agenda must keep pace with the increased understanding of mental health and mental illnesses in late life and must be based on models of practice that are not only cost-effective but help maintain and improve biopsychosocial functioning and empower older adults and their families to become an integral part of care (Finkel et al., 1993; Greene, 1993).

During the past decade, concern for the family as a system, coupled with an increasing concern for advocacy and the consumer rights of citizens, has led to a focus on the participation of such consumers and their family members in the decision-making processes surrounding mental health services (NASMHPD, 1993). This trend has unrealized potential as a means for improving access to mental health care for older adults and is central to a national agenda.

Although many researchers (Lawton et al., 1989; Pearlin, Lieberman, Menaghan, & Mullen, 1981; Zarit, Reever, & Bach-Peterson,

TABLE 1   Suggested Items for a National Agenda for the Elderly Mentally Ill and Their Families

---

Policy issues

Promote collaboration between aging network agencies and mainstream mental health initiatives.

Promote increased awareness of mental health services among families of older adults with mental illness.

Explore more opportunities to combine physical care with psychiatric consultation and treatment.

Improve clinical collaboration between families who have an older member with mental illness and mental health professionals.

Include families in treatment sessions to examine means of collaboration in problem-solving strategies.

Ensure a viable continuum of care; promote a stronger link between community-based and long-term nursing home care.

Offer professional training and continuing mental health education for mental health professionals.

Initiate additional culturally sensitive services for older ethnic minority clients.

Retain a balance among primary caregivers, government sponsored programs, and privatized care.

Research and knowledge-building measures

Further research the caregiving needs of families of later years with chronically mentally ill relatives.

Conduct more research to determine the fit between people at risk and the type of treatment needed; advocate for treatments not available.

Research possible cost-saving ideas such as the viability of brief treatment.

Project the attitudes of future cohorts toward mental health care.

Determine best practice models of training mental health professionals that are more responsive to the needs of families.

1980) have long recognized the family's role in providing care to elderly family members, still more needs to be done to ensure that families have a formal role in the health care system (Pfeiffer, 1990). With recognition of family-specific care and a further realization of their partnership with professionals, family members can become better advocates in increasing access to mental health care for older adults.

REFERENCES

Allen, J. E. (1994). *Key federal requirements for nursing facilities*. New York: Springer.

American Psychiatric Association. (1994). *Ethnic minority elderly: A task force report of the American Psychiatric Association*. Washington, DC: Author.

Antonucci, T., & Cantor, C. (1991). Strengthening the family support system for older minority persons. *Minority elders: Longevity, economics, and health*. Washington, DC: Gerontological Society of America.

Barry, P. B., & Moskowitz, M. A. (1988). The diagnosis of reversible dementia in elderly: A critical review. *Archives of Internal Medicine, 148,* 1915-1918.

Beckett, J. O., & Coley, S. M. (1987). Ecological intervention with the elderly: A case example. *Journal of Gerontological Social Work, 11,* 137-157.

Bernheim, K. (1987). Family consumerism: Coping with the winds of change. In A. B. Hatfield & H. P. Lefley (Eds.), *Families of the mentally ill* (pp. 244-260). New York: Guilford.

Bernstein, M. A., & Jenkins, S. (1991). A continuum of care for people who are elderly and mentally ill. *Innovations and Research in Clinical Services, Community Support, and Rehabilitation, 1,* 10-12.

Blenkner, M. (1965). Social work and family relationships in later life with some thoughts on filial maturity. In E. Shanas & G. E. Streib (Eds.), *Social structure and the family*. Englewood Cliffs, NJ: Prentice-Hall.

Borson, S. B., Liptzin, B., Nininger, J., & Rabins, P. V. (1989). *Nursing homes and the mentally ill elderly: A Report on the Task Force on Nursing Homes and the Mentally Ill Elderly*. Washington, DC: American Psychiatric Association.

Brody, E. (1981). Women in the middle and family care to older people. *The Gerontologist, 21,* 471-480.

Brody, E. M. (1986). Parent care as a normative family stress. *The Gerontologist, 25,* 19-29.

Brody, E. (1989). The family at risk. In E. Light & B. D. Lebowitz (Eds.), *Alzheimer's disease treatment and family stress: Directions for research* (DHHS Publication No. ADM 89-1569, pp. 2-49). Washington, DC: U.S. Government Printing Office.

Buckwalter, K. C., McLeran, H., Mitchell, S., & Andrews, P. H. (1988). Responding to mental health needs of the elderly in rural areas: A collaborative geriatric education center model. *Gerontology and Geriatrics Education, 8,* 69-80.

Buckwalter, K. C., Smith, M., Zevenbergen, P., & Russell, D. (1991). Mental health services of the rural elderly outreach program. *The Gerontologist, 31,* 408-412.

Campbell, R., & Chenoweth, B. (1981). Health education as a basis for social support. *The Gerontologist, 21,* 619-627.

Cantor, M. H. (1983). A strain among caregivers: A study of experience in the United States. *The Gerontologist, 23,* 597-604.

Carter, J. H. (1978). The Black aged: A strategy for future mental health services. *Journal of the American Geriatrics Society, 26,* 553-556.

Colenda, C. C., & van Dooren, H. (1993). Opportunities for improving community mental health services for elderly persons. *Hospital and Community Psychiatry, 44,* 531-533.

Connell, C. M. (1994). Impact of spouse caregiving on health behaviors and physical and mental health status. *American Journal of Alzheimer's Care and Related Disorders and Research,* 26-36.

Coyne, A. C., & Gjertsen, R. (1993). Characteristics of older adults referred to a psychiatric emergency outreach service. *Journal of Mental Health Administration, 20,* 208-211.

Creasey, G. L., & Jarvis, P. A. (1989). Grandparents with Alzheimer's disease: Effects of parental burden. *Family Therapy, 16,* 79-85.

Crose, R., Duffy, M., Warren, J., & Franklin, B. (1987). Project OASIS: Volunteer mental health paraprofessionals serving nursing home residents. *The Gerontologist, 27,* 359-362.

Dyck, D., & Florio, E. (1994). *Clinical characteristics and service needs of elderly referred to a community mental health center: An evaluation of the gatekeeper case finding technique, an interim report.* Spokane, WA: Washington Institute for Mental Illness Research and Training.

Family Caregiver Alliance. (1992a). *Advocacy tips for caregivers.* San Francisco: Author.

Family Caregiver Alliance. (1992b). *Fact sheet, selected caregiver statistics.* San Francisco: Author.

Filinson, R. (1988). A model for church-based services for frail elderly persons and their families. *The Gerontologist, 28,* 483-485.

Finkel, S., Dye, C., Garcia, A., Gatz, M., Greene, R., Hay, D. P., Smyer, M., & Wykle, M. L. (1993). *Report of the Interdisciplinary Coordination Group on Mental Health and the Elderly.* Washington, DC: National Institute of Mental Health.

Freddolino, P. P., & Moxley, D. P. (1992). Clinical care update: Refining an advocacy model for homeless people coping with psychiatric disabilities. *Community Mental Health Journal, 28,* 337-352.

Freund, P. D. (1993). Professional role(s) in the empowerment process: Working with mental health consumers. *Psychosocial Rehabilitation Journal, 16,* 65-73.

Gatz, M. (1993). Intergenerational issues. In S. Finkel, C. Dye, A. Garcia, M. Gatz, R. Greene, D. P. Hay, M. Smyer, & M. L. Wykle. (1993). *Report of the Interdisciplinary Coordination Group on Mental Health and the Elderly.* Washington, DC: National Institute of Mental Health.

Gatz, M., & Smyer, M. A. (1992). The mental health system and older adults in the 1990s. *American Psychologist, 47,* 741-751.

Gibson, J. W., Rabkin, J., & Munson, R. (1992). Critical issues in serving the developmentally disabled elderly. *Journal of Gerontological Social Work, 19*(1), 35-49.

Grady, S., & Maynard, C. (1987). Building ties: A mental health and aging project. *The Gerontologist, 27,* 428-429.

Greene, R. R. (1986). *Social work with the aged and their families.* New York: Aldine de Gruyter.

Greene, R. R. (1989). A life systems approach to understanding parent-child relationships in aging families. *Journal of Family Psychotherapy, 5*(1/2), 57-68.

Greene, R. R. (1993). Public information, prevention, and health promotion. In S. Finkel, C. Dye, A. Garcia, M. Gatz, R. Greene, D. P Hay, M. Smyer, & M. L. Wykle. (1993). *Report of the Interdisciplinary Coordination Group on Mental Health and the Elderly.* Washington, DC: National Institute of Mental Health.

Hagebak, J. E., & Hagebak, B. R. (1980). Serving the mental health needs of the elderly: The case for removing barriers and improving service integration. *Community Mental Health Journal, 16*, 263-275.

Hatfield, A. B. (1987). Coping and adaptation: A conceptual framework for understanding families. In A. B. Hatfield & H. P. Lefley (Eds.), *Families of the mentally ill* (pp. 60-84). New York: Guilford.

Hatfield, A. B., & Lefley, H. P. (Eds.). (1987). *Families of the mentally ill.* New York: Guilford.

Havel, J. T. (1992). Associations and public interest groups as advocates. *Administration and Policy in Mental Health, 20*(1), 27-44.

Howell, M. (1986). Old age in the retarded—A new program. *Journal of the American Geriatrics Society, 34*, 71-72.

Institute of Medicine. (1986). *Improving the quality of care in nursing homes.* Washington, DC: National Academy Press.

Intagliata, J. (1992). Improving the quality of community care for the chronically mentally disabled. In S. M. Rose (Ed.), *Case management social work practice* (pp. 25-55). New York: Longman.

Jackson, J. S., Antonucci, T. C., & Gibson, R. C. (1990). Cultural, racial, and ethnic minority influences on aging. In J. E. Birren & K. W. Schaie (Eds.), *Handbook of the psychology of aging* (3rd ed., pp. 103-123). San Diego, CA: Academic Press.

Kane, R. A. (1989, July). Case management in long term care: It can be as ethical and effective as we want it to be. Paper presented at the Pennsylvania Care Management Institute on Ethics and Care Management: A Delicate Balance, Philadelphia.

Kasper, J. A., Steinwachs, D. M., & Skinner, E. A. (1992). Family perspectives on the service needs of people with serious and persistent mental illness. Part II: Needs for assistance and needs that go unmet. *Innovations and Research in Clinical Services, Community Support, and Rehabilitation, 1*(4), 21-34.

Kent, K. L. (1990). Elders and community mental-health centers. *Generations, 14*(1), 19-21.

Kisthardt, W. E. (1992). A strengths model of case management: The principles and functions of a helping partnership with persons with persistent mental illness. In D. Saleebey (Ed.), *The strengths perspective in social work practice* (pp. 59-83). New York: Longman.

Knight, B. G. (1994). Providing clinical interpretations to older clients and their families. In M. Storandt & G. R. VandenBos (Eds.), *Neuropsychological assessment of dementia and depression in older adults: A clinician's guide* (pp. 141-154). Washington, DC: American Psychological Association.

Koyonagi, C. (1988). *Operation help: A mental health advocate's guide to Medicaid.* Alexandria, VA: National Mental Health Association.

Lawton, M. P., Brody, E. M., & Saperstein, A. R. (1989). A controlled study of respite service for caregivers of Alzheimer's patients. *The Gerontologist, 29*, 8-16.

Lebowitz, B. D. (1993). Mental health and aging: Federal perspectives. *Generations, 19*, (1), 65-68.

Lefley, H. P. (1987). Aging parents as caregivers of mentally ill adult children: An emerging social problem. *Hospital and Community Psychiatry, 38*, 1063-1070.

Libassi, M. F. (1992). The chronically mentally ill: A practice approach. In S. M. Rose (Ed.), *Case management social work practice* (pp. 77-90). New York: Longman.

Light, E., and Lebowitz, B. D. (Eds.). (1991). *The elderly with chronic mental illness.* New York: Springer.

Light, E., Niederehe, G., & Lebowitz, B. (1994). *Stress effects of family caregivers of Alzheimer's patients: Research and intervention.* New York: Springer.

Liptzin, B., Grob, M. C., & Eisen, S. V. (1988). Family burden of demented and depressed elderly psychiatric inpatients. *The Gerontologist, 28,* 397-401.

McLean, S. (1987) Assessing dementia: Part 1. Difficulties, definitions, and differential diagnosis. Review. *Australian and New Zealand Journal of Psychiatry, 21,* 142-174.

Meeks, S., Carstensen, L. L., Stafford, P. B., & Brenner, L. L., (1990). Mental health needs of the chronically mentally ill elderly. *Psychology and Aging, 5,* 163-171.

Mellins, C. A., Blum, M. J., Boyd-Davis, S. L., & Gatz, M. (1993). Family network perspective on caregiving. *Generations,* 21-24.

Menolascino, F. J., & Potter, J. F. (1989). Delivery of services in rural settings to the elderly mentally retarded–mentally ill. *International Journal of Aging and Human Development, 28,* 261-276.

Moxley, D. P., & Freddolino, P. P. (1990). A model of advocacy for promoting client self-determination in psychosocial rehabilitation. *Psychosocial Rehabilitation Journal, 14*(2), 69-82.

National Aging Dissemination Center (1992). *Administration on Aging compendium of products on elder rights.* Washington, DC: Author.

National Alliance for the Mentally Ill Training Matters. (1991). *Newsletter of the NAMI curriculum and training network, 1,* 2-3.

National Association of State Mental Health Program Directors. (1993). Putting their money where their mouths are: SMHA support of consumers and family run programs. *NASMHPD Studies Update, 92,* 720.

Ooms, T., Hara, S., & Owen, T. (1992). Service integration and coordination at the family/client level—A family impact. In *Family centered social policy: The emerging agenda.* Washington, DC: American Association for Marriage and Family Therapy.

Padgett, D. K., Patrick, C., Burns, B. J., & Schlesinger, H. J. (1994). Ethnicity and the use of outpatient mental health services in a national insured population. *American Journal of Mental Health, 84,* 222-226.

Parks, S. H., & Pilisuk, M. (1991). Caregiver burden: Gender and psychological costs of caregiving. *American Journal of Orthopsychiatry, 61,* 501-509.

Pearlin, L. I., Lieberman, M., Menaghan, E., & Mullen, J. T. (1981). The stress process. *Journal of Health and Social Behavior, 22,* 337-356.

Pearson, J., Verma, S., & Nellett, C. (1988). Elderly psychiatric patient status and caregiver perceptions as predictors of caregiver burden. *The Gerontologist, 28,* 79-83.

Pfeiffer, E. (1990). Why caregivers need care, too. *Senior Patient,* 30-40.

Piazza, J. (1989). Toward health: A staff learns to use mentally ill clients, families, and communities as advisors. *Clinical Social Work Journal, 17,* 259-270.

Pruchno, R. A., Blow, F. C., & Smyer, M. A. (1984). Life events and interdependent lives. *Human Development, 27,* 31-41.

Rabins, P. (1992). Prevention of mental disorder in the elderly: Current perspectives and future prospects. *Journal of the American Geriatrics Society, 40,* 727-733.

Rapp, C. A. (1992). The strengths perspective of case management with persons suffering from severe mental illness. In D. Saleebey (Ed.), *The strengths perspective in social work practice* (pp. 45-58). New York: Longman.

Rappaport, J. (1985). The power of empowerment language. *Social Policy, 16,* 15-21.

Raschko, R. (1994, April). *Living alone with dementia: Impact of the elderly services program at Spokane Community Mental Health Center.* Paper presented at the 44th Annual Conference of the National Council on Aging, Washington, DC.

Rickards, L. D. (1992). Professional and organized provider associations. *Administration and Policy in Mental Health, 20*(1), 11-25.

Rose, S. M. (1992). Case management: An advocacy/empowerment design. In S. M. Rose (Ed.), *Case management social work practice* (pp. 271-297). New York: Longman.

Ross, E. C. (1992). Success and failure of advocacy groups: A legislative perspective. *Administration and Policy in Mental Health, 20*(1), 57-66.

Rovner, B. W., German, P. S., Burton, L. C., & Clark, R. (1993). Underutilization of physical and mental health services prior to nursing home admission. *American Journal of Geriatric Psychiatry, 1,* 160-164.

Roybal, E. R. (1988). Mental health and aging: The need for an expanded federal response. *American Psychologist, 43,* 189-194.

Rubenstein, D. P., & Pepper, B. (1993). *Elders assert their rights: A guide for residents, family members and advocates to the legal rights of elderly people with mental disabilities in nursing homes.* Washington, DC: Bazelon Center for Mental Health Law, American Association of Retired Persons.

Rubenstein, D. P., Rovner, B. W., & Pepper, B. (1992). *Mental disability law and the elderly, Issue Paper #3: What federal law requires for nursing home residents' psychological well-being.* Washington, DC: Mental Health Law Project.

Rubin, E. H., Zorumski, C. F., & Bourke, W. J. (1988). Overlapping symptoms of geriatric depression and Alzheimer-type dementia. *Hospital and Community Psychiatry, 39,* 1074-1079.

Sanchez, C. D. (1992). Mental health issues: The elderly Hispanic. *Journal of Geriatric Psychiatry, 25*(1), 69-84.

Scogin, F., Hamblin, D., & Beutler, L. (1987). Bibliotherapy for depressed older adults: A self-help alternative. *The Gerontologist, 27,* 383-387.

Shanas, E. (1979). The family as a social support system in old age. *The Gerontologist, 19,* 169-174.

Sherman, P. S., & Porter, R. (1991). Mental health consumers as case management aides. *Hospital and Community Psychiatry, 42,* 494-498.

Silverstone, B., & Burack-Weiss, A. (1983). *Social work practice with the frail elderly and their families.* Springfield, IL: Thomas.

Skinner, E. A., Steinwachs, D. M., & Kasper, J. A. (1992). Family perspectives on the service needs of people with serious and persistent mental illness. Part I: Characteristics of families and consumers. *Innovations and Research in Clinical Services, Community Support, and Rehabilitation, 1*(3), 23-30.

Smith, D. A. (1985). Geriatric mental health care by family physicians. *Journal of Family Practice, 21,* 435-436.

Smyer, M. A., & Birkel, R. C. (1991). Research focused on intervention with families of the chronically mentally ill elderly. In E. Light & B. D. Lebowitz (Eds.), *The elderly with chronic mental illness* (pp. 111-130). New York: Springer.

Sotomayor, M. (1991). *Empowering Hispanic families: A critical issue for the '90s.* Milwaukee, WI: Family Service of America.

Spaniol, L. (1987). Coping strategies of family caregivers. In A. B. Hatfield and H. Lefley (Eds). *Families of the mentally ill: Coping and adaptation* (pp. 208-224). New York: Guilford.

Spaniol, L., Jung, H., Zipple, A., & Fitzgerald, S. (1987). Families as a resource in the rehabilitation of the severely mentally ill. In A. B. Hatfield & H. P. Lefley (Eds)., *Families of the mentally ill* (pp. 167-190). New York: Guilford.

Spaniol, L., & Zipple, A. M. (1988). Family and professional perceptions of family needs and coping strengths. *Rehabilitation Psychology, 33,* 37-45.

Spaniol, L., Zipple, A. M., & Fitzgerald, S. (1984). How professionals can share power with families: Practical approaches to working with families of the mentally ill. *Psychosocial Rehabilitation Journal, 8*(2), 77-84.

Spaniol, L., Zipple, A. M., & Lockwood, D. (1993). The role of the family in psychiatric rehabilitation. *Innovations and Research in Clinical Services, Community Support, and Rehabilitation, 2*(4), 27-34.

Spark, G., & Brody, E. (1972). The aged are family members. In C. Sager & H. Kaplan (Eds.), *Progress in group and family therapy* (pp. 712-725). New York: Brunner Mazel.

Speer, D. C., Williams, J., West, H., & Dupree, L. (1991). Brief report: Older adult users of outpatient mental health services. *Community Mental Health Journal, 27,* 69-76.

Starrett, R. A., Decker, J. T., Redhorse, J. (1984, November). The informal mental health networks of the Hispanic elderly. Paper presented at the annual program meeting of the Western Gerontological Society, San Antonio, TX.

Stockdill, J. W. (1992). A government managers' view of mental health advocacy groups. *Administration and Policy in Mental Health, 20*(1), 45-56.

Stone, R., & Kemper, P. (1989). Spouses and children of disabled elders: How large a constituency for long-term care reform? *Milbank Quarterly, 67,* 485-506.

Sullivan, W. P. (1992). Reconsidering the environment as a helping resource. In D. Saleebey (Ed.), *The strengths perspective in social work practice* (pp. 148-157). New York: Longman.

Tennessee Alliance for the Mentally Ill. (1994). Handbook of mental health services presented to NAMI conference. *TAMI Newsletter, 8*(2), 1-6.

Terkelson, K. G. (1987a). The evolution of family responses to mental illness through time. In A. B. Hatfield & H. P. Lefley (Eds.), *Families of the mentally ill* (pp. 151-166). New York: Guilford.

Terkelson, K. G. (1987b). The meaning of mental illness to the family. In A. B. Hatfield & H. P. Lefley (Eds.), *Families of the mentally ill* (pp. 128-150). New York: Guilford.

U.S. House of Representatives, Select Committee on Aging, Subcommittee on Human Services. (1987). *Exploding the myths: Caregiving in America* (Committee Publication No. 99-611). Washington, DC: U.S. Government Printing Office.

U.S. House of Representatives, Select Committee on Aging, Subcommittee on Human Services. (1988). *Mental health and the elderly: Issues in service delivery to the Hispanic and black community. Part I.* Washington, DC: U.S. Government Printing Office.

Warren, C. A., & Levy, K. A. (1991). Electroconvulsive therapy and the elderly. *Journal of Aging Studies, 5,* 309-327.

Weick, A., & Pope, L. (1990). Knowing what's best: A new look at self-determination. *Social Casework, 69,* 10-18.

Whitlatch, C. J., Zarit, S. H., & von Eye, A. (1991). Efficacy of interventions with caregivers: A reanalysis. *The Gerontologist, 31,* 9-14.

Witheridge, T. (1992). The assertive community treatment worker. In S. M. Rose, *Case management social work practice* (pp. 101-111). New York: Longman.

Wragge, R. E., & Jeste, D. V. (1989). Overview of depression and psychoses in Alzheimer's disease. *American Journal of Psychiatry, 146,* 577-587.

Zarit, S. H. (1989). Current and future directions in family caregiving research. *The Gerontologist, 29,* 481-483.

Zarit, S. H., Anthony, C. R., & Boutselis, M. (1987). Interventions with families of dementia patients: Comparison of two approaches. *Psychology and Aging, 2,* 225-232.

Zarit, S. H., Orr, N. K., & Zarit, J. M. (1985). *The hidden victims of Alzheimer's disease: Families under stress.* New York: New York University Press.

Zarit, S. H., & Pearlin, L. (1993) Caregiving systems: Informal and formal helpers. S. H. Zarit, & W. Schail (eds.). *Social structures and aging.* Hillsdale, NJ: Laurence Erlbaum Associates, Inc.

Zarit, S. H., Reever, K. E., & Bach-Peterson, J. (1980). Relatives of the impaired aged: Correlates of feelings of burden. *The Gerontologist, 20,* 649-655.

Zipple, A. M., & Spaniol, L. (1987). Current education and supportive models. In A. B. Hatfield & H. P. Lefley (Eds.), *Families of the mentally ill* (pp. 261-278). New York: Guilford.

CHAPTER 9

Models for Mental
Health Service Delivery
to Older Adults

Bob G. Knight and Brian Kaskie

The principal goal of this chapter is to compare and contrast the effectiveness of different systems of care in meeting the mental health needs of older adults. To analyze the pros and cons of different systems, it is first necessary to describe briefly the varieties of services that may be needed by the different groups of older adults who need mental health care: the severely mentally ill older adults, acutely distressed older adults, elderly people with dementia, and older adults with substance abuse problems. In the following section the existence of effective mental health intervention is noted, and basic principles that can be used to analyze the different approaches to providing and funding care are drawn from the literature on mental health systems and services. With these principles as background, the advantages and disadvantages of fee-for-service Medicare models, managed care models, and public sector services are discussed.

POPULATIONS OF OLDER ADULTS WHO NEED
MENTAL HEALTH SERVICES

In a discussion of mental health service delivery models for older adults, a helpful beginning is a description of the various populations of older people who may need mental health services. Discussions of the epidemiology of specific disorders (Jeste, Naimark, Halpain, & Lindamer, this volume; Schneider, this volume) and of the problems in access to services (Estes, this volume) can be found elsewhere. Our intent is to clarify which groups need services and to demonstrate that different groups may need different types of services.

Severely Mentally Ill Elderly People

Severely mentally ill elderly people include those with schizophrenic and paranoid disorders as well as bipolar disorder and some severe or chronic cases of major depressive disorder. Historically, older persons have tended to be overrepresented in inpatient psychiatric units (Redick & Taube, 1980), and they still account for about 16% of all psychiatric inpatients (Stiles, 1994). Older patients have tended to remain in inpatient units longer as well, thus taking up an even more disproportionate amount of services. Redick and Taube (1980) cited national data showing that average stays in state and county psychiatric hospitals were more than twice as long for geriatric inpatients as for younger adult inpatients. These facts have typically been attributed to the rising prevalence of organic brain syndrome diagnoses in late life. However, one of the few studies available—Conwell, Nelson, Kim, and Mazure (1989)—showed a predominance of depressive disorders in geriatric admissions to the Yale-New Haven Hospital psychiatric unit. Knight and Carter (1990) reported that most older adults admitted to the inpatient unit in their study in Ventura County, California, suffered from psychosis or affective disorders. Severe mental illnesses are also present in long-term care settings; it is estimated that 30% of residents of nursing homes have a chronic mental disorder, excluding dementia (Shadish, 1989).

There has been an increasing research focus on the characteristics and needs of the older seriously mentally ill adult (Light & Lebowitz, 1991; Miller & Cohen, 1987). There has also been an increasing recognition of this group as a necessary focus of future program and policy development in mental health and aging (Gatz & Smyer, 1992; Lebowitz & Niederehe, 1992). Elderly people with serious mental illness are likely to need inpatient services, partial hospitalization, and outpatient care.

Acutely Distressed Older Adults

The psychological problems of this population are likely to include depression, anxiety, phobias, and adjustment disorders. These problems are also likely to be comorbid with medical illness and may therefore complicate medical treatment and lead to unnecessary medical visits and costs (Lave, 1990). Older adults in acute psychological distress are generally assumed to be best served in outpatient mental health settings.

However, the most widely discussed issue in outreach to older adults is that acutely distressed elderly people underuse outpatient mental health services relative to the representation of older adults in the population. In 1983, elderly people comprised 11% of the population and 6% of users of community mental health centers (Fleming, Richards, Santos, & West, 1986); representation was lower in other clinics and lower still in private practices. In recent years, more elderly people have begun to use mental health services. In 1990, the Inventory of Mental Health Organizations showed that older adults were 9.72% of outpatient mental health clinic clients and 11.87% of clients in publicly supported clinics (Stiles, 1994). These increases suggest that progress has been made in meeting the needs of acutely distressed older adults, especially in public clinics. On the other hand, services for older adults are more likely to be dropped than to be added to community-based mental health programs (Estes, Linkins, & Kane, 1994).

Utilization studies from surveys by the National Institute of Mental Health provide yet another perspective on the low use of outpatient mental health services by elderly people. For all adults, only 15% to 20% of those with mental disorders sought help, and only 8% to 12% visited a mental health specialist. On the other hand, about 33% of those with mental health visits had no mental disorder. Although elderly people had a low utilization rate, their rate was not lower than that of the youngest adults, those aged 18 to 24 (Shapiro et al., 1984). The utilization of mental health services varied across the three cities surveyed and by age of clients. These data point out that the need for services has all too often been incorrectly assumed to correspond with proportionate level of use; and low utilization by elderly people was consequently interpreted as specific to older adults as a target population. Perhaps the problem of low utilization of outpatient services by elderly people should be reconceptualized as being similar to problems in other populations targeted for outreach.

Elderly People With Dementia

Dementia affects about 50% of elderly residents in nursing homes (Shadish, 1989) and large numbers of elderly people in residential care facilities and community-based long-term care. Outpatient services may also benefit older people in early stages of dementia as well as caregivers of older people in all stages of dementia.

The greater prevalence of dementia in the elderly population, as compared to younger adults means that all mental health service systems must decide whether elderly people with cognitive impairment, which is often but not always due to irreversible brain impairment, are mental health clients. This decision has varied state by state, as has the decision to separate the mental health service system from the systems for developmentally disabled people and those with substance abuse problems. The decision will affect the type and scope of programming for the elderly. Because they have different needs, older adults with dementing illnesses and those with acute psychological disorders or psychoses require different types of services. It is critically important not to confuse the two and especially not to assume that any elderly person with emotional, cognitive, or behavioral problems is necessarily cognitively impaired.

On the other hand, some older adults with dementia develop behavioral problems in the middle stages of their decline for which the treatment consists of psychotropic medications and behavioral interventions. These treatments are typically provided in the mental health system to people whose brain impairment (schizophrenia, once called *dementia praecox*) began earlier in life. In addition, with the brain-impaired older person, as with others who are severely disabled, the caregiver may be in need of mental health services to be able to continue to provide in-home care for the patient.

EFFECTIVENESS OF INTERVENTIONS

Before examining the problems in care delivery, it is worth noting that doubt about the effectiveness of intervention is *not* one of the problems; there is broad consensus that interventions are effective for mental disorders in later life.

Jeste (1991) and Jeste et al. (this volume) have provided a review of interventions with chronically mentally ill elderly people. Also, Knight and Carter (1990) described an intensive case management program that reduced the length of geropsychiatric unit stays to that of younger patients, with consequent high cost-effectiveness. Recent meta-analyses show roughly equivalent effect sizes for antidepressant medications (mean d = .57, Schneider, 1994) and for psychological interventions (mean d = .78, Scogin & McElreath, 1994) in the treatment of depression in later life. Kamholz and Gottlieb (1990) described effective psychopharmacologic interventions for older adults with dementia; Teri and Gallagher-Thompson (1991) and Fisher and Carstensen (1990) reviewed effective strategies in behavioral management for older adults with dementia. Individual psychoeducational interventions (mean d = .58) and respite care (mean d = .63) have been found effective in reducing distress among family caregivers of dementia patients (Knight, Lutzky, & Macofsky-Urban, 1993).

The effectiveness of mental health services with the targeted populations has been established.

COMPLEXITY OF CARE DELIVERY

Two major complexities prevent older adults from receiving care in the most appropriate location. First is the complexity of assessing mental health problems in older adults. Assessment is widely recognized as complex because of the array of possible presenting problems and the high rates of comorbidity. Clearly, someone who is frail and confused cannot be expected to self-diagnose accurately and then enter the system through the right doorway. Hence, outreach with accurate assessment and valid referral is necessary. Moreover, some elderly people may simply not see their problems as psychological, or they may be unaware of the existence of outpatient therapy (Lasoki & Thelan, 1987; Powers & Powers, 1991; Waxman, Carner, & Klein, 1984).

The second complexity is that older adults with mental health problems are embedded in a variety of distinct care systems at both institutional and community-based levels: medical care, long-term care for the elderly, mental health services, aging-network services, and possibly dementia care services (Knight, 1991).

Acknowledging these complexities, our analysis departs from the familiar "coordination of services" and "gaps in the system" arguments in two ways: First, we recognize that these multiple care systems operate on different principles, creating a confusing service world for both the older client and the service provider. There are gaps because different systems exist for different purposes (medical care, mental health treatment, frailty) and have developed in response to different historical pressures—not because someone overlooked elements while rationally laying out a system of care to meet all the needs of older adults.

Secondly, we observe that failures to coordinate are dictated more often by economic pressures than by failures in planning or personal failings of providers. Resources have been scarce, and they have become scarcer in the post-tax-revolt era. Amid the shrinking array of services, elderly people (especially those who need mental health services) suffer from the "last-in, first-out" principle. Older adults were targeted as a special population for mental health services late in the Carter administration, shortly before cutbacks began. Services for adults are often asked to cut back barely existing programs.

Under such conditions, the economic pressure is to compete rather than cooperate, and to limit services to existing clients rather than accept clients who may "belong" to some other system. Unfortunately for the clients, the system they belong to may not take them either. Gatz and Smyer (1992) noted that "everyone and no one is responsible for the clients" (p. 744). Ensuring appropriate care for older adults with mental health problems becomes a matter of securing appropriate services from a multiplicity of competing systems, each with its own internal operating principles.

PRINCIPLES OF CARE

Fortunately there are guidelines on what approach to take in providing more appropriate services to older adults. Knight, Rickards, Rabins, Buckwalter, and Smith (in press) have reviewed a variety of mental health programs for older adults with a range of mental health problems. The programs included community mental health services in Spokane, Washington; Cedar Rapids, Iowa; and Ventura County, California, as well as a multiservice program at Long Island Jewish Hospital in New York and a psychiatric consultation service to apartment buildings that are subsidized by the Department of Housing and Urban Development for elderly people in Baltimore. The services spanned urban and rural areas and used a variety of approaches for coordination of care.

These programs have shown that it is possible to provide high-quality, community-based mental health services to mentally ill elderly people. The programs also share some features that are key elements of successful community-based programs in mental health and aging:

1. All emphasize accurate diagnosis of older adults.
2. All are interdisciplinary and treatment focused.
3. All use active case-finding methods and community education approaches to bring clients in.
4. All collaborate actively with other agencies that serve older adults (in three cases with postal carriers, meter readers, and other "community gatekeepers"; Raschko, 1990).
5. All deliver mental health services to older adults at home.

In addition, the Department of Veterans Affairs (VA) provides models for hospital-based care (Cooley, in press). Like the community-based programs, VA mental health services emphasize accurate assessment, active treatment, and interdisciplinary services. Many VA mental health services are provided in medical settings (e.g., acute wards, chronic care, nursing homes) as well as in psychiatric units. Home care services are also a part of the VA continuum of care. Furthermore, VA has played a major role in developing training in geriatric mental health across the constituent disciplines.

A final principle of care for services to older adults is that they must be affordable. Until the past few years, most program development in mental health services for the elderly took place in contexts that do not rely entirely on either fee for service or on Medicare funding with the associated copayment from the client. Other sources of funds have included state funding for mental health services, community mental health system funding, VA funding, training grants, research grants, and various private, nonprofit agencies. Programs funded in this manner can provide service at little or not cost to the older client. These sources can be motivated by perceived client need, interest in creative program development, and training goals.

IMPACT OF PAYMENT SYSTEMS ON SERVICE DELIVERY

The privatization movement in mental health care that began in 1980 is characterized by increasing reliance on private practice providers and organized for-profit systems that are driven by market forces such as demand for services and the need to make a profit from providing them (Kiesler, 1993; Kiesler & Simpkins, 1991; Simons, 1989). Estes (1992) described developments in health care policy during this era as leading to the development of a "medical-industrial complex" comparable to the military–industrial complex; Kiesler (1992) argued that mental health policy is a small footnote to health care policy.

The ultimate source of money for mental health services for the elderly is still government funding, but the service delivery systems are driven by different forces and are likely to achieve differing policy outcomes. In this section, we describe briefly the forces that shape the development of mental health services for the elderly in the private sector, which relies on fee-for-service reimbursement, in the private managed care sector, and in the public sector.

Fee-for-Service Medicare Reimbursement

In 1988, $2.5 billion of total Medicare spending ($90.5 billion) was spent on mental health care, $2.2 billion on Part A (inpatient services). That $2.5 billion was less than 3% of the Medicare budget, versus to 20% to 30% of private insurance spent on mental health (Sherman, 1992). Slightly earlier, the National Institute of Mental Health estimated in 1984 that 51.2% of Medicare-funded mental health services went to disabled adults under 65 years of age. Medicare has spent very little on mental health care, half of that goes to younger adults, and the total outlay is disproportionately spent on inpatient care.

The changes brought about by the 1989 Omnibus Budget Reconciliation Act (OBRA) have led to increases in Medicare spending on inpatient psychiatric care, however, including an expanding number of geropsychiatric inpatient units (Michigan Office of Services to the Elderly, 1992; Wagner, 1994). Partial hospitalization services for older adults have exploded, increasing by 50% between 1986 and 1990 (Stiles, 1994). Healthcare Financial Management Association (1994) reported that the Medicare billing in the state of California increased by $250 million during 1993 and that average per diem costs of partial hospitalization sometimes exceeded those of inpatient programs. Outpatient mental health services increased by 20% in the same 4-year period (Stiles, 1994).

Since the 1989 OBRA changes took effect, one source of growth in outpatient mental health care has been the proliferation of group programs that schedule and bill for outpatient visits to nursing homes. In combination, the increase in mental health services from 1992 to 1994 under Medicare has been estimated at 25%, and Medicaid mental health expenditures showed a similar increase during the same period. This increase is, in part, a tribute to the flexibility of private services, which respond quickly to changes in the marketplace—in this case, the loosening of mental health payments at a time when both public and private insurance sources were placing increasing restrictions on medical services (Simons, 1989).

In terms of the principles of care outlined above, fee-for-service medicare reimbursement has the advantage of emphasizing assessment and encouraging the development of services at several levels of care throughout the nation. The ability of fee-for-service Medicare to produce rapid changes in service delivery to older adults by a wide spectrum of service entities with minimal administrative overhead is its greatest strength.

On the negative side, Medicare regulations have tended to discourage home visits for mental health services, if not eliminate them altogether (Knight, 1994). Interdisciplinary cooperation in the form of communication with the primary care physician is encouraged, but such communication cannot be said to amount to working in an interdisciplinary team setting. Medicare's emphasis on inpatient care tends to exacerbate the existing imbalance of older adults in inpatient versus outpatient care and is bad mental health policy in any case, since outpatient care is generally more effective and less expensive (Kiesler, 1992, 1993).

Furthermore, financial intermediaries in the Medicare program have begun to question some of the expansion in mental health services. Health Financial Management Association (1994) reported that fees charged for 20 partial hospitalization programs have been disputed by Blue Cross of California. Similar challenges were reported by Mutual of Omaha in the Midwest. The intermediaries object to billing practices and to the transporting of older adults with dementia from nursing homes to partial hospitalization sites. Anecdotal evidence suggests that similar problems occur in outpatient services in nursing homes: Verbal psychotherapy has been reported for nonverbal older adults with dementia and providers have billed 15 therapy sessions in 1 day. The extent of fraud is unknown but clearly needs further study. The appropriateness of certain mental health services for older adults in various stages of dementia needs to be determined and built into oversight procedures.

While assessment is encouraged, its accuracy may be compromised by the desire to increase income. Kiesler (1991), using national data, showed that the Medicare Diagnostic Related Groups (DRG) system led to a doubling of diagnoses of major depressive disorder between 1980 and 1985, diagnoses that he argued were a result of "gaming the system"—that is, the less serious, depressive spectrum diagnoses were changed to the more severe one, which justifies hospital admission and longer treatment time. Anecdotal evidence suggests that a troublesome issue is faced in diagnosing residents of nursing homes: If dementia is diagnosed, most financial intermediaries make no payment for mental health services; if depression is diagnosed, payment is processed. Since there is no requirement for expertise in assessment of older adults, the accuracy of diagnoses under this system is unregulated and unknown.

In summary, the Medicare fee-for-service reimbursement model seems to have expanded mental health service delivery to older adults dramatically, encouraged the privatization of mental health care for older adults, and encouraged inpatient over outpatient options. (The inpatient-outpatient imbalance may have been corrected to some extent by the rapid growth of partial hospitalization programs and outpatient services since 1990, some of which serve older adults in nursing homes.)

Managed Care

The rapid growth of fee-for-service medical care and the difficulties inherent in controlling quality and quantity of services reimbursed under this system have led to an increasing reliance on managed care models in general medical services and for medical services reimbursed under Medicare. These models have recently begun to affect mental health services for older adults.

Managed health options, especially health maintenance organizations (HMOs), have been a rapidly increasing part of the health care coverage of older Americans since 1980. Approximately 10% of older Americans have opted to receive their Medicare-funded health care through HMOs.

HMOs exist to provide overall health care management for a defined population. Since the HMO is paid per capita rather than per visit, the HMO is motivated to achieve cost savings for its group of enrollees. These cost savings are based on several factors (Wetle & Mark, 1990):

1. Since the care providers are not paid on a unit-of-service basis, there is no motivation to overprovide services.

2. There is a financial incentive to maintain the health of the population (i.e, to provide preventive services).

3. Less expensive services can be substituted for more expensive ones (e.g., outpatient care for inpatient care, primary care for specialist care, nonphysician care for physician care).

From the provider's perspective, a primary motivation for including mental health services in HMOs is the potential for a cost-offset effect—the possibility that mental health services contribute to saving medical costs. This possibility is thought to be even greater in older populations because of pervasive comorbidity, prevention of institutionalization, and greater functional impact of mental health problems in the older population (Lave, 1990). Manning, Leibowitz, Goldberg, Rogers, and Newhome (1984) showed that the costs-offset effect is largely due to decreases in hospital admission rates and average days per admission.

The use of mental health "carve outs" (that is, subcontracting to an organization of mental health specialists) to cover the mental health component of managed care is a growing trend as well.

Inpact on mental health services

What is the likely impact of the managed care model on services? For the general population of mental health users, Norquist and Wells (1991) have shown that HMO enrollees have significantly fewer visits per user to specialty mental health providers. Mental health service users in HMOs are more likely to be treated by less expensive providers, to be seen by nonmedical therapists (mainly social workers), and to receive group and family therapy and are less likely to receive individual psychotherapy (Wells, Manning, & Benjamin, 1986).

Wetle and Mark (1990) also pointed out that focusing on defined psychiatric services misses the focus of mental health care in HMOs. The cost-containment rationale means that care for mental health care in HMOs is focused on high health service users with mental health symptoms. Intervention may be limited to assessment that clarifies the non-medical cause of presented symptoms or to the type of care described above. The medically ill elderly with psychological problems complicating medical care are the primary target population for HMO mental health services. Shifting to managed care implies serving this group, *not* the older adults that public policy has focused on in the past.

Two current policy problems in California may point to other potential problems. The Alzheimer's disease diagnostic and treatment centers in California are state-funded centers that are under the auspices of university medical schools and provide diagnosis and services for patients with Alzheimer's disease and their families. The centers have recently expressed concern about the trend toward HMO enrollment of the elderly, citing three problems: (a) Many HMO clinics lack diagnostic expertise in dementing illnesses; (b) HMO reimbursement rates do not support the costs of medical education in medical center settings; and (c) some HMOs have used questionable recruiting strategies, including enrolling cognitively impaired older adults who are not competent to sign contracts.

The second revolves around the shift of the Medi-Cal system (Medicaid in California) to a managed care option. The mental health portion of the system is currently being planned as a carve-out, with the mental health managed care money going to the counties (the entities currently responsible for mental health care). This plan has led to some concern on both sides. Local mental health directors want to maintain responsibility for mental health services to seriously mentally ill people, believing that HMOs do not have a good track record with that population. HMOs are concerned that the local mental health programs will not provide services to Medicaid-covered individuals with relatively minor mental health problems that complicate medical care. Both sides are also concerned about coordination of cases between medical providers in one system and mental health providers in another.

At present, the overall picture of mental health services in HMOs suggests preferences for outpatient care, less expensive providers, limited numbers of visits, and group and family interventions (Mechanic & Aiken, 1989; Wetle & Mark, 1990). There is also a tendency to emphasize the role of primary care physicians and therefore, perhaps unintentionally, the use of psychotropic drugs as the primary form of intervention. For example, Burns and Taube (1990) pointed out that for all mental health care (not just HMOs), mental health care in the general health sector consists primarily of prescribing psychotropic medications (the ratio of drugs to psychotherapy is 4:1) in that service sector.

There are no known successful models of HMO care to severely mentally ill elderly people, who probably need a different model of care.

Consonance With Geriatric Mental Health Principles

How does managed care compare with the practice rules developed in the geriatric mental health literature? One strength of the HMO model in application to older adults is the preference for group and family therapy in the delivery of mental health services. Another strength of HMOs is the high potential for interdisciplinary, coordinated care within a single managed health system. In principle, mental health and physical health care could be completely integrated, with shared record keeping, a single-source pharmacy for better medication coordination, and providers united by concern for the patient's long-term health. However, the tendency toward carve-out, whatever the advantages for other populations and other reasons, vitiates this advantage of HMOs for the elderly population.

HMOs are weak in meeting the needs of mentally ill elderly people, for specialized assessment, outreach, and home visits.

Although there is no systematically collected evidence on assessment of mental disorders in older patients in HMOs, the complexity of accurate assessment in older adults runs counter to the HMOs' emphasis on use of nonspecialized service providers. Kaiser Permanente's Interregional Committee on Aging is working on plans that call for increased screening of older adults at the primary care level. The focus appears to be on recognizing depression, primarily as a complicating factor in medical care management.

HMOs are also not well suited organizationally for active outreach and case-finding approaches. When a guiding principle of an organization is cost containment, seeking out patients who are not actively seeking services is counterproductive. To the extent that older adults underutilize outpatient services in relation to their need and may not even recognize their own need for mental health services, the public sector approach that defines older adults as a special service population requiring specialized services is likely to be more effective.

This principle cuts the other way as well. As noted by Wetle & Mark (1990), the HMOs ability to save money depends on preexisting overuse and inefficient use of services; if services are actually underused, there is no "fat" to cut. New services for previously unserved patients will be new services and will therefore create new expense. The exceptions for managed care mental health services for older adults would be the medical cost offset and the possibility of reducing inpatient mental health service usage (which, of course, can be reduced only if it has been available in the past).

Serious mental illness and specialty treatment of mental disorders in older adults are not a pressing concern at this time in the HMO sector. We echo Robinson (1990), who ended a review of mental health components in long-term care models (including Social-HMOs) with these words:

> The treatment of mental illness is not a priority in any of the long term care models. Moreover, referral sources (senior centers, hospitals, area agencies on aging) typically underrepresent or screen out individuals with diagnosed mental illnesses. Program evaluations have reported relatively little information on mental status even though most recognized that cognitive impairment is a strong predictor of nursing home placement. (p. 172)

In summary, the move to managed care options in health care for older adults entails a number of implicit policy decisions about mental health services for elderly people. These decisions are seldom considered or debated on their specific merits. Because quality care for older adults depends on expertise in assessment and treatment, guidelines must be created to ensure that such expertise will be available. Without outside guidance, the managed care model is unlikely to engage in active case-finding, provide specialty dementia care, or provide services to older adults with schizophrenia and other psychoses. While there are potential advantages to managed care, they are unlikely to develop without more active attention from researchers, consumer advocates, and policy analysts.

STATE POLICY AND PROGRAM DEVELOPMENT

First, it is worth noting that most of the examples of model program development discussed above are public sector programs from federal, state, and county levels. Mental health programs and policy are historically a public sector concern, mainly at the state level, and services for seriously mentally ill people will likely remain in the public sector (Mechanic, 1993). As noted above, the public sector has higher rates of service utilization by older adults; further, public agencies have been found to be twice as likely to provide outreach services as nonprofit private agencies (Estes et al, 1994). However, as noted by Mechanic (1993), with regard to programs for seriously mentally ill people, while the public sector is capable of producing occasional examples of a model program, these programs rarely proliferate to the point of constituting a national program of effective services.

While private sector services tend to be driven by money (in the case of mental health services for elderly people, the money is public money), public sector services are often determined by policies set by legislative committees, the executive branch, and interest groups. With a few exceptions, such as the Mental Health and Aging Coalition in Oklahoma—which targeted specific objectives such as funding geriatric coordinators and community mental health centers and the activity of the California Senate Subcommittee on Aging with regard to dementia care—activity in mental health and aging at the state level has been driven primarily by the executive branch. The lack of a large and well-funded consumer or interest group lobby has been cited as a reason for the disarray of mental health policy for chronically mentally ill people in general (Mechanic & Rochefort, 1990; Shadish, 1989) and for elderly people in particular (Gatz & Smyer, 1992).

In trying to improve the current system of services, some state-level bureaucrats have initiated reforms by coordinating mental health programs with other aging services or by targeting in specific community mental health centers program development. For example, Indiana has successfully coordinated mental health care with an area agency on aging (AAA). In particular, the Lake County Mental Health Center provides the local AAA with a professional staff member 1 day a week. This staff member provides education and referrals to the older adults who use AAA services and express a need for mental health care. In another example, Michigan has initiated a similar service coordination program, called Building Ties. However, in a survey of 281 community mental health centers across the country, Lebowitz, Light, and Bailey (1987) reported that only 23% expressed a formal relationship with the local AAA.

In most states, however, there is only one staff member who is the bureaucratic expert on these issues. In many states, this staff person may not even be allocated 100% of the time to aging and mental health. He or she may also be responsible for other aging programs such as nursing home regulations or mental health programs such as rural community outreach. Furthermore, several states appear to have no resident expert on these issues at all. In these cases, policies for older adults are developed in conjunction with policies related to other populations or are not developed at all.

Since the state executive branches have been the main source of policy development and implementation, all 50 states would clearly benefit from an increase in the number of staff or an increase in the expertise of existing bureaucrats. This approach expands on Knight's finding (1986) that the primary predictor of service provision to older adults in local programs in California was the presence of designated staff to serve them. At the state planning and development level as well, it appears that with more professionals available, more job responsibilities can be divided and more specific activities pursued.

An example of an initiative that addresses this problem is the postdoctoral training program sponsored by the National Association of State Mental Health Program Directors (NASMHPD). In 1993, one fellow of that association was researching aging issues, and in 1994, two more were recruited. Ideally, this sort of career development may eventually create the bureaucratic critical mass that can stimulate reform across a variety of state mental health agencies.

In summary, we note that public sector services provide program development and training for the entire mental health services system. The care of seriously mentally ill elderly people is likely to remain in the public sector. These services are, and always have been, state-level policy decisions (except between 1963 and 1981; see Mechanic, 1993). Care for other groups is provided with public funds and controlled by federal public policy decisions but is provided by the private sector. At present, public sector decision making on mental health and aging is largely confined to the executive branch and appears to be successful when there are bureaucrats who are committed to these issues. For future development, the nation needs a greater number of trained and concerned personnel in the executive branch and greater involvement of legislators and consumer advocacy groups to ensure the appropriate expansion of services for older adults with mental health problems.

QUALITY ASSURANCE AND SERVICE MONITORING

As Shadish (1989) argued with regard to chronically mentally ill adults in general, quality in privatized services is controlled by consumers and by government regulation. He argued that with regard to seriously mentally ill people, both controls have typically been lacking. Consumers of mental health services often have few alternatives to choose from, and the choices are often made for them by care providers. The government has shown little interest in regulating the private sector provision of mental health care.

These problems are present at least for elderly people with dementia or chronic mentally illness with regard to choices of mental health service options. Given that older adults in general are thought to be uninformed about mental health problems and their treatment (Gatz &

Smyer, 1992; Knight 1989), the same is probably true of older adults with acute psychological problems such as anxiety and depression. For those who are acutely distressed, consumer advocates may be more effective in monitoring quality of care and attempts to overprovide service, but they are unlikely to recognize failure to provide services for depression, psychological factors complicating medical conditions, and so on.

If consumer choice cannot ensure quality in this market, then the government—which is paying the bills, has to take a more active role in regulating the quality of services. It may be useful to conceptualize this oversight function in terms of accepted contract management principles, suggesting that performance standards be built into contracts and that contracts be carefully monitored (e.g., Rehfuss, 1989), rather than in terms of increasing governmental regulations. Consumer advocacy groups can also play a role in ensuring quality of services by monitoring both private and public sector services and giving consumers an organized voice in the planning and development process.

SUMMARY AND RECOMMENDATIONS

To achieve some order amid the chaos, policy and program planning decisions are required in the planning for 21st-century geriatric mental health care. Policy initiatives can be conceptually organized by subpopulation and by mode of payment for services. In addition crosscutting policy issues require attention regardless of the decisions about who will be served or what method of payment is used.

Subpopulation Issues

Severely mentally ill elderly people

This group of older adults with psychoses was largely neglected until the past few years. They (along with all adults with psychoses) have traditionally been the responsibility of state and local governments. It seems unlikely that this responsibility will shift to the private sector, largely because the needs of severely mentally ill adults are greater than are covered by Medicare and Medicaid and so do not allow for profit taking (Shadish, 1989; Sharfstein, Stoline, & Goldman, 1993). For planning and advocacy, it is important to focus attention on state-level decision making regarding services for this population.

For older adults in general, deinstitutionalization in the past often meant transinstitutionalization into nursing homes (Shadish, 1989). The presumably unintended effect of the 1987 OBRA changes that mandate mental health screenings in nursing homes is likely to be the removal from nursing homes of older adults with psychotic diagnoses and without medical comorbidity (Gatz & Smyer, 1992). A critical current and future question is where these individuals can go to receive appropriate care.

In each state the population of seriously mentally ill older adults needs more specific planning attention in the executive and legislative branches of government. Programs such as NASMHPD's postdoctoral training in state policy should be expanded at both state and national levels to include positions in legislatures and consumer groups as well as in the executive branch. Attention to this group by consumer advocacy organizations such as the American Association of Retired Persons and the National Alliance for the Mentally Ill will also be essential to the development of effective public services.

In short, a coherent policy on the public responsibility for seriously mentally ill people is needed, and that policy must include attention to the needs of older adults with serious mental illness.

Acutely distressed older adults

The provision of services to this population has been privatized, so the principal policy question is how to use public funds to encourage, or effective contract management to ensure, the provision of appropriate services. Though these services appear to be expanding rapidly, it is unclear whether they are expanding well. That is, there is essentially no information on the quality of assessments or treatments or even on the appropriateness of care models. The Health Care Financing Administration, the Center for Mental Health Services, the National Institute of Mental Health, the National Institute on Aging, and other relevant federal agencies, as well as advocacy groups for consumers and providers, must monitor and control this process in an intentional manner (also see recommendations for payment models below).

Elderly people with dementia

The expansion of privatized services appears to include the provision of services to substantial, if not clearly known, percentages of older adults with dementia. Expert psychological assessment, medication management, and behavioral interventions to this population would be examples of professionally appropriate services that serve public interest goals. The widespread provision of incompetent assessment, medication interventions, and psychological interventions would be both undesirable and needlessly expensive.

Since an older adult with dementia is unlikely to be able to give either truly informed consent or exercise meaningful free choice in the marketplace, it is essential that such services be monitored by the public sector with attention to both professional competency and fraud.

Payment Models

In any discussion of payment models for mental health services to older adults, it is important not to lose sight of the fact that most payment originates in the public sector. The issue is more correctly described in terms of contracting out to the private sector versus direct public provision of services.

Public sector provision of services has the advantage of being focused on the needs of the mentally ill people rather than on the demand for service or profit motivation. At its best, this focus on need can lead to the design and implementation of new service models. The public sector can be told to function as the service provider for those the private sector cannot afford to treat on account of either poverty or complexity of problems (e.g., serious mental illness). The public sector has traditionally provided much of the training for mental health professionals and has been a prime mover in specialized training in geriatric mental health (e.g., Cooley, in press, described VA's role in training geropsychologists). The typically cited disadvantages of the public sector have been expense, inefficiencies, and slowness (Simons, 1989).

Fee-for-service Medicare has the advantage of being able to mobilize enormous changes in service delivery systems very quickly. The lack of effective systems for monitoring quality and controlling costs is a disadvantage to this approach. Kiesler (1992) argued that fee-for-service Medicare has the additional disadvantages of imposing health care principles on mental health services: The system is responsive to providers (physicians and hospitals) and favors short-term inpatient care over outpatient services and psychosocial interventions.

The HMO model has the potential advantages of favoring outpatient treatment and prevention and fostering an interdisciplinary approach to care for older adults, who frequently have both psychological and physical disorders. The drawbacks to the HMO model are the disincentives for specialist care and the disincentives for active outreach to find clients who do not self-identify.

Recommendations

The challenge for the 21st century may well be the creation of a rational, intentional mental health care policy for the older adult population. The stakeholders in this policy would be the payment sources (federal and state governments), consumers, and the range of providers (private for-profit organizations, private nonprofits, and governmental units). Research and gerontological professional expertise should be incorporated in planning this intentional policy.

Medicare policy could be designed to achieve public policy goals and monitored to ensure that intended consequences are being actualized. If Medicare policy were conceptualized as an incentive system that could be used to shape the activities of service providers to achieve public goals and consumer mental health, an intentional system could be developed to target those goals.

In our view, such a system would include an emphasis on expert and accurate assessment, outreach and case identification, interdisciplinary teamwork, home visits, and appropriate treatments. Services could be targeted to the more severely mentally ill people by offering appropriately larger payment incentives. Services to older adults with dementia could be appropriately targeted with regulatory oversight to discourage fraud. Payment incentives could be designed to encourage appropriate levels of care, favoring outpatient services and prevention to the extent possible. Rather than choosing among fee-for-service, managed care, and direct public sector provision of services, the challenge would be to create payment incentives that would shape the behavior of the total collection of systems and individual entrepreneurs toward the provision of quality mental health services for the various populations of older adults who need them. The incentive system so designed would be no less complex than the current one, but it could serve public and consumer interests rather than provider motivations.

REFERENCES

Burns, B. J., & Taube, C. A. (1990). Mental health services in general medical care and in nursing homes. In B. S. Fogel, A. Furino, & G. L. Gottlieb (Eds.), *Mental health policy for older Americans: Protecting minds at risk* (pp. 63-84). Washington, DC: American Psychiatric Press.

Conwell, Y., Nelson, J. C., Kim, K., & Mazure, C. M. (1989). Elderly patients admitted to the psychiatric unit of a general hospital. *Journal of the American Geriatrics Society, 37,* 35-41.

Cooley, S. (in press). Geropsychology training and services in the Department of Veterans Affairs. In B. Knight, L. Teri, J. Santos, & P. Wohlford (Eds.), *Applying geropsychology to services for older adults: Implications for training and practice.* Washington, DC: American Psychological Association.

Estes, C. (1992, November). *The aging enterprise revisited.* Donald P. Kent Award Lecture at the meeting of the Gerontological Society of America, Washington, DC.

Estes, C. L., Linkins, K. W., & Kane, K. (1994, November). *Mental health services and the elderly: Organizations in transition.* Paper presented at the meeting of the Gerontological Society of America, Atlanta, GA.

Fisher, J. E., & Carstensen, L. L. (1990). Behavioral management of the dementias. *Clinical Psychology Review,* 611-629.

Fleming, A. S., Richards, L. D., Santos, J. F., & West, P. R. (1986). *Mental health services for the elderly, Vol. 3.* Washington, DC: Retirement Research Foundation.

Gatz, M., & Smyer, M. A. (1992). The mental health system and older adults in the 1990s. *American Psychologist, 47,* 741-751.

Healthcare Financial Management Association. (1994). Partial hospitalization may face medicare fraud, kickback problems. *Healthcare Financial Ventures Report, 3*(17), 1-2.

Jeste, D. (1991). Neuroleptic treatment of chronically mentally ill elderly: Suggestions for further research. In E. Light & B. D. Lebowitz (Eds.), *The elderly with chronic mental illness.* (pp. 16-30). New York: Springer.

Kamholz, B., & Gottlieb, G. L. (1990). The nature and efficacy of interventions for depression and dementia. In B. S. Fogel, A. Furino, & G. L. Gottlieb (Eds.), *Mental health policy for older Americans: Protecting minds at risk* (pp. 37-62). Washington, DC: American Psychiatric Press.

Kiesler, C. A. (1991). Changes in general hospital psychiatric care, 1980–1985. *American Psychologist, 46,* 416-421.

Kiesler, C. A. (1992). U.S. mental health policy: Doomed to fail. *American Psychologist, 47,* 1077-1082.

Kiesler, C. A. (1993). Mental health policy and mental hospitalization. *Current Directions in Psychological Science, 2,* 93-95.

Kiesler, C. A., & Simpkins, C. (1991). The de facto national system of psychiatric inpatient care. *American Psychologist, 46,* 579-584.

Knight, B. G. (1986). Management variables as predictors of service utilization by the elderly in mental health. *International Journal of Aging and Human Development, 23,* 141-148.

Knight, B. G. (1989). *Outreach with the elderly: Community education, assessment, and therapy.* New York: New York University Press.

Knight, B. G. (1991). Outreach to older adults: Matching programs to specific needs [Monograph]. In N. Cohen (Ed.), *Psychiatric outreach to the mentally ill.* (pp. 93-112). San Francisco: Jossey-Bass.

Knight, B. G. (1994). Home delivered mental health services: An idea whose time has come? [Editorial]. *The Gerontologist, 34,* 149.

Knight, B. G., & Carter, P. M. (1990). Reduction of psychiatric inpatient stay for older adults by intensive case management. *The Gerontologist, 30,* 510-515.

Knight, B. G., Lutzky, S. M., & Macofsky-Urban, F. (1993). A meta- analytic review of interventions for caregiver distress: Recommendations for future research. *The Gerontologist, 33,* 240-249.

Knight, B. G., Rickards, L., Rabins, P., Buckwalter, K., & Smith, M. (in press). Community-based services for mentally ill elderly. In B. Knight, L. Teri, J. Santos, & P. Wohlford (Eds.), *Applying geropsychology to services for older adults: Implications for training and practice.* Washington, DC: American Psychological Association.

Lasoski, M. C., & Thelen, M. H. (1987). Attitudes of older and middle-aged persons toward mental health intervention. *The Gerontologist, 27,* 288-292.

Lave, J. R. (1990). The cost-offset effect. In B. S. Fogel, A. Furino, & G. L. Gottlieb (Eds.), *Mental health policy for older Americans: Protecting minds at risk* (pp. 125-134). Washington, DC: American Psychiatric Press.

Lebowitz, B. D., Light, E., & Bailey, F. (1987). Mental health center services for the elderly: Impact of coordination with area agencies on aging. *The Gerontologist, 27,* 699-702.

Lebowitz, B. D., & Niederehe, G. (1992). Concepts and issues in mental health and aging. In J. E. Birren, R. B. Sloane, & G. D. Cohen (Eds.), *Handbook of mental health and aging* (2nd ed., pp. 3-27). San Diego, CA: Academic Press.

Light, E., & Lebowitz, B. D. (Eds.). (1991). *The elderly with chronic mental illness.* New York: Springer.

Manning, W. G., Leibowitz, A., Goldberg, G. A., Rogers, W. H., & Newhome, J. P. (1984). A controlled trial of the effect of a prepaid group practice on the use of services. *New England Journal of Medicine, 310,* 1505-1510.

Mechanic, D. (1993). Mental health services in the context of health insurance reform. *Milbank Quarterly, 71,* 349-364.

Mechanic, D., & Aiken, L. H. (1989). Capitation in mental health: Potentials and cautions. In D. Mechanic & L. H. Aikens (Eds.), *Paying for services: Promises and pitfalls of capitation.* San Francisco: Jossey-Bass.

Mechanic, D., & Rochefort, D. A. (1990). Deinstitutionalization: An appraisal of reform. *American Sociological Review, 16,* 301-327.

Mental Health and Aging Coalition (1993). *Oklahoma Mental Health and Aging Coalition.* Norman, OK: Deighton.

Michigan Office of Services to the Elderly (1992). *Meeting the demographic imperative.* Lansing: Michigan Department of Mental Health.

Miller, N. E., & Cohen, G. D. (Eds.). (1987). *Schizophrenia and aging.* New York: Guilford.

Norquist, G. S., & Wells, K. B. (1991). How do HMOs reduce outpatient mental health care costs? *American Journal of Psychiatry, 148,* 96-101.

Powers, S. M., & Powers, E. A. (1991). *Factors which predict older adults' knowledge of psychological difficulties and of mental health services.* Final report submitted to American Association of Retired Persons Andrus Foundation, Greensboro, NC.

Raschko, R. (1990). The gatekeeper model for the isolated, at-risk elderly. In N. Cohen (Ed.), *Psychiatry takes to the streets.* New York: Guilford.

Redick, R. A., & Taube, C. A. (1980). Demography and mental health care of the aged. In J. E. Birren & R. B. Sloane (Eds.), *Handbook of mental health and aging* (pp. 57-74). Englewood Cliffs, NJ: Prentice-Hall.

Rehfuss, J. (1989). Maintaining quality and accountability in a period of privatization. In R. E. Cleary & N. L. Henry (Eds.), *Managing public programs: Balancing politics, administration, and public needs.* San Francisco: Jossey-Bass.

Robinson, G. K. (1990). The psychiatric component of long term care. In B. S. Fogel, A. Furino, & G. L. Gottlieb (Eds.), *Mental health policy for older Americans: Protecting minds at risk* (pp. 157-178). Washington, DC: American Psychiatric Press.

Schneider, L. S. (1994). Meta-analysis from a clinician's perspective. In L. S. Schneider, C. F. Reynolds, B. D. Lebowitz, & A. J. Friedhoff (Eds.), *Diagnosis and treatment of depression in late life: Results of the NIH Consensus Development Conference* (pp. 361-374). Washington, DC: American Psychiatric Press.

Scogin, F., & McElreath, L. (1994). Efficacy of psychosocial treatments for geriatric depression: A quantitative review. *Journal of Consulting and Clinical Psychology, 62,* 69-74.

Shadish, W. R. (1989). Private sector care for chronically mentally ill individuals: The more things change, the more they stay the same. *American Psychologist, 44,* 1142-1147.

Shapiro, S., Skinner, E. A., Kessler, L. G., Von Korff, M., German, P. S., Tischler, G. L., Leaf, P. S., Benham, L., Cotter, L., & Regler, D. A. (1984). Utilization of health and mental health services. *Archives of General Psychiatry, 41,* 971-978.

Sharfstein, S. S., Stoline, A. M., & Goldman, H. H. (1993). Psychiatric care and health insurance reform. *American Journal of Psychiatry, 150,* 7-17.

Sherman, J. (1992). *Medicare's mental health benefits: Coverage, utilization, and expenditures.* Washington, DC: American Association of Retired Persons.

Simons, L. R. (1989). Privatization and the mental health system: A private sector view. *American Psychologist, 44,* 1138-1141.

Stiles, P. G. (1994, Nov). *Utilization of ambulatory mental health services by the elderly: A preliminary report on the effects of recent Medicare reimbursement changes.* Paper presented at the meeting of the Gerontological Society of America, Atlanta, GA.

Teri, L., & Gallagher-Thompson, D. (1991). Cognitive-behavioral interventions for treatment of depression in Alzheimer's patients. *The Gerontologist, 31,* 413-416.

Wagner, B. (1994). Innovations in the geriatric continuum of care. *Continuum, 1,* 51-58.

Waxman, H. M., Carner, E. A., & Klein, M. (1984). Underutilizing of mental health professionals by community elderly. *The Gerontologist, 24,* 23-30.

Wells, K. B., Manning, W. G., & Benjamin, B. (1986). Use of outpatient mental health services in HMO and fee for services plans: Results from a randomized controlled trial. *Health Services Research, 21,* 452-474.

Wetle, T., & Mark, H. (1990). Managed care. In B. S. Fogel, A. Furino, & G. L. Gottlieb (Eds.), *Mental health policy for older Americans: Protecting minds at risk* (pp. 221-238). Washington, DC: American Psychiatric Press.

CHAPTER 10

Infrastructure Requirements for Research in Late-Life Mental Disorders

Ira R. Katz

What infrastructure is needed to enable research in mental health and aging? Over the past decade, substantial progress has been made in translating research findings into clinical practice. However, this area is now in transition as a result of changing demographics, flux in the structure and funding of health care, growing opportunities derived from basic research, and evolving changes in agencies that fund mental health research. This chapter examines these issues in order to recommend infrastructure requirements and emphasizes that clinical research is essential to meet changing needs in the treatment of late-life mental disorders.

LATE-LIFE MENTAL DISORDERS: DEFINING THE AREA

The mental disorders of late life consist of a spectrum of psychiatric disorders, including depressions and other affective disorders, anxiety disorders, schizophrenia and other psychoses, and severe personality disorders, as well as Alzheimer's disease, vascular dementia, other dementias,

The author thanks Richard Veith, Gabe Maletta, and Kathleen C. Buckwalter for their comments on an earlier draft.

and delirium. They include both disorders with the initial onset in late life and those chronic and recurrent disorders that have been longstanding problems. In addition to diseases that have traditionally been recognized, evidence is increasing that they include milder disorders, such as subsyndromal depressions that have long been neglected. Although late-life mental disorders differ widely in symptoms and severity, common properties include their substantial impact on well-being, quality of life, self-care, health care utilization, morbidity, and mortality; their effects on family caregivers; and their occurrence within the context of the general medical problems of late life.

As defined above, the mental disorders of late life include problems that have been of concern to different groups of patients, families, advocates, and policy makers. Those concerned with the problems of aging patients with severe and chronic disorders such as schizophrenia (e.g., the National Alliance for the Mentally Ill), those interested primarily in Alzheimer's disease and related disorders (e.g., the Alzheimer's Association), and those concerned with depressions or delirium occurring as complications of general medical conditions have, to some extent, represented distinct traditions and constituencies. In spite of these distinctions, it is important to recognize that the value of new knowledge on the relationships between brain and behavior and the benefits of new treatments, as well as recurring problems such as the stigmatization of mental illness and the inequities in Medicare funding for treatment, are shared across all the mental disorders.

On the other hand, there may be concerns that a definition based on a list of disorders, no matter how extensive, may be too narrow because it excludes consideration of expectable life transitions such as retirement and bereavement. As the goals of mental health care shift to include a focus on prevention (Horne & Blazer, 1992; Katz, Streim, & Parmelee, 1994), the need to attend to normative events becomes more apparent for both research and practice. These transitions may be viewed as critical issues for research designed to develop and evaluate interventions to prevent depression and other disorders. An exclusive focus on mental disorders also can deemphasize the extensive interactions between health and behavior that are increasingly recognized as determinants of wellness or disease. The growing evidence that health psychology and behavioral medicine can be important components of clinical practice complements the issues discussed here in demonstrating the importance of clinical mental health research.

THE DEMOGRAPHIC IMPERATIVE

The aging of America's population, with the highest rates of growth among the oldest old, is a well-known trend that represents a major challenge for the design and delivery of health care and supportive services for emerging generations of older adults. The implications of an aging population and the resulting steep rise in the incidence of Alzheimer's disease have been widely discussed (Khachaturian, 1992). In addition, the suggestion that the current cohort of middle-aged and younger adults is more vulnerable to depression than today's elderly provides other grounds for expecting that the mental disorders of the elderly will increase faster than other age-related problems (Wickramaratne, Weissman, Leaf, & Holford, 1989). We can expect an explosive increase in the occurrence of depression among future generations of older adults as more and more individuals become exposed to age-related risk factors for major depression. Similarly, patients with lifelong histories of chronic schizophrenia are, for the first time, surviving into old age in significant numbers; as a result, new concerns are emerging about their care. Increasing numbers of individuals with histories (and possible residual effects) of substance abuse will be experiencing the stresses of aging. Targeting research on these issues will be necessary to allow us to prepare for a future marked by increasing mental health needs for older adults.

CHANGES IN THE HEALTH CARE SYSTEM

Whether or not national health care reform is enacted in the near future, the country's health care system will be undergoing profound changes. These evolving changes raise concerns about how mental health care can be structured to ensure that all patients and families in need can gain access to appropriate services. These changes will also affect the current structure of disease-centered research on patient populations (Lebowitz & Gottlieb, 1995).

Tertiary care academic medical centers, public institutions, voluntary and private hospitals, and Department of Veterans Affairs medical centers are all undergoing budget cutbacks and reorganizations. They all have questions about their roles within evolving systems for the delivery of general medical care. For mental health care, institutional planning is further complicated by managed care programs that separate psychiatric treatment from the rest of medical care. Few institutions have formulated long-range plans regarding their commitment to mental health care. Moreover, the academic medical centers are becoming increasingly concerned about their ability to support a research mission in the face of increasing pressures on the funds available for treatment, inpatient or outpatient. Thus, planning for the future of both mental health care and clinical research has become a "back burner" issue in many institutions. In the current environment, mental health research is in danger because it is, in effect, twice removed from the major concerns of the institutions that have been its traditional hosts, in the first place due to separating mental health from other health care, and in the second place due to subordination of research to treatment.

Insurance carriers are placing constraints on patients' options for both inpatient and outpatient mental health care that limit their access to the traditional sites for mental health research. To an increasing extent, mental health care is being provided in the form of brief treatment with nonacademic providers organized into networks established by managed care insurers or "carve-out" carriers. Those patients who are seen in academic or research centers are increasingly skewed to those with the most severe disorders and those who do not respond to first-line treatments. All of this raises concerns about the viability of current strategies for gaining access to patients for mental health research and for providing the clinical infrastructure in which research can take place. Although Medicare was essentially unaffected in recent plans for health care reform, the increasing enrollment of Medicare recipients in managed care programs makes these issues highly relevant for those concerned about the elderly.

There are positive opportunities as well. The information systems and coordination of care that are key components of efficient managed care programs can facilitate the accessibility of primary care patients for mental health research. Within such systems there are, in principle, possibilities for designing new forms of population-based clinical research in which clinical features, natural history, biology, and treatment responses are studied in representative samples of patients with specific disorders.

NEW KNOWLEDGE

Ongoing research activities in basic neurobiology and in human genetics can be expected to make important opportunities available for research advances in geriatric mental health. For example, rapid advances in understanding the molecular biology of amyloid followed the biochemical characterization of its protein structure. This, in turn, accelerated clinical molecular genetics research that led to identification of subtypes of familial Alzheimer's disease and to increasing progress on mapping the defects (Haass, Hung, Selkie, & Teplow, 1994; Selkoe, 1994). The Decade of the Brain and the Human Genome Project are important initiatives that are likely to develop ideas and principles with the potential for improving clinical care. Cashing in on these major investments by translating basic findings into clinical applications will require a strong commitment to clinical, as well as basic, research.

Without a doubt, advances in mental health and aging will require interactions between basic and clinical research. Without firm knowledge of disease, it is not possible to translate basic knowledge derived from laboratory studies into improvements in clinical care. Conversely, clinical insight and experience are necessary to guide the development of hypotheses and models in the laboratory. For example, gains in our knowledge of the neurochemistry of schizophrenia were totally dependent on the discovery of the efficacy of neuroleptics. Discoveries related to the genetic basis of Alzheimer's disease would have been impossible without the advances in diagnosis and knowledge of the age-dependent incidence that have been gained from clinical research in the past decade (Corder et al., 1993). At present, studies investigating the potential influences of estrogen on cognitive functioning are proceeding rapidly in both clinical and basic arenas (Gibbs, 1994; Paganini-Hill & Henderson, 1994; Sherwin, 1994), and as a result, rapid progress in this area is highly likely. It is erroneous and dangerous to suggest that there is antagonism between clinical and basic science research or to imply that clinical research is inferior to basic science (or vice versa). The two are complementary, and the flow of information is in both directions.

Concerns about optimizing the interactions between basic science, clinical research, and clinical care are not limited to the impact of basic biology on medical care. Advances in the basic social and behavioral sciences can also have a profound impact on understanding mechanisms leading to disease and on the conceptualization and design of interventions to prevent or treat disorders.

WIDER IMPLICATIONS OF RESEARCH ON LATE-LIFE MENTAL HEALTH

Clinical research on the mental disorders of late life can make significant contributions to clinical knowledge for younger adult patients and can provide important leads for basic research. An example of an area in which research on aging has led the mental health field is in the relationship between depression and medical illness. Classic findings from family studies demonstrated that older patients with depressive disorders with their initial onset in late life do not have increased rates of depression in their families that could suggest genetic causes, but instead tend to develop depression in the context of chronic medical illness (Hopkinson, 1964; Mendlewicz, 1976). Studies on older adults can therefore elucidate nongenetic mechanisms for the pathogenesis of depression that may complement the genetic mechanisms that may be more common in younger patients. Moreover, what is learned about the role of general medical illness in the pathogenesis of late-life depression will be relevant to developing clinical treatments for the largely ignored population of younger and middle aged adults with psychiatric and medical comorbidity.

Similarly, research in recent years has demonstrated that the onset of schizophrenia in late life is an uncommon but real occurrence (Jeste et al., 1988). Clinical research on such patients represents an opportunity to gain insight into the pathogenesis of schizophrenia, both by identifying nongenetic causes associated with age-related changes in the brain and by identifying factors that can be associated with delayed onset of the disease in vulnerable individuals. The finding that early-onset schizophrenia is primarily a disease of men while late-onset schizophrenia occurs primarily in women (Pearlson & Rabins, 1988) may represent a clue suggesting that estrogens may somehow protect vulnerable individuals against the development of schizophrenia. Thus, studies on gender differences in rates of pathology and responses to treatment are important from a basic biological as well as a clinical and social perspective.

CHANGING APPROACHES TO THE INFRASTRUCTURE FOR CLINICAL CARE

Changes in demography, health care financing, and public health policy have resulted in a dramatic shift in the *locus* of care but only recently in the *focus* of care for the mentally ill elderly. Application of preventive, curative, and rehabilitative concepts to the elderly is still not widely accepted, implemented, or reimbursed (Hall & Buckwalter, 1990). As mental health care develops, it is possible to define four separable locations that should be considered in planning for both clinical care and for research: mental health services as a component of primary care, community services for patients with chronic and severe mental disorders, mental health services in residential care settings, and clinical neuroscience in tertiary care settings.

Mental Health Services in Primary Care

The reasons for focusing on the recognition and treatment of mental disorders in primary care follow from the accessibility of patients and from the improved coordination of care that can result when mental disorders and medical conditions are treated in the same setting. The most poignant case for strengthening the mental health components of primary care comes from the observation that the vast majority of older patients who had committed suicide had consulted their physicians within a few weeks of their deaths (Conwell, 1994). Thus, the possibilities for preventing needless tragedy through optimizing methods for recognizing and treating depression are apparent. The development of practice guidelines for the identification and treatment of depression (Agency for Health Care Policy and Research, 1993; Reynolds, Schneider, Lebowitz, & Kupfer, 1994) and for the recognition of dementia in primary care should, over the long run, stimulate further developments in this area.

Historically, the most common treatments for mental disorders identified in primary care, regardless of diagnosis, have been prescriptions of benzodiazepines (Burns & Taube, 1990). Major efforts at provider and patient education regarding the recognition and diagnosis of depression as well as the development of antidepressant medications that allow safer and more convenient delivery of adequate treatment should improve the specificity of treatment for affective illness. The delivery of psychotherapy to primary care patients with mental disorders, however, remains a challenge. Current research demonstrates that it is feasible to introduce trained psychotherapists into the structure of a primary care practice. This approach can perhaps serve as a model for delivering psychosocial treatment to primary care patients in a manner that can overcome the stigma that is often associated with entering the mental health care system (Schulberg & Burns, 1988).

The value of combining primary medical care and mental health services applies both to patients with mental disorders (primarily anxiety disorders and depression) whose primary problems are general medical conditions and to those with disability arising from serious mental disorders (Alzheimer's disease, schizophrenia, and bipolar disorder) complicated by the routine chronic or recurrent general medical disorders of late life. For the former, the challenge is to make mental health care more accessible; this requires overcoming barriers such as ageism, stigma, a lack of mental health providers with geriatric experience, and negative reimbursement schedules (Gottlieb, 1994). For the latter, it is to overcome mental-illness-related barriers to the delivery of general medical services; this also requires overcoming stigma, stereotypes, and physicians' discomfort and lack of knowledge in working with patients with mental disorders.

For patients with Alzheimer's disease, the practice of primary care must be modified to meet the needs of patients who have difficulty reporting symptoms of illness or side effects of medications and may manifest symptoms of medical illness or physical discomfort through disturbances of behavior. It is also necessary to design systems for primary care that recognize the needs of family caregivers as well as the patients themselves. For older patients with schizophrenia, it is necessary to develop systems in which the patients' frequent problems with social skills and physicians' difficulties in understanding the psychotic disorders do not compromise

263

general medical care. There is now a cohort of middle-aged and elderly schizophrenia patients who have spent most of their adult lives in the community. As these patients age, they are at risk for disability resulting from the common medical disorders of late life. In spite of the obvious nature of this problem, little attention has been devoted to developing models for preventing physical disability or for maintaining patients with psychiatric-medical comorbidity in the community. A proposal for modifying care to meet the general medical and mental health needs of both classes of patients would be for the geriatric psychiatrist to assume the role of the primary care physician or for the mental health facility to be redesigned to include elements of primary care. Another approach to bridging the gap between the medical and mental health needs of aging patients would be to incorporate advanced practice nurses with both geriatric and psychiatric training into primary care systems.

Community Services for Patients With Chronic and Severe Mental Disorders

We are now seeing far more patients with chronic mental disorders who survive into older age, probably as a result of both general improvements in health and life circumstances and the proliferation of community-based services appropriate to the needs of those with chronic mental disorders. Although the actual number of these individuals will increase with the aging of the underlying population, the research base essential to our knowledge of the nature, course, treatment, and outcome of chronic mental disorders in late life is severely limited.

Maintaining individuals with severe mental disorders in the community requires the availability of extensive supports for both patients and caregivers. Case management, structured and supportive day programs, caregiver education and support, respite services, homemakers or home health aides, and easy access to psychiatric treatment when psychotic or behavioral symptoms compromise care arrangements are important both for patients with Alzheimer's disease and for elderly patients with schizophrenia. Thus, the elements of care required for the two patient groups are similar. Those charged with the delivery of services must attend to the needs of both classes of patients with chronic mental illness: patients with schizophrenia or manic depressive disorder, who have early-onset disease, and others, primarily those with Alzheimer's disease and other dementias, whose illness begins in late life. Research is required to evaluate models for providing care for both groups and to consider how their needs can be managed within a shared system for community care.

Mental Health Services in Residential Care

Epidemiological studies consistently demonstrate that 80% to 90% of long-term care residents in nursing homes have diagnosable mental disorders (Rovner & Katz, 1993). As a result, the historic models for conceptualizing nursing homes either as retirement homes or as step-down facilities for medical-surgical patients are inadequate. Most frontline staff members in nursing homes have little knowledge about the aging process and are ill prepared to deal with the psychological symptoms and behavioral problems experienced by many residents. The mental health problems of nursing home residents clearly influence the care they receive and the amount of nursing time they require (Fries, Mehr, Schneider, Foley, & Burke, 1993). There is a need to incorporate mental health care into the basic structure of nursing home care and to make professional services available to patients with specific problems. We must reimburse nursing homes in a manner that permits them to deliver psychosocial services to mentally impaired residents. Furthermore, professional standards are needed to specify and mandate adequate levels of mental health care in this population.

Most mental disorders in nursing homes are Alzheimer's disease and related dementias. The proliferation of special care units and the ongoing research to evaluate their effectiveness demonstrate the importance of redesigning nursing homes to meet the needs of their residents (Coons, 1991; Office of Technology Assessment, 1992). There is also a need to develop more effective strategies for managing the behavioral disturbances that are common among cognitively impaired patients in long-term care. Because psychiatric symptoms and behavioral disturbances often compromise the ability of family caregivers to manage patients in the community (Steele, Rovner, Chas, & Folstein, 1990), nursing home residents are likely to be overrepresented with respect to individuals who have severe behavioral symptoms that are not responsive to first-line approaches to treatment and management.

At least 50% of cognitively intact residents of nursing homes have clinically significant depressive symptoms (Katz & Parmelee, 1994). The magnitude of this problem argues strongly for the need to reinvent the nursing home's approach to caring for cognitively intact patients who require long-term care because of disabling medical conditions. The positive effects of interventions that increase the residents' sense of control have been demonstrated in small-scale studies (Rodin, 1991); the need for further research on another type of special care unit designed to enhance autonomy and control for cognitively intact residents is apparent. There are also needs for clinical research designed to develop both pharmacologic and psychosocial treatments for depression among physically ill, frail elderly patients and for health service research designed to develop models to facilitate the delivery of professional mental health services in nursing homes.

Subacute Care, Rehabilitation, and Convalescence

Reductions in lengths of stay for older patients in acute care hospitals have led to the increased use of nursing homes as step-down units for rehabilitation and convalescent care. In fact, the growth of these services and the economics of subacute care have led to concerns that long-term care for patients with Alzheimer's disease may be squeezed out of nursing homes.

Whether services are provided in nursing homes or inpatient facilities, the importance of the mental health components of the rehabilitation process must be recognized. For example, both depression and cognitive impairment can interfere with patients' participation in physical or occupational therapy and consequently with their ability to regain independence. Even for patients who do not require specific rehabilitative services, nutritional deficits or fatigability associated with depression can slow their recuperation from acute illnesses. Accordingly, there is a need to develop models for incorporating mental health services into subacute care and to develop standards of care that recognize patients' mental health needs as well as their problems in physical functioning.

Community Alternatives for Long-Term Care

For every person currently in institutional care, there are an estimated four more in the community who require some form of long-term care. By 2000, it is projected, that 18% of the elderly (more than 5 million people) will have some impairment that requires the help of others. About 5% (or 1.75 million) of these people will be in nursing homes or other institutions, but a staggering 3.5 million who need long-term care will not. How will they be cared for? By whom? (Maas, Buckwalter, & Tripp-Reimer, in press)

Approaches to this looming problem include (a) reducing the need for home care by improving the health of older people; (b) finding and paying for alternative forms of home care when disability and frailty preclude continued independence and self-care; (c) effecting better service integration across the total continuum of care and better coordination of different care providers who subscribe to a biopsychosocial view of health care that includes mental health, medical, and social components (Ory & Duncker, 1992).

Most nursing homes violate all of the elements traditionally associated with the culturally relevant definitions of "home," in that residents have little control over what people they live with, who comes and goes in their personal space, and other aspects of the environment such as furnishings and appointments (Wilson, 1994). Various residential care models are in part a response to the medical model emphasis in most long-term care facilities and the need to develop alternatives to nursing home care. These include a spectrum of state-licensed residential living environments such as foster care homes, family homes, personal care homes, residential care facilities, and assisted living arrangements. Other programs—including day care, caregiver supports, respite care, and short-term inpatient or residential care during acute exacerbations of illness—can also serve as alternatives to long-term care in nursing homes. Further research is needed at two levels: to demonstrate the effectiveness of programs across the entire spectrum of long-term care alternatives and to evaluate the costs and trade-offs that would result from increased Medicare or Medicaid funding of community alternatives to nursing homes.

Long-Term Care for Schizophrenia Patients

The current dialogue about national health care reform represents an opportunity to reevaluate the care of older schizophrenia patients, both those living with varying degrees of support in the community and the few who are long-term inpatients in public facilities. Questions about how community services for these patients should be covered under managed care systems and about the nature of the inpatient or residential care services required for those patients who are currently hospitalized should prompt both clinical and health services research.

Clinical Neuroscience in Tertiary Care Settings

Although the distinction between "high-tech" and "high-touch" care must be considered artificial, it is clear that some elements of care require specialized tertiary care services. How well patients with dementia can be evaluated in primary care rather than specialized settings is an area of active debate. However, regardless of the general pattern of care that is established, atypical and complex cases will continue to require referral to tertiary care settings. In addition, specialized centers will remain critical for developing and investigating experimental treatment for Alzheimer's disease and other dementias. Tertiary care settings are also necessary for the evaluation and treatment of mood disorders, anxiety disorders, psychoses, and behavioral problems that do not respond to first-line treatment and for the treatment of mental disorders that coexist with severe medical illnesses. Tertiary care clinical neuroscience programs must involve both inpatient and outpatient services, and both consultative and ongoing care. The nature of the services required, the thresholds, and the indications for moving from primary care, community, or long-term care to more specialized settings must be investigated.

OPPORTUNITIES, RATIONALE, AND AGENDA FOR CLINICAL RESEARCH

Although improving clinical care and adapting to changes in the population and the health care system will require clinical, basic, and health services or outcomes research, it is clinical research (i.e., disease-related research conducted on patient populations) that is likely to be the most productive at this time. Mental disorders are the most human of diseases, and they must be understood primarily in terms of their impact on subjective experience and on complex behaviors such as social interactions and adaptive functioning within the human community. While basic molecular and cellular research are extraordinarily powerful tools, they cannot, in principle, be mobilized toward the study of mental disorders until it is possible to map subjective experience or complex behaviors onto underlying neurobiology or until valid animal models for specific disorders can be developed. Further clinical research, including studies of biological markers and investigations of the specificity of drug responses in the populations of greatest interest, is needed before animal models relevant to understanding mental health in the elderly can be validated.

We are all aware of the "iron lung" metaphor, which states that development of a polio vaccine and the elimination of polio as a major public health problem were a direct result of basic virology research. The metaphor suggests that if research on polio had been limited to clinical studies on affected patients, we would by now have perfected the iron lung, but we would still need it. However, the metaphor does not apply to research on mental disorders in general or to those of late life in particular. At present, the state of knowledge is such that each of what we consider to be specific mental disorders is, in fact, a heterogeneous state. If clinicians concerned about preventing paralysis had not been able to distinguish between the effects of polio, an infectious disease; Guillain-Barré syndrome, a disorder related to immune activity; familial periodic paralysis, a genetically determined metabolic disorder; and stroke, a circulatory disturbance, they would never have been able to develop a polio vaccine and to establish its effectiveness. A breakthrough of the magnitude of the polio vaccine will require a commitment to both clinical and basic research. The important questions about research priorities should be about how activities in the two domains can be coordinated to ensure that basic scientists are probing systems that are relevant to human disease and that clinical investigators are translating emerging basic knowledge into clinically relevant hypotheses.

In addition, health services research is needed to develop and evaluate models for the delivery of mental health services at the primary care interface, in community programs for the chronically and severely ill, in long-term care, and in tertiary care clinical neuroscience programs, as well as to establish how these components of care can best be coordinated. In each component of care, differences in delivery of care in rural and urban settings and to different cultural and racial groups should be examined.

We are aware that the research findings that may be most compelling to policy makers are those that use large-scale data sets to evaluate the outcomes of treatment, primarily in terms of costs. Based upon findings from clinical studies, it is possible, for example, to hypothesize that facilitating the access of patients with depression and medical comorbidity or those with dementia and behavioral disturbances to mental health care by decreasing Medicare copayment requirements would represent an investment that would decrease overall care costs (Katz et al., 1994).

Although results of treatment-outcomes research designed to test these hypotheses could be of major importance, there must be concerns about the validity of available methods for conducting such studies in patients with the mental disorders of late life. The current care system is marked by the stigmatization of mental disorders, inadequate attention to diagnoses of mental disorders in primary care patients, and concerns about the specificity with which psychotherapeutic medications are prescribed by primary care physicians. Thus, the markers for mental disorders and their treatment that could serve as a basis for large-scale outcomes research must be considered questionable. At the current state of knowledge, relying on outcomes research or effectiveness studies for guiding treatment for older patients could be profoundly misleading. Moreover, in light of the paucity of data on the efficacy of treatment for mental disorders in older patients, it is important to consolidate the body of knowledge on the efficacy of treatments and on differences in treatment responses between patient groups differing in age, gender, age of initial onset, ethnicity, and medical comorbidity. In parallel, studies at the boundaries between clinical and health services research are needed to develop markers for mental disorders and the outcomes of treatment that are applicable to elderly patients to enable larger scale studies of the effectiveness of treatment.

Clinical research can be divided into components devoted directly to improving clinical treatments (treatment- or outcomes-related clinical research) and those that take a less direct path through the pursuit of more basic knowledge (fundamentals-oriented clinical research) (Jeste, 1994). Fundamentals-oriented clinical research extends the traditional goals of clinical research both by promoting the refinement of theory and method and by identifying basic mechanisms of pathophysiology, etiology, and normal function. It is therefore an essential component of a clinical research agenda.

Research questions related to improving care are obvious. A feasible and necessary research agenda includes clinical trials of both pharmacotherapy and psychotherapy for the spectrum of mental disorders that occur in late life. Other components of treatment-related clinical research should include those directed toward developing mechanisms for pharmacokinetic, physiological, cognitive, and behavioral monitoring of patients during treatment to optimize the safety of interventions as well as their efficacy. Developing predictors of positive responses to specific treatment is an area of obvious practical importance as well as a mechanism for validating subtypes of apparently similar disorders. There is also increasing recognition that effective care includes both helping people get better and helping them stay better and that there is a need for evaluating the risks versus the benefits of longer term continuation and maintenance treatments. For example, the value of maintenance treatment to prevent recurrences of depression in young and healthy adults is well established, and early findings on maintenance treatment in older patients are beginning to confirm its value for them. However, the difficulties in delivering maintenance treatment to patients with significant medical illness remain to be evaluated.

Current questions in fundamentals-oriented clinical research extend to wider problems in basic science, gerontology, and psychopathology. Important areas for investigation are the symptoms of Alzheimer's disease, delirium, depression, and schizophrenia.

Ongoing research on the cognitive deficits in patients with Alzheimer's disease and related disorders has led to considerable basic knowledge in cognitive psychology and in the brain mechanisms underlying cognition. Studies on the determinants and correlates of the noncognitive psychiatric symptoms in Alzheimer's disease can extend this knowledge and can provide information on the relationships between emotion and cognition, the neural basis of emotion, and the cognitive and neural underpinnings of the psychoses. Studies of the disruptive behavioral symptoms that occur in patients with dementia can provide insight into the cognitive and biological roots of behaviors that support interactions.

Studies on delirium can provide information on the vulnerability of consciousness, cognition, and perception to metabolic activity in the brain as well as on how homeostatic mechanisms are affected by aging and disease.

Studies on early- versus late-onset depression in older patients can provide insight into the genetic and nongenetic mechanisms that give rise to similar symptoms. The increased physiological variance that occurs in association with depression in older patients with psychiatric-medical comorbidity can help explain possible structural and metabolic mechanisms underlying primary mood disorders. Studies on the association between minor or subsyndromal depressions and comorbid medical or neurological conditions can elucidate basic mechanisms associated with the regulation of affect.

Finally, as discussed, studies of late-onset schizophrenia can provide clues to alternative nongenetic causes of disease or to mechanisms that delay the expression of genetic vulnerability.

INFRASTRUCTURE REQUIREMENTS TO ENABLE RESEARCH

To facilitate research on each of the major mental disorders of late life, with a focus on how the nature of the disorders and their responses to interventions differ with age and treatment setting, requires both treatment-oriented and fundamentals-oriented clinical research. Extensive opportunities are anticipated for reciprocal interactions of clinical research with both basic science and health services research. At present, however, the state of knowledge in the field requires a major focus on disease-oriented research conducted directly with patient populations.

Research Funding

Review of the scientific press over the past 2 years reveals widespread concerns that clinical research is under siege (Gavaghan, 1994).

Both basic biomedical sciences and health services research have champions within the National Institutes of Health (NIH) directorship or in Congress. There are concerns that funding for clinical research is being squeezed from both sides. In addition, news reports about clinical research have focused less on major advances and more on problems in the management of large-scale therapeutic trials and on questions about funding of science through federal agencies versus drug companies versus the health care industry. It is important, however, to recognize that mental health research of necessity emphasizes the assessment of human patient populations and that the research of the greatest importance to older patients—that on patients with psychiatric-medical comorbidity or behavioral complications of dementia—has historically been of little interest to industry. Thus, advocacy by those concerned with improving the care of older patients with mental disorders is needed to ensure that federal research agencies and major foundations support clinical research in general and in this field in particular.

Other concerns are emerging in other agencies. The Department of Veterans Affairs, for example, is currently evaluating a significant shift in resources toward primary care. This shift, however, does not mean that the department's support of aging and mental health research should be diminished. In fact, many of the research issues discussed above are directly relevant to optimizing the effectiveness and economics of treatment and prevention for an aging primary care population.

Review of Research Proposals

The major source of funding for research on mental disorders and mental health has been the National Institute of Mental Health (NIMH). Currently, as a consequence of NIMH's move from the Alcohol, Drug Abuse, and Mental Health Administration to NIH, there are discussions about how the NIMH structure for the review of research grant proposals will be incorporated into the Division of Research Grants at NIH. A key requirement with respect to the mental health care of older adults must be a mechanism for ensuring that NIH research proposals as well as proposals within other federal agencies (e.g., the Department of Veterans Affairs, the Agency for Health Care Policy Research, the Health Care Financing

Administration) are reviewed by those knowledgeable about the clinical realities, theoretical issues, and methodological concerns related to mental health and aging. Only such a mechanism can ensure that science of the highest quality is recognized and that the research funded will lead to both fundamental knowledge about disease and improved outcomes from clinical care.

Academic Medical Centers and the Decentralization of Research

The debate over national health care reform raised questions about the future of academic medical centers in a health care system that is rapidly evolving toward managed care and capitated payment for services. Although the costs of providing services in these centers are often greater than those in community facilities, medical centers play critical roles in professional training and research. Specifically, in a field such as mental health and aging, the stable, multidisciplinary teams of investigators available at academic medical centers are needed to allow research to respond rapidly to emergent issues. It is therefore in the national interest that these centers survive.

The academic medical centers will remain for some time the primary sites for intensive biological research on late-life mental disorders. Such studies require expensive laboratories and instruments (e.g., sophisticated instruments for neuroimaging) that are available only at institutions with a critical mass of biomedical research. Even in these settings, however, the conduct of these studies will become increasingly difficult as pressures increase to reduce the length of both inpatient and outpatient treatment and to limit the clinical use of neuroimaging and laboratory tests. As a result of changes in the health care system, it is likely that intensive biological research in mental health will become increasingly expensive and that the number of centers that can mobilize the resources needed to support it will decrease. Consequently, a proactive approach is needed to ensure that the potential for conducting this research can be maintained.

As discussed above, it is also becoming apparent that the academic medical center represents only one component of the evolving systems of mental health care needed to serve the elderly. Because most patients with mental disorders receive their care in other settings, researchers evaluating responses to treatment must be concerned about the interactions between diagnoses and care settings as determinants of outcomes. A further concern is that patients seen in tertiary care settings are increasingly unrepresentative of those who receive mental health services in primary, community, or long-term care settings. There is a need to reevaluate and revise the traditional approach to clinical research, in which investigators on the staffs of university-based hospitals and clinics conduct research on the patient populations of their own institutions.

University-based clinical research has been productive largely because the academic medical centers have had critical masses of both investigators and relevant patients. This coupling, however, may be less common in the future. When clinical research is conducted in settings where investigators are essentially guests, there must be concerns about how investigators will interact with clinicians and how the burden on the host site can be minimized and costs reimbursed. The future of clinical research will require the coordinated activities of interdisciplinary groups of investigators conducting studies on increasingly decentralized patient populations. Establishing research of this type and maintaining it over time will require enabling resources such as those of NIMH clinical research centers, or Department of Veterans Affairs geriatric research education and clinical centers or proposed mental illness research, educational, and clinical centers. These centers have their own established infrastructures, and funding designed to enable research rather than to support specific studies. As a result, they are the entities best suited to the rapid translation of basic findings into clinical hypotheses and protocols. Stabilization of their funding is necessary to enable clinical research to evolve in parallel with basic science.

Similar structures are needed to enable research on the effects of mental health interventions in the elderly. Agencies concerned with health services and effectiveness research should specifically target mechanisms such as AHCPR's patient outcomes research teams (PORTs) to address key questions in mental health and aging, including the outcomes and cost savings associated with treatment of depression in patients with significant medical comorbidity and treatment of the psychotic, affective, and behavioral symptoms associated with Alzheimer's disease and related dementias.

Interactions With the Single Payer

One of the elements of the recent debate on health care reforms was a proposal that a fixed percentage of the costs of health care insurance be set aside to increase the funding available for biomedical research. In geriatrics and gerontology, the federal government's Medicare programs are essentially the sole payer for acute medical care, and the federal contribution to nursing home care through Medicaid programs represents approximately 25% of the total national costs for nursing homes. Advances in clinical care through research on topics such as the treatment of depression, caregiver support, and the management of psychotic, affective, and behavioral complications of dementia could translate over a relatively short time into major cost savings. Putting a fixed percentage of the federal costs of medical and long-term care for the elderly into a fund for research in geriatrics and gerontology would be a prudent investment. These funds should be used to augment existing mechanisms that support research designed to improve clinical care for the elderly. Current experience suggests that these would be primarily NIH programs, but they would include those of other agencies, such as the Department of Veterans Affairs.

Other interactions between late-life mental health and the sole payer for geriatric health services could facilitate research designed to improve the outcomes and cost-effectiveness of care. A process that would allow funding through Medicare for the patient care costs that accompany clinical research would facilitate such studies and would result in more effective clinical use of Medicare money.

Interactions With State and Local Governments

The role of state governments in the support of the infrastructure needed for clinical research and the willingness of state and local health, mental health, or aging agencies to support and collaborate with clinical investigators vary widely. Support of research should be encouraged at all levels to ensure that developing knowledge is relevant to the care of all patients.

Research Training

The most critical element of the research infrastructure required to enable research in this, or any, area is the availability of rigorously trained investigators. Some have suggested that funds available for supporting biomedical research are decreasing and that, in an era of contracting resources, it is more important to continue support of established, productive investigators than to support the development of new ones. These concerns, however, are shortsighted. The continuity of the research enterprise requires a continuous flow of investigators at various stages of development. Cutting off funds for training in a period of scarcity would lead to a generation gap with long-term effects on the field that could not be reversed by increasing investments in the future.

Key questions about research training include how to keep an appropriate balance between clinical and basic investigators, how to attract and keep investigators in a changing and frequently inhospitable environment, and how to keep investigators with clinical training from fleeing to more stable and lucrative practice positions. For laboratory investigators, there are questions about the extent to which training should be directed toward disease-related applications as well as about basic principles and methods. If the translation of advances in basic science into gains in clinical treatment is to occur, investigators with depth of knowledge in both domains must be developed. As discussed above, questions about the interactions between basic and clinical research apply to the social and behavioral as well as the biological and molecular domains.

There are ongoing questions about how clinical investigators can best be educated and kept informed about basic advances. There is also a need to focus on the complementary issue of how students and trainees in the more basic sciences can best be educated about clinical disorders. Funding of programs for short-term training of basic scientists in clinical realities is likely to increase the extent to which basic investigations focus on areas of potential clinical relevance and to facilitate the process of information transfer.

Increased support of research training and research career development, both direct salary support and indirect support through the funding of pilot and small grant programs, is critical if this field is to adapt to the changing care environment. Although there must be questions about whether the limited amounts of training and career development support should be made available to more people or used to provide more stable and enduring support for those who show the greatest promise and productivity, it is clear that mechanisms for providing long-term support (such as the NIH program of "K" awards for investigators in early, mid, and established career levels) have profoundly affected the field.

As outlined above, biomedical and behavioral research, basic and clinical, can be considered the research and development (R & D) component of the health care industry; as in any industry, an investment of a fixed percentage of overall costs in R & D would constitute prudent management. By extension, research training should be considered the R & D component of the biomedical research industry, and a fixed percentage of research funds (perhaps 15% by analogy with other industries) should be invested in training and career development programs.

SUMMARY AND KEY RECOMMENDATIONS

Research on the mental disorders of late life has become a mature field with rigorous methods and high standards for the review of research proposals and publications. Although, as emphasized above, much remains unknown, the field has developed to the point where further investments in research will bring substantial benefit, both for improving the lives of older people and for increasing our understanding of basic mechanisms. Key recommendations with respect to support for research on mental disorders of the elderly include:

1. Advances in the care of patients with the mental disorders of late life will require that federal agencies and foundations strongly support clinical research.

2. Future advances in clinical care and prevention will require bidirectional, reciprocal interactions between clinical research and basic research components, including social and behavioral as well as molecular and biological science.

3. Recognition and funding of research proposals with the greatest potential to advance basic and clinical knowledge will require mechanisms to ensure that research proposals are reviewed by those knowledgeable about mental health and aging.

4. A fixed component of Medicare costs for medical care for the

elderly and federal Medicaid contributions for nursing home care should be set aside to increase the funds available for research in geriatrics and gerontology in general and for mental health and aging specifically.

5. Medicare should develop mechanisms to facilitate clinical research designed to improve the efficacy and cost-effectiveness of treatment in the elderly through support of research-related patient care costs. Mechanisms should be developed to allow concurrent review of the scientific merit of proposals for funding of research and patient care.

6. In a rapidly changing health care environment, there is an increasing need for conducting clinical research on the mental disorders of late life in primary, community, and long-term care settings as well as in tertiary care centers.

7. The continuity of the research enterprise requires a firm commitment to research training and career development programs. A fixed component of the federal budget for research should be dedicated to research training.

REFERENCES

Agency for Health Care Policy and Research. (1993). *Depression in primary care: Volume 1. Detection and diagnosis. Volume 2. Treatment of major depression* (AHCPR Publication No. 93-0551). Rockville, MD: Author.

Burns, B. J., & Taube, C. A. (1990). Mental health services in general medical care and in nursing homes. In B. S. Fogel, A. Furino, & G. L. Gottlieb (Eds.), *Mental health policy for older Americans: Protecting minds at risk* (pp. 63-83). Washington, DC: American Psychiatric Press.

Conwell, Y. (1994). Suicide in elderly patients. In L. S. Schneider, C. F. Reynolds, III, B. D. Lebowitz, & A. J. Friedhoff (Eds.), *Diagnosis and treatment of late life depression: Results of the NIH Consensus Development Conference* (pp. 397-418). Washington, DC: American Psychiatric Press.

Coons, D. H. (1991). *Specialized dementia care units.* Baltimore: Johns Hopkins University Press.

Corder, E. H., Saunders, A. M., Strittmatter, W. J., Schmechel, D. E., Gaskell, P. C., Small, G. W., Roses, A. D., & Haines, J. L. (1993). Gene dose of apolipoprotein E type 4 allele and the risk of Alzheimer's disease in late onset families. *Science, 261,* 828-829.

Fries, B. E., Mehr, D. R., Schneider, D., Foley, W. J., & Burke, R. (1993). Mental dysfunction and resource use in nursing homes. *Medical Care, 31,* 898-920.

Gavaghan, H. (1994). Varmus speaks out on need to boost clinical research. *Nature, 372,* 118.

Gibbs, R. B. (1994). Estrogen and nerve growth factor related systems in brain: Effects on basal forebrain cholinergic neurons and implications for learning and memory processes and aging. *Annals of the New York Academy of Sciences, 743,* 165-196.

Gottlieb, G. L. (1994). Barriers to care for older adults with depression. In L. S. Schneider, C. F. Reynolds, III, B. D. Lebowitz, & A. J. Friedhoff (Eds.), *Diagnosis and treatment of late life depression: Results of the NIH Consensus Development Conference* (pp. 375-396). Washington, DC: American Psychiatric Press.

Haass, C., Hung, A. Y., Selkoe, D. J., & Teplow, D. B. (1994). Mutations associated with a locus for familial Alzheimer's disease result in alternative processing of amyloid-beta protein. *Journal of Biological Chemistry, 269,* 17741-17748.

Hall, G. R., & Buckwalter, K. C. (1990). From almshouse to dedicated unit: Care of the institutionalized elderly with behavioral problems. *Archives of Psychiatric Nursing, 4,* 3-11.

Hopkinson, G. (1964). A genetic study of affective illness in patients over 50. *British Journal of Psychiatry, 110,* 244-254.

Horne, A., & Blazer, D. G. (1992). The prevention of major depression in the elderly. *Clinical Geriatric Medicine, 8,* 159-172.

Jeste, D. V. (1994). Fundamentals-oriented clinical research—The need for reconsideration. *American Journal of Geriatric Psychiatry, 4,* 282-284.

Jeste, D. V., Harris, M. J., Pearlson, G. D., Rabins, P., Lesser, I. M., Miller, B., Coles, C., & Yassa, R. (1988). Late onset schizophrenia: Studying clinical validity. *Psychological Clinics of North America, 11,* 1-13.

Katz, I. R., & Parmelee, P. A. (1994). Depression in elderly patients in residential care settings. In L. S. Schneider, C. F. Reynolds, III, B. D. Lebowitz, & A. J. Friedhoff (Eds.), *Diagnosis and treatment of late life depression: Results of the NIH Consensus Development Conference* (pp. 437-462). Washington, DC: American Psychiatric Press.

Katz, I. R., Streim, J., & Parmelee, P. (1994). Prevention of depression, recurrences, and complications in late life. *Preventive Medicine, 23,* 743-750.

Khachaturian, Z. (1992). The 5-5, 10-10 plan for Alzheimer's disease. *Neurobiology of Aging, 13,* 197-198.

Lebowitz, B. D., & Gottlieb, G. L. (1995). Clinical research in the managed care environment. *American Journal of Geriatric Psychiatry, 3,* 21-29.

Maas, M., Buckwalter, K. C., & Tripp-Reimer, T. (in press). Equity of access to long-term care: A critical aspect of health care reform. *Nursing Outlook.*

Mendlewicz, J. (1976). The age factor in depressive illness: Some genetic consideration. *Journal of Gerontology, 31,* 300-303.

Office of Technology Assessment. (1992). *Specialized care units for people with Alzheimer's disease and other dementias.* Washington, DC: U.S. Government Printing Office.

Ory, M. G., & Duncker, A. P. (1992). *In-home care for older people: Health and supportive services.* Newbury Park, CA: Sage.

Paganini-Hill, A., & Henderson, V. W. (1994). Estrogen deficiency and risk of Alzheimer's disease in women. *American Journal of Epidemiology, 140,* 255-261.

Pearlson, G. D., & Rabins, P. V. (1988). The late-onset psychoses: Possible risk factors. *Psychiatric Clinics of North America, 11,* 15-33.

Reynolds, C. F., III, Schneider, L. S., Lebowitz, B. D., & Kupfer, D. J. (1994). Treatment of depression in elderly patients: Guidelines for primary care. In L. S. Schneider, C. F. Reynolds, III, B. D. Lebowitz, & A. J. Friedhoff (Eds.), *Diagnosis and treatment of late life depression: Results of the NIH Consensus Development Conference* (pp. 463-490). Washington, DC: American Psychiatric Press.

Rodin, J. (1991). Control-relevant interventions to enhance health in older adults. *Experimental Aging Research, 17,* 90-91.

Rovner, B. W., & Katz, I. R. (1993). Psychiatric disorders in the nursing home: A selective review of studies related to clinical care. *International Journal of Geriatric Psychiatry, 8,* 75-87.

Schulberg, H. C., & Burns, B. J. (1988). Mental disorders in primary care: Epidemiological, diagnostic, and treatment research directions. *General Hospital Psychiatry, 10,* 79-87.

Selkoe, D. (1994). Normal and abnormal biology of the beta-amyloid precursor protein. *Annual Review of Neuroscience, 17,* 489-517.

Sherwin, B. B. (1994). Estrogen effects on memory in women. *Annals of New York Academy of Sciences, 743,* 213-230.

Steele, C., Rovner, B., Chase, G. A., & Folstein, M. (1990). Psychiatric symptoms and nursing home placement of patients with Alzheimer's disease. *American Journal of Psychiatry, 147,* 1049-1051.

Wickramaratne, P. J., Weissman, M. M., Leaf, P. J., & Holford, T. R. (1989). Age, period, and cohort effects on the risk of major depression: Results from five United States communities. *Journal of Clinical Epidemiology, 42,* 333-343.

Wilson, K. B. (1994). Assisted living: Model program may signify the future. *Long-Term Care Quality Newsletter, 6,* 1-4.

CHAPTER 11

Education and Training of Mental Health Service Providers

Margaret Gatz and Sanford I. Finkel

During the past 15 years, partly as a consequence of the 1981 White House Conference on Aging and the associated Mini-Conference on the Mental Health of Older Americans, mental health professionals have increased efforts to provide services to older adults. Still for reasons that include continued growth in the numbers of older adults who need services, continued lack of sufficient training at all levels, major alterations in the delivery of health care, and a pattern of economic disincentives for service providers to specialize in geriatrics and for older adults to see trained professionals, we must conclude that the mental health needs of older adults are not now being adequately met and that they will not be adequately met in 2000, 2010, or 2020.

FUTURE MENTAL HEALTH PROFILE OF OLDER AMERICANS

In 1993, the National Advisory Mental Health Council generated an estimate of the prevalence of mental disorders in persons of all ages and prepared a report on service needs for these disorders. Relying on data from the Epidemiologic Catchment Area (ECA) Survey, the council reported that, within any given year, 22% of adults met criteria for a diagnosable mental disorder. Newer data from the National Comorbidity Survey show that about 30% of persons under age 55 meet criteria for at least one disorder during 1 year, suggesting that the prevalence of mental disorders may be greater than had been thought (Kessler et al., 1994).

For older adults, who were not singled out in the National Advisory Mental Health Council estimate or included in the National Comorbidity Survey, prevalence figures can be derived from (a) rates of anxiety and affective disorders, alcohol and drug abuse, and schizophrenia reported in the ECA data for persons over age 65 living in the community (Regier et al., 1988); (b) rates of dementia from recent population surveys (e.g., Ritchie, Kildea, & Robine, 1992); and (c) rates of disorder in long-term care settings, based on the National Nursing Home Survey (U.S. National Center for Health Statistics, 1989). On this basis, we estimate the 1-year prevalence of all mental disorders among persons age 65 and older at 20% to 22% (Gatz & Smyer, 1992). Other sources, such as the report of the Department of Health and Human Services (HHS) to Congress, *Personnel for Health Needs of the Elderly Through the Year 2020* (National Institute on Aging, 1987), indicate that 18% to 28% of the elderly population have significant psychiatric symptoms.

By the year 2000, there will be nearly 35 million Americans age 65 and older. If current prevalence rates for mental disorders are applied, then more than 7.5 million of those individuals could be expected to have mental health problems warranting professional attention.

There are two reasons to adjust these assumptions upward, particularly as we look ahead to the year 2020. First, the evidence suggests a cohort difference in rates of mental disorders (Klerman & Weissman, 1989). Therefore, as baby boomers become elderly, the prevalence of mental disorders such as anxiety and depression could double among persons age 65 and older. Second, depending on assumptions about life expectancy, by 2010 the number of Americans age 85 and older could be more than twice the number in 1990 (U.S. Bureau of the Census, 1992). It is this age group that experiences the highest rates of dementing disorders. It seems likely that dementia will figure prominently among the chronic disorders creating the biggest pressure on future health care resources (E. L. Schneider & Guralnik, 1990).

THE MENTAL HEALTH CARE SYSTEM IN THE YEAR 2000

It is impossible to consider training needs for the year 2000 without a discussion of trends in the mental health care system that will make the delivery of care quite different by 2000 or 2010 from delivery of care in 1990 or even today. Changes in the mental health care system will accompany whatever health care reform occurs. The form of changes will likely reflect the movement already taking place toward managed care (see chapters by Knight & Kaskie, Katz, and Estes, this volume).

It seems likely that, in the future, as is true today, many older adults with mental health problems will be seen by various nonspecialists—for example, physicians in internal medicine, clinical psychologists without special training in aging, nursing personnel without gerontological credentials, and staff in long-term care settings. It is estimated that, in the community, only 32% of persons who need mental health care receive treatment from mental health professionals. Another 31% are treated by primary care physicians, predominantly with psychotropic medication, and 37% receive no care (Burns & Taube, 1990; George, Blazer, Winfield-Laird, Leaf, & Fischbach, 1988). These treatment trends may become *more* pronounced if primary care physicians in a managed care system are not sufficiently sensitive to mental health issues in older patients and so do not identify mental health problems or make appropriate referrals.

Under Medicare there has never been any incentive for community-based care; incentives in insurance programs have instead favored inpatient care. As pressure increases to limit acute-care hospital stays, including psychiatric services at general hospitals, mentally ill older adults will have fewer options (Koenig, George, & Schneider, 1994).

Mental health practitioners who do see older adults with mental health problems will be under pressure to use cost-effective, empirically based treatments. This pressure is likely to translate to more use of medication or electroconvulsive therapy, limitations on use of psychosocial interventions (despite research evidence of effectiveness), and greater involvement of master's-level counselors and other professionals with lower hourly rates.

CURRENT NUMBERS OF PROFESSIONALS AND PROJECTED NEEDS

The following sections are devoted to the four traditional mental health professions: psychiatry, psychology, nursing, and social work. In each section, we summarize what is known about (a) projections about numbers of trained personnel who will be needed in the year 2000, (b) current numbers of specialists in aging, (c) credentialing of geriatric experts, and (d) availability of specialized training. At this point, the metrics are not comparable across all professions, but they do provide a sense of the state of each discipline. We do not devote similar attention to other disciplines—for example, occupational therapy—but the Association for Gerontology in Higher Education maintains a national database of programs in aging across a wide variety of disciplines. Professional certificates are a particularly interesting mechanism, as they permit a nurse, social worker, day care center staff member, residential care provider, or program administrator to obtain a specialization in aging.

Psychiatry

An expert panel has recommended that, by 2000, every medical school have three to five academic geriatricians and geropsychiatrists able to teach medical students and train residents (Rowe et al., 1987). This translates to about 450 geropsychiatrists, who would provide leadership in education, training, and research, and 1,650 geriatricians, for a total of 2,100 faculty members. Another 3,000-4,000 physicians trained in geropsychiatry will be needed for direct patient care. This figure is based on an estimate of 1 geropsychiatrist per 10,000 older adults by the year 2000.

Currently, there are approximately 35,000 psychiatrists in the United States, of whom more than 5,000 list geriatric or gerontologic psychiatry as one of their three primary interests in psychiatry. The American Association for Geriatric Psychiatry has more than 1,400 psychiatrist members. However, only a few hundred have completed specialty training, and approximately 1,000 psychiatrists have passed the examination granting them specialty status in geriatric psychiatry.

Less than 20 years ago, there was only one geriatric psychiatry fellowship program in the United States. Ten years ago there were nine. In 1994, 37 such programs applied for official accreditation in geriatric psychiatry, and, at least 15 additional programs existed that had not yet applied.

In 1990, geriatric psychiatry achieved subspecialty status, and the first examination in geriatric psychiatry was offered, sponsored by the American Board of Psychiatry and Neurology. Actually, this subspecialty status is a modified one—unlike child psychiatry, which is a standard subspecialization category. The geriatric psychiatry subspecialty is defined by a Certificate of Added Qualifications, indicating that a generalist in psychiatry has acquired added qualifications in geriatric psychiatry. The purpose of the additional training is to strengthen the capability of the general psychiatrist in addressing the mental health needs of the elderly and to encourage academic leadership (Cohen, 1989).

Ideally, the outcome of this certification process would be significant growth of an expert faculty in geriatric psychiatry, significant growth in research focused on the mental health problems of older adults, improved skills of psychiatrists who work with older patients in general, enhanced public awareness of the nature of mental illness in later life and the value of psychogeriatric interventions, and heightened awareness of policy makers about the state of the art in psychogeriatrics in relation to the development of more effective policies addressing the mental health needs of older persons.

Psychology

The projected need for psychologists to serve older adults in the year 2000 is 7,495 full-time equivalents (FTE). This number is derived by using the need-based approach developed for the 1980 mini-conference (VandenBos, 1979), assuming that 22% of the elderly population will need the services of a mental health professional, that median length of care is 4.5 hours of professional services, that full time is defined as 1,152 hours of direct service per year, and that psychology will provide one quarter of the needed services.

Only imperfect methods are available for estimating current numbers of psychologists who serve older adults. For example, there are 16,000 psychologists listed in the current *National Register of Health Service Providers in Psychology*. A recent survey of a national sample drawn from the *Register* indicates that 10% of the average caseload consists of individuals age 65 and older (James & Haley, in press). If specializing in clinical geropsychology is defined as devoting at least half one's practice to older adults and their families, then it is estimated that 4.4% of psychologists in the *Register,* or just over 700 individuals, would qualify (Gatz, Karel, & Wolkenstein, 1991). It is notable that only a quarter of those serving older adults had specialized training in clinical geropsychology. Finally, the newly organized section for geropsychology in the Division of Clinical Psychology of the American Psychological Association now has 238 members.

In April 1992, the National Conference on Clinical Training in Psychology: Improving Services for Older Adults was held (Knight, Teri, Santos, & Wohlford, in press). Following the conference, the Task Force on Qualifications for Practice in Clinical and Applied Geropsychology was established to spell out the foundations for setting in motion various forms of credentialing through which psychologists competent to serve older adults would be formally recognized.

Two recent surveys determined that 16 to 20 clinical and counseling psychology training programs offer specialized training in aging (Blieszner, 1994; Dawson & Santos, 1994). In other words, about 10% of accredited professional psychology programs offer some sort of emphasis in aging for doctoral students. At the doctoral level, more important than creating specialists is ensuring that all students receive some exposure to gerontological content. On this front, progress is slow. About 30% of programs have a faculty member who offers an elective course in aging. However, an increasing number of clinical internships do offer rotations in aging. Thus, a greater proportion of practitioners in the future may have some clinical experience with elderly patients.

Nursing

By 2000, it is estimated that 1.7 million FTE registered nurses (RNs), 0.5 million FTE licensed practical nurses (LPNs), and 1 million nursing aides will be needed, with about 35% of the efforts of RNs and

50% of the efforts of LPNs devoted to individuals age 65 and older (Health Resources and Services Administration, 1991). The difference reflects the proportion of LPNs to RNs working in nursing homes. The projected need for the year 2000 is 19,000 gerontological nurse practitioners and clinical specialists in gerontological nursing (Dye, 1993).

A certification program of the American Nurses Association (ANA) provides current numbers of registered providers trained in aging: There are 10,282 gerontological nurses (generalists), 601 gerontological clinical nurse specialists, and 1,698 gerontological nurse practitioners (O'Neal, 1994). There is no separate certification in geropsychiatric nursing; the numbers cited here refer to specializing in all medical care for the aged.

It is also possible to estimate the numbers of nurses without special certification in gerontology who provide services to older adults. Of 4,439 adult nurse practitioners, 18% have a practice largely with older adults. There are 5,653 adult psychiatric clinical specialists, who constitute an important cadre for meeting the mental health needs of the aged (O'Neal, 1994).

The practice skills and knowledge necessary for meeting the nursing needs of older adults are well defined through the Standards and Scope of Gerontological Nursing Practice issued in 1987 by the ANA. Core competencies for gerontological nursing at both undergraduate and graduate (specialist in gerontological nursing) levels have been developed by consensus. Also available is a statement of content for geropsychiatric nursing curricula.

It is possible to identify educational programs that offer specialized training in aging. Of 637 programs at the baccalaureate level, about 14% have required content in gerontological nursing. Of 274 programs at the graduate level, 26% offer advanced preparation in gerontological nursing. Finally, of approximately 200 nurse practitioner programs, students may focus on gerontological nursing in only about 20% (Dye, 1993; O'Neal, 1994).

A key strategy for improving the availability of services is to provide continuing education for nurses now practicing. Special projects have been piloted to provide training in geriatrics, through both didactic modules and clinical experiences, targeting groups such as nursing aides, nurse managers, and faculties in schools of nursing.

Social Work

It is projected that 40,000 to 50,000 full-time social workers will be needed to serve the older population by 2000, increasing to 60,000 or 70,000 by 2020. In contrast, in 1984, there were 5,570 social workers employed in roles directly related to older persons (Dye, 1993; National Institute on Aging, 1987). These numbers refer to all gerontological social work services, not specifically to services related to mental health.

Currently, there is no national certification for social workers who provide services for the elderly, although the matter is under consideration (Mellor & Solomon, 1992).

The best current estimate is that 34% of master's degree programs have concentrations in aging and another 33% offer at least one course in aging. However, 53% of graduate programs in social work have no field faculty in aging, and 21% have no classroom faculty with expertise in aging. At the undergraduate level, 9% of programs have a concentration in aging, and another 11% offer at least one course in aging. However, less than 25% of all undergraduate students in social work take courses in aging, and only 10% of faculty report having any special preparation in the field of aging (Dye, 1993; Mellor & Solomon, 1992).

This educational lag is attributable to lack of trained faculty, lack of training sites, student and faculty resistance, a curriculum that is too full, and a view of the elderly as a low-priority population. Thus, Geriatric Education Centers (GECs) started at two schools of social work are an extremely important recent development (Mellor & Solomon, 1992). Augmenting a prior master's degree program in social work or gerontological social work, the GEC provides a nondegree gerontology program in a continuing education format, with an interdisciplinary educational focus. Associates return to their own organizations and serve as educators or trainers for other health care workers.

BEST STRATEGIES FOR TRAINING MENTAL HEALTH PROFESSIONALS AND BUILDING AN INFRASTRUCTURE OF SERVICE PROVIDERS

We suggest guidelines for curriculum development and for ensuring an infrastructure of service providers trained to meet the mental health needs of older adults. These guidelines are directed primarily at the four traditional mental health professions and at building an infrastructure that will supply enough trainers, incorporate a wide range of providers, and enhance access to the mental health system.

Several guidelines relate to the philosophy and content of training and the nature of clinical experience:

1. Training programs should prepare practitioners for working in interdisciplinary settings and in a variety of roles, including consultation, education, and supervision.

2. The training of personnel to serve the mental health needs of older adults should reflect a continuum of care and multiple points of entry, consistent with the ways older adults interact with the mental health system.

3. Training programs should convey a philosophy of intervention that encompasses prevention, assessment, treatment, and rehabilitation.

4. The curriculum should encompass an understanding of normal aging as well as psychopathology.

With the national movement toward interprofessional education and training in the helping professions (Julian & Lyons, 1992), greater attention should be paid to integration across disciplines. All trainees must become familiar with six areas of knowledge (see, for example, Eisdorfer & Cohen, 1982; Santos & VandenBos, 1982):

The first area is *normal aging*, including physiological changes, cognitive changes, personality development, spiritual matters, and the interpersonal and social context. The interpersonal and social context includes demographics, special considerations with regard to ethnic-minority elderly (see Baker, Lavizzo-Mourey, & Jones, 1993; Cohen, 1993; Kemp, Staples, & Lopez-Acqueres, 1987), retirement, intergenerational issues and family caregiving, and social isolation. Trainees are introduced to a biopsychosocial perspective in which it is recognized that alterations in one area are likely to affect others.

The second area of knowledge is *psychopathology and assessment*. Diagnoses that should be encompassed include reversible and irreversible dementia, depression and suicide, delirium, paranoid disorders, schizophrenia, chemical dependency, anxiety disorders (including phobias and panic disorders), sexual dysfunctions, personality disorders, and sleep disorders. The trainee should be taught not only diagnostic criteria but also epidemiology of the disorders.

Assessment information is gathered from the person as well as from both formal and informal supports. Here, the biopsychosocial perspective continues to be relevant—for example, a stroke may precipitate a depression; social isolation can affect nutrition or contribute to alcoholism, in turn affecting mental status; and dementia can lead to poor dental care and significant dental problems (see Cohen, 1992).

The third area of knowledge for trainees is *intervention*. Prevention implies a reduction of risk through education, social support, and removal of environmental or psychosocial stressors (Berg & Cassells, 1990; Smyer, this volume; Waters, this volume). Treatment includes identifying cases and applying empirically validated interventions. Rehabilitation includes restoring functioning and maximizing independence and decision making.

In the area of treatment, the trainee should be knowledgeable in a range of psychotherapies and should be familiar with the relevant literature on outcomes. For example, empirically validated treatments are available for anxiety, depression, and behavioral symptoms related to dementia in older adults (Schneider, this volume; Smyer, Zarit, & Qualls, 1990). The trainee should also have knowledge of somatic therapies and the relevant research on outcomes.

The fourth topic with which trainees need to become familiar is *interprofessional functioning*. This area incorporates a comprehensive view of the different professions and different care settings, including the ability to interface with nonpsychiatric physicians, other health care professionals (e.g., clinical pharmacists or occupational therapists), and other professionals and organizations (area agencies on aging, community social service organizations, local chapters of the Alzheimer's Association, clergy, or managers at apartment complexes for the aged). The trainee must also be knowledgeable about economic and policy shifts within the society that affect older adults—for example, managed care, managed competition, HMOs, capitation, and malpractice issues. Finally, the trainee must gain the ability to advocate when appropriate.

Fifth, trainees must focus explicitly on *attitudes and ethics*. This area includes understanding the patient-therapist relationship, such as awareness of transference-countertransference issues and the ability to deal with death, dying, and bereavement, as well as knowledge and sensitivity toward ethical and legal matters such as physician-assisted suicide and euthanasia, durable powers of attorney, living wills, competency, and undue influence.

The sixth area of knowledge and skills is *research and evaluation*, so that trainees may contribute to the knowledge base, in the interest of improving the quality of health care intervention strategies, assessment tools, and services.

All trainees should also have experience with older adults across a representative range of sites for mental health service delivery to older adults. For example, rotations might be provided through (a) an inpatient geriatric psychiatry program; (b) a multidisciplinary outpatient program that provides individual, group, and family psychotherapies, as well as medical evaluation and management; (c) a day care program, typically specializing in Alzheimer's disease and other dementias; (d) a nursing home and other community long-term care settings; (e) a community-based program that includes outreach and in-home evaluations (e.g., Abraham et al., 1993) and support groups for family caregivers; and (f) consultation or liaison experience with departments of geriatric medicine and neurology, and placement with special services such as a geriatric chemical-dependency program.

In short, trainees from the four mental health professions not only would become specialists but also would be positioned to become trainers of others who have contact with older adults.

Additional guidelines concern the infrastructure:

1. To increase the number of service providers, strategies must include (a) specialty training programs in gerontological mental health, (b) training in the context of regular degree programs in the core professions, and (c) advanced workshops, continuing education, and supervised experience for professionals now in practice.

2. Because older adults are treated through the general health sector, there is urgency in making sure that all students in medicine, psychology, nursing, and social work are exposed to training with elderly populations.

3. A top priority is faculty development in all four mental health disciplines.

As indicated previously, the number of service providers will fall far short of projected need for professionals by 2000. Specialty training is particularly important for the creation of new faculty. These faculty will teach in specialty training programs, infuse gerontological content into the core curriculum for practitioners who will not be specializing in aging, develop certificate programs for existing practitioners to become credentialed in geriatrics, and involve themselves in clinical research to improve assessment, treatment, and prevention for mental disorders of older adults.

However, encouraging specialty tracks is by itself insufficient, both in terms of attracting sufficient numbers of trainees to the field and in relation to older adults' patterns of use of services, especially the central role of the primary care physician. Therefore, the incorporation of aging into the regular curriculum for psychiatric and nonpsychiatric physicians, clinical psychologists, nurses, and social workers is urged.

Including aging in the regular curriculum should decrease the number of graduates of medical schools, or clinical psychology programs or nursing programs, who have absolutely no exposure to aging. For instance, less than 10 years ago, it was estimated that, although 75% of U.S. medical schools offered elective geriatric courses, only 4% of medical students took a course in aging (Arie, Jones, & Smith, 1985). Exposure must be coupled with serious efforts to make the material interesting, rather than tediously presenting statistics about the profound mental health needs of older adults or attempting to expose the students' supposed age-ism. Students can readily be shown how interests that they already hold, such as neuropsychology or quality of life in cancer patients, could be interestingly applied to an aged patient population (cf. Gatz & Pearson, 1986).

Another target group for increasing the number of providers with expertise in aging comprise professionals already in practice. A key target is the primary care physician. For example, the American Medical Association recently underwrote costs for a series of 1-day seminars across the country on geriatric depression and suicide. In addition, many local chapters of the Alzheimer's Association offer speakers to physician groups. Some professionals are interested in becoming proficient in working with older adults, because of on-the-job exposure to an older patient population, because of experiences with their own parents, or in relation to their own aging. Finally, changes in Medicare to expand to more types of practitioners may encourage more newly eligible practitioners to see older adults. Ensuring their competence with this population is therefore imperative.

RESOURCES PERTINENT TO TRAINING MENTAL HEALTH PROFESSIONALS IN AGING

Governmental programs that fund training for geriatric mental health professionals include the Department of Veterans Affairs (VA), the National Institute on Aging (NIA), the National Institute of Mental Health (NIMH), the Center for Mental Health Service (CMHS), the Health Resources and Services Administration (HRSA), and the Administration on Aging (AoA).

The VA realized the tremendous effect that aging of World War II veterans would have on its programming and in 1975 started establishing Geriatric Research, Evaluation, and Clinical Centers (GRECCs) to encourage biomedical, clinical, and health services research and to provide training for students from various disciplines (Goodwin & Morley, 1994). There are 16 GRECC sites, each affiliated with a university-based geriatrics program and 12 Interdisciplinary Team Training Programs (ITTPs). The VA is a major source of funding for geriatric physicians, including geriatric psychiatrists, and has programs for psychology, social work, nursing, pharmacy, occupational therapy, and audiology; at some sites, it also has training programs for nursing aides.

The NIA has developed programs to fund and train researchers to study the biomedical, social, clinical, and behavioral aspects of aging. Beyond its mechanisms for research grants, research career development awards, and research training grants, some of the most relevant funding opportunities include (a) the Geriatric Leadership Academic Award (K07) to support a faculty member to coordinate the development of training and research programs in geriatrics and gerontology; (b) the Clinical Investigator and NIA Academic Awards (K08), Individual Physician Scientist Award

(K11), and Physician Scientist Award Programs (K12), which provide funding for investigators with clinical training to develop as researchers; and (c) a Senior Fellowship Award (F33).

The NIMH program supports training in psychogeriatric research skills in all disciplines. Funding is provided through these mechanisms: (a) institutional training grant awards for pre- and postdoctoral research training fellowships (T32); (b) short-term training grant awards (T35); (c) individual pre- and postdoctoral awards (F30, F31, F32); (d) the Clinical Mental Health Academic Award (K07), the Scientist Development Award for Clinicians (K20), and the Scientist Development Award (K21), which offer additional training to individual faculty members; and (e) research scientist awards (K05) and research scientist development awards (K02).

The CMHS has the elderly as one of five priority populations. In the past, it has provided institutional pre- and postdoctoral clinical training grant awards (T01). Since 1981, these awards have required service payback by all trainees receiving support. Because of reduced funding, the last awards were made in September 1994.

The HRSA supports 22 centers dedicated to the study of aging, known as Geriatric Education Centers. These focus on improving training and providing continuing medical education courses for faculty.

The AoA provides training grants for more limited purposes across a wide range of providers. For example, in fiscal year 1993, the AoA funded three mental health training projects. The targets of training included non-mental-health service providers, caregivers, and volunteers, toward the goals of improving interagency coordination and increasing access to appropriate services, especially for the rural elderly,

The private sector also contributes to training and research. For example, the American Federation of Aging Research (AFAR) administers the Paul Beeson Physician Faculty Scholars in Aging Research Program, funded with donations from the John A. Hartford Foundation, the Commonwealth Fund, and the Alliance for Aging Research. AFAR also administers the Hartford/AFAR Medical Student Geriatric Scholars program and the Merck/AFAR Fellowship program. The Brookdale Foundation has a National Fellowship Program that funds scholars in a variety of disciplines. The Charles A. Dana Foundation provides funds to train geriatricians who want to conduct research on common illnesses in the elderly. Other funded training programs are sponsored by Pfizer Pharmaceuticals and the Travelers Companies Foundation.

The possibility of providing specialized training in mental health and aging is supported by the enormous growth of knowledge and curricular resources in the field. Scientific journals are one important example of this growth. Ten years ago, the only specialty journal in geriatric psychiatry was the *Journal of Geriatric Psychiatry*. Since then, many journals have been introduced: *International Psychogeriatrics, International Journal of Geriatric Psychiatry, Journal of Geriatric Psychiatry and Neurology, Clinical Gerontologist, Journal of Clinical Geropsychology, Alzheimer Disease & Associated Disorders*, and *Journal of Mental Health and Aging*. Several other journals not specific to mental health and aging also carry relevant articles—for example, *Journal of Gerontological Nursing, Journal of Gerontological Social Work, Psychology and Aging, The Gerontologist*, and *Journal of the American Geriatrics Society*.

Twenty years ago, the bookshelf of a professional in mental health and aging held very few volumes, and there were no major textbooks in geriatric psychiatry. Today, there are more than a dozen textbooks in geriatric psychiatry; several handbooks (e.g., the *Handbook of Mental Health and Aging* [Birren, Sloane, & Cohen, 1992] and the *Handbook of Clinical Gerontology* [Carstensen & Edelstein, 1987; Carstensen, Edelstein, & Dornbrand, in press]); reports from NIH-sponsored consensus conferences on key disorders (the most recent example is the volume on depression edited by L. S. Schneider, Reynolds, Lebowitz, & Friedhoff, 1994); and numerous guides to key topics such as psychotherapy with older adults (Knight, 1986), memory and cognitive assessment batteries (Storandt & VandenBos, 1994), and working with caregivers (Zarit, Orr, & Zarit, 1985).

There are also burgeoning resources for professionals in mental health and aging to use in training practitioners and in working with volunteers and family caregivers, who are critical to identifying older persons with mental health problems and to providing support in the community. For instance, several universities have developed multimedia educational programs, often through their extension services (Schmall & Pratt, 1993). Information about these materials is often poorly disseminated; a clearinghouse might be of value.

BARRIERS TO TRAINING MORE PROFESSIONALS TO MEET THE MENTAL HEALTH SERVICE NEEDS OF OLDER ADULTS

In 1982, the U. S. General Accounting Office issued a major document officially recognizing the fact that older adults were underserved by the mental health system. Three sources of barriers were indicated (in part reflecting institutional and professional ageism): systemic factors, service providers, and older adults themselves. Systemic barriers include insufficient special outreach, absence of collaboration with other agencies, and problems related to financing and reimbursement. Service provider barriers include the belief that children should have priority because later problems can be prevented in children but not in older adults, a preference for psychotherapy over the mixture of strategies called for when treating older adults and their families, and a lack of education and training. Barriers among older adults include fear of the implications of their symptoms.

Systematic barriers posed by the economics of reimbursement not only keep older adults from receiving services but also discourage professionals from obtaining the training to competently treat the problems of older adults. Although the annual cap on outpatient mental health services under Medicare Part B has been repealed, the 50% coinsurance payment rate is a barrier to needed care and prevents many elderly persons in need of treatment from seeking mental health care. Under Medicare, only mental illness is not allocated the usual 80% Part B coverage for illness. With legislative changes in the Omnibus Budget Reconciliation Act of 1989 (OBRA 1989) and OBRA 1990, Medicare now pays directly for qualified mental health services provided by clinical psychologists and clinical social workers. OBRA 1987 substantially improved funding for training and upgrading mental health services provided in long-term care settings. However, an inherent tension continues between federal policy requiring the identification of persons with primary diagnoses of severe mental illness or mental retardation under the Preadmission Screening and Annual Resident Review process and assurance of adequate funding to provide the specialized services that nursing home residents with mental illness or mental retardation need.

Of particular concern is the impact of Medicare physician and nonphysician payment rules on the provision of mental health services to the elderly. In 1989, Congress adopted a new Resource-Based Relative Value Scale (RBRVS) methodology used to determine payment under the national Medicare fee schedule for physicians and other health care services. The RBRVS fee schedule poses special problems for psychiatry as well as for psychology and social work, which have fees linked to psychiatry. Current payment rules create barriers and disincentives to the provision of needed mental health care, particularly to patients in nursing home facilities (Burns, et al., 1993).

The complexity of the problems of older adults, which require more professional time to assess and to treat, is not reflected in reimbursement (Koenig et al., 1994). This factor makes practice with older adults less attractive. There are also biases in the treatments that may be reimbursed. For example, cognitive-behavioral treatment (CBT) for depression has considerable basis in research. Several studies have shown CBT to be as effective as pharmacotherapy, except in severely vegetative cases, where a combined program may be beneficial in both alleviating the depression and preventing further episodes. The positive features of CBT are that side effects of medication are avoided and skills are learned that help prevent future depression. However, it is extremely difficult to secure reimbursement for psychosocial treatments (Berg & Cassells, 1990).

RECOMMENDATIONS FOR ENSURING AN INFRASTRUCTURE OF TRAINED MENTAL HEALTH SERVICE PROVIDERS TO MEET THE MENTAL HEALTH NEEDS OF AN AGING POPULATION

1. All general medical and professional mental health training programs should include both course work and clinical experience sufficient to expose the trainee to gerontology and geriatrics. This requirement is intended to extend not only to psychiatrists, psychologists, social workers, and psychiatric nurses, but also to general practice physicians, registered nurses, marriage and family therapists, master's-level mental health counselors, and others in the health care system who are likely to encounter older adults in need of mental health services.

2. All licensure, relicensure, certification, or recertification of mental health professionals should include content in mental health and aging. At the same time, continuing education minicourses and supervised experience should be made available to provide the essential content.

3. Certification should be established in disciplines that now have no method of identifying practitioners who are competent to serve older adults.

4. Emphasis must be placed on the development of faculty with expertise in mental health and aging, through encouraging qualified individuals to pursue academic careers in geriatric psychiatry, clinical geropsychology, gerontological social work, or gerontological nursing. Various career development awards and training grant mechanisms should be made available toward this goal.

5. The content of training should be sensitive to the evolution of health care financing and delivery, including interprofessional models; the rationale for preventive intervention; and expansion of the knowledge base necessary for cure and prevention of mental disorders of later life.

REFERENCES

Abraham, I. L., Buckwalter, K. C., Snustad, D. G., Smullen, E. D., Thompson-Heisterman, A. A., Neese, J. B., & Smith, M. (1993). Psychogeriatric outreach to rural families: The Iowa and Virginia models. *International Psychogeriatrics, 5,* 203-211.

American Nurses' Association. (1987). Task force to revise a statement on the scope of gerontological nursing practice and standards of gerontological nursing practice. *Standards and Scope of Gerontological Nursing Practice.* Kansas City, MO: Author.

Arie, T., Jones, R., & Smith, C. (1985). The educational potential of old age psychiatric services. In T. Arie (Ed.), *Recent advances in psychogeriatrics: Vol. 1* (pp. 97-207). Edinburgh: Churchill Livingstone.

Baker, F. M., Lavizzo-Mourey, R., & Jones, B. E. (1993). Acute care of the African American elder. *Journal of Geriatric Psychiatry and Neurology, 6,* 66-71.

Berg, R. L., & Cassells, J. S. (1990). *The second 50 years: Promoting health and preventing disability.* Washington, DC: National Academy Press.

Birren, J. E., Sloane, R. B., & Cohen, G. D. (Eds.) (1992). *Handbook of mental health and aging.* (2nd ed.) San Diego: Academic Press.

Blieszner, R. (1994, May). *A guide to doctoral study in the psychology of development and aging, including clinical psychology [and] postdoctoral opportunities.* Washington, DC: American Psychological Association, Division 20.

Burns, B. J., & Taube, C. A. (1990). Mental health services in general medical care and nursing homes. In B. S. Fogel, A. Furino, & G. Gottlieb (Eds.), *Protecting minds at risk* (pp. 63-84). Washington, DC: American Psychiatric Association.

Burns, B. J., Wagner, H. R., Taube, J. E., Magaziner, J., Permutt, T., & Landerman, L. R. (1993). Mental health service use by the elderly in nursing homes. *American Journal of Public Health, 83,* 331-337.

Carstensen, L. L., & Edelstein, B. A. (1987) (Eds.) *Handbook of clinical gerontology.* Oxford, England: Pergamon Press.

Carstensen, L. L., Edelstein, B. A., & Dornbrand, L. (Eds.) (in press). *The practical handbook of clinical gerontology.* Newbury Park, CA: Sage.

Cohen, G. D. (1989). The movement toward subspecialty status for geriatric psychiatry in the United States. *International Psychogeriatrics, 1,* 201-206.

Cohen, G. D. (1992). The future of mental health and aging. In J. E. Birren, R. B. Sloane, & G. D. Cohen (Eds.), *Handbook of mental health and aging* (2nd ed., pp. 893-912). San Diego, CA: Academic Press.

Cohen, G. D. (1993). African American issues in geriatric psychiatry: A perspective on research opportunities. *Journal of Geriatric Psychiatry and Neurology, 6,* 195-199.

Council for the National Register of Health Service Providers in Psychology. (1987). *National register of health service providers in psychology.* Washington, DC: Author.

Dawson, G. D., & Santos, J. F. (1994). *National survey project: Funding for geriatric health and mental health care trainees.* Notre Dame, IN: University of Notre Dame.

Dye, C. (1993). Training. In, S. I. Finkel, C. Dye, A. Garcia, M. Gatz, R. Greene, D. P. Hays, M. Smyer, & M. L. Wykle. *Report of the interdisciplinary coordination group on mental health and the elderly.* (pp. 26-33). Washington, DC: National Institute of Mental Health.

Eisdorfer, C., & Cohen, D. (1982). *Mental health care of the aging: A multidisciplinary curriculum for professional training.* New York: Springer.

Gatz, M., Karel, M. J., & Wolkenstein, B. (1991). Survey of providers of psychological services to older adults. *Professional Psychology: Research and Practice, 22,* 413-415.

Gatz, M., & Pearson, C. G. (1986) Training clinical psychology students in aging. *Gerontology and Geriatrics Education, 6,* 15-25.

Gatz, M., & Smyer, M. (1992). The mental health system and older adults in the 1990s. *American Psychologist, 47,* 741-751.

George, L. K., Blazer, D. F., Winfield-Laird, I., Leaf, P. J., & Fischbach, R. L. (1988). Psychiatric disorders and mental health service use in later life: Evidence from the Epidemiologic Catchment Area Program. In J. Brody & G. Maddox (Eds.), *Epidemiology and aging* (pp. 189-219). New York: Springer.

Goodwin, M., & Morley, J. E. (1994). Geriatric research, education, and clinical centers: Their impact in the development of American geriatrics. *Journal of the American Geriatrics Society, 42,* 1012-1019.

Health Resources and Services Administration, Division of Nursing. (1991). *Eighth report to the President and Congress on the status of health personnel in the United States.* Washington, DC: U.S. Department of Health and Human Services.

James, J. W., & Haley, W. E. (in press). Age and health bias in practicing clinical psychologists. *Psychology and Aging.*

Julian, D. A., & Lyons, T. S. (1992). A strategic planning model for human services: Problem solving at the local level. *Evaluation and Program Planning, 15,* 247-254.

Kemp, B. J., Staples, F., & Lopez-Acqueres, W. (1987). Epidemiology of depression and dysphoria in an elderly Hispanic population. *Journal of the American Geriatrics Society, 35,* 920-926.

Kessler, R. C., McGonagle, K. A., Zhao, S., Nelson, C. B., Hughes, M., Eshleman, S., Wittchen, H. U., & Kendler, K. S. (1994). Lifetime and 12-month prevalence of *DSM-III-R* psychiatric disorders in the United States: Results from the National Comorbidity Survey. *Archives of General Psychiatry, 51,* 8-19.

Klerman, G. L., & Weissman, M. M. (1989). Increasing rates of depression. *Journal of the American Medical Association, 261,* 2229-2235.

Knight, B. (1986). *Psychotherapy with older adults.* Newbury Park, CA: Sage.

Knight, B. G., Teri, L., Santos, J., & Wohlford, P. (Eds.). (in press). *Mental health services for older adults: Implications for training and practice.* Washington, DC: American Psychological Association.

Koenig, H. G., George, L. K., & Schneider, R. (1994). Mental health care for older adults in the year 2020: A dangerous and avoided topic. *The Gerontologist, 34,* 674-679.

Mellor, M. J., & Solomon, R. (Eds.). (1992). *Geriatric social work.* New York: Haworth.

National Advisory Mental Health Council. (1993). Health care reform for Americans with severe mental illnesses: Report of the National Advisory Mental Health Council. *American Journal of Psychiatry, 150,* 1447-1465.

National Institute on Aging. (1987). *Personnel for health needs of the elderly through the year 2020* (NIH Publication No. 87-2950). Washington, DC: U.S. Government Printing Office.

O'Neal, D. (1994, November). Memorandum. Washington, DC: American Nurses Association.

Regier, D. A., Boyd, J. H., Burke, J. D., Rae, D. S., Myers, J. K., Kramer, M., Robins, L. N., George, L. K., Karno, M., & Locke, B. Z. (1988). One-month prevalence of mental disorders in the United States. *Archives of General Psychiatry, 45,* 977-986.

Ritchie, K., Kildea, D., & Robine, J. M. (1992). The relationship between age and the prevalence of senile dementia: A meta-analysis of recent data. *International Journal of Epidemiology, 21,* 763-769.

Rowe, J. W., Grossman, E., Bond, E., and the Institute of Medicine Committee on Leadership for Academic Geriatric Medicine. (1987). Special report: Academic geriatrics for the year 2000. *New England Journal of Medicine, 316,* 1425-1428.

Santos, J. F., & VandenBos, G. R. (Eds.). (1982). *Psychology and the older adult: Challenges for training in the 1980s.* Washington, DC: American Psychological Association.

Schmall, V., & Pratt, C. (1993). Community education on mental health in later life: Findings from an evaluation of a series of three model programs. *Journal of Mental Health Administration, 20,* 190-200.

Schneider, E. L., & Guralnik, J. M. (1990). The aging of America. *Journal of the American Medical Association, 263,* 2335-2040.

Schneider, L. S., Reynolds, C. F., III, Lebowitz, B. D., & Friedhoff, A. J. (Eds.). (1994). *Diagnosis and treatment of depression in late life.* Washington, DC: American Psychiatric Press.

Smyer, M. A., Zarit, S. H., & Qualls, S. H. (1990). Psychological intervention with the aging individual. In J. E. Birren & K. W. Schaie (Eds.), *Handbook of the psychology of aging* (pp. 375-404). San Diego, CA: Academic Press.

Storandt, M. A., & VandenBos, G. R. (Eds.). (1994). *Neuropsychological assessment of dementia and depression in older adults: A clinician's guide.* Washington, DC: American Psychological Association.

U.S. Bureau of the Census. (1992). *Sixty-five plus in America* (Current Population Reports, Special Studies, P23-178RV). Washington, DC: U.S. Government Printing Office.

U.S. General Accounting Office. (1982, September). *The elderly remain in need of mental health services* (GAO/HRD-82-112). Gaithersburg, MD: Author.

U.S. National Center for Health Statistics (1989). *National nursing home survey* (DHHS Publication No. PHS 89-1758, Series 13, No. 97). Washington, DC: U.S. Government Printing Office.

VandenBos, G. R. (1979, September). *A service need-based approach to the projection of mental health personnel needs*. Washington, DC: American Psychological Association.

Zarit, S. H., Orr, N. K., & Zarit, J. M. (1985). *The hidden victims of Alzheimer's disease: Families under stress*. New York: New York University Press.

CHAPTER 12

Mental Health Services for the Elderly: Key Policy Elements

Carroll L. Estes

Access to mental health services has long been a problem for the elderly. A variety of barriers have combined to create this problem: (a) the fragmented and uncoordinated development and implementation of federal and state mental health policy for the aged; (b) a lack of public financing for mental health services and particularly noninstitutional care (Estes et al., 1994); and (c) social, cultural, and economic issues. The literature portrays a fragmented mental health system in which shifting policies and economic considerations largely prescribe the type of care, if any, that the elderly receive (Gatz & Smyer, 1992; Binney & Swan, 1991).

This chapter examines utilization of mental health services, barriers to services, and funding and revenue sources. Key elements of mental health policy and recent changes in mental health service delivery are outlined. The chapter concludes with a discussion of research needs in mental health services and aging.

The author gratefully acknowledges the assistance and ideas of Laura Keegan, Karen Linkins, Elinore Lurie, Elizabeth Binney, Kathryn Kane, and Grace Yoo. The AARP/ Andrus Foundation provided support for research that contributed to the chapter, and three reviewers (Trudy Persky, Mary Jo Gibson, and Sara Honn Qualls) provided invaluable suggestions, many of which are incorporated.

CARROLL L. ESTES

MENTAL ILLNESS AND THE OLDER ADULT

In late life, a significant proportion of patients with mental illness remain unrecognized and untreated (Birren, Sloane, & Cohen, 1992), often overshadowed by problems of the young, which appear both more urgent and potentially more capable of solution. Mental disorders in the elderly are also overshadowed by their medical illnesses. Already-constrained mental health priorities, resources, and targeting largely center on other, younger generations (Estes et al., 1994). Although the elderly tend to have lower prevalence rates of mental disorders than younger groups (with the exception of dementia), mental illness in late life is significant: The proportion of adults age 65 and over with mental disorders, both in institutions and in the community, is approximately 22% (Gatz & Smyer, 1992), while the proportion among the nursing home population is approximately two thirds (Burns et al., 1993). The U. S. General Accounting Office (1992) reported that 18% to 25% of older persons have mental disorders.

The elderly are often viewed as a homogeneous group; however, multiple variables can alter the picture of mental health in later life. The National Institute of Mental Health (NIMH) Epidemiological Catchment Area (ECA) studies suggest that the incidence and prevalence of psychiatric disorders are affected by age, gender, ethnicity, geographic location, social status, and type of residence (Roughan, 1993). Gender can have a significant effect on mental health; for example, women are twice as likely as men to suffer from depression (Roughan, 1993) and are more likely to suffer from anxiety disorders (Bliwise, McCall, & Swan, 1987). In addition, women's access to mental health care is constrained by the fact that they are more likely to be economically disadvantaged. In old age, the economic hardships faced by women are augmented by the fact that they live 7 years longer than men and are much more likely than older men to be widowed, to live alone, to be institutionalized (Goldstein & Perkins, 1993), and to receive a lower income from all sources. Minority older women are especially compromised by these conditions (Jones & Estes, in press).

Poverty is associated with mental illness (Bruce & McNamara, 1992; Cohen, 1989; Lurie, 1987; Sanchez, 1992). Minorities are also far more likely than Whites to be poor in old age. Approximately one third

304

of Blacks 65 and older are poor. Older Hispanics have higher rates of illiteracy and poverty than Whites (McCombs, 1993), and minorities may have additional stressors such as limited communication skills, limited education, low social status, inadequate housing, and greater health problems (Sanchez, 1992). The growing number and proportion of minorities in the U.S. population (in some cases projected to constitute the majority of the population, as with Hispanics in California [Baker, 1992]) signify the import of developing culturally competent services and eliminating service barriers for minorities (McCombs, 1993).

TRENDS AND ISSUES

Patterns of Mental Health Service Utilization

Older adults are more likely to use inpatient than outpatient services, are more likely to use general hospitals than other treatment sites, and are highly likely to be treated by general medical practitioners rather than mental health professionals (Goldstrom, 1993). These patterns hold serious implications for the elderly, influencing the appropriateness and effectiveness of treatment. Important factors constraining utilization of mental health services are stigma and general misinformation about mental health problems among the public.

In contrast to the often stated priority of the mental health system for community-based treatment (Swan & McCall, 1987), 70% of all mental health expenditures are for inpatient care (Gatz & Smyer, 1992). This is a result of reimbursement policies of public and private insurers. After a deductible is reached for the limited number of elderly who are eligible, both Medicare and private insurance reimburse fully for hospitalization, again within limits. However, outpatient care is only partially covered, providing major incentives for the use of hospital care. In 1986, the elderly made up 8.7% of all inpatient, but only 3.1% of all outpatient, admissions, (Goldstrom, 1993). Gatz and Smyer (1992) describe the predicament of older adults who need mental health care in the 1990s as one marked by overreliance on inpatient treatment, increased use of general hospitals as treatment sites, inadequate integration with the nursing home industry, and insufficient mental health referrals from general medical providers.

These patterns of institutional care result in part from mental health policy and from "perverse economic incentives and multiple payers" (Frisman & McGuire, 1989, p. 119) that leave the mental health system fragmented and uncoordinated. Swan and McCall (1987) describe the mental health network as a "non-system of health care" (p. 111).

Older adults who seek care for mental health problems are likely to do so outside the mental health sector. Burns and Taube (1990) report that only 56% of the service use by the elderly for mental disorders is provided through the mental health sector; 44% is provided in the general health sector. These utilization patterns may have serious consequences for older adults: The majority of the elderly who seek care from the general health sector see internists or family practitioners, who as a group tend to overlook mental illness (Goldstein, 1994). Many primary care physicians rely excessively on medication, spend little time on counseling, and make few referrals to mental health professionals (Gottlieb, 1992). In a study of medical residents, primary care physicians indicated that they deal with their patients' mental health problems themselves and refer only those with the most severe symptoms (Feinson, 1990); however, older adults reported that the most important factor in making them more willing to utilize mental health services would be the recommendation of the family doctor. The elderly also demonstrate a very high usage of prescription drugs compared to other age groups (Frieman, Cunningham, & Cornelius, 1994).

Inpatient Services

According to Goldstrom (1993), in 1986 the majority of psychiatric inpatient care (64.5%) for persons age 65 and older was provided in general hospitals. When general hospital care of the mentally ill elderly occurs outside of designated psychiatric inpatient units, they are likely to receive care from nonpsychiatric physicians. In addition, psychiatric liaison services tend to be underused, particularly by older patients (Swan & McCall, 1987).

Nursing homes are not included in most statistics for inpatient admissions, probably because they have not been integrated into the mental health system. However, nursing homes are a major destination for mentally ill elderly. Burns et al. (1993) found mental illness among elderly nursing home residents at the rate of 64%; however, only about 4.5% received any mental health treatment in a given 1-month period. When they did receive treatment, it was likely to be psychotropic medication, which was most often prescribed (sometimes inappropriately) by general practitioners. These are 1985 data, collected before the Omnibus Budget Reconciliation Act (OBRA) of 1987 reforms mandated preadmission screening and treatment for mental illness, and it is not known whether nursing home residents have fared better since then. The OBRA policy on a restraint-free environment defines psychotropic medications in some cases as chemical restraints that must be reduced over time. Residents may be "subjected to medication reductions until their symptomatology and distress returns, then . . . cycled through an in-patient psychiatric unit for medical stabilization" (S. H. Qualls, personal communication, 1994). Potential negative consequences include fear among nursing home staff about using psychotropic drugs, the screening out by nursing homes of elderly with mental disorders, and the presence of unqualified mental health providers (e.g., surveyors and staff with bachelor's or master's degrees) playing key roles in the mental health services given (Lombardo, 1994). E. E. Lurie (personal communication, 1994) suggests that current mental health provision in nursing homes is limited to drug therapy with limited monitoring or monitoring by nonpsychiatrists. Few nursing homes employ either mental health professionals or general medical physicians trained to treat mental illness.

Outpatient services

The elderly receive disproportionately fewer outpatient services than other groups from community mental health centers, psychiatric clinics, and private therapists. The number of older adults receiving services in the community was disproportionately low in relation to their numbers in the community (Goldstrom, 1993). Goldstrom (1993) found that in 1986 mentally ill older adults were likely to use general hospital services, their second most common destination after multiservice mental health organizations. The short-term treatment provided in general hospitals may leave unaddressed the elderly's comprehensive service needs for social support, continuity of care, case management, and long-term therapy.

Only 15% of community mental health providers named the elderly as a target group for outreach, signaling a relatively low level of commitment toward the aged in terms of organizational priority and mission among community mental health providers (Estes et al., 1994). The data underscore the importance of outreach to older persons (Estes et al., 1994; Gurian, 1982), geriatric mobile teams, and models of service delivery tailored to particular needs (Knight, 1991).

Community care is delivered largely by nonpsychiatric physicians rather than by professionally trained mental health providers. This situation is due in part to the coincidence of physical and mental illness in late life and the fact that many elderly will not consult a professional unless physical manifestations are present (Swan & McCall, 1987). In a study of older adults, only one third of respondents said they would report symptoms of depression to a health professional, but 72% said they would report cardiovascular symptoms (Feinson, 1990). Nonpsychiatric physicians are less likely to diagnose or treat mental disorders and are generally unlikely to refer patients to mental health professionals. When they do treat mental disorders, they are more likely to prescribe psychotropic medications; although prevalence rates for mental disorders are lower among the elderly than among other age groups, the elderly are the largest consumers of psychotropic and anxiolytic drugs (Bliwise et al., 1987; Roughan, 1993). This disparity calls for training of primary care and other physicians to improve their capacity to identify, manage, and refer older patients who present psychiatric symptoms.

The elderly underutilize both private psychiatrists and community mental health services. Although psychiatrists are dominant in the hiearchy of the general mental health sector and provide 5.5% of all outpatient mental health services, older adults account for only 2.7% of psychiatrist services (Swan & McCall, 1987). When older people do receive care from psychiatrists, those who receive office visits are more likely to receive medications and brief visits than standard or extended visits (E. E. Lurie, personal communication, 1994).

The elderly are more likely to receive medical health services in public than in private nonprofit agencies (Estes et al., 1994), probably because funding demands that public providers accept the most difficult or unprofitable clients. In a recent study by Estes et al. (1994), 40% of community mental health providers identified non–health-related services (e.g., transportation, home help) as unmet needs, suggesting that the comprehensive needs of the elderly—physical, mental, and social—are not being met. In the face of an increasingly "corporatized" mental health system, these trends are likely to continue. There are economic disincentives for providers to treat the elderly, to provide continuity of care, and to provide community-based outpatient, rather than inpatient, care. Reform and research, then, should concentrate on identifying and removing the disincentives that deter access to services for the elderly.

Attempts to make the mental health delivery system more comprehensive and less fragmented have been most visible in the growth of managed care and in President Clinton's proposed national health care reform that did not pass. Concerns over rising costs have led both private and public mental health sectors to seek new ways to manage the system (Cuffel, Snowden, Maslad, & Piccagli, 1994). Managed care plans claim to offer cost efficiency, simplified care, and financing (Dougherty, 1988). However, the desire by government, private insurers, and employers to control the rising costs of medical care has made managed care synonymous with cost containment rather than a program geared toward providing appropriate and efficient care to patients (Dorwart & Epstein, 1993). The rapid growth of managed care in the 1990s and the "carving out" and contracting of managed care for mental health services are two trends that are expected to affect and further limit utilization of mental health services, with unknown effects on the elderly. Dougherty (1988) points out that health maintenance organizations (HMOs) have chosen to concentrate on delivering mental health care to acute, nondisabled patients, much as the traditional mental health system has done. Scheffler, Grogan, Cuffel, and Penner (1993) point to potential problems with managed care, including a lack of continuity of care, a lack of diagnostic testing for mental illness, and inappropriate or inadequate treatment delivery for severe mental illness.

Barriers to mental health services

Numerous experts have argued that mental health services are underutilized in later life (Sherman, 1992). A study by Shapiro et al. (1985) found that 7.8% of community-dwelling elderly persons in a Baltimore

ECA survey required mental health services and that 62.6% did not receive the care they needed. From this it was inferred nationwide that approximately 2.4 million noninstitutionalized elderly currently need mental health services and slightly more than 1.5 million may not be receiving the care they need.

This underutilization has been attributed to a number of factors, including reluctance on the part of elders to seek mental health care due to fear of stigma, as well as ageist attitudes among mental health professionals, inadequate detection of mental illness among the elderly by mental health professionals, economic disincentives for patients to use services, barriers to access, low rates of referral by general practitioners, and limited knowledge about the availability of services (Colenda & van Dooren, 1993; Feinson, 1990).

Minorities are underserved because of all of these factors, as well as cultural stigma regarding mental illness and perceptions of discriminatory treatment (McCombs, 1993). Data are sparse regarding the mental health needs, utilization, and expenditures of minority elderly, suggesting an important research agenda in this area. Additional barriers to access for minority elderly are language differences, financial problems, and the lack of knowledgeable providers (McCombs, 1993). Another major problem of access to mental health services relates to geographic location, primarily rural setting. Barriers to mental health services in rural areas include the lack of trained professionals, organizational barriers, and geographic financial and psychological factors (Smith, 1993).

The two major destinations for mentally ill older adults are nursing homes and general hospitals (Gatz & Smyer, 1992; Goldman, Taube, & Jenks, 1987). Board-and-care facilities are growing in significance, and home visits by mental health workers are expected to grow. Although mental health policy since deinstitutionalization has purported to stress treating mental illness on an outpatient basis (Kiesler & Sibulkin, 1987), 70% of all mental health expenditures are for inpatient care (Gatz & Smyer, 1992). A 1985 study found that the elderly received about 6% of all community mental health services, that 45% of the community mental health centers (CMHCs) had no aging-specific programs, and that fewer than 45% of the CMHCs had staff trained in geriatric service delivery (Flemming, Buchanan, Santos, & Rickards, 1986).

These patterns have not, until recently, been counteracted by advocacy for the mentally ill elderly. A historical lack of cooperation exists between the aging network and the mental health system (Gatz & Smyer, 1992): For the most part, aging organizations have not advocated for the mentally ill elderly (Shane, 1987). For example, because nursing home reform requires the screening out of the mentally ill from other elderly, the Alzheimer's Association has lobbied to dissociate the disease from the label of mental illness and has distanced itself from the mental health system. Recent activity of the Coalition for Mental Health and Aging has been devoted to increasing the visibility of older adults' mental health needs (Rickards, 1993). In some instances, ties between area agencies on aging (AAAs) and CMHCs have been found to serve the elderly well (Gatz & Smyer, 1992). Affiliation with an AAA has been found to be a significant factor affecting the breadth of service provision to the elderly and predicting higher percentages of elders in provider caseloads (Lebowitz, Light, & Bailey, 1987).

Funding and Revenue Sources

Funding for mental health services reflects the fragmentation of mental health policy itself. Although states finance the largest proportion of mental health services, public funding and especially federal funding for mental health services increased with deinstitutionalization. Federal funds, including Medicare, the federal share of Medicaid, and block grant funds accounted for 26% of total funding in 1990 (Rice, Kelman, Miller, & Dunmeyer, 1990), while state and local funds accounted for 28%. These figures understate the states' influence of mental health services because block grant funds transferred to the states are shown as a federal contribution (Rice et al., 1990). The remaining 46% of mental health funding came from out-of-pocket payments, private insurance, and philanthropy. Reimbursement and financial policies governing this mixture of public and private funds have had a serious impact on access to mental health care, often favoring inpatient over outpatient care, medically oriented over psychologically oriented care, acute over chronic care, and more restrictive over less restrictive alternatives (Swan & Gerard, 1987). Reimbursement practices reward short-term inpatient treatment and penalize other types of services (Katz & Cancro, 1982).

CARROLL L. ESTES

Medicare

Because Medicare was enacted with a focus on acute illness, it has posed special problems in terms of mental disorders and health service delivery (Gottlieb, 1993). Medicare accounted for only about 7% of the $23 billion spent on mental health in 1988 (Center for Mental Health Services & NIMH, 1992). Medicare has, from its inception, severely restricted mental health coverage in psychiatric facilities; for example, coverage for any type of psychiatric hospitalization is limited to 90 days per benefit period. Beneficiaries may use an additional 60 "lifetime reserve days" only once. However, because there is no such limit for psychiatric care in general hospitals, where coverage is similar to other conditions, a shift of psychiatric care to general hospitals has been reported (Gottlieb, 1993). Interestingly, there is no limit on lifetime days for anything else under Medicare (Gottlieb, 1993). Although mental health benefits were liberalized with the 1987 and 1989 federal budget reconciliation bills, Medicare coverage is restricted and excludes two important benefits: (a) custodial care for Alzheimer's patients and those not requiring skilled nursing care and (b) outpatient prescription (e.g., psychotropic) drugs (Sherman, 1992).

Although mental health benefits are covered under both Part A and Part B of Medicare, less than 3% of Medicare expenditures went to mental health care in 1988 (Sherman, 1992). Most of that ($2.2 billion) was used for Part A (inpatient services), with only $300 million for Part B. Medicare Part B, a voluntary enrollment program in which the elderly pay a monthly premium, covers 80% of allowable physician costs and outpatient services. There is a 20% copayment fee for in-patient psychiatric services in a hospital setting (Sherman, 1992). For most outpatient mental health services, a 50% copayment rate is required, although OBRA 1987 and 1989 expanded the covered limit by removing the annual dollar limit on outpatient services (Dorwart & Epstein, 1993). Gottlieb (1993) described these funding restrictions as "stigma . . . institutionally and governmentally imposed because mental health services are treated quite differently than general health services" (p. 88).

Medicare Part B also requires a 20% coinsurance payment for initial mental health diagnostic services. In 1990, copayments for visits to change or monitor psychiatric medications were reduced to 20%, the same as other health services. OBRA 1987 also added coverage for ambulatory treatment and expanded coverage to pay for treatment provided by clinical psychologists and social workers in addition to that provided by physicians (White, 1991). Nevertheless, the remaining 50% copayment is still a serious barrier to many elderly; outpatient mental health care amounts to less than 0.1% of total Medicare costs (Dorwart & Epstein, 1993; McGuire, 1989), suggesting an underuse of mental health services by Medicare beneficiaries. Additionally, although disabled persons under age 65 account for 9.5% of the overall Medicare population, 39% of Medicare discharges with mental illness were from this population (Dorwart & Epstein, 1993; Lave & Goldman, 1990), suggesting an even greater underuse of mental health services by elderly Medicare beneficiaries.

Medicaid

Medicaid accounted for 13% of total mental health expenditures in 1988 (Center for Mental Health Services & NIMH, 1992), and the federal share of Medicaid represents the majority of federal funding for mental health. A significant characteristic of Medicaid funding is its wide variability across states. About 15% of total Medicaid dollars are spent on mental illness, with the bulk spent on skilled nursing facilities and intermediate care facilities (more than $2 billion), general hospital psychiatric care (about $2 billion), and state psychiatric hospital care (almost $1 billion). The remainder goes to community-based facilities and physicians' visits (Taube, Goldman, & Salkever, 1990). These expenditures suggest that Medicaid encourages institutionalization (Estes & Harrington, 1981; Sharfstein, 1982; Stotsky & Stotsky, 1983; Swan, Fox, & Estes, 1986) and the use of general hospital care. Although often described as inadequate, Medicaid rates come closer to covering costs for inpatient care than ambulatory care, and some patients may be admitted to hospitals unnecessarily because outpatient services are seen as either unprofitable or unavailable (Dorwart & Epstein, 1993).

States' shares of total mental health funding vary between 17% and 50% (Dorwart & Epstein, 1993), depending on the size and wealth of the state. States have discretion over Medicaid fund disbursement, ensuring that coverage is fragmented, with varying eligibility, reimbursement, service limits, and benefit policies (Swan et al., 1986). Taube et al. (1990) suggest a tension between the state Medicaid authority, which promotes cost containment, and the overarching interest of the state mental health authority. They find too few covered service benefits for nonhospital community providers, but a paradoxical effort toward cost containment in this area.

Mental Health Policy

The fragmented nature of the current mental health system is the outcome of federal and state policies that have left the mental health system uncoordinated and generally unable to implement needed programs and services, particularly where the elderly are concerned (Swan, Bergthold, & Estes, 1988; Swan & Gerard, 1987). The failure of President Clinton's health reform in 1994 has exacerbated the uncertainty for mental health services in the future.

One of the most significant changes in the mental health system in the past several decades was deinstitutionalization, which began in the early 1960s when Social Security was expanded to cover the health needs of the elderly under Medicare and the poor under Medicaid (Estes & Harrington, 1981). These programs meant that the poor elderly, who previously resided in state mental hospitals because they were senile or similarly disabled, were now eligible for Medicaid and could be moved into nursing homes and board-and-care homes where the federal government would share the cost. Both Medicaid and Supplemental Security Income were to play an important role in enabling this deinstitutionalization to occur. States began to shift older patients to nursing homes to promote cost savings in their programs. The trend was significant: In 1963, among the institutionalized elderly, 48% of the mentally ill over age 65 were in state institutions and the rest were in nursing homes. Six years later, only 25% were in state hospitals, and 75% were in nursing homes (Dorwart & Epstein, 1993). In the general population, prior to deinstitutionalization, 77% of mental illness episodes were inpatient; the remainder were outpatient. By 1975, only 27% were inpatient, 70% were outpatient, and 3% were day treatment (Brown & Cooksey, 1989). These percentages have since remained relatively stable.

Along with deinstitutionalization came the rise of community-based mental health care. CMHCs were established in 1963, funded originally by federal seed money. The Community Mental Health Centers Act of 1975 mandated special services to, among others, the elderly, children and adolescents, and substance abusers (Goldman & Frank, 1990). By the 1970s—the height of deinstitutionalization—CMHC caseloads increased 600% (Manderscheid, Witkin, Rosenstein, & Bass, 1984).

However, with the passage of the Reagan administration's Omnibus Budget Reconciliation Act of 1981 (OBRA), community mental health took a substantive turn. The initiation of a mental health block grant in alcohol, drug abuse, and mental health (ADM) combined ten categorical programs previously funded on a project or state formula basis. This change transferred authority of the disbursement of federal CMHC funds to the states. Along with a reduction in mandated services (including the repeal of the mandate for specialized geriatric service), states were given broad discretion in the use of federal funds (Hadley & Culhane, 1993). States were no longer required to match federal funds as before, which in some cases resulted in less overall money directed to some or all of the programs combined in the ADM grant. There was an off-the-top reduction in federal program funds previously allocated to areas that were consolidated (Rochefort & Logan, 1989), and funding was shifted from mental health to drug abuse. Overall funding decreased 21% (Estes & Wood, 1984), which reportedly led to reduced professional staffing, increased caseloads, service reorganization to target chronically mentally ill and insured clients, and fewer services to children, the elderly, and the uninsured, as well as to a decline in federal revenues being offset by state funds and private-pay clients (Drolen, 1990; Estes & Wood, 1984; Jerrel & Larsen as cited in Hadley & Culhane, 1993).

The impact of the ADM block grant was so significant that, after 1981, CMHCs were essentially redefined out of existence. According to *Mental Health, United States, 1992*, CMHCs were reclassified under the category "ambulatory mental health organizations," of which there are three major types: freestanding psychiatric outpatient clinics, which provide only outpatient service; freestanding partial care organizations, which provide only partial care services; and multiservice mental health organizations, which emphasize the provision of outpatient services but also provide partial care services or inpatient or residential treatment services (Center for Mental Health Services & NIMH, 1992).

In addition to eliminating mandated services and cutting funding, OBRA 1981 had the effect of creating additional barriers to access. In a study by Estes and Wood (1984), one third of agencies surveyed reported implementing one or more policy changes that created barriers to access, such as tightening eligibility (36.1%), initiating fees or copayments (33.3%), increasing fees or copayments (50%), reducing volume (36.1%), or eliminating services (41.7%). At the same time, however, demand for services and the number of clientele, especially those over age 75, were increasing in a majority of agencies.

During the 1980s, demands for mental health services increased as a result of deinstitutionalization, which contributed to the wave of homelessness (Brown, 1985). These events were followed by the demise of the CMHC movement (Kenig, 1992) and the implementation in 1983 of Medicare prospective payment through diagnosis-related groups. Patients who were released "quicker and sicker" often had needs for mental as well as physical posthospital care.

Following state hospital deinstitutionalization, the nursing home became an important institution for those with mental illness. Provisions of OBRA 1987 were intended to avoid transinstitutionalization—that is, recycling former mental hospital patients into other forms of institutional care (Gatz & Smyer, 1992). The act mandated preadmission screening and an annual review for all potential and existing nursing home residents using the following criteria:

1. Residents who are mentally ill or retarded who do not need nursing services should be moved to a more appropriate setting.

2. Residents who are mentally ill or retarded who have lived in a nursing home less than 30 months, but who need active psychiatric treatment, should be moved to a more appropriate setting.

3. Residents who are mentally ill and in need of treatment and have resided in a nursing home for more than 30 months may be allowed to stay.

Estimates of the effects of OBRA 1987 on nursing home residents vary: Freiman, Arons, Goldman, and Burns (1990) and Lair, Smyer,

Goldman, and Arons (1989) suggest that 2.4% to 5.5% of the nursing home population in Medicare-certified facilities would be excluded. Eichmann, Griffin, Lyons, Larson, and Finkel (1992) suggest that a much higher 18% would require immediate discharge because, according to the regulations, dementia alone does not qualify mentally ill patients for nursing home care; that is, they must also need nursing care according to a medical diagnosis other than dementia. Eichmann et al. further argued that the fact that states must provide active treatment for residents who are mentally ill and pay for said treatment from nonfederal Medicaid funds may promote yet another wave of deinstitutionalization, this time from nursing homes. Smith and Jensen (1990) suggested that if the purpose of OBRA 1987 changes is to find patients who are not receiving adequate and specialized mental health care, then the number of discharges or refusals is likely to be small. However, if a target reduction in federal fiscal responsibility is the object, the criteria need simply be expanded.

Processes of Change in the Delivery of Mental Health Services

Estes et al. (1994) have identified seven processes of change in the delivery of mental health services as a consequence of policy and funding changes, particularly those of the last two decades. Each process has implications not only for mental health service delivery in general, but also for access by the elderly to these services.

Rationalization

The rationalization of mental health care—aimed at improving productivity and efficiency—is marked by several elements, including the diversification of the industry, the specialization of services, and the emergence of managed care and case management (Estes et al., 1994). The current mental health system has been transformed from a relatively comprehensive system of care to one that is complex and fragmented (Surles, 1991), as evidenced by the expansion and restructuring of the industry, the widespread development of multisite and multifacility systems (Brown, 1985; Estes et al., 1994), and the vertical and horizontal integration across services (Estes et al., 1994). Currently the most sweeping form of rationalization is the wave of managed care and contracting for mental health services, both of which are expected to dramatically influence the use and cost of these services. A particular dilemma is that there is no standardization in the way mental health services are provided under those service trends (Gottlieb, 1993).

Privatization

Privatization, which refers to the growth in nonprofit and for-profit facilities and the decline in public facilities, is an outgrowth of larger trends in the American health care system (Dorwart & Epstein, 1993; Estes & Alford, 1990). Changing patterns of payment for services have contributed to a shift from separate public and private systems of care to a mixed system in which mental health providers of all types rely on mixed sources of revenue (Dorwart & Epstein, 1993). Mental health policies have thus become more market oriented in their approach, with economic reasoning increasingly applied (Brown & Cooksey, 1989) and the behavior of insurers, employers, and practitioners increasingly privatized—that is, focused on their own well-being rather than their broader societal role (Dorwart & Epstein, 1993).

Other pressures for privatization include competition, the growth of multifacility systems (Brown & Cooksey, 1989; Dorwart & Epstein, 1993), and the reluctance of most states to replace their closing psychiatric hospital beds with permanent state funds for community services. As a consequence, general hospital psychiatric units and the private psychiatric hospitals, have "moved to the center of the treatment arena" (Kenig, 1992, p. 190). As public funds available for mental health services have diminished, state and local agencies have sought efficiency increases by purchasing mental health services in the private sector (Hu, Cuffel, & Masland, 1994). Proponents argue that this trend increases cost efficiency, flexibility, and consumer choice and quality. Critics point to problems with contracting out to the private sector. Hu et al. suggest that contracting increases efficiency in the provision of certain, but not all, public mental health services. With strong fiscal incentives, public providers may be encouraged to cut costs by denying services or reducing the quality of services. Since public providers are already the sector of last resort, numerous mentally ill

318

individuals may fall through ever-widening cracks. Private production of public goods limits the government's right of intervention (Scheffler, 1992), drawing "public" providers further from their original goals. Additionally, competitive bidding can lead to discontinuities in care. If every year the purchase of service contracts is led by a competitive bid without regard for continuity of client treatment, disruption can occur (Paulson, 1988).

Competition

The number of mental health organizations increased steadily between 1970 and 1988 from 3,005 to 4,930 (Center for Mental Health Services & NIMH, 1992). The number of inpatient service providers almost doubled, and the number providing both outpatient and partial care services increased. With funding uncertainty, cost containment, and privatization, competition has increased for scarce funds, referrals, and patients for whom reimbursement is assured (Dorwart & Epstein, 1993; Estes et al. 1994).

Deinstitutionalization

Three waves of deinstitutionalization can be identified. The first was the deinstitutionalization of the mentally ill elderly from state mental hospitals in the 1960s (Brown, 1985); the second is a form of deinstitutionalization through early discharge of elderly patients from acute care hospitals under Medicare prospective payment (Eichmann et al., 1992; Estes & Swan, 1993); the third is the potential deinstitutionalization of the mentally ill elderly from nursing homes with the implementation of selected regulatory requirements under OBRA 1987, coupled with the lack of a cohesive system of alternatives (Estes et al., 1994; Lombardo, 1994).

Transinstitutionalization

The corollary of deinstitutionalization is transinstitutionalization, as the mentally ill move from one facility or location to another. Brown (1985) refers to this process as one in which the location and some of the

319

characteristics of institutional living change, but the underlying control and rigidity remain. This process is influenced by changes in Medicare and Medicaid policy and, as such, affects the elderly in particular. During the first wave of deinstitutionalization, state hospitals had an economic incentive to transinstitutionalize elderly patients into nursing and board-and-care homes, as well as dump them into the community (Persky, 1992).

Medicalization

Current financing and reimbursement policies tend to favor medically oriented over psychologically oriented care (Swan & Gerard, 1987) and inpatient over outpatient services, thus "reaffirming the medical/psychiatric role as the primary source for mental illness treatment" (Kenig, 1992, p. 190). This medicalization of the mental health field reflects larger trends in health care (Estes & Binney, 1988), evidenced in the convergence of the biological and psychodynamic arenas relevant to aging (Cohen, 1989). Also, as preferential treatment is given to those who are chronically mentally ill or who can be treated on a short-term basis through drugs and short-term institutionalization, resources are diverted from the socially supportive continuity of care needed by elderly with problems such as depression and anxiety (two of the most prevalent disorders in older adults). Medicalization also contributes to overreliance on psychotropic drugs, which are often prescribed inappropriately (Bliwise et al., 1987; Brown, 1985; Burns et al., 1993; Gottlieb, 1992).

Informalization

Binney, Estes, and Humphers (1993) suggest that as certain groups of mentally ill are denied treatment because of policy and funding shifts, patients sometimes drop out of the formal delivery system into the informal sector of the home and family. Homelessness represents a severe type of informalization, as patients drop or are forced out of the system altogether. Estimates are that one third of the homeless are chronically mentally ill. Much more needs to be known about the mental health profiles and service patterns of the population.

SUMMARY OF RECOMMENDATIONS

Research

A substantial future research agenda is required. Studies are needed on the structure and performance of mental health delivery in terms of access, quality, and cost. Data are needed on the range and scope of services needed and utilized by older adults, with particular attention to issues of race, ethnicity, social class, and gender. Little is known about whether or how the elderly are served by providers of different types (for-profit, nonprofit, and public) or about the effects of current reimbursement and policy on service utilization and access by elders. Community-level studies are required to examine the interorganizational relationships between local mental health providers and providers of other services to the elderly in the continuum of long-term care, such as nursing home, adult day, and home care; hospitalization; social services; and housing. Research is needed to assess the extent and effects of deinstitutionalization and transinstitutionalization for specific populations and diagnostic groups.

More specifically, research is needed to address the following questions:

1. How do different types of practice settings (e.g., for-profit, nonprofit, and public agencies; independent vs. multifacility-linked agencies) and structures (e.g., managed care vs. traditional fee-for-service and HMO models) influence the outcome of mental health care for elders?

2. What are the treatment and outcome differences, if any, for elders receiving outpatient and inpatient mental health care from mental health specialists and from other providers?

3. How do managed care and managed care organizations, as well as other fiscal and environmental conditions in the private and public mental health system affect the access, cost, and quality of mental health services?

4. What are the nature and effects of the relationships between institutional and community-based mental health and managed care, and between home care and mental health provider organizations and agencies in the provision of mental health services to the elderly?

5. How have managed "carve-outs" in mental health affected the utilization, as a measure of access, of mental health services by at-risk elderly? How are such programs structured, and which types of programs have increased utilization of needed services by the elderly?

6. What demographic, organizational, environmental, or policy factors explain referral to and receipt of mental health services by the elderly? How is the receipt of mental health services linked to other types of long-term care services? What are the constraints or barriers to referral and utilization of mental health services, including gender, race, ethnicity, and social class?

At the policy and systems levels, additional research questions must be addressed:

1. What are the characteristics of the mental health delivery system for the elderly (structure, volume, and distribution of service)?

2. What are the implications of federal, state, and local policy on mental health services access, utilization, and cost for the elderly?

3. What is the extent of coverage for mental health services in supplemental health insurance policies, and how does it affect access to mental health services by Medicare beneficiaries?

4. What are the effects on mental health care utilization and expenditures of Medicare policy (e.g., OBRA 1987 and OBRA 1989) and other medical provisions, including the 50% coinsurance for many outpatient mental health services, such as counseling and psychotherapy?

5. What are the effects of Medicaid policy changes on the cost, quality, and access of mental health services for elders and for particular subgroups of older persons (e.g., minorities, women, low income)?

Mental Health Policy

In the absence of a coherent, comprehensive mental health policy for the elderly, older adults will continue to be overlooked in an increasingly fragmented, "corporatized" service delivery system. The unique needs of the elderly—both physical and mental—need to be addressed, and systems of general, long term, and mental health care need to work together with, not independently of, each other. Policies and funding strategies at both the federal and the state levels must permit adequate care for the physical, social, and mental needs of the elderly (Lurie, Swan, et al., 1987).

The mental health field is increasingly experiencing restructuring and cost-containment pressures similar to those that confront the health care delivery system as a whole. Given the variability of benefits and resource commitments across the states, mental health systems reform is needed to assure universal access to the comprehensive mental health benefits that older persons need. Such benefits include continuity of care, basic therapies such as treatment and counseling for depression, and sustained mental health treatment that takes the physical needs of the elderly into account. Close cooperation is needed between the medical and psychosocial disciplines, since the elderly often require treatment in both spheres, and special attention should be paid to the long-term, severely disabled population, in order to accommodate the needs of these oldest, sickest, and least compliant patients. Finally, specific requirements and financing of psychogeriatric services such as those incorporated in the now abolished Community Mental Health Centers Act of 1975 need to be reconsidered in light of other health and mental health reform initiatives that emerge in 1995 and beyond.

REFERENCES

Baker, F. M. (1992). Ethnic minority elders: A mental health research agenda. *Hospital and Community Psychiatry, 43,* 337-342.

Binney, E. A., Estes, C. L., & Humphers, S. (1993). The long term care crisis: Elders trapped in the no care zone. *Informalization and Community Care.* (pp. 166-169). Newbury Park, CA: Sage.

Binney, E. A., & Swan, J. (1991). The political economy of mental health care for the elderly. In C. L. Estes & M. Minkler (Eds.), *Critical Perspectives on Aging: The Political and Moral Economy of Growing Old.* (pp. 165-188). Amityville, NY: Baywood Publishing, Inc.

Birren, J. E., Sloane, R. B., & Cohen, G. D. (Eds.). (1992). *Handbook of mental health and aging* (2nd ed.). San Diego, CA: Academic Press.

Bliwise, N. G., McCall, M. E., & Swan, S. J. (1987). The epidemiology of mental illness in late life. In E. E. Lurie, J. H. Swan et al. (Eds.), *Serving the mentally ill elderly: Problems and perspectives.* Lexington, MA: Lexington/Heath.

Brown, P. (1985). *The transfer of care: Psychiatric deinstitutionalization and its aftermath.* London: Routledge and Kegan Paul.

Brown, P., & Cooksey, E. (1989). Mental health monopoly: Corporate trends in mental health services. *Social Science and Medicine, 28,* 1129-1138.

Bruce, M. L., & McNamara, R. (1992). Psychiatric status among the homebound elderly: An epidemiologic perspective. *Journal of the American Geriatrics Society, 40*, 561-566.

Burns, B., Wagner, H. R., Taube, J. E., Magaziner, J., Permutt, T., & Landerman, L. R. (1993). Mental health service use by the elderly in nursing homes. *American Journal of Public Health, 83*, 331-337.

Burns, B., & Taube, C. A. (1990). Mental health services in general medical care and nursing homes. In B. S. Fogel, A. Furino, & G. Gottlieb (Eds.), *Mental health policy for older Americans: Protecting minds at risk*. Washington, DC: American Psychiatric Association.

Center for Mental Health Services & National Institute of Mental Health. (1992). *Mental health, United States, 1992* (DHHS Publication No. SMA 92-1942). Washington, DC: U.S. Government Printing Office.

Cohen, G. (1989). The interface of mental and physical health phenomena in later life: New directions in geriatric psychiatry. *Gerontology and Geriatrics Education, 9*, 27-38.

Colenda, C. C., & van Dooren, H. (1993). Opportunities for improving community mental health services for elderly persons. *Hospital and Community Psychiatry, 44*, 531-533.

Cuffel, B. J., Snowden, L., Masland, M. C., & Piccagli, G. (1994). *Managed mental health care in the public sector* (working paper). Berkeley, CA: Institute for Mental Health Services Research.

Dorwart, R. A., & Epstein, L. (1993). *The privatization of mental health care*. Westport, CT: Auburn House.

Dougherty, C. (1988). Mind, money, and morality: Ethical dimensions of economic change in American psychiatry. *Hastings Center Report, 18*, 15-20.

Drolen, C. S. (1990). Current community mental health center operations: Entrepreneurship or business as usual? *Community Mental Health Journal, 26*,(6), 547-559.

Eichmann, M. A., Griffin, B. P., Lyons, J. S., Larson, D. B., & Finkel, S. (1992). An estimation of the impact of OBRA 1987 on nursing home care in the United States. *Hospital and Community Psychiatry, 43*, 781-789.

Estes, C. L., & Alford, R. (1990). Systemic crisis and the nonprofit sector: Toward a political economy of the nonprofit health and social services sector. *Theory and Society, 19*, 173-198.

Estes, C. L., & Binney, E. A. (1988). The biomedicalization of aging: Dangers and dilemmas. *The Gerontologist, 29*, 587-596.

Estes, C. L., Binney, E. A., Linkins, K. W., et al. (1994). *Community mental health services and the elderly: Structure, access and outreach*. Final report to AARP/Andrus Foundation, University of California, Institute for Health and Aging, San Francisco.

Estes, C. L., & Harrington, C. A. (1981). Fiscal crisis, deinstitutionalization, and the elderly. *American Behavioral Scientist, 24*, 811-826.

Estes, C. L., Swan, J. H., et al. (1993). *The long term care crisis*. Newbury Park, CA: Sage.

Estes, C. L., & Wood, J. B. (1984). A preliminary assessment of the impact of block grants on community mental health centers. *Hospital and Community Psychiatry, 35*, 1125-1129.

Feinson, M. C. (1990). Underutilization of community mental health services by elders: Examining policy barriers. *Medicine and Law, 9*, 1044-1051.

Flemming, A. S., Buchanan, J. G., Santos, J. F., & Rickards, L. D. (1986). *Mental health services for the elderly: Report of a survey of community mental health centers. Vol. 3.* Washington, DC: Action Committee to Implement the Mental Health Recommendations of the 1981 White House Conference on Aging.

Freiman, M. P., Arons, B. S., Goldman, H., & Burns, B. J. (1990). Nursing home reform and the mentally ill. *Health Affairs, 9,* 47-60.

Freiman, M. P., Cunningham, P. J., & Cornelius, L. J. (1994). *Use and expenditures for the treatment of mental health problems* (AHCPR Publication No. 94-0085; National Medical Expenditure Survey Research Findings 22). Rockville, MD: Author.

Frisman, L. K., & McGuire, T. G. (1989). The economics of long-term care for the mentally ill. *Journal of Social Issues, 45,* 119-130.

Gatz, M., & Smyer, M. A. (1992). The mental health system and older adults in the l990s. *American Psychologist, 46,* 741-751.

Goldman, H. H., & Frank, R. G. (1990). Division of responsibility among payers. In B. Fogel, A. Furino, & G. L. Gottlieb (Eds.), *Mental health policy for older Americans: Protecting minds at risk* (pp. 85-96). Washington, DC: American Psychiatric Press.

Goldman, H. H., Taube, C. A., & Jenks, S. (1987). The organization of the psychiatric inpatient services system. *Medical Care, 25*(Suppl.), 6-21.

Goldstein, M. Z. (1994). Taking another look at the older patient and the mental health system. *Hospital and Community Psychiatry, 45,* 117-119.

Goldstein, M. Z., & Perkins, C. A. (1993). Mental health and the aging woman. *Clinics in Geriatric Medicine, 9,* 191-196.

Goldstrom, I. (1993). Unpublished from the 1986 Data Client/Patient Sample Survey of inpatient/outpatient and partial care program.

Gottlieb, G. L. (1992). Economic issues and geriatric mental health care. In J. E. Birren, R. B. Sloane, & G. D. Cohen (Eds.), *Handbook of mental health and aging* (2nd ed., pp. 873-893). San Diego, CA: Academic Press.

Gottlieb, G. L. (1993, July 15). *Mental health and aging* (Forum before U.S. Senate Special Committee on Aging, No. 103-10, pp. 84-90). Washington, DC: U.S. Government Printing Office.

Gurian, B. (1982). Mental health outreach and consultation services for the elderly. *Hospital and Community Psychiatry, 33,* 142-146.

Hadley, T. R., & Culhane, D. P. (1993). The status of community mental health centers 10 years into block grant financing. *Community Mental Health Journal, 29,* 95-102.

Hu, T., Cuffel, B. J., & Masland, M. C. (1994). *The effect of contracting on the cost of public mental health services in California* (working paper). Berkeley, CA: Institute for Mental Health Services Research.

Jones, V. Y., & Estes, C. L. (in press). Older women: Income, retirement and health. In S. Ruzek, V. Olesen, & A. Clark (Eds.), *Women's health: Dynamics of diversity.* San Francisco: Department of Social and Behavioral Sciences.

Katz, S. E., & Cancro, R. (1982). The metamorphosis of the county psychiatric service. *Hospital and Community Psychiatry, 33,* 728-731.

Kiesler, C. A., & Sibulkin, A. E. (1987). *Medical hospitalization: Myths and facts about a national crisis.* Newbury Park, CA: Sage.

Kenig, S. (1992). *Who pays? Who plays? Who cares? A case study in applied sociology, political economy, and the community mental health centers movement.* Amityville, NY: Baywood.

Knight, R. (1991, Winter). Outreach to older adults: Matching programs to specific needs. *New Directions for Mental Health Services.*

Lair, T. J., Smyer, M. A., Goldman, H., & Arons, B. (1989, November). *Mental illness and the impact of nursing home reform: Estimates from the National Medical Expenditure Survey.* Paper presented at the annual meeting of the Gerontological Society of America, Minneapolis, MN.

Lave, J. R., & Goldman, H. H. (1990). Medicare financing for mental health care. *Health Affairs, 9,* 19-30.

Lebowitz, B., Light, E., & Bailey, F. (1987). Mental health center services for the elderly: The impact of coordination with area agencies on aging. *The Gerontologist, 27,* 699-702.

Lombardo, N. E. (1994). *Barriers to mental health services for nursing home residents* (Series 9401). Washington DC: American Association of Retired Persons Public Policy Institute.

Lurie, E. E. (1987). The interrelationship of physical and mental illness in the elderly. In E. E. Lurie, J. Swan et al. (Eds.), *Serving the mentally ill elderly: Problems and perspectives.* Lexington, MA: Lexington/Heath.

Lurie, E. E., Swan, J., et al. (1987). *Serving the mentally ill elderly: Problems and perspectives.* Lexington, MA: Lexington/Heath.

Manderscheid, R. W., Witkin, M. J., Rosenstein, M. J., & Bass, R. D. (1984). A review of trends in mental health services. *Hospital and Community Psychiatry, 35,* 673-674.

McCombs, H. G. (1993). Access of minority elderly to mental health services. *Mental health and aging* (Forum before the U.S. Senate Special Committee on Aging, No. 103-10, pp. 67-73). Washington, DC: U.S. Government Printing Office.

McGuire, T. G. (1989). Outpatient benefits for mental health services in Medicare: Alignment with the private sector? *American Psychologist, 44,* 818-824.

National Institutes of Health. (1992). Consensus development panel on depression in late life. *Journal of the American Medical Association, 268,* (8), 1018-1024.

Paulson, R. (1988). People and garbage are not the same: Issues in contracting for public mental health services. *Community Mental Health Journal, 24,* 91-102.

Persky, T. (1992). *A study of Philadelphia's licensed personal care homes: Characteristics of the homes and profile of elderly residents.* Philadelphia, PA.

Rice, D. P., Kelman, S., Miller, L. S., & Dunmeyer, S. (1990). *The economic costs of alcohol and drug abuse and mental illness.* San Francisco: University of California Institute for Health and Aging.

Rickards, L. D. (1993). The coalition on mental health and aging. In Mental health and aging: Progress and prospects. *Generations: Journal of the American Society on Aging,* Winter/Spring, 81-82.

Rochefort, D. A., & Logan, B. M. (1989). The alcohol, drug abuse, and mental health block grant: Origins, design, and impact. In D. A. Rochefort (Ed.), *Mental health policy in the United States* (pp. 143-170). New York: Greenwood.

Roughan, P. (1993). Mental health and psychiatric disorders in older women. *Clinics in Geriatric Medicine, 9,* 173-190.

Sanchez, C. D. (1992). Mental health issues: The elderly Hispanic. *Journal of Geriatric Psychiatry, 25,* 69-84

Scheffler, R. (1992). *An empirical analysis of "contracting out" in California mental health departments* (working paper). Berkeley, CA: Institute for Mental Health Services Research.

Scheffler, R., Grogan, C., Cuffel, B., & Penner, S. (1993). *A specialized mental health plan for persons with severe mental illness under managed competition* (working paper). Berkeley, CA: Institute for Mental Health Services Research.

Shane, P. (1987). Linkages between the mental health and aging systems from the perspective of the aging network. In E. E. Lurie, J. H. Swan et al. (Eds.), *Serving the mentally ill elderly: Problems and perspectives* (pp. 179-202). Lexington, MA: Lexington/Heath.

Shapiro, S., Skinner, E. A., Kramer, M., et al. (1985). Measuring need for mental health services in a general population. *Medical Care, 23,* 1033-1043.

Sharfstein, S. S. (1982). Medicaid cutbacks and block grants: Crisis or opportunity for community mental health? *American Journal of Psychiatry, 139,* 66-70.

Sherman, J. (1992). *Medicare's mental health benefits: Coverage, utilization, and expenditures* (No. 9206). Washington, DC: American Association of Retired Persons Public Policy Institute.

Smith, D., & Jensen S. (1990). *OBRA—Its effect on the mentally ill in South Dakota nursing homes.*

Smith, M. (1993). Access to mental health services in rural settings. *Mental health and aging* (Forum before the U.S. Senate Special Committee on Aging, No. 103-10, pp. 78-82). Washington, DC: U.S. Government Printing Office.

Stotsky, B. A., & Stotsky, E. S. (1983). Nursing homes: Improving a flawed community facility. *Hospital and Community Psychiatry, 34,* 238-242.

Surles, R. (1991). Toward a national mental health policy. *Psychiatric Quarterly, 62,* 267-275.

Swan, J. H., Bergthold, L., & Estes, C. L. (1988). Community mental health in an era of hospital prospective payment. In C. L. Estes, & J. B. Wood (Eds.), *Organizational and community responses to Medicare policy: Consequences for health and social services for the elderly* (3 vols., final report). San Francisco: University of California, Institute for Health and Aging.

Swan, J. H., Fox, P. J., & Estes, C. L. (1986). Community mental health services and the elderly: Retrenchment or expansion? *Community Mental Health Journal, 22,* 275-285.

Swan, J. H., & Gerard, L. E. (1987). Reimbursement and funding systems. In E. E. Lurie & J. Swan (Eds.), *Serving the mentally ill elderly: Problems and perspectives* (pp. 111-138). Lexington, MA: Lexington/Heath.

Swan, J. H., & McCall, N. (1987). Mental health components and the aged. In E. E. Lurie & J. Swan et al. (Eds.), *Serving the mentally ill elderly: Problems and perspectives* (p. 111). Lexington, MA: Lexington/Heath.

Taube, C. A., Goldman, H. H., & Salkever, D. (1990). Medicaid coverage for mental illness: Balancing access and costs. *Health Affairs, 9,* 5-18.

U.S. General Accounting Office. (1992). *The elderly remain in need of mental health services* (GAO/HRD-B2-112). Gaithersburg, MD: U.S. Government Printing Office.

White, J. (1991). Mental healthcare: Access, excess, and fragmentation. *Health Progress, 72,* 12-14.

APPENDIX A

Resolutions of the White House Mini-Conference on Emerging Issues in Mental Health and Aging

I n the next two decades, the United States will undergo a major demographic shift. Currently, 12% of adults are over age 65—the largest proportion in our nation's history. By 2025, this proportion is estimated to increase to 20%. There is a pressing need to understand the social and economic impact of this enormous demographic change. An area of particular importance is how a range of mental health issues will affect our midlife and older population.

The purpose of the White House Mini-Conference on Emerging Issues in Mental Health and Aging was to make resolutions to address a number of mental health issues that may change in significant ways and assume even greater importance as the population ages. The conference, held February 24–26, 1995, at the Embassy Suites Hotel in Washington, DC, focused on emerging issues within major mental health and aging areas. Conference attendees addressed the following four major areas:

- *Promoting recognition of mental health as an integral component of general health and personal well-being*

There have been major advances in the understanding and treatment of mental disorders, yet the resources our society devotes to address mental disorders continue to fall far short of what is needed, particularly when compared with the resources that are expended on physical conditions. It is essential to identify the reasons behind this pattern so that strategies for improving it can be developed.

- *Promoting optimal mental health as people age*

The majority of older adults do not have mental disorders. However, the process of aging requires continual adaptation in the face of changing personal circumstances. It is essential that our aging population be educated to recognize both the scope and the limits of their personal resources and to seek and receive the services they need to cope effectively with changes, so that they may continue functioning at the highest possible level.

- *Expanding and consolidating the scientific knowledge base of late-life mental disorders*

A review of the strengths and limitations of the research knowledge base related to late-life mental disorders and the infrastructure available to meet changing needs in the treatment of these disorders is needed to determine their current status. Prevention of and early interventions in mental illness, with a particular emphasis on cultural and ethnic differences among the cohorts, also need review.

- *Increasing access to mental health services*

Key elements of access include community-based service models, with particular emphasis on increasing the involvement of consumers and family; patterns of education and training of mental health service providers, including both the mental health and social service disciplines; and the preparation of nontraditional service providers, such as the clergy and those who serve "gatekeeper" functions.

MAIN RESOLUTION

During the May 1995 White House Conference on Aging, the following main resolution was brought forth to consolidate a full set of resolutions written and approved by participants in the White House Mini-Conference on Emerging Issues in Mental Health and Aging. The full set of resolutions can be found beginning on page 341. This resolution does not necessarily reflect the positions of the individual participants in the White House Conference on Aging Mini-Conference on Emerging Issues in Mental Health and Aging or of the organizations or agencies that they represent.

Meeting Mental Health Needs

WHEREAS quality of life and optimal functioning depend upon physical and mental health; and

WHEREAS research indicates the efficacy of mental health interventions, illness prevention, and health promotion produce positive health outcomes; and

WHEREAS substantial numbers of older persons residing in the community have mental health needs and approximately half of nursing home residents have serious mental disorders that are often undiagnosed and untreated; and

WHEREAS there is an insufficient supply of practitioners, including primary care providers, who are adequately prepared in the promotion of optimal mental health and the recognition and treatment of mental disorders among diverse populations; and

WHEREAS older adults are experienced, knowledgeable, and effective resources for meeting their own and others' mental health needs.

Resolution Statements

THEREFORE BE IT RESOLVED THAT the 1995 White House Conference on Aging (WHCoA) support policies that:

    a. Ensure access to an affordable, comprehensive range of quality mental and physical health care, including outreach, in-home, preventive, acute, and long-term care services,

b. Amend all statutes that regulate public and private health and long-term care insurance plans to achieve parity in coverage and reimbursement for mental and physical health disorders, eliminate exclusions based on preexisting conditions, set standards for health plans, and ensure consumer rights,

c. Expand education and training programs (a) for all providers to include the development of faculty with clinical research expertise in mental health and aging, aging and mental health content, and continuing education in mental health and aging; (b) for older adults, their families and caregivers, and (c) for nontraditional urban and rural gatekeepers to ensure access for those most at risk,

d. Support an expedited mental health and aging research agenda that includes funding for basic, clinical, and services research and ensures that findings are widely disseminated, and

BE IT FURTHER RESOLVED THAT federal, state, and local public policies recognize older adults as a primary resource for maintenance and achievement of mental health, and that consumers be significantly involved in the planning and development of mental health research, systems, services, and programs.

FORWARDED RESOLUTIONS

At the direction of participants in the White House Mini-Conference on Emerging Issues in Mental Health and Aging, members of the planning committee revised and collapsed the full set of approved resolutions beginning on page 341 into one in each of five primary topic areas and submitted them to the White House Conference on Aging. The forwarded resolutions do not necessarily reflect the positions of individual participants in the Mini-Conference on Emerging Issues in Mental Health and Aging or of the organizations or agencies that they represent.

Mental Health and Aging Policy

WHEREAS optimal functioning in society depends upon both the physical and mental capacity of its citizens, and the coexistence of mental and physical illness impairs the functioning and quality of life of older adults, leading to increased social and economic dependence; and

WHEREAS research indicates that a substantial number of older persons residing in the community have a mental disorder, and more than half of nursing home residents have serious mental disorders that are often undiagnosed and/or untreated; and

WHEREAS mental disorders can amplify the negative effects associated with other medical conditions, cause considerable excess disability and mortality, and are associated with older Americans having the highest suicide rate of any age group in the United States; and

WHEREAS most Americans do not have access to comprehensive, integrated mental and physical health services, and older persons with mental disorders are greatly underserved by both public and private mental health systems; and

WHEREAS current federal, state, and private reimbursement policies discourage appropriate access to mental health services by paying a lower percentage for mental health services and by allowing mental health services under Medicaid to be offered as an optional rather than a mandatory service; and

WHEREAS current federal, state, and private reimbursement policies discourage appropriate access to mental health treatment by providing fewer benefits for mental health than physical health care, by allowing Medicaid to offer mental health as optional rather than as mandatory services, and by Medicare and Medicaid reimbursement policies that are biased toward institutional rather than community-based care; and

WHEREAS private fee-for-service insurance and managed care systems have limited and reduced access to outpatient mental health care by restricting benefits packages and excluding coverage for persons with preexisting conditions; and

WHEREAS there is ample research evidence of the benefits and efficacy of mental health interventions for older persons; and

WHEREAS there are validated mental health promotion methods and techniques, which can be a cost-effective means to contain medical expenses.

Resolution Statements

THEREFORE BE IT RESOLVED THAT the federal government take steps to ensure that all older persons have access to an affordable, comprehensive range of mental and physical health services, including preventive, acute, and long-term care services. These steps should include:

    a. Congress and state legislatures amending all statutes that regulate public and private health and long-term care insurance programs so that reimbursement for services to treat mental disorders reaches parity with reimbursement for services to treat physical illnesses,

    b. insurance reform to eliminate discriminatory practices including exclusion based on preexisting conditions,

    c. coordination of mental health services with acute and long-term health care and aging network services,

    d. the creation of mechanisms to protect consumers by setting standards for health plans and ensuring consumer rights,

    e. mandated coverage of a package of services at a level no less than the core mental health services now required under the Community Mental Health Services Act of 1963, including outreach and in-home mental health services, and

BE IT FURTHER RESOLVED THAT states certify health insurance plans to ensure the inclusion of these principles and monitor quality, access, and availability of mental health care in both the public and private sectors, foster collaboration between and among state and local mental health and aging services programs, and expand their state mental health agency priority populations to include older adults.

Access to Mental Health Care

WHEREAS there are great diversities within the older population, with rapidly growing segments being the oldest old, the poorest, and members of ethnic and cultural minority groups; and

WHEREAS the presentation of mental disorders and the appropriateness of services varies among diverse populations; and

WHEREAS many older citizens do not recognize and identify their own service needs or do not know how to access and use the service delivery system; and

WHEREAS mental health services for older adults tend to focus on the diagnosis and treatment of illness with inadequate attention to early identification of high-risk individuals, preventive measures, and the promotion of optimal mental health; and

WHEREAS there is evidence that illness prevention and health promotion models produce positive health outcomes; and

WHEREAS older adults typically use primary care providers as a point of entry to the health care delivery system, and primary care physicians are not adequately prepared to identify mental health needs and available resources to meet those needs; and

WHEREAS the existing federal, state, and private funding streams for mental health services are separate, uncoordinated, and fragmented; and

WHEREAS current federal, state, and private funding sources discourage appropriate access to mental health services by paying a lower percentage for these services under Medicare and by providing optional rather than mandatory coverage for mental health services under Medicaid; and

WHEREAS current federal and state policies are biased toward institutional care and against the provision of mental health services in the least restrictive settings, and discourage prevention, health promotion, active case finding, and outreach; and

WHEREAS managed care is rapidly revolutionizing the health care delivery system and bringing about a diversity of standards and benefit structures.

Resolution Statements

THEREFORE BE IT RESOLVED THAT Congress amend Medicare, Medicaid, and other federal funding programs to encourage a wide range of coordinated, affordable, and culturally appropriate public and private integrated health and mental health services that promote the dignity, autonomy, independence, and well-being of older adults with mental health needs, provided without discrimination or bias; and

BE IT FURTHER RESOLVED THAT Congress provide funding to systems of community-based mental health care to establish and maintain culturally sensitive case-finding strategies, including (a) the training of nontraditional, urban, and rural community "gate-keepers," examples of whom are employees of utility companies, banks, civil servants, and postal workers; and (b) routine administration of screening for cognitive, behavioral, and emotional disorders by health care providers such as primary care physicians and nurse practitioners; and

BE IT FURTHER RESOLVED THAT appropriate public and private funding sources provide for the development, demonstration, evaluation, and rapid translation into practice of prevention and health promotion models; that these models be made an integral part of primary and secondary health care services; that these models provide for early identification of high-risk individuals; and that these models be holistic (including alternative approaches), be accessible and culturally acceptable, and be available in a range of settings; and

BE IT FURTHER RESOLVED THAT there be a federally supported consensus conference to develop and promulgate a set of federal standards of practice for primary care providers and managed care systems that incorporate multidimensional assessment and collaborative service provision to meet consumer mental health needs.

Education and Training in Mental Health and Aging

WHEREAS the older population will increase in the next three decades, especially the oldest old and minority populations; and

WHEREAS mental disorders such as depression, dementia, delirium, and substance abuse are highly prevalent among older Americans, yet are underrecognized by health care practitioners; and

WHEREAS untreated mental disorders cause morbidity, disability, and mortality, including suicide; and

WHEREAS the recognition and treatment of mental disorders can prevent disability; promote a higher level of health, social, and economic functioning; reduce family and caregiver stress; and prevent premature death; and

WHEREAS providing education regarding aging issues to professionals and to the general public is a key component of promoting optimal mental health; and

WHEREAS persons providing care and services to the elderly possess widely varying skills and knowledge; and

WHEREAS there is currently an insufficient supply of health and mental health practitioners, including primary care providers, who have received adequate preparation in the recognition and treatment of mental illness among diverse populations[1]; and

WHEREAS there is currently an insufficient supply of researchers trained in mental health and aging.

---

[1]Diversity encompasses age, gender, ethnicity, culture, and socioeconomic status.

Resolution Statements

THEREFORE BE IT RESOLVED THAT Congress and the states maintain and expand funded mental health and aging education and training programs; and

BE IT FURTHER RESOLVED THAT mental health and aging education, training, and research training be funded by the private sector as well as federal and state governments and that this training include (a) exposure to issues of mental health and aging as part of training for all health care and other service providers; (b) continuing education for all such providers; (c) preparation of clinical providers with expertise in mental health and aging; (d) development of faculty with expertise in mental health and aging issues; and (e) development of faculty with research expertise in mental health and aging; and

BE IT FURTHER RESOLVED THAT other stakeholders, including older adults, their families, caregivers, and paraprofessionals receive appropriate training in mental health and aging; and

BE IT FURTHER RESOLVED THAT public policy ensure that health and mental health practitioner programs and clinical settings emphasize the importance of interdisciplinary collaboration in the provision of mental health services and the importance of including individuals, their families, and caregivers in the treatment process; and

BE IT FURTHER RESOLVED THAT each of the health care professions establish standards for minimal competence in mental health and aging and criteria for credentialing practitioners as specialists in mental health and aging; and

BE IT FURTHER RESOLVED THAT states establish mechanisms to require content on mental health and aging in the education and training of all professional disciplines serving the elderly and that such training be a condition required for licensure, relicensure, and certification or recertification.

Research Agenda for Mental Health and Aging

WHEREAS the mental disorders of late life represent major burdens to older Americans, their families, and communities in terms of direct cost of care, suffering, disability, institutionalization, and the amplification of morbidity and increased mortality from coexisting general medical conditions, (e.g., depression coexisting with cardiovascular disease and strokes); and

WHEREAS the burdens of late-life mental health challenges and disorders disproportionately affect the oldest old and reach into all of the diverse communities and settings in which older people live and receive care; and

WHEREAS the elderly population will double from the current level of 12% to 20% by the year 2025; and

WHEREAS the public health impact of late-life mental disorders will increase at a rate even faster than the elderly population as a whole due to the selective growth in the numbers of those who are oldest, most frail, and most vulnerable; and

WHEREAS research is currently generating unprecedented advances in understanding the mechanisms of disease and in developing effective treatments; and

WHEREAS significant areas important to building an adequate knowledge base have been underestimated (such as the oldest old, the socioeconomically vulnerable, and ethnic minorities as well as the conditions and characteristics that protect and enhance mental health).

Resolution Statements

THEREFORE BE IT RESOLVED THAT the federal government support an expedited mental health and aging research agenda and ensure that findings are widely disseminated; and

BE IT FURTHER RESOLVED THAT Congress appropriate a doubling in terms of constant dollars in funding for basic, clinical, and services research in mental health and aging over the next decade through 12% annual increases to enhance the development of effective preventive and treatment interventions to meet the needs of current and future generations of older individuals.

Consumer Involvement in Mental Health and Aging

WHEREAS older adults of all races, cultures, and socioeconomic circumstances are themselves a primary source of information about the status and factors of their mental health; and

WHEREAS older adults as a group are an experienced, knowledgeable, and effective resource for meeting their own mental health needs, as well as for helping others with similar needs; and

WHEREAS there is no national, organized voice specific to mentally ill *older* adults; and

WHEREAS it is nationally recognized that issues of access, comprehensiveness, and quality of mental health services depend in considerable part on consumer and family involvement, participation, and advocacy; and

WHEREAS there is a lack of education, training, and support for families and caregivers on caring for older persons with mental illness.

Resolution statements

THEREFORE BE IT RESOLVED THAT public policy at the national, state, and local levels recognize older adults as a primary resource for the maintenance and achievement of mental health, and that consumers be significantly involved in the planning and development of mental health research, systems, and programs; and

BE IT FURTHER RESOLVED THAT care be consumer focused,

involving a partnership among providers, consumers, and significant others; and

BE IT FURTHER RESOLVED THAT an active constituency of consumers and significant others for purposes of advocacy in the care and treatment of mentally ill *older* adults be strengthened; and

BE IT FURTHER RESOLVED THAT the federal and state governments and the private sector initiate a continuum of educational efforts ranging from a public awareness program on the issues of mental health and aging to specific competency-based preparation for all providers, including paraprofessionals and professionals.

CONSENSUS RESOLUTIONS

During the closing session of the Mini-Conference, participants reached consensus in adopting the following resolutions. The resolutions of the White House Conference on Aging Mini-Conference on Emerging Issues in Mental Health and Aging are the collective efforts of the participants. They do not necessarily reflect the positions of the individual participants or of the organizations or agencies that they represent.

TOPIC: The need for multidimensional health assessment and collaborative service delivery at the primary care level

Statement of Issue 1

WHEREAS health is a multidimensional construct that must be addressed from a variety of perspectives, including mental health and quality of life; and

WHEREAS older adults typically use primary care providers as a point of entry to the health care delivery system; and

WHEREAS primary care providers must be adequately prepared to identify mental health needs and available resources to meet those needs; and

WHEREAS managed care is rapidly revolutionizing the health care delivery system and bringing about a diversity of standards and benefit structures.

Resolution Statement 1

THEREFORE BE IT RESOLVED THAT there be a federally supported consensus conference to develop and promulgate a set of federal standards of practice for primary care providers that incorporate multidimensional assessment and collaborative service provision to meet consumer mental health needs.

TOPIC: Need for research addressing the relationships between the mental and physical components of health

Statement of Issue 2

WHEREAS the advances in clinical and basic research in mental health and aging have been the foundation and driving force in the delivery of care; and

WHEREAS there is a need for research models for community-based through long-term care that examine mental health services as an essential component of health services; and

WHEREAS the current empirical knowledge base is based on select portions of the population and does not adequately reflect the heterogeneity of the elderly population as a whole; and

WHEREAS it is estimated that the aging population will double from the current level of 12% to 25% by the year 2010 and that the burden of mental disorders will increase at an even faster pace; and

WHEREAS mental disorders are highly prevalent among older Americans and will increase in the next three decades, yet are often undetected; and

WHEREAS federally funded research advances in the last decade have led to effective treatment and management of these illnesses; and

WHEREAS most Americans do not have access to comprehensive, integrated mental and physical health services; and

WHEREAS optimal functioning in society depends on both physical and mental capacity, and the co-occurrence of mental and physical illness makes it difficult for older adults to function, leading to increased social and economic dependence; and

WHEREAS mental disorders can amplify the negative effects of other medical conditions and cause considerable morbidity, disability, and mortality; and

WHEREAS research and its dissemination and application are essential to building effective service programs for older adults; and

WHEREAS more research is needed on the relative effectiveness and cost of interventions in specific populations.

Resolution Statement 2

THEREFORE BE IT RESOLVED THAT Congress increase federal funding as follows:

    a. to represent a real rate of growth annually,
    b. for research on the interrelationships between the mental and physical components of health at the basic, clinical, and service research levels to promote optimal lifelong health and well-being,
    c. to overcome barriers to the prevention, recognition, and treatment of mental disorders among midlife and older Americans,
    d. to identify methods to disseminate and apply research findings in a variety of educational and practice settings,

e. to ensure that this research reflects the diversity and true complexity of the elderly population, and

f. to expand the range of effective mental health interventions for all older Americans, particularly for at-risk and underserved populations.

TOPIC: Need for increased understanding about the multidimensional components of health

Statement of Issue 3

WHEREAS older adults may underutilize mental health services because of the stigma attached to mental health services, reflecting a general lack of understanding about mental health among the American public; and

WHEREAS currently there is fragmentation among physical, mental, and social services; and

WHEREAS it is critical to recognize that mental health is an essential component of general health in order to better comprehend quality health care; and

WHEREAS research findings about quality health care are inadequately communicated and underutilized by the general public and service providers.

Resolution Statement 3

THEREFORE BE IT RESOLVED THAT public and private initiatives fund the education of the general public, trainers, and service providers on the multidimensional nature of health in order to increase general understanding, empower consumers, promote the transfer of knowledge from research findings to practice, and enhance service integration among providers.

TOPIC: Education and training

Statement of Issue 4

WHEREAS mental disorders such as depression, dementia, delirium, and substance abuse are highly prevalent among older Americans, yet are underrecognized by health care practitioners; and

WHEREAS the older population will increase in the next three decades, especially the oldest old and minority populations; and

WHEREAS there is a serious lack of knowledge and understanding of mental disorders and their impact on the total well-being of older individuals among the general population; and

WHEREAS untreated mental disorders cause morbidity, disability, and mortality, including suicide, and the recognition and treatment of mental disorders can prevent disability; promote a higher level of health, social, and economic functioning; reduce family and caregiver stress; and prevent premature death; and

WHEREAS federally funded research advances in the last decade have led to effective treatment and management of mental disorders; and

WHEREAS health and mental health practitioners, including primary care providers, do not receive sufficient education and training to recognize and treat mental illness among diverse populations.

Resolution Statement 4

THEREFORE BE IT RESOLVED THAT public policy ensure that health and mental health practitioner schools, universities, and clinical settings provide improved education and training for students, providers, and the general public in the prevention, recognition, and treatment of mental illness in diverse older populations; and

BE IT FURTHER RESOLVED THAT this education and training emphasize the importance of interdisciplinary collaboration in the provision of mental health services and the importance of including individuals, their families, and caregivers in the treatment process.

TOPIC: Integrating health and mental health services

Statement of Issue 5

WHEREAS optimal functioning in society depends on both physical and mental capacity; and

WHEREAS the coexistence of mental and physical illness impairs the functioning of older adults, leading to increased social and economic dependence; and

WHEREAS most Americans do not have access to comprehensive, integrated mental and physical health services; and

WHEREAS mental disorders, for example depression and substance abuse, can amplify the negative effects associated with other medical conditions and cause considerable excess morbidity, disability, and mortality; and

WHEREAS the presentation of mental disorders and the appropriateness of prevention and treatment services may vary among diverse populations.

Resolution Statement 5

THEREFORE BE IT RESOLVED THAT public policy ensure that all Americans have access to an affordable, comprehensive range of integrated mental and physical health services, including preventive, acute, and long-term care services; and

BE IT FURTHER RESOLVED THAT providers deliver services in a manner that respects the individual, is adapted to the diversity of the population, and that supports the maintenance of health in addition to managing the acute phase of an illness; and

BE IT FURTHER RESOLVED THAT mental health services provided through capitated and other managed health care plans not be "carved out," and reimbursement for mental health services have parity with reimbursement for physical health services in all health care systems.

TOPIC: Mental illness prevention and health promotion

Statement of Issue 6

WHEREAS mental health services for older adults tend to focus on the diagnosis and treatment of illness with inadequate attention to early identification of high-risk individuals, preventive measures, and the promotion of optimal mental health; and

WHEREAS there are numerous missed opportunities for illness prevention and health promotion activities within the family setting, the community setting, and primary health care settings; and

WHEREAS there is evidence that illness prevention and health promotion models have produced positive health outcomes; and

WHEREAS there has been inadequate funding for prevention and promotion services and for studying the outcomes of these services.

Resolution Statement 6

THEREFORE BE IT RESOLVED THAT mental health promotion and illness prevention be made an integral part of primary and secondary health care services; and

BE IT FURTHER RESOLVED THAT appropriate public and private funding sources provide for the development, demonstration, evaluation, and rapid translation into practice of mental illness prevention and health promotion models; that these models provide for early identification of high-risk individuals; and that these models be holistic (including alternative medicine and other approaches), be accessible and culturally acceptable, and be available in a range of settings.

TOPIC: Ethnic, cultural, and intergenerational differences in promoting mental health service use and preventing illness

Statement of Issue 7

WHEREAS ethnic, cultural, and intergenerational barriers prevent many older citizens from using mental health services; and

WHEREAS current mental health services are designed primarily for the white, middle-class culture; and

WHEREAS there are no recognized national models of intergenerational mental health services and, few if, any that capitalize on ethnic and cultural strengths of individuals, families, and communities; and

WHEREAS current health and mental health professional training curricula contain limited education on ethnic, cultural, and intergenerational diversity.

Resolution Statement 7

THEREFORE BE IT RESOLVED THAT all professional schools and universities include education regarding ethnic, cultural, and intergenerational differences in the training of health and mental health professionals in order to promote optimal mental health, and that all mental health services be accessible, culturally acceptable, and available in a range of settings.

TOPIC: Education and training in mental health promotion and illness prevention

Statement of Issue 8

WHEREAS the number of persons trained to provide mental health services to older adults and their families is inadequate for present and future needs; and

WHEREAS education and training for mental health professionals tend to focus on the diagnosis and treatment of mental illness rather than promotion of mental health; and

WHEREAS mental health services are generally viewed by the public as appropriate only for mentally ill persons.

Resolution Statement 8

THEREFORE BE IT RESOLVED THAT both preservice education and in-service training for all health care professionals include knowledge and skills in the promotion of mental health and prevention of mental illness, and that various professional groups be encouraged to develop certifications in gerontological mental health; and

BE IT FURTHER RESOLVED THAT other stakeholders, including older adults, their caregivers, and paraprofessionals receive appropriate training; and

BE IT FURTHER RESOLVED THAT funding for such education and training come from the private sector as well as federal and state governments.

TOPIC: Research

Statement of Issue 9

WHEREAS the older population is estimated to double from its present level of 12% to 25% by the year 2025; and

WHEREAS optimal mental health in advanced age is beneficial to younger generations as well as to older individuals; and

WHEREAS established knowledge of optimal mental health and of the factors promoting it is currently inadequate.

Resolution Statement 9

THEREFORE BE IT RESOLVED THAT there be an immediate 50% increase in funding, with 12% annual increments thereafter, for research that identifies the criteria and processes of optimal mental health and the conditions that protect and enhance the mental health of midlife and older Americans of diverse social, economic, racial, and cultural backgrounds.

TOPIC: Parity

Statement of Issue 10

WHEREAS mental health and physical health are inseparable; and

WHEREAS there are validated mental health promotion methods and techniques, some of which are not approved as reimbursable services under federal and state laws and by private health insurers; and

WHEREAS optimal mental health promotion is provided by many professional disciplines, paraprofessionals, and volunteers; and

WHEREAS the promotion of optimal mental health can be a cost-effective way to contain medical expenses.

Resolution Statement 10

THEREFORE BE IT RESOLVED THAT Congress and state legislators amend all public health care and long-term care insurance mechanisms so that reimbursement for mental illnesses and mental health promotion reaches parity with service coverage for physical health; and

BE IT FURTHER RESOLVED THAT Congress and state legislators amend all laws that regulate private health care and long-term care insurance so that reimbursement for mental illnesses and for mental health promotion reaches parity with service coverage for physical health.

TOPIC: Support systems

Statement of Issue 11

WHEREAS there are great diversities among the older population, with rapidly growing segments being the oldest old, the poorest, and members of minority groups; and

WHEREAS these groups are at high risk of exposure to environmental, lifestyle, economic, and other factors that adversely affect the development and maintenance of optimal mental health; and

WHEREAS the mental health of older individuals, especially the oldest old, the poor, and members of minority groups, is severely compromised by uncertainties in their financial security and ability to obtain and pay for basic human needs such as shelter, health care, and food.

Resolution Statement 11

THEREFORE BE IT RESOLVED THAT Congress and state legislators enact legislation to ensure that a broad array of affordable and culturally appropriate public and private services that promote mental health and prevent and/or treat mental illnesses are made available to all segments of the older population without discrimination or bias; and

BE IT FURTHER RESOLVED THAT Congress and state legislators protect all older Americans from decreases and discrimination in Medicaid,

Medicare, Social Security, and Department of Veterans Affairs and the Older Americans Act programs.

TOPIC: Funding of research on mental health and aging

Statement of Issue 12[2]

WHEREAS common sense and life experience dictate that state of mind has a significant effect on physical health; and

WHEREAS research has shown that mental disorders have an adverse effect on the course and costs of physical illness in later life; and

---

[2]Notes:

* Research on the course of hospitalization for cardiac and surgical patients with concomitant mental health problems has shown that mental health and aging interventions have reduced hospital stay by as much as 30%, while increasing immediate post-discharge return to home two-fold, such outcomes being associated with significant cost savings beyond reduced patient and family burden.

* Research has shown that there is a 3- to 5-fold increase in mortality during the 6- to 12-month period following a heart attack in patients untreated for co-existing depression.

* Research has shown that over 80% of nursing home residents have mental disorder diagnoses—the underattention to which has resulted in significantly compromised quality of life for residents and considerable anguish for family members.

* Research has shown that older depressed family caregivers of Alzheimer patients have significant changes in their immune systems associated with increased frequency of physical illness, increased physician visits, and increased use of medications.

* Research has shown that suicide rates are greatest in the 65 and older age group, with the highest rates in aging white males.

* "Dementia" is by definition a behavioral term, as discussed in the NIH Consensus Conference Report on the Differential Diagnosis of Dementing Disorders (Number 6, 1987; Bethesda, MD: National Institutes of Health). Because the manifestations of dementia are behavioral (altered intellectual functioning, altered coping, problem behaviors in general), the interventions drawn upon are by necessity behavioral—defining the need for more mental health and aging research, the domain most focused on treating behavioral dysfunction in later life.

* The only way to ultimately reduce the risk factors driving the need for long-term care is through research breakthroughs because, despite how effective the delivery of care becomes, the demographic revolution is producing increased cases; only research breakthroughs can lead to decreased cases in the major disorders creating the need for long-term care.

WHEREAS an expanded mental health and aging research agenda is needed to expand our understanding of the biological, behavioral, and social factors that cause disease and disability and that will lead to new and more effective mental health and aging prevention and treatment strategies to improve overall health and the costs of care; and

WHEREAS mental health changes are the greatest factors influencing the need for long-term care, and mental health and aging research is needed to develop interventions that prolong independence and reduce the need for long-term care, thereby lowering patient suffering, family burden, and societal costs; and

WHEREAS the country is trying to effect positive health care reform and long-term care improvements by the beginning of the next century; and

WHEREAS the elderly population is estimated to double from the current level of 12% to 25% by the year 2010; and

WHEREAS the public health burden of late-life mental disorders will increase at an even faster pace because of the accelerated growth of the oldest and most frail populations; and

WHEREAS current levels of research funding allow only a small proportion of meritorious proposals to be funded; and

WHEREAS unprecedented progress in providing treatment and understanding of the mechanisms of disease processes and outcomes has resulted from research.

Resolution Statement 12

THEREFORE BE IT RESOLVED THAT Congress appropriate a doubling of research funding in constant dollars for mental health and aging research within the next decade, which will require a 12% annual increase.

TOPIC: Research training in mental health and aging

Statement of Issue 13

WHEREAS studies conducted by researchers trained in mental health and aging provide the essential knowledge needed to treat older adults with mental health problems in both the primary care and specialized mental health settings; and

WHEREAS there is a severe shortage of well-trained personnel across a variety of disciplines to conduct basic, clinical, health services, and policy research on critical aging and mental health issues; and

WHEREAS federal research training funding levels represent less than 4% of the total research budget, and these levels have been declining as a proportion of the budget over the past decade; and

WHEREAS given the current demographic revolution, federal, state, local, and private funding sources must give priority to preserving and strengthening the programs, teachers, academic and clinical settings, and other support that will attract into the field and prepare future researchers in aging and mental health.

Resolution Statement 13

THEREFORE BE IT RESOLVED THAT Congress legislate regular increases to bring federal support for research training in mental health and aging to the level of 10% of the total research budget within the next decade.

TOPIC: Special research needs in mental health and aging

Statement of Issue 14

WHEREAS the vast majority of older adults with mental health problems are seen in the primary/general health care setting and settings other than specialized mental health services, and most often exhibit multiple comorbid conditions and functional disabilities; and

WHEREAS an adequate knowledge base is lacking regarding the unique clinical characteristics and care needs of these patients, as well as of ethnic minority patients and other underserved and underresearched subgroups of the elderly; and

WHEREAS the generation of relevant research ideas and the application of research findings is enhanced by a close linkage among researchers, practitioners, and consumer groups.

Resolution Statement 14

THEREFORE BE IT RESOLVED THAT special federal funds be made available and innovative research initiatives be undertaken to build the capacity to expand research into understudied settings and underserved populations of the elderly, to enhance the research/practice interface, and to disseminate and apply research findings in a variety of educational and practice settings.

TOPIC: Special research needs in mental health and aging

Statement of Issue 15

WHEREAS the elderly population is estimated to double from the current level of 12% to 25% by the year 2010; and

WHEREAS the public health burden of late-life mental disorders will increase at an even faster pace because of the accelerated growth of the oldest and most frail populations; and

WHEREAS current levels of research funding allow only a small proportion of meritorious proposals to be funded; and

WHEREAS unprecedented progress in providing treatment and understanding of the mechanisms of disease processes and outcomes has resulted from research.

Resolution Statement 15

THEREFORE BE IT RESOLVED THAT Congress shall appropriate a doubling of research funding in constant dollars (12 percent annual increase), which is proportional to the increase of public health need, dedicated to research on mental health and aging through the year 2010.

TOPIC: Special research needs in mental health and aging

Statement of Issue 16

WHEREAS mental health and mental illness in later life result from interactions among individual history and functioning, family history and functioning, and community contexts; and

WHEREAS there is increasing cultural, ethnic, and geographic diversity among the elderly, their families, and the contexts in which they live; and

WHEREAS the mentally ill elderly seek services in a diverse range of settings such as primary care, long-term care, senior housing, and others.

Resolution Statement 16

THEREFORE BE IT RESOLVED THAT mental health services research and clinical research initiatives be established by appropriate funding agencies to identify the optimal conditions to prevent and/or decrease excess disability of mental disorders in later life and effectively treat them in a range of settings.

TOPIC: Special research needs in mental health and aging

Statement of Issue 17

WHEREAS a variety of formal and informal service providers are in a key position to identify and refer the mentally ill elderly for treatment; and

WHEREAS in addition to expanding the supply of geriatric mental health specialty providers, it is essential to amplify professional expertise through disseminating knowledge and skills to formal and informal service providers; and

WHEREAS technological developments are emerging that can extend the expertise of professionals.

Resolution Statement 17

THEREFORE BE IT RESOLVED THAT research mechanisms be developed to assess the effectiveness of methods designed to overcome the impact of geographic, cultural, and attitudinal barriers to increase public awareness and professional recognition of serious mental illness among older adults.

TOPIC: Health care financing and service systems

Statement of Issue 18

WHEREAS current federal and state polices encourage institutional mental health services and discourage mental health services provided in least-restrictive, community-based settings, such as prevention, active case finding, outreach, community-based intervention, and home visits; and

WHEREAS the existing federal, state and private funding streams are separate, uncoordinated, and fragmented.

Resolution Statement 18

THEREFORE BE IT RESOLVED THAT Congress amend Medicare, Medicaid, and other federal funding programs to encourage a wide range of services that promote the dignity, autonomy, independence, and well-being of older adults with mental health needs, with such services covered at parity with other health care services.

TOPIC: Outreach and intervention

Statement of Issue 19

WHEREAS older citizens living in the community with serious mental health problems most often do not recognize and identify their own service needs or how to access and use the service delivery system, requiring assistance in accomplishing these tasks; and

WHEREAS these same older citizens live alone or with someone who is unable to provide this invaluable function.

Resolution Statement 19

THEREFORE BE IT RESOLVED THAT Congress provide funding to systems of community-based mental health care to establish and maintain culturally sensitive case-finding strategies, including:

a. the training of nontraditional, urban, and rural community "gatekeepers," such as employees of utility companies, banks, civil servants, postal workers, apartment managers, pharmacists, emergency medical technicians, clergy, and volunteers, and
b. increase the routine administration of screening for cognitive, behavioral, and emotional disorders by health care providers, especially those in primary care settings.

TOPIC: Mental health and aging services research

Statement of Issue 20

WHEREAS mental health services research in the aging field lacks models for access and delivery of mental health services at the primary care interface, in long-term care settings, and in community-based mental health programs; and

WHEREAS there is a need to examine access issues in urban and rural settings and among various ethnic groups, genders, residences, and mental statuses; and

WHEREAS new systems of health care and long-term care are developing that have not been adequately studied.

Resolution Statement 20

THEREFORE BE IT RESOLVED THAT the federal government support an expedited mental health and aging health services research agenda that examines the effects of the restructuring of mental health care systems on access, outcomes, and quality of care and that is widely disseminated to policy makers at all levels of government, program administrators, practitioners, advocates, and consumers.

TOPIC: Ensuring equitable access to mental health care

Statement of Issue 21

WHEREAS research indicates that between 18% and 25% of the elderly living in the community have a mental disorder; and

WHEREAS more then 50% of nursing home residents have serious mental disorders, often undiagnosed and untreated; and

WHEREAS seniors with mental disorders are greatly underserved by both the public and private mental health systems; and

WHEREAS the suicide rate for older Americans is 20% of all suicides, which is the highest rate of any age group in the United States; and

WHEREAS there is evidence of the benefits and efficacy of mental health interventions for older persons; and

WHEREAS only 3% of Medicare expenditures are for mental health services; and

WHEREAS there is a lack of parity between reimbursement for mental health and other health services under Medicare; and

WHEREAS under both Medicare and Medicaid there is a bias toward the funding of care for mental disorders in the elderly in institutions rather than community-based care; and

WHEREAS private insurance and managed care have limited and reduced access to outpatient mental health care and exclude persons and/or benefits for preexisting conditions; and

WHEREAS there is an underrepresentation of elderly consumer involvement in mental health planning and systems development.

Resolution Statement 21

THEREFORE BE IT RESOLVED THAT the federal government take steps to ensure the development of a system of universal, accessible, affordable, and culturally competent mental health care that incorporates:

    a. parity of mental health care with other health services,

    b. insurance reform to eliminate discriminatory insurance practices, including exclusion based on preexisting conditions,

    c. integration of mental health services with acute and long-term care and other aging network services,

    d. the setting of quality assurance and performance standards, including access, client outcomes, and consumer satisfaction,

    e. mechanisms to protect consumers by setting planned standards and consumer rights,

    f. a package of services no less than the core mental health services now required in the Community Mental Health Services Act of 1963 and to include outreach and in-home mental health services,

    g. in any federal/state health care partnerships, the above principles must apply; and

BE IT FURTHER RESOLVED THAT states certify health insurance plans to ensure the inclusion of these principles and monitor quality access and availability of mental health care in both the public and private sectors, foster collaboration between and among state and local mental health and aging services programs, and expand their state mental health agency priority populations to include mental health services for the elderly; and

BE IT FURTHER RESOLVED THAT local jurisdictions place priority on providing mental health care to their elderly residents.

TOPIC: Consumer involvement

Statement of Issue 22

WHEREAS older adults of diverse populations and circumstances are themselves the primary source of information about the status and factors of their mental health; and

WHEREAS older adults as a group are an experienced, knowledgeable, and effective resource for meeting their own mental health needs, as well as for helping others with similar needs; and

WHEREAS comprehensive community mental health care for elders is largely nonexistent in most American communities; and

WHEREAS there is no national organized voice specific to mentally ill older adults; and

WHEREAS there is a nationally recognized need for consumer and family involvement in health care; and

WHEREAS issues of access, comprehensiveness, and quality depend in considerable part on consumer and family involvement, participation, and advocacy; and

WHEREAS the industrial health complex will increasingly have to consider quality consumer outcomes as well as fiscal outcomes; and

WHEREAS arbitrary decisions are made about treatment, sometimes without consumer involvement or redress.

Resolution Statement 22

THEREFORE BE IT RESOLVED THAT public policy at the national, state, and local levels recognize older adults as a primary resource for the maintenance and achievement of mental health; and

BE IT FURTHER RESOLVED THAT consumers be involved in the planning and development of mental health systems and programs and that care be consumer focused, involving a partnership among providers, consumers, and significant others; and

BE IT FURTHER RESOLVED THAT public policy foster an active constituency of consumers and significant others for purposes of advocacy in the care and treatment of mentally ill older adults.

TOPIC: Education and training in mental health promotion and illness prevention

Statement of Issue 23

WHEREAS the number of persons trained to provide mental health services to older adults and their families is inadequate for present and future needs; and

WHEREAS providing education regarding aging issues to professionals and to the general public is a key component of promoting optimal mental health as people age; and

WHEREAS despite the core of knowledge about the competencies required to promote mental health throughout the aging process, the education and training for mental health professionals tends to focus on the diagnosis and treatment of mental illness rather than promotion of mental health; and

WHEREAS persons providing care and services to the elderly possess widely varying skills and knowledge that may be inadequate to respond effectively to older persons' mental health needs.

Resolution Statement 23

THEREFORE BE IT RESOLVED THAT the Department of Health and Human Services initiate a continuum of educational efforts ranging from a public awareness program on the issues of mental health and aging to specific competency-based training for all providers including lay persons, paraprofessionals, and professionals.

TOPIC: Education and training for mental health and aging

Statement of Issue 24

WHEREAS access to quality mental health services depends on there being trained providers; and

WHEREAS there is currently an insufficient supply of service providers with training in mental health and aging and in the needs of cultural and linguistic minorities; and

WHEREAS training must encompass (a) exposure to issues of mental health and aging as part of training for all health care and other service providers; (b) continuing education for all such providers; (c) preparation of clinical providers with expertise in mental health and aging; and (d) development of faculty with expertise in mental health and aging; and

WHEREAS there is a need for interagency training for staff in mental health and aging agencies; and

WHEREAS there is a lack of education, training, and support for families/caregivers on caring for older persons with mental illness; and

WHEREAS consumers and family caregivers have unique needs for information on mental health and aging.

WHEREAS there is often a reliance on families and significant others to provide care to older persons with psychiatric disorders; and

WHEREAS many older persons with significant mental health problems receive mental health care from nonspecialists (about 31% are seen by primary care physicians).

Resolution Statement 24

THEREFORE BE IT RESOLVED THAT Congress maintain and expand federally funded mental health and aging training mechanisms (such as the National Institutes of Health, HRSA, SAMHSA, and the Veterans Administration); and

BE IT FURTHER RESOLVED THAT states establish mechanisms to require content in mental health and aging for licensure, relicensure, and certification or recertification for all professionals providing services to the elderly; and

BE IT FURTHER RESOLVED THAT each of the health care professions establish standards for minimal competence in mental health and aging and criteria for credentialing as a specialist in mental health and aging; and

BE IT FURTHER RESOLVED THAT a campaign of public education be initiated at the federal, state, and local levels on mental health and aging for the general public, consumers, families, and caregivers.

Members of the Planning Committee for the White House Mini-Conference

Rita Munley Gallagher, PhD, RN,C
American Nurses Association
Planning Committee Co-chair

Susan Cooley, PhD
Department of Veterans Affairs
Planning Committee Co-chair

Members

Nathan Billig, MD
American Psychiatric Association,
   American Association for Geriatric
   Psychiatry

Joyce Berry, PhD, JD
Center for Mental Health Services,
   Substance Abuse and Mental
   Health Administration

Stuart Broad, JD
National Association of State Mental
   Health Program Directors

Mildred Brooks-McDow
Center for Mental Health Services,
   Substance Abuse and Mental
   Health Administration

Carol Bush, PhD
Center for Mental Health Services,
   Substance Abuse and Mental
   Health Administration

Gloria Cavanaugh
American Society on Aging

Pamela Cohen, JD
Bazelon Center for Mental Health
   Law

Nancy Coleman, MSW, MA
American Society on Aging

Karen Hoehn, MPM
Mental Health Policy Resource
   Center

Krista Hopkins, BA
National Mental Health Association

Stanley Jacobson, EdD
United Seniors Health Cooperative

Nancy Story Kilpatrick, MA
Center for Substance Abuse
    Treatment, Substance Abuse and
    Mental Health Administration

Enid Light, PhD
National Institute of Mental Health,
    National Institutes of Health

Anne Long Morris, EdD
American Occupational Therapy
    Association

Donald Moses, MSW
Department of Veterans Affairs

Janet O'Keeffe, Dr. P.H.
American Psychological Association

Bob Rawlings
National Association of State Mental
    Health Directors

Larry Rickards, PhD
Center for Mental Health Services,
    Substance Abuse and Mental
    Health Administration

Anita Rosen, PhD
National Association of Social
    Workers

Pat Schwallie-Giddis
American Counseling Association

Paul Wohlford, PhD
Center for Mental Health Services,
    Substance Abuse and Mental
    Health Administration

Staff

Charlotte Mahoney, MSW
American Association of Retired
    Persons

Ruth J. L. Richard, MA
American Association of Retired
    Persons

Ida Fairley, BS
American Association of Retired
    Persons

APPENDIX C

Delegates Attending the White House Mini-Conference

Shirley Bagley, MS, National Institute on Aging, National Institutes of Health

Sharon Baker, LSWA, National Association of Area Agencies on Aging

Carolyn Baum, PhD, American Occupational Therapy Association

Fred Blow, PhD, National Institute on Alcohol Abuse and Alcoholism

Bette Bonder, PhD, American Occupational Therapy Association

Marilyn J. Bonjean, EdD, American Association for Marriage and Family Therapy

Beatrice Braun, MD, American Association of Retired Persons

Mildred Brooks-McDow, MSW, Administration on Aging

Lovola Burgess, MA, American Association of Retired Persons

Gene Cohen, MD, PhD, American Psychiatric Association

Pamela Cohen, JD, Bazelon Center for Mental Health Law

Virginia Dize, MS, National Association of State Units on Aging

Susan Dore, National Alliance for the Mentally Ill

Calvin Fields, MA, Association for Gerontology and Human Development in Historically Black Colleges and Universities

Sanford Finkel, MD, American Psychiatric Association

Lorene Fischer, MA, FAAN, American Nurses Association

Michael Franch, PhD, Alzheimer's Association

Linda Gantt, PhD, National Coalition of Arts Therapies Associations

Robyn Golden, LCSW, American Society on the Aging

Edith Gomberg, PhD, National Institute on Alcohol Abuse and Alcoholism

Richard T. Greer, National Alliance for the Mentally Ill

George Grossberg, MD, American Geriatrics Society

Diane Gruszewski, MA, MSW, National Community Mental Healthcare Council

James Jackson, PhD, American Psychological Association

Charlene Kampfe, PhD, American Counseling Association

Ira Katz, MD, American Association for Geriatric Psychiatry

Ruth Knee, ACSW, MSW, National Association of Social Workers

Greta Krahn, EdD, American Counseling Association

Ellen M. LaCapria, DC, MA, National Coalition of Arts Therapies Associations

Barry Lebowitz, PhD, National Institute of Mental Health, National Institutes of Health

Suzanne Lego, PhD, CS, FAAN, American Nurses Association

Mingyew Leung, MPP, American Association for Marriage and Family Therapy

Enid Light, PhD, National Institute of Mental Health

Nancy Emerson Lombardo, PhD, Alzheimer's Association

Brian Lutz, Administration on Aging

John Lyle, Federal Council on the Aging

Willard Mays, National Association of State Mental Health Program Directors

Alixe McNeill, MPA, National Council on Aging

Baila Miller, PhD, American Sociological Association

E. Veronica Pace, MSW, United Seniors Health Cooperative

Sidney Paul, MSSW, National Mental Health Association

Trudy Persky, MSW, National Association of Area Agencies on Aging

John Pickering, JD, Bazelon Center for Mental Health Law

Ray Raschko, MSW, Federal Council on the Aging

Bob Rawlings, National Association of State Mental Health Program Directors

Burton Reifler, MD, MPH, American Geriatrics Society

Larry Rickards, PhD, Center for Mental Health Services, Substance Abuse and Mental Health Administration

Gail Robinson, PhD, Mental Health Policy Resource Center

Ruth Robinson, Delegate-at-large

J. Knox Singleton, MEd, LPC, NCC, United Seniors Health Cooperative

Stanley Slater, MD, National Institute on Aging, National Institutes of Health

Sally Steiner, MSW/CSW, National Association of State Units on Aging

Joel Streim, MD, American Association for Geriatric Psychiatry

Henry Tomes, PhD, Delegate-at-large

Miriam Torres, MS, CED, National Hispanic Council on Aging

Laura Trejo, MSG, MPA, American Society on Aging

Modesto A. Ulerio, MA, National Hispanic Council on Aging

Paul Veith, MD, Department of Veterans Affairs

Paul Wohlford, PhD, Center for Mental Health Services, Substance Abuse and Mental Health Services Administration

Steven Zarit, PhD, American Psychological Association

Antonette Zeiss, PhD, Department of Veterans Affairs

Joan Ellen Zweben, PhD, Center for Substance Abuse Treatment, Substance Abuse and Mental Health Services Administration

APPENDIX D

Members of the Coalition on Mental Health and Aging[1]

ADMINISTRATION ON AGING
Bruce Craig
Aging Program Specialist
330 Independence Avenue, SW,
    Room 4661
Washington, DC 20201
(202) 619-3458
FAX (202) 619-3759

Nancy Wartow
Aging Program Specialist
330 Independence Avenue, SW,
    Room 4661
Washington, DC 20201
(202) 619-1058
FAX (202) 619-3759

ALZHEIMER'S ASSOCIATION
Steve McConnell
Senior Vice President for Public
    Policy
1319 F Street, NW, Suite 500
Washington, DC 20004
(202) 393-7737
FAX (202) 393-2109

**AMERICAN ASSOCIATION
FOR GERIATRIC PSYCHIATRY**
Nathan Billig, MD
Professor of Psychiatry
Georgetown University Medical
    Center
3800 Reservoir Road, NW
Washington, DC 20007
(202) 687-8537
FAX (202) 687-6658

Sanford I. Finkel, MD
Director
Gero-Psychiatric Services

Northwestern Memorial Hospital
446 E. Ontario Street, Suite 840
Chicago, IL 60611
(312) 908-9481
FAX (312) 908-6276

Janet Pailet, JD
Executive Director
1910 Woodmont Avenue, 7th Floor
Bethesda, MD 20814
(301) 654-7850
FAX (301) 654-4137

**AMERICAN ASSOCIATION
FOR MARRIAGE AND FAMILY
THERAPY**
Mingyew Leung
Government Relations Associate
1100 17th Street, NW, 10th Floor
Washington, DC 20036
(202) 467-5117
FAX (202) 223-2329

**AMERICAN ASSOCIATION OF
HOMES AND SERVICES FOR
THE AGING**
Susan Pettey, JD
Director, Health Policy, Policy, and
    Governmental Affairs
901 E Street, NW, Suite 500
Washington, DC 20004-2037
(202) 508-9451
FAX (202) 783-2255

**AMERICAN ASSOCIATION OF
RETIRED PERSONS**
Lovola Burgess
Immediate Past President
c/o National Activities
601 E Street, NW
Washington, DC 20049
(202) 434-2440
FAX (202) 434-6794

**AMERICAN COUNSELING
ASSOCIATION**
Mary Ellison
Special Projects Administrative
    Assistant
5999 Stevenson Avenue
Alexandria, VA 22304
(703) 823-9800 ext. 204
(703) 823-0252

Greta Krahn
ACA Liaison to the Coalition of
    Mental Health and Aging
1709 SE 49th Avenue
Portland, OR 97215
(503) 371-0636
FAX (503) 371-7607

Helen Stidham
Assistant Executive Director
5999 Stevenson Avenue
Alexandria, VA 22304
(703) 823-9800 ext. 216
FAX (703) 823-0252

**AMERICAN GERIATRICS
SOCIETY**
Marc Zisselman, MD
Staff Psychiatrist
The Division of Geriatric Psychiatry
    at Thomas Jefferson University
Wills Eye Hospital, 8th Floor
900 Walnut Street
Philadelphia, PA 19107
(215) 928-3029
FAX (215) 928-1317

**AMERICAN MEDICAL
ASSOCIATION**
Larry Goldman, MD
Director, Department of Mental
    Health

515 North State Street
Chicago, IL 60610
(312) 464-5067 (direct) or
(312) 464-5000 (main)
FAX (312) 464-5841 or
(312) 464-5842

**AMERICAN NURSES
ASSOCIATION**
Rita Munley Gallagher, PhD, RN,C
Senior Policy Fellow
600 Maryland Avenue, SW, Suite 100
Washington, DC 20024
(202) 651-7062
FAX (202) 651-7001

**AMERICAN OCCUPATIONAL
THERAPY ASSOCIATION,
INC.**
Ann Long Morris, EdD
Geriatric Program Manager
4720 Montgomery Lane
P.O. Box 31220
Bethesda, MD 20824-1220
(301) 652-2682
FAX (301) 652-7711

**AMERICAN
ORTHOPSYCHIATRIC
ASSOCIATION, INC.**
Ernest Herman
Executive Director
330 7th Avenue, 18th Floor
New York, NY 10001
(212) 564-5930 (work) or
(301) 986-5338 (home)
FAX (301) 443-6885

**AMERICAN PSYCHIATRIC
ASSOCIATION**
Nathan Billig, MD
Director, Geriatric Psychiatry Service

Georgetown University Hospital
3800 University Hospital
Washington, DC 20007-2197
(202) 687-8537
FAX (202) 687-6658

**AMERICAN PSYCHOLOGICAL
ASSOCIATION**
Anita Brown, PhD
Assistant Executive Director for Policy
Training and Research
750 First Street, NE
Washington, DC 20002-4242
(202) 336-5878
FAX (202) 336-5797

Janet O'Keeffe, Dr. P.H.
Assistant Director for Public Interest
  Policy
750 First Street, NE
Washington, DC 20002-4242
(202) 336-5934
FAX (202) 336-6063

Michael A. Smyer, PhD
Dean, Graduate School of Arts and
  Sciences
Associate Vice President for Research
McGuinn 221
Boston College
Chestnut Hill, MA 02167
(617) 552-3268
FAX (617) 552-3700

**AMERICAN SOCIETY ON
AGING**
Gloria Cavanaugh
Executive Director
833 Market Street, Suite 511
San Francisco, CA 94103-1824
(415) 974-9600
FAX (415) 974-0300

Nancy Coleman
American Bar Association
Director, Commission on Legal
  Problems of the Elderly
740 15th Street, NW
8th Floor
Washington, DC 20005
(202) 662-8685
FAX (202) 662-1032

AMERICAN SOCIOLOGICAL ASSOCIATION

Ramon Porrecilha, PhD
Director of Minority Affairs Program
1722 N Street, NW
Contact Person: Frances Foster
Washington, DC 20036
(202) 833-3410 ext. 322
FAX (202) 785-0146

ASSOCIATION FOR ADULT DEVELOPMENT AND AGING

Jana L. Raup
Director
1634 Revel Downs Drive
Annapolis, MD 21401
(410) 280-8775
FAX (410) 573-1426

ASSOCIATION FOR GERONTOLOGY AND HUMAN DEVELOPMENT IN HISTORICALLY BLACK COLLEGES AND UNIVERSITIES

Calvin Fields
Treasurer
1424 K Street, NW, Suite 601
Washington, DC 20005

(202) 628-5322
FAX (202) 628-0939

BAZELON CENTER FOR MENTAL HEALTH LAW

Pamela Cohen, JD
Staff Attorney
1101 15th Street, NW, Suite 1212
Washington, DC 20005-5002
(202) 467-5730
FAX (202) 223-0409

DEPARTMENT OF VETERANS AFFAIRS

Susan Cooley, PhD
Chief, Research and Evaluation
Office of Geriatrics and Extended
  Care (114B)
810 Vermont Avenue, NW
Washington, DC 20420
(202) 565-7531
FAX (202) 535-7006

Donald G. Moses
Chief, Social Services
Mental Health and Behavioral
  Sciences (111J)
810 Vermont Avenue, NW
Washington, DC 20420
(202) 565-7266
FAX (202) 523-1900

Gary Small, MD
Coordinator, Geriatrics Psychiatric
  Fellowship Program
Veterans Affairs
Medical Center
11301 Wilshire Boulevard
W. Los Angeles, CA 90073
(310) 825-0291
FAX (310) 825-6792

**FEDERAL COUNCIL ON
THE AGING**
Brian Lutz
Executive Director
4657 Cohen Building
330 Independence Avenue, SW
Washington, DC 20201
(202) 619-2451
FAX (202) 619-3759

**MENTAL HEALTH POLICY
RESOURCE CENTER**
Karen E. Hoehn
Policy Associate for Federal Affairs
1730 Rhode Island Avenue, NW,
  Suite 308
Washington, DC 20036
(202) 775-8826
FAX (202) 659-7613

Leslie Scallet, JD
Executive Director
1730 Rhode Island Avenue, NW,
  Suite 308
Washington, DC 20036
(202) 775-8826
FAX (202) 659-7613

**NATIONAL ACADEMY ON
AGING**
Robert B. Friedland
Director
1275 K Street, NW
Washington, DC 20005
(202) 408-3375
FAX (202) 842-1150

**NATIONAL ALLIANCE FOR
THE MENTALLY ILL**
Bob Bohlman
Director, Government Relations
200 N. Clede Road, #1015
Arlington, VA 22203-3754
(703) 524-7600
FAX (703) 524-9094

Dixie Reding
Manager, Depressive Illness Project
200 N. Glebe Road, #1015
Arlington, VA 22203
(703) 524-7600
FAX (703) 524-9094

**NATIONAL ASSOCIATION OF
AREA AGENCIES ON AGING**
Janice Jackson Fiegener
Legislative Director
1112 16th Street, NW, Suite 100
Washington, DC 20036
(202) 296-8130
FAX (202) 296-8134

**NATIONAL ASSOCIATION OF
RETIRED FEDERAL
EMPLOYEES**
Dan Adcock
Legislative Representative
1533 New Hampshire Avenue, NW,
  Suite 100
Washington, DC 20036-1279
(202) 234-0832 ext. 315
FAX (202) 797-9697

**NATIONAL ASSOCIATION OF
SOCIAL WORKERS**
Anita Rosen, PhD
Senior Staff Associate
750 First Street, NE, Suite 700
Washington, DC 20002
(202) 336-8342
FAX (202) 336-8327

**NATIONAL ASSOCIATION OF
STATE MENTAL HEALTH
PROGRAM DIRECTORS**
Roy Praschil
Assistant Executive Director for
  Divisional Operation

66 Canal Center Plaza, Suite 302
Alexandria, VA 22314
(703) 739-9333 ext. 20
FAX (703) 548-9517

Bob Rawlings
Director, OBRA and Long-Term
  Care
Department of Mental Health and
  Substance Abuse Services
P.O. Box 53277
Oklahoma City, OK 73151-3277
(405) 522-3854
FAX (405) 522-3650

**NATIONAL ASSOCIATION OF
STATE UNITS ON AGING**
Virginia Dize
Senior Program Associate
1225 I Street, NW, Suite 725
Washington, DC 20005
(202) 898-2578
FAX (202) 898-2583

**NATIONAL CAUCUS AND
CENTER ON BLACK AGED**
Linda Jackson
Project Director
1424 K Street, NW, Suite 500
Washington, DC 20005
(202) 637-8400
FAX (202) 347-0895

**NATIONAL COALITION OF
ARTS THERAPIES
ASSOCIATIONS**
Linda Gantt
Federal Legislative Chair NCATA
c/o American Dance Therapy
  Association
2000 Century Plaza, Suite 108,
  Columbia, MD 21044

(410) 997-4040
Mail Information to: Route 1, Lake
  O'Woods
Bruceton Mills, WV 26525
(304) 379-3301 (telephone and FAX)

**NATIONAL COALITION OF
HISPANIC HEALTH AND
HUMAN SERVICES
ORGANIZATION (COSSMHO)**
Helen Munoz
Project Director
1501 16th Street, NW, Suite 1053
Washington, DC 20036
(202) 387-5000
FAX (202) 797-4353

**NATIONAL COMMUNITY
MENTAL HEALTHCARE
COUNCIL**
Sandi Wurtz
Government Relations Associate
Capitol Hill Office
900 2nd Street, NE, Suite 216
Washington, DC 20002
(202) 842-1240
FAX (202) 842-1247

**NATIONAL COUNCIL OF
SENIOR CITIZENS**
John Lawniczak
Senior Health Policy Analyst
1331 F Street, NW
Washington, DC 20004
(202) 624-9535
FAX (202) 624-9595

**NATIONAL COUNCIL ON
AGING**
Alixe P. McNeill
Senior Program Manager
409 Third Street, WE

Second Floor
Washington, DC 20024
(202) 479-6671 or (202) 479-1200
FAX (202) 479-0735

Donna Wagner, PhD
Vice President, Programs
409 Third Street, SW, 2nd Floor
Washington, DC 20024
(202) 479-0735
FAX (202) 479-0735

NATIONAL HISPANIC COUNCIL ON AGING

Marta Sotomayo, PhD
President
2713 Ontario Road, NW
Washington, DC 20009
(202) 745-2521 or (202) 265-1288
FAX (202) 745-2522

NATIONAL INSTITUTE OF ALCOHOL AND ALCOHOLISM

Gayle Boyd, PhD
Program Director for Research on
   Youth and Aging
6000 Executive Blvd., Room 505
Rockville, MD 20892
(301) 443-8766
FAX (301) 443-9334

NATIONAL INSTITUTE OF MENTAL HEALTH

Harold Goldstein, PhD
Director of Training, D/ART
   Program
Prevention Research Branch
5600 Fishers Lane
Room 14C02
Rockville, MD 20857

(301) 443-4140
FAX (301) 443-4045

Barry Lebowitz, PhD
Chief of the Mental Health Disorders
   of the Aging
Research Branch
5600 Fishers Lane
Room 18-105, Parklawn Building
Rockville, MD 20857
(301) 443-1185
FAX (301) 594-6784

Enid Light, PhD
Head, Services Research Program
Head, Alzheimer's Disease
Family Stress Program
5600 Fishers Lane
Room 18-105, Parklawn Building
Rockville, MD 20857
(301) 443-1185
FAX (301) 594-6784

Louis Steinberg, PhD
Chief of Legislative and Constituent
   Relations Branch
5600 Fishers Lane, 17C-20
Rockville, MD 20857
(301) 443-3175
FAX (301) 443-7264

NATIONAL INSTITUTE ON AGING

Stanley Slater, MD
Deputy Associate Director for
   Geriatrics
Geriatrics Program
NIA/NIH
7201 Wisconsin Avenue
Bethesda, MD 20872
(301) 496-6761
FAX (301) 402-1784

NATIONAL MENTAL HEALTH ASSOCIATION
Krista Hopkins
Prevention Specialist
1021 Prince Street
Alexandria, VA 22314-2971
(703) 838-7511
FAX (703) 684-5968

Colleen Reilly
Director, Community Education
1021 Prince Street
Alexandria, VA 22314-2971
(703) 838-7516
FAX (703) 684-5968

SAMHSA CENTER FOR MENTAL HEALTH SERVICES (U.S. Public Health Services)
Joyce Berry, PhD, JD
Director, Division of State and
    Community Systems Development
5600 Fishers Lane
Room 15C-26
Rockville, MD 20857
(301) 443-7712
FAX (301) 443-7926

Carol Bush, PhD
Chief, State Planning and Systems
    Development Branch
5600 Fishers Lane, 150
Rockville, MD 20857
(301) 443-4257
FAX (301) 443-4926

Larry Rickards, PhD
Director of Intergovernmental
    Initiatives
Homeless Programs Branch
5600 Fishers Lane

Room 11C-05
Rockville, MD 20857
(301) 443-3707
FAX (301) 443-0541

Paul Wohlford, PhD
Chief, Psychology Education Program
5600 Fishers Lane
Room 15C-18
Rockville, MD 20857
(301) 443-3503

SAMHSA CENTER FOR SUBSTANCE ABUSE TREATMENT (U.S. Public Health Services)
Nancy S. Kilpatrick
Public Affairs Analyst
Office of Scientific Analysis and
    Evaluation
Rockwell 2, 6th Floor
5600 Fishers Lane
Rockville, MD 20857
(301) 443-8522
FAX (301) 480-3144

UNITED SENIORS HEALTH COOPERATIVE
Stanley Jacobson, EdD
Board Member
1800 R Street, NW
Suite C5
Washington, DC 20009
(202) 332-1320

Edmond Worthy
President
1331 H Street, NW
Washington, DC 20005
(202) 393-6222
FAX (202) 783-0588

COALITION STAFF
Charlotte Mahoney
Ida Fairley
Ruth J. L. Richard
Betty Davis
Carol Cober
AARP
Social Outreach and Support
601 E Street, NW
Washington, Dc 20049

About the Editor

Margaret Gatz is Professor of Psychology at the University of Southern California. For the past 15 years, she has led the specialization track in aging within the university's clinical psychology training program. Her scholarly and research interests encompass genetic and environmental factors in the etiology and manifestation of dementia, age-related change in depressive symptoms, integration of preventive and life-span development theories, and evaluation of the effects of interventions. Since 1992, she has been Associate Editor of *Psychology and Aging,* and she was an associate editor for the third and fourth editions of the *Handbook of the Psychology of Aging.*